The Greatest Boxing Stories Ever Told

Thirty-Six Incredible Tales from the Ring

EDITED BY
JEFF SILVERMAN

THE LYONS PRESS
Guilford, Connecticut
An imprint of The Globe Pequot Press

Copyright © 2002 by Jeff Silverman

First Lyons Press paperback edition, 2004

The Lyons Press is an imprint of The Globe Pequot Press.

10 9 8 7 6 5 4 3 2

Printed in the United States of America

ISBN 1-59228-479-5 (paperback)

Library of Congress Cataloging-in-Publication Data is available on file.

Dedication

In memory of Allan Malamud

Acknowledgments

Thanks, as usual, to Tony Lyons for making the match, Nick Lyons for his superb corner work, and Mark Weinstein for going the distance editorially; to Steve Wollenberg for his advice from opening bell to final decision-making; and, most of all, to Abby Van Pelt for putting up with another of my adventures into anthological punch-drunkenness without so much as a hint that she's ready to throw in the towel.

Contents

Introduction

Boxing is like every other sport, only more so. I'm not being facetious. Let's take off the gloves and consider it for a bit.

What are sports about? We could certainly make a case for the high ideals of competition, character-building, sportsmanship, health, fitness, and the kinds of momentous life lessons which hold, as the Duke of Wellington suggested, that the seeds that won the Battle of Waterloo were planted on the playing fields of Eton. Sure, sports are about that. But, Grantland Rice's poetic notions of how we play the game aside, we know something else, something more basic. Sports are about a tally sheet. In an age of spin doctoring, image control, plausable deniability, passing the buck, and language so thick with obfuscation that even parsing what the meaning of "is" is can present something of a challenge, we continue to look to sports to do what they do best: Cut through all that garbage and give us—unequivocally—the score.

They tell us who won. They tell us who lost. They tell us who the better man or woman or team was. Could anything be clearer? Just this. Sports also provide a safe and acceptable playground for us to channel the aggressions we'd rather relegate to the sub-basement of our human natures—either actively through our own participation or vicariously from our seats in the stands.

Look no further, then, for why boxing—the ur-sport, born the moment one cave guy challenged another with "Wanna fight about it?", and easily the most fundamental—has been around so long. It tells us—bad officiating aside—who won and who lost in the rawest way: the loser's generally flat on his back or looking like he should be. Two combatants in a ring, each trying to pummel the other, each trying to avoid the blows, each trying to prove himself, each trying to walk away unhurt and unscathed and on his own steam, is as stripped down and primal as any sport can get. It is instantly and universally understood. Unlike its athletic brethren, boxing needs no translations or explanations as it moves from culture to culture across time and around the globe. Imagine saying that about cricket to an American or baseball to the Vietnamese. The fights, in their purest sense, are pure. They form a crucible for all that can ennoble—consider Ali-Frazier III—and repulse—the dive, the fix, the corruption, and Mike Tyson—our sports and our spirits.

Boxing is a hard game. At its root—to enter the realm of words for a second—it's also a verb. Boxers fight and fighters box, and, of course, vice versa. Nothing need be inserted between subject and action; they are one and the same. Nobody plays boxing, like they play ball or golf, because boxing isn't something to play around with. It's volatile, like matches, and we don't play with them either. What happens inside the ropes is a moment-to-moment test of courage and mortality. And though we call it a game, it's not one, really; in truth, when we talk about the fight game, we're talking more about the forces at work outside the ring than the combat that takes place within it. To play at this would lessen it. Why not just taunt danger?

It's no wonder, then, that writers as diverse, intense, and adept in their footwork as O. Henry, Norman Mailer, Ralph Ellison, A.J. Liebling, Jack London, Ring Lardner, Richard Ford, Irwin Shaw, Damon Runyon, James Baldwin, Joyce Carol Oates, Dashiell Hammett, Rod Serling, and Paul Gallico have been lured at some points in their distinguished careers into this dark and smokey arena. What a canvas the sweet science has given them to fill. What a venue it's presented for sparring with the highs and lows of the human condition.

In seeking out THE GREATEST BOXING STORIES EVER TOLD, I've tried to assemble a collection that reflects all of that, a varied and complementary stable mixing old and new, light and heavy, cynical and laudatory, fact and fancy, poetry and pith. It arrives with a lot of politically incorrect language and a crafty population of champions and chumps, renegades and rapscallions, some brash, some humble, some brave, some fearful, some filled with hope, some on the brink of tossing in the towel. All, to say the obvious, pack a punch. All, in their own way, are knockouts. The hard part wasn't picking the winners, but relegating so much of a long and shining literature to the undercard.

Still, I find myself dancing around the heavyweight braggadocio advertised by the title. Are these the greatest, the true nonpareils? Just raising the question exposes the endeavor's glass jaw, but I'll say this with absolute confidence: Each tale that follows is, indeed, a contender . . . with enough swagger and class to go the distance with the bravado.

Wanna fight about it?

Jeff Silverman
Spring, 2002

The
Greatest
Boxing Stories
Ever Told

In the Face

RICHARD FORD

Good writers will go to pretty much any length to find their verities, but how many are truly willing to take it on the chin for their art? Of course, if the writer is Richard Ford, the Pulitzer-Prize winning master of *Independence Day*, *The Sportswriter*, and *A Multitude of Sins*, he knows how to dish it out, too, as he does in the stunning essay that he used to introduce a 1996 volume that featured the extraordinary ring images of the late *New York Daily News* photographer Charles Hoff.

🥊   🥊   🥊   🥊

I've hit a lot of people in the face in my life. Too many, I'm sure. Where I grew up, in Mississippi, in the fifties, to be willing to hit another person in the face with your fist meant something. It meant you were, well— brave. It meant you were experienced, too. It also meant you were brash, winningly impulsive, considerate of but not intimidated by consequence, admittedly but not too admittedly theatrical, and probably dangerous. As a frank, willed act, hitting was a move toward adulthood, the place we were all headed—a step in the right direction.

I have likewise been hit in the face myself by others, also quite a few times. Usually just before or just after the former experience. Being hit in the face *goes with* doing the hitting yourself; and while much less to be wished for, it is also (or was) important. It signaled some of those same approved character values (along with rugged resilience), and one had to be willing to endure it.

I can't with accuracy say where this hitting impulse came from, although it wasn't, I'm sure, mere peer pressure. My grandfather was a boxer,

3

and to be "quick with your fists" was always a good trait in his view. He referred to hitting someone as "biffing." "I biffed him," he would say, then nod and sometimes even smile, which meant it was good, or at least admirably mischievous. Once, in Memphis, in 1956, at a college football game in Crump Stadium, he "biffed" a man right in front of me—some drunk he got tired of and who, as we were heading up the steep concrete steps toward an exit, had kicked his heel not once but twice. The biff he delivered that day was a short, heavy boxer's punch from the shoulder. Technically a hook. There was only one blow, but the other guy, a man in a felt hat (it was autumn), took it on the chin and went over backward, and right down the concrete steps into the midst of some other people. He was biffed. We just kept going.

There were other times he did that, too: once, right in the lobby of the hotel he ran—putting a man down on the carpet with two rather clubbing blows that seemed to me to originate in his legs. I don't remember what the man had done. Another time was at a hunting camp. A man we were riding with in a pickup truck somehow allowed a deer rifle to discharge inside the cab with us and blow a hole through the door—a very, very loud noise. The man was our host and was, naturally enough, drunk. But it scared us all nearly to death, and my grandfather, whose boxing name was Kid Richard, managed to biff this man by reaching over me and connecting right across the truck seat. It was ten o'clock at night. We were parked in a soybean field, hoping to see some deer. I never thought about any of it much afterward except to think that what he—my grandfather—did was unarguably the best response.

Later, when I was sixteen, and my father had suddenly died, my grandfather escorted me to the YMCA—this was in Little Rock—and there, along with the boys training for the Golden Gloves, he worked out the solid mechanics of hitting for me. The need for compactness. The proper tight fist. The confident step forward. The focus of the eyes. The virtue of the three-punch combination. And it was there and then that he taught me to "cut" a punch—the snapping, inward, quarter-rotation of the fist, performed at the precise moment of impact, and believed by him (rightly or wrongly) to magnify an otherwise hard jolt into a form of detonation. Following this, and for a while, I tried out all I'd learned on the Golden Gloves boys with some not very positive effects to myself. They were, after all, stringy, small-eyed, stingy-mouthed boys from rural Arkansas, with more to lose than I had—which is to say, they were tougher. In years to come, however, I tried to practice all I'd learned, always made the inward cut, took the step forward, always looked where I was hitting. These, I considered, were the crucial aspects of the science. Insider's knowledge. A part of who I was.

I, of course, remember the first occasion on which I was hit in my own face—hit, that is, by someone who meant to hurt me: break my cheek or my nose (which happened), knock my teeth out, ruin my vision, cut me, deliver me to unconsciousness—kill me, at least figuratively. Ronnie Post was my opponent's name. It was 1959. We were fifteen, and had experienced a disagreement over some trivial school business. (We later seemed to like each other.) But he and his friend, a smirky boy named Johnny Petite, found me after class one day and set on me with a torrent of blows. Others were present, too, and I did some wild, inexpert swinging myself—nothing like I would later learn. None of it, of course, lasted very long or did terrible damage, which is usual with such events. There was no spectacle. No one "boxed." But I got hit a lot, and I remember the feeling of the very first punch, which I saw coming yet could not avoid. The feeling was like a sound more than a shock you'd feel—two big cymbals being clanged right behind my head, then almost immediately the sensation of cold traveling from my neck all the way down into my toes. It didn't particularly hurt or knock me down. (It's not so easy to knock a person down.) And it didn't scare me. I may even have bragged about it later. But when I think about it now, thirty-seven years later, I can hear that cymbals' sound, and I go light-headed and cold again, as if the air all around me had suddenly gotten rarer.

Over the years since then, there have been other occasions for this sort of blunt but pointed response to the world's contingent signals—all responses I think now to be regrettable, and (to me) not very interestingly explainable. (Though I'm certain it's not just a "male thing," since I've seen women do it, too, and have unhappily enough even had it done to me by women a time or two.) But I once hit my best friend at the time flush in the cheek in between downs in a football game where we were playing shirts and skins. We were never friends after that. I once hit a fraternity brother a cheap shot in the nose because he'd humiliated me in public, plus I simply didn't like him. At a dinner after a friend's funeral, of all places, I punched one of the other mourners who due to his excessive style of mourning was making life and grief worse for everybody, and "needed" it, or so I felt. And many, many years ago, on a Saturday afternoon in the middle of May, on a public street in Jackson, Mississippi, I bent over and kissed another boy's bare butt for the express purpose of keeping him from hitting me. (There is very little to learn from all this, I'm afraid, other than where glory does not reside.)

I can't speak for the larger culture, but it's been true all my life that when I've been faced with what seems to me to be an absolutely unfair, undeserved, and insoluble dilemma, I have thought about hitting it or its human emissary in the face. I've felt this about writers of certain unfair book reviews. I've felt it about other story writers whom I considered perfidious and due for some suffering. I've felt it about my wife on a couple of occasions. I once took a reckless swing at my own father, a punch that missed but brought on very bad consequences for me. I even felt it about my neighbor across the street, who in the heat of an argument over nothing less than a barking dog, hit me in the face very hard, provoking me (or so I judged it) to hit him until he was a bloody mess on the sidewalk. I was forty-eight years old when that happened—an adult in every way.

Even today when, by vow, I don't do it anymore, hitting in the face is still an act the possibility of which I *retain*—an idea—one of those unerasable, personal facts we carry around in deep memory and sometimes re-inventory every day, and that represent the seemingly realest, least unequivocal realities we can claim access to. These are segments of our bottom line, which for each of us is always comprised of plenty we're not happy about. Oddly enough, I don't think about hitting much when I attend an actual boxing match—something I like to do less and less—but where plenty of hitting happens. Boxing *seems* to be about so much more than hitting—about not getting hit, about certain attempts at grace, even about compassion or pathos or dignity. Though hitting in the face *may be* all boxing's about—that and money—and its devotees have simply fashioned suave mechanisms of language to defend against its painful redundancy. This is probably why Liebling, who knew it well, wrote less about boxing than about boxers, and why he called it a science, not an art: because, in essence, hitting in the face is finally not particularly interesting, inasmuch as it lacks even the smallest grain of optimism.

Part of my bottom line is that to myself I'm a man—fairly, unfairly, uninterestingly, stupidly—who could be willing to hit you in the face. And there are still moments when I think this or that—some enmity, some affront, some inequity or malfeasance—will conclude in blows. Possibly I am all unwholesome violence inside, and what I need is therapy or to start life over again on a better tack. Or possibly there's just a meanness in the world and, as Auden wrote once, "We are not any of us very nice." But that thought—hitting—thrilling and awful at the same time, is still one crudely important calibration for what's serious to me, and a guide albeit extreme to how I *could* confront the serious if I had to. In this way, I suppose it is a part of my inner dramaturgy, and relatable as interior dramas as well as many perversions are, to a sense of justice. And in the end, I have to think, it's simply better and more generally informative that I know all of this, and take caution from it, forebearance, empathy, than that I know nothing about it at all.

from On Boxing

JOYCE CAROL OATES

A trenchant—and prolific—observer of modern life, novelist/essayist/poet/ short story writer Joyce Carol Oates was introduced to the fights in the '50s when her father took her to a Golden Gloves tournament in Buffalo. In 1987, she set down her decades of serious thought on the ring in a passionate, eloquent and learned booklength essay, *On Boxing*, which went beyond the surface of sport to explore "The Sweet Science" as metaphor, madness spectacle, and history, all of which make an appearance in this excerpt.

T o the untrained eye most boxing matches appear not merely savage but mad. As the eye becomes trained, however, the spectator begins to see the complex patterns that underlie the "madness;" what seems to be merely confusing action is understood to be coherent and intelligent, frequently inspired. Even the spectator who dislikes violence in principle can come to admire highly skillful boxing—to admire it beyond all "sane" proportions. A brilliant boxing match, quicksilver in its motions, transpiring far more rapidly than the mind can absorb, can have the power that Emily Dickinson attributed to great poetry: you know it's great when it takes the top of your head off. (The physical imagery Dickinson employs is peculiarly apt in this context.)

This early impression—that boxing is "mad," or mimics the actions of madness—seems to me no less valid, however, for being, by degrees, substantially modified. It is never erased, never entirely forgotten or overcome; it simply sinks beneath the threshold of consciousness, as the most terrifying and heartrending of our lives' experiences sink beneath the level of consciousness by way of familiarity or deliberate suppression. So one knows, but does not (consciously) know, certain intransigent facts about the human condition. One does not (consciously) know, but one *knows*. All boxing fans, however accustomed to the sport, however many decades have been invested in their obsession, know that boxing is sheerly madness, for all its occasional beauty. That knowledge is our common bond and sometimes—dare it be uttered?—our common shame.

To watch boxing closely, and seriously, is to risk moments of what might be called animal panic—a sense not only that something very ugly is happening but that, by watching it, one is an accomplice. This awareness, or revelation, or weakness, or hairline split in one's cuticle of a self can come at any instant, unanticipated and unbidden; though of course it tends to sweep over the viewer when he is watching a really violent match. I feel it as vertigo—breathlessness—a repugnance beyond language: a sheerly physical loathing. That it is also, or even primarily, self-loathing goes without saying.

For boxing really isn't metaphor, it is the thing in itself. And my predilection for watching matches on tape, when the outcomes are known, doesn't alter the fact that, as the matches occurred, they occurred in the present tense, and for one time only. The rest is subterfuge—the intellectual's uneasy "control" of his material.

Impossible to see the old, early fights of Dempsey's and not to feel this *frisson* of dread, despite the poor quality of the films, the somewhat antic rhythms of the human figures. Or, I would guess, the trilogy of Zale-Graziano fights about which people speak in awe forty years later. For one man of my acquaintance it was a fight of Joe Louis', against a long-forgotten opponent. For another, one of the "great" dirty matches of Willie Pep and Sandy Saddler—"little white perfection / and death in red plaid trunks" as the poet Philip Levine has written of that infamous duo. There was Duk Koo-Kim, there was Johnny Owen, in an earlier decade luckless Benny Paret, trapped in the ropes as referee Ruby Goldstein stood frozen, unable to interfere . . .

For one friend of mine it was a bloody fight fought by the lightweight contender Bobby Chacon that filled him with horror—though, ironically, Chacon came back to win the match (as Chacon was once apt to do). For another friend, a fellow novelist, enamored of boxing since boyhood, it was the Hagler-Hearns fight of 1985—he was frightened by his own ecstatic participation in it.

At such times one thinks: What is happening? why are we here? what does this mean? can't this be stopped? My terror at seeing Floyd Patterson battered into insensibility by Sonny Liston was not assuaged by my rational understanding that the event had taken place long ago and that, in fact, Patterson is in fine health at the present time, training an adopted son to box. (Liston of course has been dead for years—he died of a heroin overdose, aged thirty-eight, in "suspicious" circumstances.) More justified, perhaps, was my sickened sense that boxing is, simply, wrong, a mistake, an outlaw activity for some reason under the protectorate of the law, when, a few weeks ago in March 1986, I sat in the midst of a suddenly very quiet closed-circuit television audience in a suburban Trenton hall watching bantamweight Richie Sandoval as he lay flat and unmoving on his back . . . very likely dead of a savage beating the referee had not, for some reason, stopped in time. My conviction was that anything was preferable to boxing, anything was preferable to seeing another minute of it, for instance standing outside in the parking lot for the remainder of the evening and staring at the stained asphalt . . .

A friend who is a sportswriter was horrified by the same fight. In a letter he spoke of his intermittent disgust for the sport he has been watching most of his life, and writing about for years: "It's all a bit like bad love—putting up with the pain, waiting for the sequel to the last good moment. And like bad love, there comes the point of being worn out, when the reward of the good moment doesn't seem worth all the trouble . . ."

Yet we don't give up on boxing, it isn't that easy. Perhaps it's like tasting blood. Or, more discreetly put, love commingled with hate is more powerful than love. Or hate.

> Dustin Hoffman recalls a boxing match he had seen as a
> boy: as the triumphant boxer left the ring to pass up the aisle,
> an ecstatic fight fan, male, followed closely after him, wiping
> all he could of the sweat from the boxer's body onto himself.

An observer is struck by boxing's intense preoccupation with its own history; its continuous homage to a gallery of heroes—or are they saints? At Muhammad Ali's Deer Lake, Pennsylvania, training camp the names of heavyweight champions—Louis, Marciano, Liston, Patterson, et al.—were painted in white letters on massive iconographic boulders. "Jack Dempsey" named himself for the middleweight champion Jack Dempsey (1884–91—known as Dempsey "The Nonpareil" because he outboxed every man he fought). "Sugar Ray" Leonard named himself boldly after "Sugar Ray" Robinson—an act of audacity that did not prove embarrassing. If Marvin Hagler shaves his head, the image of Rubin "Hurricane" Carter comes to mind, and, beyond him, that of Jack Johnson himself—the first and very likely the greatest of defiantly *black* boxers, whom Cassius Clay/Muhammad Ali admired as well. So frequently are a few names evoked—Dempsey, Louis, Marciano, Pep, Robinson—one might think these boxers were our contemporaries and not champions of eras long past.

If boxing exhausts most of its practitioners in a Darwinian struggle for survival like virtually no other, it so honors a very few, so enshrines them in the glamour of immortality, surely the danger is justified? As in any religion, present and past are magically one; Time, even death, are defeated. The dead immortals are always with us, not only their names and the hazy outlines of careers recalled, but individual bouts, moments when decisive punches were thrown and caught, the size of a boxer's fist, the measurement of his reach, his age when he began and when he retired, his record of wins, losses, draws. The uppercut Jack Johnson used against Stanley Ketchel in 1909—the famous Fitzsimmons "shift" of 1897 (when Fitzsimmons defeated Gentleman Jim Corbett for the heavyweight title)—the wicked left hook with which Jack Dempsey caught a distracted Jack Sharkey in 1927—Rocky Marciano's several right-hand knockout punches—Cassius Clay's mystery punch in the first minute of the first round of his second match with Sonny Liston—the left hook of Joe Frazier that knocked Muhammad Ali on his back in the fifteenth round of their first fight: all are commemorated. The typical boxing writer's imagination is not so much stimulated by his subject as enflamed. Dream matches are routinely fantasized in which boxers of different eras meet one another—Marciano-Dempsey, Louis-Ali, Hagler-Robinson, the 1961 Sonny Liston and the 1973 George Foreman. Boxers of different weights are thrown together—how would Willie Pep or Benny Leonard or Roberto Durán have done against Joe Louis, *equipped with the necessary poundage?* Though preoccupation with past records is common to most sports there is something unusually intense about it in boxing, perhaps because, in boxing, the individual is so very alone, or seems so. Like the saint he gives the impression of having arrived at his redemption by unflagging solitary effort.

The boxing past exists in an uncannily real and vital relationship with the present. The dead are not dead, or not merely dead. When, for instance, Larry Holmes made his ill-advised attempt to equal Rocky Marciano's record (forty-nine wins, no losses) it seemed suddenly that Marciano was living again, his name and photograph in all the papers, interviews with his family published. Michael Spinks resurrected not only Billy Conn, the light-heavyweight champion who was defeated in a famous match by Joe Louis in 1941 (and again in 1946) but any number of other light-heavyweight

champions who were defeated by heavyweight champions—Georges Carpentier, Tommy Loughran, Joey Maxim, the indefatigable Archie Moore. The
spectacular first round of the Hagler-Hearns match provoked reminiscences
of "the greatest first rounds of all time." (Number one remains Dempsey-
Firpo, 1923.) *The Ring's* Hall of Fame—to which controversial Jake LaMotta
was only recently elected—corresponds to the pantheon of saints elected by
the Vatican except it is in fact more finely calibrated, its saints arranged under
various groupings and subgroupings, and its balloting highly complex. (Indeed, no intellectual journal in the states is more scrupulously attentive to
its history than this famous boxing magazine, founded by Nat Fleischer in
1922, in which past, present, and a hypothesized future are tirelessly examined, and in which one finds articles on such subjects as "The Greatest Disap-
pointments in Ring History," "The Greatest Mismatches," "The Greatest Left
Hooks," "When a Good Little Man *Did* Defeat a Good Big Man.")

It is as if by way of the most strenuous exigencies of the physical self
a boxer can—sometimes—transcend the merely physical; he can, if he is
lucky, be absolved of his mortality. The instinct is of course closely allied with
the desire for fame and riches (those legendary champions with their purple
Cadillacs!) but is not finally identical with it. If the boxing ring is an altar it is
not an altar of sacrifice solely but one of consecration and redemption.
Sometimes.

Ring Around the Writers

GEORGE PLIMPTON

In the service of a good story, George Plimpton's quarterbacked the Lions, teed it up at Cypress Point, minded net for the Boston Bruins, and pitched to Hall-of-Famers Richie Ashburn, Frank Robinson, and Ernie Banks—all with brilliantly humanizing and embarrassingly funny results. En route to his encounter between the ropes with former light-heavyweight champion Archie Moore, Plimpton went toe to toe—in these pages from *Shadow Box*—with the gloved exploits of an impressive stable of literary pugs, several of whom you'll encounter in other pages of this volume.

A nother large class of persons who ventured into the ring against champion boxers was composed of authors. Ostensibly these writers had a reason for doing so: they wanted to go through the experience of confrontation in order to write about it. Perhaps the best known of the literary pugilistic amateurs was the author Paul Gallico—the famous chapter "The Feel" from his book *Farewell to Sport* was what inspired me to try my hand at participatory journalism—who as a cub reporter assigned to the training camp at Saratoga, N.Y., where Jack Dempsey was preparing for the Luis Firpo fight, persuaded the champion to go one round with him. He wanted to find out what it felt like to be in the ring with Dempsey. Gallico had never boxed before, but he felt that four years' rowing in a Columbia racing shell would stand him in good physical stead. It did not at all. Dempsey, who quite simply did not like to have other people in the ring with him, stalked him and pole-axed him. ". . . a ripping in my head and the sudden blackness, and the next thing I knew, I was sitting on the canvas . . . with my legs collapsed under me, grinning idiotically. How often since have I seen that same silly, goofy look on the face of a dropped fighter . . . and understood it. I held on to the floor with both hands, because the ring and the audience outside were making a complete clockwise revolution, came to a stop, and went back again counterclockwise."

Even earlier than Gallico in the New York newspaper field was a journalist named Albert Payson Terhune, who subsequently became famous for his fiction about dogs, especially collies. For twenty-one years he was a reporter on the Pulitzer-owned New York *Evening World* (he started in 1894 at fifteen dollars a week). He scored a great journalistic coup when he happened to be on hand in June, 1906, to see Harry Thaw shoot Stanford White in the Madison Square Roof Garden. He rushed to a phone booth, and, bodily removing a man who was inside talking to his girlfriend, he phoned in to the paper what was then called a "flash," which made the next editions.

His managing editor at the *World* was a big, gruff, intensely disliked man named Nelson Hersh. Terhune was called into his office one day and asked to take on a somewhat unusual assignment for the feature page—to box three rounds against the six best heavyweights of the day and write about his experiences. The six were Jim Corbett, Kid McCoy, Gus Ruhlin, Jim Jeffries, Bob Fitzsimmons, and Tom Sharkey.

Terhune jumped at the chance. He was an excellent amateur fighter (he had been trained as a youngster by an ex-fighter named Professor McDermott, the Daddy of Footwork); he was built like a heavyweight—six foot four and so strong that he was always called on to act as a pallbearer when a member of the *Evening World* staff died. Not only did he know most of the fighters he had been asked to box, but he had already sparred with some of them. He saw his assignment as an easy way of coming up with six good features for his paper.

To his surprise, each of his opponents—even those he thought of as friends—really whacked him around. By the time he had finished with the six sparring matches, his left hand was broken, two teeth were gone, and his face was puffed and stitched. He said of the experience, "I used to limp back to the office in a deplorable condition to write my daily tale of the carnage."

What Terhune did not know was that Hersh, who hurried over to get a firsthand account of the day's bloodletting every time his reporter staggered into the building, had been around to see each of the professional fighters in advance, offering a half-page feature story to the boxer who knocked Terhune out. Apparently, he wanted a story which truly described what it was like to be in the ring with a champion, no holds barred.

Terhune eventually found out about the bribe (a staff member fessed up a year later) but there is no record that he went in and socked his managing editor around as a result. Certainly it was to his credit as a fighter that he never went down for good against any of the six, and perhaps it was enough compensation to remember what Corbett had told him after their set-to—that he was the best amateur in the country.

Ernest Hemingway was, of course, an active boxer from his early newspaper days with the Kansas City *Star*. He sparred whenever he had the chance. Indeed, his friendship with F. Scott Fitzgerald supposedly evaporated as a result of an incident during a sparring session between Hemingway and the Canadian writer Morley Callaghan in the America Club following a lobster thermidor lunch at Prunier's. Fitzgerald got so excited watching the proceedings that he let a round, which was supposed to last one minute, go four, at the end of which Hemingway got caught by a counterpunch and was dumped, bloodied, on his back on the canvas.

One of the best men Hemingway sparred against was Tom Heeney, who fought Gene Tunney for the championship in 1928, just before Tunney's retirement. Hemingway was fond of saying that his Heeney scuffles—which took place on the beach at Bimini—were so ferocious that finally Heeney said, "Hey, Ernie, the two of us ought to quit this . . . or get paid for what we're doing." The story got better with each telling. George Brown was predictably skeptical. Imagining the two of them on the beach, he laughed and said the only way Hemingway could have hit Heeney was if the professional got bogged down in the sand and couldn't move. This could well have been the case. Heeney was very large indeed. Mary Hemingway told me once that years later she and her husband, driving up from Key West, had stopped in a bar Heeney was running in Miami at the time. Miss Mary had not met Heeney before. "He was an absolutely *vast* man," she remembered. "I didn't think he could have walked on a beach without dropping in. I had a trick at the time of being able to heft quite big men off the ground—sneaking up behind them, locking my arms around their middles, and hoisting them up an inch or so off the floor. I tried it on Heeney—he was deep in conversation with Ernest—but I couldn't budge him . . . not even a millimeter. He was like a tree rooted to the floor. I'm not sure that he even noticed."

I had often heard a rumor that Hemingway had sparred with Tunney himself and had had such an ugly time that he never talked about it. I checked it out with Tunney's son and I could see why. It happened at the Finca Vigia, Hemingway's home outside Havana, where Hemingway was always trying to get Tunney, whenever he came to visit, to spar bare-fisted, especially if the two had polished off some of the frozen daiquiries that were brought out in a thermos from the Floridita Bar in town; Tunney would grumble and get up on occasion to do it, though mostly he looked up at Hemingway from his armchair and said no. He had once hurt Eddie Egan, the president of the New York State Boxing Commission, quite badly in a sparring session—Egan had hurt *him* with a sneaky punch, and he had retaliated and popped the commissioner with some exceedingly stiff shots and had damaged him—and he knew that the same sort of thing could happen with Hemingway. The problem was that neither Hemingway nor Egan knew how to spar; neither could resist taking advantage of an opening. There *were* amateurs Tunney enjoyed sparring with—Bernard F. Gimbel, my friend Peter's father, and James Forrestal, among others—excellent exercise, shuffling around, half shadowboxing, half sparring—but the thought of fooling with Hemingway always made Tunney wince. Sure enough, on this occasion at the *finca,* the two began shuffling around the big living room, and Hemingway did what Tunney half expected: he threw a low punch, perhaps out of clumsiness, but it hurt. It outraged Tunney. He feinted his opponent's guard down, and then threw a whistling punch, bringing it up just a millimeter short of Hemingway's face, so that the fist and the ridge of bare knuckles completely filled the other's field of vision, the punch arriving there almost instantaneously, so that immutable evidence was provided that if Tunney had let it continue its course, Hemingway's facial structure—nose, cheekbones, front teeth, and the rest—would have snapped and collapsed inwardly, and Tunney looked down the length of his arm into Hemingway's eyes and said, *"Don't you ever do that again!"* This simple child-warning admonition was delivered with such venom and authority that on subsequent occasions at the *finca,* Hemingway would get up and look at his friend, and pad around, and Tunney could see that he had it on his mind to ask him to spar, but he never did.

Among Hemingway's contemporaries, A. J. Liebling, the great *New Yorker* writer (especially on the subjects of food and boxing), enjoyed sparring with professional fighters; indeed, he was a habitué at George Brown's gym on Fifty-seventh Street, where he moved ponderously around on goutish legs but was possessed (according to Brown) of an excellent left hook when he could move himself into position, rather like a battleship jockeying around in a fjord, to throw it. He boxed Philadelphia Jack O'Brien on one occasion, and he wrote a lovely paragraph in his book on boxing, *The Sweet Science,* commemorating his membership in the brotherhood:

"It is through Jack O'Brien, the *Arbiter Elegantiarum Philadelphiae,* that I trace my rapport with the historic past through the laying-on of hands. He hit me, for pedagogical example, and he had been hit by the great Bob Fitzsimmons, from whom he won the light-heavyweight title in 1906. Jack had a scar to show for it. Fitzsimmons had been hit by Corbett, Corbett by John L. Sullivan, he by Paddy Ryan, with the bare knuckles, and Ryan by Joe Goss, his predecessor, who as a young man had felt the fist of the great Jem Mace. It is a great thrill to feel that all that separates you from the early Victorians is a series of punches on the nose. I wonder if Professor Toynbee is as intimately attuned to his sources. The Sweet Science is joined onto the past like a man's arm to his shoulder."

To my regret I had never met Mr. Liebling. He called me on the phone within an hour of my experience with Archie Moore (he had heard about it somehow)—finding me in the offices of *Sports Illustrated,* where I had gone to wind down. He wanted to know what had happened; he was glad I was interested in boxing, and he told me that he himself, after a long layoff, was going to start writing about boxing again for *The New Yorker*—the subject was one which he could not stay away from.

If we had met in person I think I would have stared at his nose, which had been poked by Philadelphia Jack O'Brien, and I like to think that he would have looked briefly at mine—perhaps still bulbous from what Archie Moore had done to it—since it was by these respective appendages that we were both pegged onto that splendid genealogical tree that led back to Jem Mace.

Of the writers of more contemporary times, Norman Mailer, of course, is an enthusiast. Mailer has sparred with a number of fighters, starting with an early father-in-law whose record in the professional ranks was 2 won and 2 lost, at which point his wife made him stop because in donnybrook fashion he either murdered his opponent (Norman reported) or *was* murdered, with neither condition endearing him to her.

Mailer's most exalted competition was Jose Torres, the world's light-heavyweight champion in the mid-sixties. One summer in Vermont, when Torres had a house down the road, they sparred almost every day out on the front lawn—two-minute rounds, with a minute of rest. "Sometimes they were one-minute rounds with two minutes of rest," Mailer remembered. "Torres occasionally gave me a hole to hit through so I couldn't get demoralized, but he didn't like it. He said it made him feel wrong. So he made me work very hard . . . it was like boxing a puma."

Once, by accident, Mailer landed a right hand, which so excited Torres, the proud instructor, that he ran around the lawn shouting, "He hit me with a right, a *right!*"

The two of them actually performed in public—on the Dick Cavett television show (Torres was promoting a book he had finished), on which Norman appeared wearing a somewhat frayed bathrobe over a sweatshirt and short pants. Torres, very fancily got up in what he would wear for a championship fight, got influenced by the public's being on hand and hit Mailer in the stomach much harder than he intended, grimacing as soon as he had done so, much as one would dropping a vase, as if he expected Norman to disintegrate on the floor. Torres was so relieved that Mailer had withstood the punch that later he called up Cus D'Amato, the distinguished fight manager, and cried out, "Cus, I hit him hard in the stomach and he didn't go down. Not *hard,* but hard."

There were others. Roger Donoghue, an excellent middleweight who cut his ring career short when an opponent with the sweet name Angel Flores died after a Madison Square Garden bout in 1951, had also sparred with Mailer. Donoghue liked his balance. He told me, "His hook off a jab isn't too good, but he can hook off a participle."

"What's that mean?" I asked.

"Which means that he's not bad, but he's a much better writer."

Donoghue had also gone four rounds with Budd Schulberg, the author of *On the Waterfront* and *The Harder They Fall.* Donoghue described Schulberg's style as follows: "He gets very low to the ground, in a huddled sort of crouch, and he peers up at you over the rim of his gloves like a woodchuck looking out of a hole. It's very hard to foul him. He looks at you sorrowfully, like he knew what you had in mind to do, and he feints you with his eyebrows."

from The Iliad

H O M E R

Hardly anything is known for certain about Homer (c. 9th century B.C.) other than this: the guy had reach.

The poet given credit for *The Iliad* and *The Odyssey* knew how to tell a story and understood the nuances of human nature. His canvas was huge, and his themes even larger: war, death, heroism, loyalty, love. Homer was nothing if not versatile.

And, it can be argued, he was the ur-sportswriter. Since his epics—which scholars suggest were dispensed orally—are the foundations of Western literature, the chronicle that follows (translated by Robert Fitzgerald) of the boxing match between Epeios and Euryalos, is thus part of the first sports report that myth and history hand down to us.

Here's the scene. The Greeks and Trojans have been fighting for a decade, and Helen, whose abduction started the whole thing, still hasn't been returned. Hector, the noble leader of the Trojan forces, has just killed Patroclus, the great friend of Achilles, the commander of the Greeks. Enraged with grief, Achilles seeks revenge. He kills Hector and desecrates his body.

Then Homer inserts a time-out.

Patroclus' pyre must be built. His body must be laid to rest. And games must be held in his honor. That was the Greek way.

Boxing is second on the day's bill, right after the chariot race. Other events included wrestling, a footrace, archery, and the javelin.

One more thing. Does Epeios' prefight boast remind you of a more contemporary ringmaster?

"Well, carry on
the funeral of your friend with competitions.
This I take kindly, and my heart is cheered
that you remember me as well disposed,
remembering, too, the honor that is due me
among Akhaians. May the gods
in fitting ways reward you for it all."

Akhilleus bent his head to Nestor's praise
and then returned across the field of Akhaians.
Now as first prize for the bruising fist fight
he led a mule to tie it in the ring,
a beast of burden, six years old, unbroken,
that would be hard to break. And for the loser
he set out a two-handled cup, then stood
and said to the Argives:

"Excellency, Agamémnon,
and other Akhaians under arms, call
on two of our most powerful men to try
for these awards in boxing.
The one Apollo helps to keep his feet—
if all Akhaians will concede the winner—
may take this working animal for his own,
while a two-handled cup goes to the loser."

At this a huge man got to his feet at once,
huge but compact, clever with his fists,
Epeiós, a son of Panopeus.
He laid hold of the stubborn mule and said:

"Step up, one of you men, and take the cup!
I think no other here will take the mule
by whipping me. I'm best, I don't mind saying.
Enough to admit I'm second-rate at war;
no man can be a master in everything.
Here is my forecast, and it's dead sure.
I'll open his face and crack his ribs. His friends

should gather and stand by to take him off
after my left and right have put him down."

At this they all grew silent. Eurýalos
alone stood up to face him, well-built son
of Lord Mêkisteus Talaïonidês,
who in the old days came to Thebes when Oidipous
had found his grave. At that time, Mêkisteus
defeated all the Kadmeíans. His son
had Diomêdês to attend him now
and cheer him on, wishing him victory.
First he cinched around him a fighter's belt
and then bound rawhide strips across his knuckles.
Both men, belted, stepped into the ring
and, toe to toe, let fly at one another,
hitting solid punches. Heavy fists
then milled together as they worked in close
with a fierce noise of grinding jaws. Their bodies
ran with sweat. Then Epeiós leapt out
with a long left hook and smashed the other's cheek
as he peered out through puffed eyes. He could keep
his feet no longer, but his legs gave way
and down he went—the way a leaping fish
falls backward in the offshore sea when north wind
ruffles it down a beach littered with seawrack:
black waves hide him. So the man left his feet
and dropped at the blow. Gallantly Epeiós
gave him a hand and pulled him up; his friends
with arms around him helped him from the ring,
scuffing his feet and spitting gouts of blood,
his head helplessly rolling side to side.
They sat him down, addled, among themselves,
and took charge of the double-handled cup.

The Fight

WILLIAM HAZLITT

Bernard Darwin, Charles's golf-writing grandson and one of the fittest essayists of the 20th century, considered William Hazlitt (1778–1830) the finest writer he'd ever read. Period. As English majors can attest, Hazlitt was a master interpreter of Shakespeare, Wordsworth, and Coleridge. The guy also knew his fights. This 1822 account seems so contemporary that, as Herbert Warren Wind, another superb chronicler of the sporting scene, once noted, "the reader finds himself wondering if it might not be an inspired idea, the next time a big fight is scheduled, to run up to Picadilly and catch a stage-coach to the stadium."

R eader, have you ever seen a fight? If not, you have a pleasure to come, at least if it is a fight like that between the Gas-man and Bill Neate. The crowd was very great when we arrived on the spot; open carriages were coming up, with streamers flying and music playing, and the country-people were pouring in over hedge and ditch in all directions, to see their hero beat or be beaten. The odds were still on Gas, but only about five to four. Gully had been down to try Neate, and had backed him considerably, which was a damper to the sanguine confidence of the adverse party. About two hundred thousand pounds were pending. The Gas says, he has lost £3000, which were promised him by different gentlemen if he had won. He had presumed too much on himself, which had made others presume on him. This spirited and formidable young fellow seems to have taken for his motto the old maxim, that "there are three things necessary to success in life—

Impudence! Impudence! Impudence!" It is so in matters of opinion, but not in the *Fancy*, which is the most practical of all things, though even here confidence is half the battle, but only half. Our friend had vapoured and swaggered too much, as if he wanted to grin and bully his adversary out of the fight. The difference of weight between the two combatants (14 stone to 12) was nothing to the sporting men. Great, heavy, clumsy, long-armed Bill Neate kicked the beam in the scale of the Gas-man's vanity. The amateurs were frightened at his big words, and thought that they would make up for the difference of six feet and five feet nine. Truly, the *Fancy* are not men of imagination. They judge of what has been, and cannot conceive of anything that is to be. The Gas-man had won hitherto; therefore he must beat a man half as big again as himself—that to a certainty. Besides, there are as many feuds, factions, prejudices, pedantic notions in the *Fancy* as in the state or in the schools. Mr. Cully is almost the only cool, sensible man among them, who exercises an unbiased discretion, and is not a slave to his passions in these matters. But enough of reflections, and to our tale.

The day, as I have said, was fine for a December morning. The grass was wet, and the ground miry, and ploughed up with multitudinous feet, except that, within the ring itself, there was a spot of virgin-green closed in and unprofaned by vulgar tread, that shone with dazzling brightness in the midday sun. For it was now noon, and we had an hour to wait. This is the trying time. It is then the heart sickens, as you think what the two champions are about, and how short a time will determine their fate. After the first blow is struck, there is no opportunity for nervous apprehensions; you are swallowed up in the immediate interest of the scene—but

> "Between the acting of a dreadful thing
> And the first motion, all the interim is
> Like a phantasma, or a hideous dream."

I found it so as I felt the sun's rays clinging to my back, and saw the white wintry clouds sink below the verge of the horizon. "So," I thought, "My fairest hopes have faded from my sight!—so will the Gas-man's glory, or that of his adversary, vanish in an hour."

The *swells* were parading in their white box-coats, the outer ring was cleared with some bruises on the heads and shins of the rustic assembly (for the *cockneys* had been distanced by the sixty-six miles); the time drew near, I had got a good stand; a bustle, a buzz ran through the crowd, and from the opposite side entered Neate, between his second and bottle-holder. He rolled along swathed in his loose greatcoat, his knock-knees bending under his huge bulk; and, with a modest cheerful air, threw his hat into the ring. He then just looked round, and began quietly to undress; when from the other side there was a similar rush and an opening made, and the Gas-man came forward with a conscious air of anticipated triumph, too much like the cock-of-the-walk. He strutted about more than became a hero, sucked oranges with a supercilious air, and threw away the skin with a toss of his head, and went up and looked at Neate, which was an act of supererogation. The only sensible thing he did was, as he strode away from the modern Ajax, to fling out his arms, as if he wanted to try whether they would do their work that day.

By this time they had stripped, and presented a strong contrast in appearance. If Neate was like Ajax, "with Atlantean shoulders, fit to bear" the pugilistic reputation of all Bristol, Hickman might be compared to Diomed, light, vigorous, elastic, and his back glistened in the sun, as he moved about, like a panther's hide. There was now a dead pause—attention was awestruck. Who at that moment, big with a great event, did not draw his breath short— did not feel his heart throb? All was ready. They tossed up for the sun, and the Gas-man won. They were led up to the *scratch*—shook hands, and went at it.

In the first round everyone thought it was all over. After making play a short time, the Gas-man flew at his adversary like a tiger, struck five blows in as many seconds, three first, and then following him as he staggered back, two more, right and left, and down he fell, a mighty ruin. There was a shout, and I said, "There is no standing this." Neate seemed like a lifeless lump of flesh and bone, round which the Gas-man's blows played with the rapidity of electricity or lightning, and you imagined he would only be lifted up to be knocked down again. It was as if Hickman held a sword or a fire in that right hand of his, and directed it against an unarmed body. They met again, and Neate seemed, not cowed, but particularly cautious. I saw his teeth clenched together and his brows knit close against the sun. He held out both his arms at full length straight before him, like two sledgehammers, and raised his left an inch or two higher. The Gas-man could not get over this guard—they struck mutually and fell, but without advantage on either side.

It was the same in the next round, but the balance of power was thus restored—the fate of the battle was suspended. No one could tell how it would end. This was the only moment in which opinion was divided; for, in the next, the Gas-man aiming a mortal blow at his adversary's neck, with his right hand, and failing from the length he had to reach, the other returned it with his left at full swing, planted a tremendous blow on his cheekbone and eyebrow, and made a red ruin of that side of his face. The Gas-man went down, and there was another shout—a roar of triumph as the waves of fortune rolled tumultuously from side to side. This was a settler. Hickman got up, and "grinned horrible a ghastly smile," yet he was evidently dashed in his opinion of himself; it was the first time he had ever been so punished; all one side of his face was perfect scarlet, and his right eye was closed in dingy blackness, as he advanced to the fight, less confident, but still determined.

After one or two more rounds, not receiving another such remembrancer, he rallied and went at it with his former impetuosity. But in vain. His strength had been weakened,—his blows could not tell at such a distance,— he was obliged to fling himself at his adversary, and could not strike from his feet; and almost as regularly as he flew at him with his right hand, Neate warded the blow, or drew back out of its reach, and felled with the return of his left. There was little cautious sparring—no half-hits—no tapping and trifling, none of the *petit-maîtreship* of the art—they were almost all knockdown blows:—the fight was a good stand-up fight. The wonder was the half-minute time. If there had been a minute or more allowed between each round, it would have been intelligible how they should by degrees recover strength and resolution; but to see two men smashed to the ground, smeared with gore, stunned, senseless, the breath eaten out of their bodies; and then, before you recover from the shock, to see them rise up with new strength and courage, stand ready to inflict or receive mortal offense, and rush upon each other "like two clouds over the Caspian"—this is the most astonishing thing of all—this is the high and heroic state of man! From this time forward the event became more certain every round; and about the twelfth it seemed as if it must have been over.

Hickman generally stood with his back to me; but in the scuffle, he had changed positions, and Neate just then made a tremendous lunge at him, and hit him full in the face. It was doubtful whether he would fall backwards or forwards; he hung suspended for a second or two, and then fell back, throwing his hands in the air, and with his face lifted up to the sky. I never saw anything more terrific than his aspect just before he fell. All traces of life, of natural expression, were gone from him. His face was like a human skull, a death's head, spouting blood. The eyes were filled with blood, the nose streamed with blood, the mouth gaped blood. He was not like an actual man, but like a preternatural, spectral appearance, or like one of the figures in Dante's *Inferno*.

Yet he fought on after this for several rounds, still striking the first desperate blow, and Neate standing on the defensive, and using the same cautious guard to the last, as if he had still all his work to do; and it was not till the Gas-man was so stunned in the seventeenth or eighteenth round, that his senses forsook him, and he could not come to time, that the battle was declared over.

Ye who despise the *Fancy,* do something to shew as much *pluck,* or as much self-possession as this, before you assume a superiority which you have never given a single proof of by any one action in the whole course of your lives!—When Gas-man came to himself, the first words he uttered were, "Where am I? What is the matter, Tom,—you have lost the battle, but you are the bravest man alive." And Jackson whispered to him, "I am collecting a purse for you, Tom."—Vain sounds, and unheard at that moment! Neate instantly went up and shook him cordially by the hand, and seeing some old acquaintance, began to flourish with his fists, calling out, "Ah, you always said I couldn't fight—What do you think now?" But all in good humor, and without any appearance of arrogance; only it was evident Bill Neate was pleased that he had won the fight.

When it was over, I asked Cribb if he did not think it was a good one? He said, *"Pretty well!"* The carrier-pigeons now mounted into the air, and one of them flew with the news of her husband's victory to the bosom of Mrs. Neate. Alas, for Mrs. Hickman!

"I Decide to Give Up Fighting"

At 5 foot seven, 160 pounds, Daniel Mendoza (1764–1836) was, by design, a natural middleweight who carried himself more like a heavyweight in several respects. Indeed, for three years at the end of the 18th century, he held the British heavyweight title, then equivalent to the heavyweight championship of the world. From there, his story just gets more interesting.

Mendoza was a man who could claim many firsts for himself. He was the first champ to pen his reminiscences—*The Memoirs of the Life of Daniel Mendoza*, in 1826, and the first to practice a sweet science emphasizing ring savvy over brute force. His 1787 volume, *The Art of Boxing*, was the sport's first real training manual. He was also the first Jew to fight for the title, the first Jew to wear the crown, and the first Jew ever to talk with King George III, though, given what we now know about the mad monarch, that doesn't seem like much to brag about. In 1954, "The Light of Israel" joined the inaugural class of inductees into the Boxing Hall of Fame.

A noted raconteur and a natural performer who regularly turned to the stage to supplement his income as a boxer and boxing instructor, Mendoza certainly knew how to work a crowd. Especially, as is evident at the end of this excerpt from his *Memoirs*, if that crowd included a young royal sparring partner. As a fighter and a presence, Mendoza—like another remarkable champion some two centuries later—had a keen understanding of the theatricality of a given moment.

The attention of sporting men and amateurs was excited, in an eminent degree, towards the contest, which was now speedily expected to take place, according to appointment between Mr. Ward and myself.

As I had, at the conclusion of the last contest with Mr. Humphreys, publicly declared my intention of engaging in no more pitched battles, no small surprise was excited at my departing from this resolution, for the purpose of engaging with one, who seemed likely to prove a successful opponent: my conduct in this instance appeared very mysterious,—to risque the ruin of the fame I had already acquired, by engaging in a contest which appeared almost impossible to terminate in my favor, and this too, after having made the public declaration before mentioned, appeared an act of the highest imprudence, indeed almost of madness, and such it was considered by most of my friends, who, though they had hitherto readily accepted such bets, as had at different times been offered, concerning my success in the various battles in which I had engaged, came forward very reluctantly on the present occasion, and the bets at this time were generally six or seven to four against me.

This contest was, however, prevented from being decided at the time and place first intended, in consequence of the following notice being published in the newspapers.

> "Margate, June 11, 1791.
>
> Whereas a boxing match, between Mendoza and Ward, has been announced, in several public papers for next Wednesday for 15th instant, I am directed by the mayor of Dover (under whose jurisdiction this place is) to take the necessary steps to prevent the same; this is therefore to give notice, that the said meetings, or any other of the kind, will not be suffered to take place, within this parish.
>
> Francis Cobb, Deputy."

It was afterwards settled we should fight at Hounslow, but we were again prevented, for a magistrate, on being apprised of the circumstance, repaired to the place, attended by a party of soldiers, and having desired the people to disperse, proceeded to read the riot act, and then declared his determination of waiting no longer than an hour before he employed the assistance of the military, to effect by force what, he observed, could not otherwise be accomplished. He accordingly took out his watch, and observed the time very minutely: after some while had elapsed, during which, the populace seemed, notwithstanding his menaces, to have increased rather than diminished, he went again to pull out his watch with the intention of seeing how the time went, when lo! a terrible disaster occurred. Some wicked fellow had taken a fancy to the worship's watch, as well as to the riot-act, and had taken the liberty of stealing them both. This will not certainly be deemed an unfortunate event, as it was the cause of the soldiers not being ordered to act, and perhaps some bloodshed was thereby prevented, for the magistrate was completely at a loss what to do—to borrow a watch was impossible, no person could be induced to lend one for such a purpose; at length he retired from the scene in disgust. The battle, however, was prevented, and was not fought till some weeks afterwards, when it took place at Swithin Bottom near Croydon.

At setting to, the bets were considerably against me, and my friends appeared very apprehensive of my being defeated, but contrary to their fears, and the general expectation of the sporting world, I came off completely victorious, after a contest of twenty-six minutes, in the course of which I received but one blow of material consequence, this was in the neck, just under the right ear, and happened soon after the commencement of the contest; the effect at the moment was so powerful as to deprive me of my senses, but in the course of a few seconds I recovered, and was enabled to set to again with unabated vigor, and finally to gain a complete victory over my antagonist, who at the conclusion of the battle, was so much overpowered, that he was unable to move, and was absolutely obliged to be carried off the stage by his second.

The expectations of my opponent's friends were, in this instance, completely disappointed. They had imagined his success so certain, that, in the gaiety of their hearts, they could not forbear exulting at the prospect of a contest, which would crown him with new laurels, and check, forever, the aspiring hopes of a rival, whose defeat would yield them the highest triumph. They treated "my presumption in daring to engage with so superior an antagonist" as they considered Mr. Ward to be, with derision and contempt. My opponent himself seemed animated with the same sentiments, and elated at the idea of gaining an easy conquest. I well recollect being asked, at the commencement of the contest, whether I had brought my coffin with me. Such was the contemptuous manner in which my opponent and his friends were pleased to treat so humble an individual as myself. The disappointment and chagrin of Mr. Ward's friends at the contest terminating so differently from what they expected, was beyond description.

For my own part, I gained more honor than money by this battle. In defeating an opponent of such superior strength, I exceeded the expectation of the most sanguine of my friends, and had the honor of coming off victorious in a contest with an antagonist whom Johnson could not beat, but as my friends had been very reluctant to accept bets on the occasion, the money gained was but trifling: I won, however, a small sum, which I staked on the contest.

A few weeks after my return to town, I had again the misfortune to experience very ill health, and, in consequence of my indisposition, was obliged to relinquish for many months the exercise of my profession. This was a very great loss to me, and I now felt most forcibly the precarious nature of a profession dependant solely on my own exertions. I was unable to attend my scholars, and, at the same time was paying a very high rent for my house and living at a very great expense.

When my health was improving, I frequently used to indulge myself with excursions into the country for the purpose of taking the air. On one of those occasions, I went for a few days to Windsor, and, during my stay in that town, had the honor of being introduced to a great personage. This happened, one evening on the terrace, where I was walking, and was suddenly surprised at being accosted by a nobleman, who, in a very abrupt manner, mentioned his intention of introducing me to His Majesty. He had scarcely spoken when the King, attended by some lords in waiting, approached the spot, upon which, I was introduced, and had a long conversation with His Majesty, who made many ingenious remarks on the pugilistic art, such as might naturally be expected to be made by a person of so comprehensive a mind and such transcendent abilities, as that illustrious personage is generally believed to possess! Before I quitted the terrace, the Princess Royal (now queen of Wirtemberg) brought one of the younger branches of the royal family to me, and asked my permission (which I of course readily granted) for this young gentleman to strike me a blow, in order that he might have to boast at a subsequent opportunity of having at an early period of his life, struck a professed pugilist on Windsor terrace.

The Higher Pragmatism

O. HENRY

An O. Henry story—think *The Gift of the Magi*, *The Ransom of Red Chief*, *After Twenty Years*, and *The Last Leaf*—demands an O. Henry ending, and William C. Porter (1862–1910) naturally supplied one for this boxing yarn published a year before his death.

🥊   🥊   🥊   🥊

S ay," said Mack, "tell me one thing—can you hand out the dope to other girls? Can you chin 'em and make matinee eyes at 'em and squeeze 'em? You know what I mean. You're just shy when it comes to this particular dame—the professional beauty—ain't that right?"

"In a way you have outlined the situation with approximate truth," I admitted.

"I thought so," said Mack grimly. "Now, that reminds me of my own case. I'll tell you about it."

I was indignant, but concealed it. What was this loafer's case or anybody's case compared with mine? Besides, I had given him a dollar and ten cents.

"Feel my muscle," said my companion suddenly, flexing his biceps. I did so mechanically. The fellows in gyms are always asking you to do that. His arm was hard as cast iron.

"Four years ago," said Mack, "I could lick any man in New York outside of the professional ring. Your case and mine is just the same. I come from the West Side—between Thirteenth and Fourteenth—I won't give the number on the door. I was a scrapper when I was ten, and when I was twenty no amateur in the city could stand up four rounds with me. 'S a fact. You know Bill McCarty? No? He managed the smokers for some of them swell clubs. Well, I knocked out everything Bill brought up before me. I was a middleweight, but could train down to a welter when necessary. I boxed all over the West Side at bouts and benefits and private entertainments, and was never put out once.

"But say, the first time I put my foot in the ring with a professional I was no more than a canned lobster. I dunno, how it was—I seemed to lose heart. I guess I got too much imagination. There was a formality and publicness about it that kind of weakened my nerve. I never won a fight in the ring. Lightweights and all kinds of scrubs used to sign up with my manager and then walk up and tap me on the wrist and see me fall. The minute I seen the crowd and a lot of gents in evening clothes down in front, and seen a professional come inside the ropes, I got as weak as ginger ale.

"Of course, it wasn't long till I couldn't get no backers, and I didn't have any more chances to fight a professional—or many amateurs, either. But lemme tell you—I was as good as most men inside the ring or out. It was just that dumb, dead feeling I had when I was up against a regular that always done me up.

"Well, sir, after I had got out of the business, I got a mighty grouch on. I used to go round town licking private citizens and all kinds of unprofessionals just to please myself. I'd lick cops in dark streets and car conductors and cab drivers and draymen whenever I could start a row with 'em. It didn't make any difference how big they were, or how much science they had, I got away with 'em. If I'd only just have had the confidence in the ring that I had beating up the best men outside of it, I'd be wearing black pearls and heliotrope silk socks today.

"One evening I was walking along near the Bowery, thinking about things, when along comes a slumming party. About six or seven they was, all in swallowtails, and these silk hats that don't shine. One of the gang kind of shoves me off the sidewalk. I hadn't had a scrap in three days, and I just says, "De-lighted! and hits him back of the ear.

"Well, we had it. That Johnnie put up as decent a little fight as you'd want to see in the moving pictures. It was on a side street and no cops around. The other guy had a lot of science, but it only took me about six minutes to lay him out.

"Some of the swallowtails dragged him up against some steps and began to fan him. Another one of 'em comes over to me and says:

"'Young man, do you know what you've done?'

"'Oh, beat it,' says I. 'I've done nothing but a little punching-bag work. Take Freddy back to Yale and tell him to quit studying sociology on the wrong side of the sidewalk.'

"'My good fellow,' says he, 'I don't know who you are, but I'd like to. You've knocked out Reddy Burns, the champion middleweight of the world! He came to New York yesterday, to try to get a match on with Jim Jeffries. If you—

"But when I come out of my faint I was laying on the floor in a drugstore saturated with aromatic spirits of ammonia. If I'd known that was Reddy Burns, I'd have got down in the gutter and crawled past him instead of handing him one like I did. Why, if I'd ever been in a ring and seen him climbing over the ropes, I'd have been all to the sal volatile.

"So that's what imagination does," concluded Mack. "And, as I said, your case and mine is simultaneous. You'll never win out. You can't go up against the professionals. I tell you, it's a park bench for yours in this romance business."

Like Father Like Son

CLARENCE RIORDAN

Subtitled *A Story About Theodore Roosevelt and His Love for Boxing*, Clarence Riordan's quaint recollection appeared in a 1930 edition of *The Ring* magazine. Established eight years earlier by the indefatigable editor and publisher Nat Fleischer, the long acknowledged "Bible of Boxing" continues to go the distance some three decades after its founder's death.

🥊　🥊　🥊　🥊

L ike Father, Like Son" is an adage as old as the hills. Down in San Juan, on the hill where the mansion of the Governor of Puerto Rico is situated, there is a young man who not only in appearance, but in practically every move he makes, reminds his intimate friends of his illustrious dad. The young man is none other than Theodore Roosevelt.

The smile, the handshake, and the energy put into his work is not the only reminder of his father. There is still a greater resemblance—his love for athletics. I was a great admirer of President Roosevelt and knew him well when he was Police Commissioner of New York City and later Governor of the Empire State. I was present many times with him at Jack Coopers' gymnasium where he would don the mitts and show his ability as a boxer.

Hence when I chanced to be in Puerto Rico recently on the day Theodore Roosevelt made his bow as Governor, I made certain to pay my respects to the son of the great Teddy. The day following the inauguration, I learned that the newly appointed Governor had put in a strenuous early morning workout in calesthenics and then a few days later he went a step further and put on the gloves for a little tilt with the island's leading boxing trainer and champion, Frankie O'Ben.

Naturally the papers went strong for this, some printing first page headlines on the Governor's athletic ability. To the Islanders, it was a big surprise to think that a Governor could find time to take a little exercise during his recreation period and to one paper, it seemed rather a shock to learn that Theodore Roosevelt, the Governor of Puerto Rico, was an ardent boxing enthusiast.

If the fellow who wrote that piece had been a New Yorker, he would have known better, for New York fight followers have often seen the Roosevelt family sitting in the first row in Madison Square Garden, directly behind the radio announcer. Those in the vicinity of the Roosevelts can vouch for the statement that there are no more ardent rooters at a good fight than the Oyster Bay celebrities, especially the fair sex of the family.

To New Yorkers, the news emanating from Puerto Rico about Roosevelt's interest in boxing does not arouse any surprise. But if a statement were published that Theodore Roosevelt, Governor of Puerto Rico, shuns boxing and thinks it degrading, that would immediately be regarded as a big news item.

The reason? Well, all of the Roosevelt boys were brought up on an athletic diet. All were taught the manly art of self defense when at school. Each had often heard his dad preach on the benefits of boxing. Therefore, when after spending his first week as Governor, Teddy announced that he had hired Puerto Rico's best trainer, Frankie O'Ben for his sparring mate, the son of the former president was simply following in the footsteps of his illustrious father.

The late Theodore Roosevelt was a remarkable man. His life had been full of varied episodes and thrilling adventures. He made his mark as an all-around athlete, a ranchman, a soldier, a hunter, and a politician, but boxing was his hobby. Never was there a child who gave less promise of strength and hardihood than Theodore Roosevelt. As a boy, the late president was referred to as a chicken-chested kid, so delicate was he that he was not permitted to play in strenuous games with other lads.

But like the son who holds the Governor's rein over Puerto Rico today, Theodore Roosevelt had grit, determination, and the courage of the fighting man. As a newspaper man who was assigned to politics on a New

York paper, I had occasion to interview Roosevelt when he occupied the Police Commissioner's office and later when he went to Albany as head of New York State. I recollect distinctly an occasion when, with half dozen other scribes, we cornered Teddy after an appeal had been made to him by the Law and Order Society to stop a fight in the old Garden and he had refused, and asked for his reasons for not taking any action.

"Because I can see nothing wrong in boxing so long as the law is obeyed," was his reply. "Boxing is a great sport. Too bad our schools don't take it up. If they did, we would have more courageous young men and less ruffians."

With that he shifted his weight to the other foot, and told us a little story of his early life and how he overcame his physical ailment. He remarked that he loved a good scrap because he admired the fighting spirit in any man. When I learned that Roosevelt, the Puerto Rican governor, was sparring with a professional boxer, for exercise, I couldn't help but think of the career of his dad. I went through my clippings, for I've kept a morgue for many years, and from there I drew out a story I had written many years ago on "Roosevelt and Boxing."

"I made my health what it is today," said he, at our interview years ago. "When I found that, physically I was not the equal of other boys, I determined to make myself as stout and able a fighting man as my Norse ancestors. When only a boy, I was sent to Moosehead Lake to rid myself of asthma. I was brought up by a maiden aunt who felt that the change of air would help my ailment and also build me up. While en route, I became acquainted with three boys who took a keen delight in teasing me. One, in particular, every now and then would thrash me until my pride was hurt and I decided I would learn to defend myself so that I could retaliate if ever the occasion again arose.

"Upon my return home, I told my father what had happened, and he willingly consented to have me take up boxing. An instructor, Tom Long, an ex-prize fighter, was engaged and for two years he trained me. At the end of that period I won his lightweight amateur tournament and I felt elated at having mastered the sport. From then on, I took a keen delight in donning the gloves with my friends. I also took up wrestling at which I became proficient. Before I left school to enter college, I had learned considerable about both sports.

"Many of the boys at school ridiculed my sailor suit and thanks to my boxing lessons, every fellow who called me a dude was forced to take his medicine. It wasn't long before I no longer was molested, for the boys all learned that I wasn't afraid of a fair-stand-up fight.

"When I went to Harvard, I joined the boxing and wrestling teams. I sparred a great deal, and also was on the track team. It didn't make any difference to me that I seldom came in first, for I got more good out of my boxing and wrestling exercises than those who beat me, because I immensely enjoyed it and never injured myself.

"When I became a member of the New York State Legislature, there was considerable commotion up at Albany by a faction that was opposed to boxing and other strenuous sports. I took issue with them. Like my father who believed that a fair, stand-up fight would do a boy a lot of good, I arose and defended boxing. I surprised, yes, and even shocked many mothers when I said:

"The boy that won't fight is not worth his salt. He is either a coward or constitutionally weak. I have taught my boys to take their own part and fight their way whenever they must. Cowardice is not in their makeup. I do not know which I should punish my boys for quicker—for cruelty or flinching. Both are abominable.

"I have never been able to sympathize with the outcry against boxing. The only objection I have to prizefighting as at present conducted is the crookedness that has attended its commercial development, but this can be easily eradicated. Outside of this, I regard boxing, professional and amateur, a healthful, vigorous sport that develops courage, keenness of mind, quickness of eye and a spirit of combativeness that fits the boy for every task that might confront him in the average lifetime. It is not half as brutalizing or demoralyzing as many forms of big business and of legal work carried on in connection with such business."

That little talk drew heaps of comment in the next day's papers, but it did not phase the great Roosevelt. He was a born fighter, just as is his son, the Governor of Puerto Rico. When the elder Roosevelt went to Harvard, he was not long in making known his prowess with the mitts. One day, while practicing in the gymnasium, he was approached by the class bully, who asked for a little set-to. Roosevelt was quick to oblige and with the gloves on, they stepped to the center to prepare for the proceedings. Teddy's opponent was anxious to beat him, and while in the act of shaking hands, he whipped over a terrific right to Roosevelt's jaw, which not only jarred the future president, but shocked him by this piece of unsportsmanship.

The students were quick to observe this foul work and immediately cries of shame and foul rent the air. Roosevelt, however, stood his ground. He smiled and raised his hand to curb the hissing. Then, to the astonishment of all, he politely held out his right hand for his opponent to grasp and to the discomforture of his rival, he stood in this position until the latter complied with the chivalry and courtesy of ring combat.

With that accomplished, Teddy, according to the person who told me this story, sailed into the bully and hammered him all over the ring. Never again did he try to slip one over on Roosevelt or any other member of the boxing fraternity. Throughout the remainder of their college days, Teddy and the fellow he whipped were the greatest of pals.

When he was governor of New York, Roosevelt, as his son recently did in Puerto Rico, hired a professional fighter to spar with him. The billiard room on the third floor of the Executive Mansion was fitted up as a gymnasium, and here the Governor spent an hour a day in wrestling, bag punching, boxing, and rope skipping.

When he was Police Commissioner, he refused to stop the Choynski-Maher battle in Madison Square Garden. Teddy sneaked into the Garden, saw the fight, enjoyed every moment of the affair, and when the contest was over, he ordered that no arrests be made.

"It was one of the greatest bouts I ever saw," were Teddy's words to the newspapermen who interviewed him at headquarters the following morning. "I can see no harm in such exhibitions.

"Why stop it and make arrests? In my opinion, it is far better for a man to know how to protect himself as these fellows did last night than it is to be forced to resort to the use of firearms, knives, or clubs."

One day Roosevelt put on the gloves with Billy Edwards, one time lightweight champion of the world. Edwards smiled as he faced the slender young student. He actually feared to strike a blow for fear he might injure the collegian. But when the gong sounded, and before Edwards realized it, young Teddy slipped by a left hook and crashed a straight left to Edwards' right eye and closed it.

It was accomplished so quickly and so suddenly, that the professional was completely taken off his guard. Edwards became furious and then tore into his opponent and almost had Teddy out when the bell sounded. However, Roosevelt took the beating courageously. He had lived up to his motto and even against such a renowned professional, he showed no signs of fear.

It was while in the White House where he had Mike Donovan, Jack Cooper, and others box, fence, and wrestle with him, that Roosevelt received an injury which blinded his left eye. While boxing with a young artillery captain, the captain struck Roosevelt a heavy blow that broke some blood vessels and throughout the remainder of his life, though few knew it, the left eye was useless.

The Governor of Puerto Rico may never reach the heights of his illustrious dad, but he is following the footsteps of Theodore Roosevelt as a great lover of outdoor life. He is an ardent follower of all sports, especially boxing.

Here is one case "Like Father, Like Son."

Cribb Repulses
Molineaux's Challenge

PIERCE EGAN

Imagine a Ring Lardner, Damon Runyon, Grantland Rice, Red Smith, and Frank Deford rolled into the essence of a single scribe and you'll begin to get a sense of the scope, influence, importance, and renown held by Pierce Egan (1770–1849) in his prime. His hugely successful novel, "Life in London" was a kind of early 19th century Baedeker to some of the city's spicier allurements; its main characters—Tom and Jerry—survive largely through the cocktail that carries their name. Still, Egan's most lasting accomplishment was creating and filling the job description we've come to know as "The Sportswriter."

His prolific and knowledgeable reportage—dispensed to an avid readership via the eponymously dubbed periodical "Pierce Egan's Book of Sports"—covered all the arenas of his day: cricket, hunting, fox-hunting, shooting, angling, cock-fighting, turf-racing, steeplechase, and, most gloriously, boxing, which he also weighed in on in every month in another journal he published called *Boxiana*. It was *The Ring* magazine of its day, and Egan filled it splendidly with results, biographical sketches, fascinating lore, marvelous observation, and deliciously inappropriate gossip.

Not surprisingly, Egan left his mark on pretty much every notable prizefight of his era. In an age of brutal, bloody, bare-knuckled, pre-Marquis of Queensberry fury, fights regularly lasted 30, 40, 50 rounds or more, as did this 1810 classic between British heavyweight champion Tom Cribb and the American challenger Tom Molineaux. (Each round ended when a combatant was either on the ground or too whipped to go on; if he couldn't get himself together to continue within 30 seconds, the bout was over.) Part of what makes this matchup, and Egan's account of it, so absorbing was that

Molineaux, a former slave who fought his way to freedom before traveling to England, was black. A good half century before the Confederates fired on Fort Sumter—and a full 98 years before Jack Johnson's thrashing of Tommy Burns would create the international hysteria for a Great White Hope—just the idea of a Molineaux victory hints at the staggering aftershocks that would likely have been felt on both sides of the Atlantic.

🥊 🥊 🥊 🥊

Since the days of the renowned Figg, when the *Venetian Gondolier* impotently threatened, on his arrival in London, to tear the Champion's Cap from the British brow, (but who was soon *convinced* of his error), it has been transferred quietly, at various times, and without murmurs, from the *nob* of one native to another, whose merit entitled him to its possession—but, that a foreigner should ever again have the temerity to put in a claim, *even* for the mere contention of obtaining the prize, much more for the honor of wearing it, or bearing it away from Great Britain, such an idea, however distant, never intruded itself into the breasts of Englishmen, and reminds us, in a more extended point of view, of the animating passage in the works of our immortal bard, so truly congenial with the native characteristic spirit of the country:

> *England never did nor never shall*
> *Lie at the proud foot of a conqueror.*

But the towering and restless ambition of Molineaux induced him to quit his home and country, and erect his hostile standard among the British heroes. The man of color dared the most formidable of her chiefs to the chance of war; when it was reserved for the subject of this memoir to chastise the bold intruder, in protecting the national practice and honor of the country, his own character from contempt and disgrace, and the whole race of English pugilists from ridicule and derision.

Tom was born on July 8, 1781, at *Hanham,* a township and chapelry, in the parish of Bitton, hundred of Langley and Swineshead, Gloucester, on the border of Somerset, situated about five miles from Bristol, and it is rather a disputed point to which of the counties that are contiguous to *Hanham* this spot belongs; therefore, whether the honor of giving birth to the Champion of England appertains to Gloucestershire or Somersetshire remains at present undecided.

Cribb left his native home at a very early period, and arrived in the Metropolis, when he was no more than thirteen years old, to follow the occupation of a bell-hanger, under the guidance of a relative; but the confined situation of *hanging bells* not exactly meeting his ideas, and being a strong athletic youth, he preferred an outdoor calling, and commenced porter at the wharfs, during which time he met with two accidents that had nearly deprived him of existence—in stepping from one coal barge to another, he fell between them, and got jammed in a dreadful manner; and in carrying a very heavy package of oranges, weighing nearly 500 pounds weight, he slipped down upon his back, and the load fell upon his chest, which occasioned him to spit blood for several days afterwards. By the excellence of his constitution, he was soon enabled to recover his strength from those severe accidents; and aided by the invigorating air of the ocean, upon which, we learn, he had the honor of serving against the enemies of his country, that fine stamina and hardihood got improved for which the name of Cribb, at the present period, stands almost unrivalled.

With the *perception* of a General—the *fortitude* of a Hero—and the *science* of a thoroughbred Professor, Tom Cribb has been enabled to obtain his numerous achievements; and no pugilist whatever entered a ring with more confidence in himself, upon all those trying occasions, than the present Champion of England; his style of fighting *(milling on the retreat)* has been somewhat disliked by several amateurs, as savoring more of policy than manliness; but this objection loses all its weight when put in comparison with his *game* or *gluttony* exhibited in every one of his conquests ...

Much as the fame of the former contests of the Champion has excited interest in the *Sporting World* they were looked upon as trifling when compared with his battle with Molineaux: and even those persons who had hitherto passed over boxing in general as beneath their notice, now seemed to take a lively interest in the issue of this fight. It appeared somewhat as a national concern; all felt for the honor of their country, and were deeply interested in the fate of their Champion, TOM CRIBB. Molineaux was viewed as a truly formidable rival: he was by no means deficient either in point of strength, courage, or agility, with his opponent; and, though but little known himself, his pedigree had been traced to be good: his father was never beaten; he was a twin brother; and the family distinguished for pugilistic traits of excellence and *bottom*. In height, Molineaux is about five feet eight and a quarter, weighing fourteen stone two pounds; while his brave opponent stands five feet ten and a half, and in weight about fourteen stone three pounds. It appears that Cribb expected to win with ease and style; and Molineaux threatened to perform wonders: it was also stated by the most experienced and best informed upon the subject, that the betting upon this occasion exceeded anything of the kind that had gone before it. Considerable odds were betted that Molineaux was disposed of in fifteen minutes, and it was considered safe betting that Cribb proved the conqueror in half an hour. The day selected for this grand *milling* exhibition was December 10, 1810, at Copthall Common, in the neighborhood of East Grinstead, Sussex, within 30 miles of the Metropolis. Notwithstanding the rain came down in torrents, and the distance from London, the *Fancy* were not to be deterred from witnessing the *mill,* and who waded through a clayey road, nearly knee-deep for five miles, with alacrity and cheerfulness, as if it had been as smooth as a bowling-green, so great was the curiosity and interest manifested upon this battle. About twelve o'clock Mr. Jackson, with his usual consideration, had the ring formed at the foot of a hill, (twenty-four feet roped,) surrounded by the numerous carriages which had conveyed the spectators thither, to ward off the chilling breezes and rain which came keenly from the eastward. Immediately upon this being completed Molineaux came forward, bowed, threw up his hat in defiance, and retired to strip; Cribb immediately followed, and they were soon brought forward by their seconds; Gulley and Joe Ward for the Champion, and Richmond and Jones for Molineaux.

First round—The first appearance of the young Roscius excited not greater attention than the *setting-to* of the above pugilists; the eyes of the spectators were stretched to their utmost, waiting for the first blow, when, after a few seconds of scientific display, the Moor put in a left-handed hit, but which did no execution. Cribb returned, but his *distance* was incorrect; however, he made a good stop, and planted a blow with his left hand under the eye of his opponent. A rally now ensued; a blow was exchanged by each of them, but of no import, when they closed, and Molineaux was thrown.

Second—The Moor rallied with a left-handed blow, which did not tell, when Cribb planted a most tremendous one over his adversary's right eyebrow, but which did not have the effect of knocking him down, he only staggered a few paces, followed up by the Champion. Desperation was now the order of the round, and the rally re-commenced with uncommon severity, in which Cribb showed the most science, although he received a dreadful blow on the mouth that made his teeth chatter again, and exhibited the first signs of *claret.* Four to one on Cribb.

Third—After a short space, occupied in sparring, Molineaux attempted a good blow on Cribb's *nob,* but the Champion parried it, and returned a right-handed hit under the Moor's lower rib, when he fell rapidly in the extreme. Still four to one.

Fourth—On setting-to Molineaux rallied, when the Champion stopped his career by a severe hit in the face, that *levelled* him, the ground being wet and slippery.

Fifth—The amateurs were uncommonly interested in this round, it was a display of such united *skill* and *bottom,* that both the combatants claimed peculiar notice from their extraordinary efforts. Molineaux rallied with uncommon fortitude, but his blows were short. Cribb returned with spirit, but the Moor knocked them off, and put in a tremendous hit on the left eye of the Champion. A rally, at half-arm's length, now followed, which excited the utmost astonishment from the resoluteness of both the heroes, who hit each other away three times, and continued this desperate *milling* for half a minute, when Molineaux fell from a feeble blow. The *knowing ones* were lost for the moment, and no bets were offered.

Sixth—The Moor planted a blow upon the *nob* of the Champion, who fell from the bad state of the ground.

Seventh—Cribb in a rally gave Molineaux a hit on the side of his head, when he went down.

Eighth—Cribb showed himself off in good style, and dealt out his blows with considerable success and effect, but experienced from the determined resolution of the Moor that he was somewhat mistaken in his ideas of the Black's capabilities, who rallied in *prime twig,* and notwithstanding the severe left-handed hits which were planted on his *nob*—the terrible punishment he had received on his body, directed by the fine skill and power of the Champion—still he stood up undismayed, proving that his courage was of no ordinary nature in exchanging several of the blows, till he fell almost in a state of stupor, from the *milling* his head had undergone. This round was equal to any that preceded it, and only different in point of duration.

Ninth—The battle had arrived at that doubtful state, and things seemed not to prove so easy and tractable as was anticipated, that the betters were rather puzzled to know how they should proceed with success. Molineaux gave such proofs of *gluttony* that four to one now made many tremble who had sported it; but still there was a ray of hope remaining from the senseless state in which the Moor appeared at the conclusion of the last round. Both the combatants appeared dreadfully punished; and Cribb's head was terribly swelled on the left side; Molineaux's *nob* was also much worse for the fight. On Cribb's displaying weakness the *flash side* were full of palpitation—it was not looked for, and operated more severe upon their minds on that account. Molineaux rallied with a spirit unexpected, bored in upon Cribb, and by a strong blow through the Champion's guard, which he planted in his face, brought him down. It would be futile here to attempt to portray the countenances of the interested part of the spectators, who appeared, as it were, panic-struck, and those who were not thoroughly acquainted with the *game* of the Champion began hastily to *hedge-off;* while others, better informed, still placed their confidence on Cribb, from what they had seen him hitherto *take.*

Tenth—Molineaux now showed symptoms of weakness; but yet rallied and bored his opponent to various parts of the ring. Cribb kept knocking him about the *nob,* but he seemed to disregard it, and kept close to his man till they both went down. The Champion now perceived what sort of a *customer* he had to deal with, and that to win judgment and caution must be resorted to; he therefore adopted his favorite and successful system of *milling on the retreat.*

Eleventh—The Moor still partial to rallying, planted several blows, but they appeared rather feeble, and did not have the desired effect; but, notwithstanding, he evinced strength enough to give Cribb a heavy fall.

Twelfth—Molineaux, immediately on *setting-to,* commenced another rally, when the Champion put in a severe body blow, but the Moor treated it with indifference, and in return not only *milled* his head, but in closing threw him.

Thirteenth—Molineaux, in boring in upon his adversary, received a severe *facer* from him, but who went down from the force of his own blow. To show the uncertainty of betting, it is necessary to state, that the odds had changed six to four on the Moor, to the no small chagrin of those who had sported their money, that Molineaux would not become the favorite during the fight.

Fourteenth—The Moor went furiously in, and run down Cribb without striking a blow, or without the latter being able to return one; however, on disengaging, the Champion was *levelled.*

Fifteenth—Cribb, on *setting-to,* planted a blow over the guard of the Moor, which occasioned a most determined rally, and those persons who were fond of viewing *milling* might now witness it in perfection; no shifting, but giving and taking were displayed on both sides, till Molineaux was knocked down from a severe hit he received in his throat.

Sixteenth—Rallying still the most prominent feature, but Molineaux went down through fatigue: Cribb appearing to the best advantage, the odds changed about till they became even, and that the Champion would win.

Seventeenth—Both the combatants, determined to do their best, entered most spiritedly into another sharp rally, when they closed, and Molineaux not only gave Cribb a desperate fall but fell upon him. Betting very shy, if any, it appearing to be any body's battle.

Eighteenth—The Champion made play, and planted with his right hand a severe blow on his opponent's body; when Molineaux returned a hit on the Champion's head, who, by a blow on the forehead, hit the Moor off his legs, but afterwards fell from the strength of his own blow. Both in an exhausted state.

Nineteenth—To distinguish the combatants by their features would have been utterly impossible, so dreadfully were both their faces beaten—but their difference of *color* supplied this sort of defect. It was really astonishing to view the determined manner in which these heroes met—Cribb, acting upon the defensive, and retreating from the blows of his antagonist, though endeavoring to put in a hit, was got by Molineaux against the ropes, which were in height about five feet, and in three rows. Molineaux with both his hands caught hold of the ropes, and held Cribb in such a singular way, that he could neither make a hit or fall down: and while the seconds were discussing the propriety of separating the combatants, which the umpires thought could not be done till one of the men were down, about two hundred persons rushed from the outer to the interior ring, and it is asserted, that if one of the Moor's fingers was not broken, it was much injured by some of them attempting to remove his hand from the ropes: all this time Molineaux was gaining his wind by laying his head on Cribb's breast, and refusing to release his victim; when the Champion, by a desperate effort to extricate himself from the rude grasp of the Moor, was at length run down to one corner of the ring, and Molineaux, having got his head under his arm, *fibbed* away most unmercifully, but his strength not being able to the intent, it otherwise must have proved fatal to Cribb, who fell from exhaustion and the severe *punishment* he had received. The bets were now decided that Molineaux did not fight half an hour; that time having expired during this round.

Twentieth—Molineaux made the most of himself, and brought his opponent down by boring and hitting.

Twenty-first—Cribb planted two blows on the head and body of his opponent, which Molineaux returned by a desperate blow in Cribb's face;

when they closed, and the Champion was thrown. The well-known *bottom* of Cribb induced his friends to back him six to four.

Twenty-second—Of no importance.

Twenty-third—The wind of both the combatants appearing some-what damaged, they sparred some time to recruit it, when Cribb put in a blow on the left eye of Molineaux, which hitherto had escaped *milling*. The Moor ran in, gave Cribb a severe hit on the body, and threw him heavily.

Twenty-fourth—Molineaux began this round with considerable spirit, and some hits were exchanged, when Cribb was thrown. The betting tolerably even.

Twenty-fifth—The effects of the last fall operated in some degree upon the feelings of Cribb, from its severity; yet the Champion endeavored to remove this impression by making play, and striving (as in the former round) to put in a hit on Molineaux's left eye, but the Moor, aware of the intent, warded it off, and in return knocked down Cribb.

Twenty-sixth—Both the combatants trying to recruit their wind and strength by scientific efforts. The Champion now endeavored to hit the right eye of Molineaux, the left having been *darkened* for some time; but the Moor warded off the blows of Cribb with agility and neatness, although he went down from a trifling hit.

Twenty-seventh—Weakness conspicuous on both sides, and, after some pulling and hauling, both fell.

Twenty-eighth—Cribb received a *leveller* in consequence of his distance being incorrect.

Twenty-ninth—The Moor was running in with spirit, but the Champion stopped his career by planting a hit upon his right eye, and, from its severe effects, he went down, which materially damaged his *peeper.* The fate of the battle might be said to be decided by this round.

Thirtieth—If anything could reflect credit upon the *skill* and *bottom* of Cribb, it was never more manifested than in this contest, in viewing what a resolute and determined hero he had to vanquish. Molineaux, in spite of every disadvantage, with a courage and ferocity unequalled, rising superior to exhaustion and fatigue, rallied his adversary with as much resolution as at the commencement of the fight, his *nob* defying all the *milling* it had received, that *punishment* appeared to have no *decisive* effect upon it, and contending nobly with Cribb right and left, knocking him away by his hits, and gallantly concluded the round by closing and throwing the Champion. The Moor was now convinced that, if he did win, he must do it off hand, as his sight was much impaired.

Thirty-first—The exertion of this last round operated most forcibly upon Molineaux, and he appeared much distressed on quitting his second, and was soon *levelled* by a blow in the throat, which Cribb very neatly put in.

Thirty-second—It was almost who should—strength was fast leaving both the combatants—they staggered against each other like inebriated men, and fell without exchanging a blow.

Thirty-third—To the astonishment of every spectator, Molineaux rallied with strength enough to bore his man down; but both their *hits* were of more *show* than effect.

Thirty-fourth—This was the last round that might be termed fighting, in which Molineaux had materially the worst of it, but the battle was continued to the 39th, when Cribb evidently appeared the best man, and, at its conclusion, the Moor, *for the first time, complained* that "he could fight no more!" but his seconds, who viewed the nicety of the point, persuaded him to try the *chance* of another round, to which request he acquiesced, when he fell from weakness, reflecting additional credit on the manhood of his brave conqueror, TOM CRIBB.

Great events are generally judged of by comparison; and, however severe the conflict might have been between *Johnson* and *Big Ben*—this battle betwixt Cribb and Molineaux was not only more formidable in its nature, but more ferocious and sanguinary. Fifty-five minutes of unprecedented *milling*, before the *Moor thought* he had had *enough!*

If anything had been wanting to establish the *fame* of Cribb, the above contest has completely decided his just pretensions to the CHAMPIONSHIP OF ENGLAND. With a coolness and confidence, almost his own, and with skill and judgment so truly rare, that he has beaten his men with more certainty than any of the professors of the gymnastic art; he was called upon to protect the honor of his country and the reputation of *English Boxing*,—a parade of words or the pomposity of high-flown diction are not necessary to record the circumstance; however, let it not be forgotten that Tom Cribb HAS DONE THIS: and let it be remembered also, that, however partial to his favorite system of *milling on the retreat*, he never resorted to its scientific effects till the necessity of the moment compelled him not to throw away the *chance*; and that, for the first ten rounds of this contest, he was the *offensive* pugilist, and, notwithstanding his *game* had always been well known, his *courage* in this instance astonished all the spectators, who expressed their admiration at his being ever ready at the mark fighting his man.

Jack Johnson vs. Jim Jeffries

The legacy of Jack London (1876–1916) is filled with contradictions. The most popular writer of his time, he's largely unread today. His greatest stories—*The Call of the Wild*, *White Fang*, *To Build a Fire*, and *The Sea Wolf*—reach for complex themes, yet they tend to be dismissed as adventure tales for teenagers. A socialist who preached individualism, he was a champion of brotherhood who subscribed to the inferiority of what he called the "colored people."

The last of those attributes is on display in London's remarkable account for *The New York Herald* of Jeffries' attempted comeback against Johnson in 1910. Jeffries had held the heavyweight crown from 1899 until he retired, undefeated, in 1904. London virtually pleaded in print for Jeffries to fight Johnson. Indeed, it was London, in his 1908 dispatch from Sydney following Johnson's 14th-round TKO of Tommy Burns to take the title that helped foment what would turn into the ballyhooed search for a Great White Hope.

London was transfixed by boxing. He liked its feel, its ambience, its characters, its grace, and its brutality. He not only covered the fights—from club encounters to title bouts—as a journalist throughout his career, he also wove it into his fiction, both in novellas (*The Abysmal Brute*, *The Game*) and short stories (*The Mexican*, *A Piece of Steak*.) Interestingly, London, anxious that he was running out of ideas for stories, bought the plot for *The Abysmal Brute* in outline form for $7.50 from a hungry young writer named Sinclair Lewis.

A final note about Johnson. His first fight after winning the title was a six-round, nontitle exhibition (though it's often listed as his first title defense) against a pug named Victor McLaglen. Though McLaglen would go on to win the heavyweight championship of the British army, his fame lay in an-

5 3

other arena. He won the 1935 Academy Award for Best Actor for his IRA turncoat in *The Informer*, and, years later, made spectacular use of his ring experience in the unforgettable fight sequence—opposite John Wayne—in *The Quiet Man*.

*   *   *   *

Reno, Nevada. July 5, 1910—Once again has Johnson sent down to defeat the chosen representative of the white race and this time the greatest of them. And as of old, it was play for Johnson. From the opening round to the closing round he never ceased his witty sallies, his exchanges of repartee with his opponent's seconds and with the audience. And, for that matter, Johnson had a funny thing or two to say to Jeffries in every round.

The golden smile was as much in evidence as ever and neither did it freeze on his face nor did it vanish. It came and went throughout the fight, spontaneously, naturally.

It was not a great battle after all, save in its setting and significance. Little Tommy Burns, down in far-off Australia, put up a faster, quicker, livelier battle than did Jeffries. The fight today was great only in its significance. In itself it wasn't great. The issue, after the fiddling of the opening rounds, was never in doubt. In the fiddling of those first rounds the honors lay with Johnson, and for the rounds after the seventh or eighth it was more Johnson, while for the closing rounds it was all Johnson.

Johnson played as usual. With his opponent not strong in attack, Johnson, blocking and defending in masterly fashion, could afford to play. And he played and fought a white man, in the white man's country, before a white man's audience. And the audience was a Jeffries audience.

When Jeffries sent in that awful rip of his the audience would madly applaud, believing it had gone home to Johnson's stomach, and Johnson, deftly interposing his elbow, would smile in irony at the audience, play-acting, making believe he thought the applause was for him—and never believing it at all.

The greatest fight of the century was a monologue delivered to twenty thousand spectators by a smiling Negro who was never in doubt and who was never serious for more than a moment at a time.

As a fighter Johnson did not show himself a wonder. He did not have to. Never once was he extended. There was no need. Jeffries could not make him extend. Jeffries never had him in trouble once. No blow Jeffries ever landed hurt his dusky opponent. Johnson came out of the fight practically undamaged. The blood on his lip was from a recent cut received in the course of training and which Jeffries managed to reopen.

Jeffries failed to lead and land. The quickness he brought into the fight quickly evaporated, and while Jeffries was dead game to the end, he was not so badly punished. What he failed to bring into the ring with him was his stamina, which he lost somewhere in the last seven years. Jeffries failed to come back. That's the whole story. His old-time vim and endurance were not there. Something has happened to him. He lost in retirement outside of the ring the stamina that the ring itself never robbed him of. As I have said, Jeffries was not badly damaged. Every day boys take worse lacings in boxing bouts than Jeffries took today.

Jeffries today disposed of one question. He could not come back. Johnson, in turn, answered another question. He has not the yellow streak. But he only answered that question for today. The ferocity of the hairy-chested caveman and grizzly giant did not intimidate the cool-headed Negro. Many thousands in the audience expected the intimidation, and were correspondingly disappointed. Johnson was not scared, let it be said here, and beyond the shadow of any doubt, not for an instant was Johnson scared. Not for a second did he show the flicker of fear that the Goliath against him might eat him up.

But the question of the yellow streak is not answered for all time. Just as Johnson has never been extended, so has he never shown the yellow streak. Just as any man may rise up, heaven alone knows where, who will extend Johnson, just so may that man bring out the yellow streak; and then again he may not. So far the burden of proof all rests on the conclusion that Johnson has no yellow streak.

And now to the battle and how it began! All praise to Tex Rickard, the gamest of sports, who pulled off the fight after countless difficulties and who, cool, calm, and quick with nervous aliveness, handled the vast crowd splendidly in his arena and wound up by refereeing the fight.

Twenty thousand filled the great arena and waited patiently under the cloud-flecked, wide Nevada sky. Of the many women present some elected to sit in the screened boxes far back from the ring, for all the world like old-time Spanish ladies at the theater. But more, many more women, sat close to the ringside beside their husbands or brothers. They were the wiser by far.

Merely to enumerate the celebrities at the ringside would be to write a sporting directory of America—at least a directory of the four-hundred sportsmen, and of many more hundreds of near four-hundreds. At four minutes to two Billy Jordan cleared the ring amid cheers and stood alone, the focal point of twenty thousand pairs of eyes, until the great William Muldoon climbed through the ropes to call ringing cheers from the twenty thousand throats for the state of Nevada, the people of Nevada, and the governor of Nevada.

Beginning with Tex Rickard, ovation after ovation was given to all the great ones, not forgetting Bob Fitzsimmons, whom Billy Jordan introduced as "The greatest warrior of them all." And so they came, great one after great one, ceaselessly, endlessly. Until they were swept away before the greatest of them all, the two men who were about to do battle.

It was half past two when Johnson entered. He came first, happy and smiling, greeting friends and acquaintances here and there and everywhere in the audience, cool as ice, waving his hand in salute, smiling, smiling, ever smiling with eyes as well as with lips, never missing a name nor a face, placid, plastic, nerveless, with never a signal of hesitancy or timidity. Yet he was keyed up, keenly observant of all that was going on, ever hearing much of the confused babble of the tongues about him—hearing, aye, and understanding, too.

There is nothing beary or primitive about this man Johnson. He is alive and quivering, every nerve fiber in his body, and brain. Withal that it is hidden so artfully or naturally under that poise of facetious calm of his. He is a marvel of sensitiveness, sensibility, and perceptiveness. He has the perfect mechanism of mind and body. His mind works like chain lightning and his body obeys with equal swiftness.

But the great madness of applause went up when Jeffries entered the ring two minutes later. A quick, superficial comparison between him and the Negro would have led to a feeling of pity for the latter. For Jeff was all that has been said of him. When he stripped and his mighty body could be seen covered with mats of hair, all the primordial adjectives ever applied to him received their vindication. Nor did his face belie him. No facial emotion played on that face, no whims of the moment, no flutterings of a lighthearted temperament.

Dark and somber and ominous was that face, solid and stolid and expressionless, with eyes that smoldered and looked savage. The man of iron, grim with determination, sat down in his corner. And the carefree Negro smiled and smiled. And that's the story of the fight. The man of iron, the grizzly giant, was grim and serious. The man of summer temperament smiled and smiled. That is the story of the whole fight. It is the story of the fight by rounds.

At the opening of the first round they did not shake hands. Knowing the two men for what they are, it can be safely postulated that this neglect was due to Jeffries or to the prompting from Jeffries' corner. But it is not good that two boxers should not shake hands before a bout. I would suggest to those protagonists of a perishing game, if they wish to preserve the game, that they make the most of these little amenities that by custom grace their sport and give it the veneer of civilization.

Both men went to work in that first round very easily. Johnson smiling, of course; Jeffries grim and determined. Johnson landed the first blow, a light one, and Jeffries in the clinches gave a faint indication of his forthcoming tactics by roughing it, by crowding the Negro around and by slightly bearing his weight upon him. It was a very easy round, with nothing of moment. Each was merely feeling the other out and both were exceedingly careful. At the conclusion of the round, Johnson tapped Jeffries playfully on the shoulder, smiled good-naturedly and went to his corner. Jeffries, in the first, showed flashes of catlike quickness.

Round Two—Jeffries advanced with a momentary assumption of famous crouch, to meet the broadly smiling Johnson. Jeffries is really human and good-natured. He proved it right here. So friendly was that smile of Johnson's, so irresistibly catching, that Jeffries, despite himself, smiled back. But Jeffries' smiles were doomed to be very few in this fight.

And right here began a repetition of what took place down in Australia when Burns fought Johnson. Each time Burns said something harsh to Johnson in the hope of making him lose his temper, Johnson responded by giving the white man a lacing. And so today. Of course, Jeffries did not talk to Johnson to amount to anything, but Corbett, in his corner, did it for Jeffries. And each time Corbett cried something in particular, Johnson promptly administered a lacing to Jeffries.

It began in the second round. Corbett, in line with his plan of irritating the Negro, called out loudly:

"He wants to fight a little, Jim."

"You bet I do," Johnson retorted, and with that he landed Jeffries a stinger with his right uppercut.

Both men were tensely careful, Jeffries trying to crowd and put his weight on in the clinches, Johnson striving more and more than the other to break out of the clinches. And at the end of this round, in his corner Johnson was laughing gleefully. Certainly Jeffries showed no signs of boring in, as had been promised by his enthusiastic supporters.

It was the same story in the third round, at the conclusion of which the irrepressible Negro was guilty of waving his hands to friends in the audience.

In this fourth round Jeffries showed up better, rushing and crowding and striking with more vim than hitherto shown. This seemed to have been caused by a sally of Johnson's, and Jeffries went at him in an angry sort of way. Promptly Jeffries rushed, and even ere they came together Johnson cried out: "Don't rush me, Jim. You hear what I'm telling you?"

No sign there of being intimated by Jeffries' first dynamic display of ferocity. All he managed to do was to reopen the training cut in Johnson's lip and to make Johnson playful. It was most anybody's round and it was certainly more Jeffries' than any preceding one.

Round Five brought Jeffries advancing with his crouch. The blood from Johnson's lip had turned his smile to a gory one, but still he smiled, and to balance things off he opened Jeffries' lip until it bled more profusely than his own. From then until the end of the fight, Jeffries' face was never free from blood, a steady stream, later flowing from his right nostril, added to by an open cut on his left cheek. Corbett's running fire of irritation served but to make Johnson smile the merrier, and to wink at him across Jeffries' shoulder in the clinches.

So far, no problems have been solved, no questions answered. The yellow streak had not appeared. Neither had Jeffries bored in, ripping awfully, nor put it over Johnson in the clinches. Yet one thing had been shown. Jeffries was not as fast as he had been. There was a shade of diminution in his speed.

Johnson signalized the opening of the sixth round by landing stinging blows to the face in one, two, three order. Johnson's quickness was startling. In response to an irritating remark from Corbett, Johnson replied suavely, "Too much on hand right now," and at the same instant he tore into Jeffries. It was Johnson's first real aggressive rush. It lasted but a second or two, but it was fierce and dandy. And at its conclusion it was manifest that Jeff's right eye was closing fast. The round ended with Johnson fighting and smiling strong, and with Jeff's nose, lip, and cheek bleeding and his eye closed. Johnson's round by a smile all the way through.

The seventh round was a mild one, opening with Jeff grim and silent and with Johnson leading and forcing. Both were careful and nothing happened, save that once they exchanged blows right niftily. So far Jeff's rough-

ing and crowding and bearing in of weight had amounted to nothing; also he
was doing less and less of it.

"It only takes one or two, Jeff," Corbett encouraged his principal in
the eighth round. Promptly Johnson landed two stingers. After a pause he
landed another. "See that?" he chirruped sweetly to Corbett in the corner.
Jeff perceptibly showed signs of slowing down in this round, rushing and
crowding less than ever. Jeff's slowing down was not due to the punishment
he had received, but to poorness of condition. He was flying the first signals
of fatigue. He was advertising, faintly, it is true, that he had not come back.

The ninth round was introduced by a suggestion from Corbett, heroically carrying out the policy that was bringing his principal to destruction.
"Make the big stiff fight," was Corbett's suggestion.

"That's right. That's what they all say," was Johnson's answer, delivered
with the true Chesterfield grace across his adversary's shoulder. In the previous rounds Jonson had not wreaked much damage with the forecasted cut,
the right uppercut.

In this round he demonstrated indubitably that he could drive the
left hand in a way that was surprising. Be it remembered that it had long been
denied that he had any sort of punch in that left of his. Incidentally, in this
round, it led all the others, and he landed a blow near Jeffries' heart that must
have been discouraging.

The tenth round showed Johnson with his unexpected left, as quick
as ever, and Jeffries going slower and slower. The conclusion of the first ten
rounds may be summed up as follows:

The fight was all in favor of Johnson, who had shown no yellow, who
had shown condition, who had shown undiminished speed, who had not
used his right uppercut much, who had developed a savage left, who had held
his own in the clinches, who had gotten the best of the infighting and all the
outfighting, who was unhurt, and who was smiling all the way.

Jeff was in bad shape: He was tired, slower than ever, his rushes had
been futile, and the sports who had placed their money against him were
jubilant.

There were men who proclaimed they saw the end. I refused to see
this end, for I had picked Jeff to win, and I was hoping hugely—for what I
did not know, but for something to happen, for anything that would turn
the tide of battle. And yet I could not hide from myself the truth, that Jeff
slowed down.

The eleventh round looked better for Jeff. Stung by a remark of Corbett's, Johnson rushed and provoked one grand rally from Jeff. It was faster fighting and more continuous than at any time in the preceding ten rounds, culminating in a fierce rally in which Jeff landed hard.

Round Twelve found Johnson, if anything, quicker and more aggressive than ever. "Thought you were going to have me wild?" Johnson queried sweetly of Corbett. As usual every remark of Corbett's brought more punishment to Jeffries. And by the end of this round the second of the two great questions was definitely answered. Jeff had not come back.

The thirteenth round was the beginning of the end. Beginning slowly enough, but stung by Corbett, Johnson put it all over him in the mouth fighting, and all over Jeff in the outfighting and the infighting. From defense to attack and back again and back and forth Johnson flashed like the amazing fight mechanism he is. Jeff was silent and sick, while as the round progressed Corbett was noticeably silent.

A few entertained the fond hope that Jeff could recuperate, but it was futile; there was no comeback in him. He was a fading, heartsick, heartbroken man.

"Talk to him, Corbett," Jeff's friends appealed in the fourteenth round, but Corbett could not talk. He had long since seen the end. And yet through this round Johnson went in for one of his characteristic loafing spells. He took it easy and played with the big gladiator, cool as a cucumber, smiling broadly as ever, and yet, as careful as ever. "Right on the hip," he grinned out once as Jeff in a desperate dying flurry managed to land a wild punch in that vicinity.

Corbett, likewise desperate, ventured a last sally. "Why don't you do something?" he cried to the loafing, laughing Johnson. "Too clever, too clever, like you," was the reply.

Round Fifteen and the end. It was pitiful. There happened to Jeff the bitterness that he had so often made others taste, but which for the first time, perforce, he was made to taste himself.

He who had never been knocked down was knocked down repeatedly. He who had never been knocked out was knocked out. Never mind the technical decision. Jeff was knocked out and through the ropes by the punch he never believed Johnson possessed—by the left and not by the right. As he lay across the lower rope while the seconds were tolled off, a cry that had in it tears and abject broken pride went up from many of the spectators.

"Don't let the Negro knock him out! Don't let the Negro knock him out!" was the oft-repeated cry.

There is little more to be said. Jeff did not come back. Johnson did not show the yellow streak. And it was Johnson's fight all the way through. Jeff was not the old Jeff at all.

Even so, it is to be doubted if this old Jeff could have put away this amazing Negro from Texas, this black man with the unfailing smile, this king of fighters and monologists.

Corbett and Berger and the others were right. They wanted Jeff to do more boxing and fighting in his training. Nevertheless, lacking the comeback, as he so patently did, this preliminary boxing and fighting would have profited him nothing. On the other hand, it would have saved his camp much of the money with which it backed him.

It was a slow fight. Faster, better fights may be seen every day of the year in any of the small clubs in the land. It is true these men were heavyweights, yet for heavyweights it was a slow fight.

It must be granted that plucky Tommy Burns put up a faster fight with Johnson a year and a half ago. Yet the American fight followers had to see this fight of today in order to appreciate what Burns did against this colored wonder.

Johnson is a wonder. No one understands him, this man who smiles. Well, the story of the fight is the story of a smile. If ever man won by nothing more fatiguing than a smile, Johnson won today.

And where now is the champion who will make Johnson extend himself, who will glaze those bright eyes, remove that smile and silence that golden repartee?

The Battle Royal

RALPH ELLISON

Though Ralph Ellison (1914–1994) published only one novel in his lifetime, that novel was choice. *Invisible Man* began rocking the foundations of American literature and American culture soon after its appearance in 1952, and if the metaphor supplied by its title remains dispiriting, the metaphors inherent in this boxing scene are absolutely Dantean in the depths they still take us.

Everyone praised me and I was invited to give the speech at a gathering of the town's leading white citizens. It was a triumph for our whole community.

It was in the main ballroom of the leading hotel. When I got there I discovered that it was on the occasion of a smoker, and was told that since I was to be there anyway I might as well take part in the battle royal to be fought by some of my schoolmates as part of the entertainment. The battle royal came first.

All of the town's big shots were there in their tuxedoes, wolfing down the buffet foods, drinking beer and whiskey, and smoking black cigars. It was a large room with a high ceiling. Chairs were arranged in neat rows around three sides of a portable boxing ring. The fourth side was clear, revealing a gleaming space of polished floor. I had some misgivings over the battle royal, by the way. Not from a distaste for fighting, but because I didn't care too much for the other fellows who were to take part. They were tough guys who seemed to have no grandfather's curse worrying their minds. No one could mistake their toughness. And besides, I suspected that fighting a battle royal might detract from the dignity of my speech. In those pre-invisible days I visualized myself as a potential Booker T. Washington. But the other fellows didn't care too much for me either, and there were nine of them. I felt superior to them in my way, and I didn't like the manner in which we were all crowded together into the servants' elevator. Nor did they like my being there. In fact, as the warmly lighted floors flashed past the elevator we had words over the fact that I, by taking part in the fight, had knocked one of their friends out of a night's work.

We were led out of the elevator through a rococo hall into an anteroom and told to get into our fighting togs. Each of us was issued a pair of boxing gloves and ushered out into the big mirrored hall, which we entered looking cautiously about us and whispering, lest we might accidentally be heard above the noise of the room. It was foggy with cigar smoke. And already the whiskey was taking effect. I was shocked to see some of the most important men of the town quite tipsy. They were all there—bankers, lawyers, judges, doctors, fire chiefs, teachers, merchants. Even one of the more fashionable pastors. Something we could not see was going on up front. A clarinet was vibrating sensuously and the men were standing up and moving eagerly forward. We were a small tight group, clustered together, our bare upper bodies touching and shining with anticipatory sweat; while up front the big shots were becoming increasingly excited over something we still could not see. Suddenly I heard the school superintendent, who had told me to come, yell, "Bring up the shines, gentlemen! Bring up the little shines!"

We were rushed up to the front of the ballroom, where it smelled even more strongly of tobacco and whiskey. Then we were pushed into place. I almost wet my pants. A sea of faces, some hostile, some amused, ringed around us, and in the center, facing us, stood a magnificent blonde—stark naked. There was dead silence. I felt a blast of cold air chill me. I tried to back away, but they were behind me and around me. Some of the boys stood with lowered heads, trembling. I felt a wave of irrational guilt and fear. My teeth chattered, my skin turned to goose flesh, my knees knocked. Yet I was strongly attracted and looked in spite of myself. Had the price of looking been blindness, I would have looked. The hair was yellow like that of a circus kewpie doll, the face heavily powdered and rouged, as though to form an abstract mask, the eyes hollow and smeared a cool blue, the color of a baboon's butt. I felt a desire to spit upon her as my eyes brushed slowly over her body. Her breasts were firm and round as the domes of East Indian temples, and I stood so close as to see the fine skin texture, and beads of pearly perspiration glistening like dew around the pink and erected buds of her nipples. I wanted at one and the same time to run from the room, to sink through the floor, or go to her and cover her from my eyes and the eyes of the others with my body; to feel the soft thighs, to caress her and destroy her, to love her and murder her, to hide from her, and yet to stroke where below the small American flag tattooed upon her belly her thighs formed a capital V. I had a notion that of all in the room she saw only me with her impersonal eyes.

And then she began to dance, a slow sensuous movement; the smoke of a hundred cigars clinging to her like the thinnest of veils. She seemed like a fair bird-girl girdled in veils calling to me from the angry surface of some gray and threatening sea. I was transported. Then I became aware of the clarinet playing and the big shots yelling at us. Some threatened us if we looked and others if we did not. On my right I saw one boy faint. And now a man grabbed a silver pitcher from a table and stepped close as he dashed ice water upon him and stood him up and forced two of us to support him as his head hung and moans issued from his thick bluish lips. Another boy began to plead to go home. He was the largest of the group, wearing dark red fighting trunks much too small to conceal the erection which projected from him as though in answer to the insinuating low-registered moaning of the clarinet. He tried to hide himself with his boxing gloves.

And all the while the blonde continued dancing, smiling faintly at the big shots who watched her with fascination, and faintly smiling at our fear. I noticed a certain merchant who followed her hungrily, his lips loose and drooling. He was a large man who wore diamond studs in a shirtfront which swelled with the ample paunch underneath, and each time the blonde swayed her undulating hips he ran his hand through the thin hair of his bald head and, with his arms upheld, his posture clumsy like that of an intoxicated panda, wound his belly in a slow and obscene grind. This creature was completely hypnotized. The music had quickened. As the dancer flung herself about with a detached expression on her face, the men began reaching out to touch her. I could see their beefy fingers sink into the soft flesh. Some of the others tried to stop them and she began to move around the floor in graceful circles, as they gave chase, slipping and sliding over the polished floor. It was mad. Chairs went crashing, drinks were spilt, as they ran laughing and howling after her. They caught her just as she reached a door, raised her from the floor, and tossed her as college boys are tossed at a hazing, and above her red, fixed-smiling lips I saw the terror and disgust in her eyes, almost like my own terror and that which I saw in some of the other boys. As I watched, they tossed her twice and her soft breasts seemed to flatten against the air and her legs flung wildly as she spun. Some of the more sober ones helped her to escape. And I started off the floor, heading for the anteroom with the rest of the boys.

Some were still crying and in hysteria. But as we tried to leave we were stopped and ordered to get into the ring. There was nothing to do but what we were told. All ten of us climbed under the ropes and allowed ourselves to be blindfolded with broad bands of white cloth. One of the men seemed to feel a bit sympathetic and tried to cheer us up as we stood with our backs against the ropes. Some of us tried to grin. "See that boy over there?" one of the men said. "I want you to run across at the bell and give it to him right in the belly. If you don't get him, I'm going to get you. I don't like his looks." Each of us was told the same. The blindfolds were put on. Yet even then I had been going over my speech. In my mind each word was as bright as flame. I felt the cloth pressed into place, and frowned so that it would be loosened when I relaxed.

But now I felt a sudden fit of blind terror. I was unused to darkness. It was as though I had suddenly found myself in a dark room filled with poisonous cottonmouths. I could hear the bleary voices yelling insistently for the battle royal to begin.

"Get going in there!"

"Let me at that big nigger!"

I strained to pick up the school superintendent's voice, as though to squeeze some security out of that slightly more familiar sound.

"Let me at those black sonsabitches!" someone yelled.

"No, Jackson, no!" another voice yelled. "Here, somebody, help me hold Jack."

"I want to get at that ginger-colored nigger. Tear him limb from limb," the first voice yelled.

I stood against the ropes trembling. For in those days, I was what they called ginger-colored, and he sounded as though he might crunch me between his teeth like a crisp ginger cookie.

Quite a struggle was going on. Chairs were being kicked about and I could hear voices grunting as with a terrific effort. I wanted to see, to see more desperately than ever before. But the blindfold was as tight as a thick skin-puckering scab and when I raised my gloved hands to push the layers of white aside a voice yelled, "Oh, no you don't, black bastard! Leave that alone!"

"Ring the bell before Jackson kills him a coon!" someone boomed in the sudden silence. And I heard the bell clang and the sound of the feet scuffling forward.

A glove smacked against my head. I pivoted, striking out stiffly as someone went past, and felt the jar ripple along the length of my arm to my shoulder. Then it seemed as though all nine of the boys had turned upon me at once. Blows pounded me from all sides while I struck out as best I could. So many blows landed upon me that I wondered if I were not the only blindfolded fighter in the ring, or if the man called Jackson hadn't succeeded in getting me after all.

Blindfolded, I could no longer control my motions. I had no dignity. I stumbled about like a baby or a drunken man. The smoke had become thicker and with each new blow it seemed to sear and further restrict my lungs. My saliva became like hot bitter glue. A glove connected with my head, filling my mouth with warm blood. It was everywhere. I could not tell if the moisture I felt upon my body was sweat or blood. A blow landed hard against the nape of my neck. I felt myself going over, my head hitting the floor. Streaks of blue light filled the black world behind the blindfold. I lay prone, pretending that I was knocked out, but felt myself seized by hands and yanked to my feet. "Get going, black boy! Mix it up!" My arms were like lead, my head smarting from blows. I managed to feel my way to the ropes and held on, trying to catch my breath. A glove landed in my midsection and I went over again, feeling as though the smoke had become a knife jabbed into my guts. Pushed this way and that by the legs milling around me, I finally pulled erect and discovered that I could see the black, sweat-washed forms weaving in the smoky-blue atmosphere like drunken dancers weaving to the rapid drum-like thuds of blows.

Everyone fought hysterically. It was complete anarchy. Everybody fought everybody else. No group fought together for long. Two, three, four, fought one, then turned to fight each other, were themselves attacked. Blows landed below the belt and in the kidney with the gloves open as well as closed, and with my eye partly opened now there was not so much terror. I moved carefully, avoiding blows, although not too many to attract attention, fighting from group to group. The boys groped about like blind, cautious crabs crouching to protect their midsections, their heads pulled in short against their shoulders, their arms stretched nervously before them, with their fists testing the smoke-filled air like the knobbed feelers of hypersensitive snails. In one corner I glimpsed a boy violently punching the air and heard him scream in pain as he smashed his hand against a ring post. For a second I saw him bent over holding his hand, then going down as a blow caught his unprotected head. I played one group against the other, slipping in and throwing a punch then stepping out of range while pushing the others into the melee to take the blows blindly aimed at me. The smoke was agonizing and there were no rounds, no bells at three minute intervals to relieve our exhaustion. The room spun round me, a swirl of lights, smoke, sweating bodies surrounded by tense white faces. I bled from both nose and mouth, the blood spattering upon my chest.

The men kept yelling, "Slug him, black boy! Knock his guts out!"

"Uppercut him! Kill him! Kill that big boy!"

Taking a fake fall, I saw a boy going down heavily beside me as though we were felled by a single blow, saw a sneaker-clad foot shoot into his groin as the two who had knocked him down stumbled upon him. I rolled out of range, feeling a twinge of nausea.

The harder we fought the more threatening the men became. And yet, I had begun to worry about my speech again. How would it go? Would they recognize my ability? What would they give me?

I was fighting automatically when suddenly I noticed that one after another of the boys was leaving the ring. I was surprised, filled with panic, as though I had been left alone with an unknown danger. Then I understood. The boys had arranged it among themselves. It was the custom for the two men left in the ring to slug it out for the winner's prize. I discovered this too late. When the bell sounded two men in tuxedoes leaped into the ring and removed the blindfold. I found myself facing Tatlock, the biggest of the gang. I felt sick at my stomach. Hardly had the bell stopped ringing in my ears than it clanged again and I saw him moving swiftly toward me. Thinking of nothing else to do I hit him smash on the nose. He kept coming, bringing the rank sharp violence of stale sweat. His face was a black blank of a face, only his eyes alive—with hate of me and aglow with a feverish terror from what had happened to us all. I became anxious. I wanted to deliver my speech and he came at me as though he meant to beat it out of me. I smashed him again and again, taking his blows as they came. Then on a sudden impulse struck him lightly and as we clinched, I whispered, "Fake like I knocked you out, you can have the prize."

"I'll break your behind," he whispered hoarsely.

"For *them?*"

"For *me,* sonofabitch!"

They were yelling for us to break it up and Tatlock spun me half around with a blow, and as a joggled camera sweeps in a reeling scene, I saw the howling red faces crouching tense beneath the cloud of blue-gray smoke. For a moment the world wavered, unraveled, flowed, then my head cleared and Tatlock bounced before me. That fluttering shadow before my eyes was his jabbing left hand. Then falling forward, my head against his damp shoulder, I whispered,

"I'll make it five dollars more."

"Go to hell!"

But his muscles relaxed a trifle beneath my pressure and I breathed, "Seven?"

"Give it to your ma," he said, ripping me beneath the heart.

And while I still held him I butted him and moved away. I felt myself bombarded with punches. I fought back with hopeless desperation. I wanted to deliver my speech more than anything else in the world, because I felt that only these men could judge truly my ability, and now this stupid clown was ruining my chances. I began fighting carefully now, moving in to punch him and out again with my greater speed. A lucky blow to his chin and I had him going too—until I heard a loud voice yell, "I got my money on the big boy."

Hearing this, I almost dropped my guard. I was confused. Should I try to win against the voice out there? Would not this go against my speech, and was not this a moment for humility, for nonresistance? A blow to my head as I danced about sent my right eye popping like a jack-in-the-box and settled my dilemma. The room went red as I fell. It was a dream fall, my body languid and fastidious as to where to land, until the floor became impatient and smashed up to meet me. A moment later I came to. An hypnotic voice said FIVE emphatically. And I lay there, hazily watching a dark red spot of my own blood shaping itself into a butterfly, glistening and soaking into the soiled gray world of the canvas.

When the voice drawled TEN I was lifted up and dragged to a chair. I sat dazed. My eye pained and swelled with each throb of my pounding heart and I wondered if now I would be allowed to speak. I was wringing wet, my mouth still bleeding. We were grouped along the wall now. The other boys ignored me as they congratulated Tatlock and speculated as to how much they would be paid. One boy whimpered over his smashed hand. Looking up front, I saw attendants in white jackets rolling the portable ring away and placing a small square rug in the vacant space surrounded by chairs. Perhaps, I thought, I will stand on the rug to deliver my speech.

Then the M.C. called to us, "Come on up here boys and get your money."

We ran forward to where the men laughed and talked in their chairs, waiting. Everyone seemed friendly now.

"There it is on the rug," the man said. I saw the rug covered with coins of all dimensions and a few crumpled bills. But what excited me, scattered here and there, were the gold pieces.

"Boys, it's all yours," the man said. "You get all you grab."

"That's right, Sambo," a blond man said, winking at me confidentially.

I trembled with excitement, forgetting my pain. I would get the gold and the bills, I thought. I would use both hands. I would throw my body against the boys nearest me to block them from the gold.

"Get down around the rug now," the man commanded, "and don't anyone touch it until I give the signal."

"This ought to be good," I heard.

As told, we got around the square rug on our knees. Slowly the man raised his freckled hand as we followed it upward with our eyes.

I heard, "These niggers look like they're about to pray!"

Then, "Ready," the man said. "Go!"

I lunged for a yellow coin lying on the blue design of the carpet, touching it and sending a surprised shriek to join those rising around me. I tried frantically to remove my hand but could not let go. A hot, violent force tore through my body, shaking me like a wet rat. The rug was electrified. The hair bristled up on my head as I shook myself free. My muscles jumped, my nerves jangled, writhed. But I saw that this was not stopping the other boys. Laughing in fear and embarrassment, some were holding back and scooping up the coins knocked off by the painful contortions of the others. The men roared above us as we struggled.

"Pick it up, goddamnit, pick it up!" someone called like a bass-voiced parrot. "Go on, get it!"

I crawled rapidly around the floor, picking up the coins, trying to avoid the coppers and to get greenbacks and the gold. Ignoring the shock by laughing, as I brushed the coins off quickly, I discovered that I could contain the electricity—a contradiction, but it works. Then the men began to push us onto the rug. Laughing embarrassedly, we struggled out of their hands and kept after the coins. We were all wet and slippery and hard to hold. Suddenly I saw a boy lifted into the air, glistening with sweat like a circus seal, and dropped, his wet back landing flush upon the charged rug, heard him yell and saw him literally dance upon his back, his elbows beating a frenzied tattoo upon the floor, his muscles twitching like the flesh of a horse stung by many flies. When he finally rolled off, his face was gray and no one stopped him when he ran from the floor amid booming laughter.

"Get the money," the M.C. called. "That's good hard American cash!"

And we snatched and grabbed, snatched and grabbed. I was careful not to come too close to the rug now, and when I felt the hot whiskey breath descend upon me like a cloud of foul air I reached out and grabbed the leg of a chair. It was occupied and I held on desperately.

"Leggo, nigger! Leggo!"

The huge face wavered down to mine as he tried to push me free. But my body was slippery and he was too drunk. It was Mr. Colcord, who owned a chain of movie houses and "entertainment palaces." Each time he grabbed me I slipped out of his hands. It became a real struggle. I feared the rug more than I did the drunk, so I held on, surprising myself for a moment by trying to topple *him* upon the rug. It was such an enormous idea that I found myself actually carrying it out. I tried not to be obvious, yet when I grabbed his leg, trying to tumble him out of the chair, he raised up roaring with laughter, and, looking at me with soberness dead in the eye, kicked me viciously in the chest. The chair leg flew out of my hand and I felt myself going and rolled. It was as though I had rolled through a bed of hot coals. It seemed a whole century would pass before I would roll free, a century in which I was seared through the deepest levels of my body to the fearful breath within me and the breath seared and heated to the point of explosion. It'll all be over in a flash, I thought as I rolled clear. It'll all be over in a flash.

But not yet, the men on the other side were waiting, red faces swollen as though from apoplexy as they bent forward in their chairs. Seeing their fingers coming toward me I rolled away as a fumbled football rolls off the receivers' fingertips, back into the coals. That time I luckily sent the rug sliding out of place and heard the cons ringing against the floor and the boys scuffling to pick them up and the M.C. calling. "All right, boys, that's all. Go get dressed and get your money."

I was limp as a dish rag. My back felt as though it had been beaten with wires.

When we had dressed the M.C. came in and gave us each five dollars, except Tatlock, who got ten for being last in the ring. Then he told us to leave. I was not to get a chance to deliver my speech, I thought. I was going out into the dim alley in despair when I was stopped and told to go back. I returned to the ballroom, where the men were pushing back their chairs and gathering in groups to talk.

The M.C. knocked on a table for quiet. "Gentlemen," he said, "we almost forgot an important part of the program. A most serious part, gentlemen. This boy was brought here to deliver a speech which he made at his graduation yesterday . . ."

"Bravo!"

"I'm told that he is the smartest boy we've got out there in Greenwood. I'm told that he knows more big words than a pocket-sized dictionary."

Much applause and laughter.

"So now, gentlemen, I want you to give him your attention."

There was still laughter as I faced them, my mouth dry, my eye throbbing. I began slowly, but evidently my throat was tense, because they began shouting, "Louder! Louder!"

"We of the younger generation extol the wisdom of that great leader and educator," I shouted, "who first spoke these flaming words of wisdom: 'A ship lost at sea for many days suddenly sighted a friendly vessel. From the mast of the unfortunate vessel was seen a signal: "Water, water, we die of thirst!" The answer from the friendly vessel came back: "Cast down your bucket where you are." The captain of the distressed vessel, at last heeding the injunction, cast down his bucket, and it came up full of fresh sparkling water from the mouth of the Amazon River.' And like him I say, and in his words, 'To those of my race who depend upon bettering their condition in a foreign land, or who underestimate the ignorance of cultivating friendly relations with the Southern white man, who is his next-door neighbor, I would say: "Cast down your bucket where you are"—cast it down in making friends in every manly way of the people of all races by whom we are surrounded . . .'"

A Visit with John L. Sullivan

NELLIE BLY

One of the most famous reporters of the late 19th century, Nellie Bly (1864–1922) had a knack for cutting any subject down to size. Less than six months after traveling to upstate New York to take on the reigning heavyweight champ John L. Sullivan for *The New York World,* she set off, on November 14, 1889, to shrink the planet. In one of the most storied excursions in the history of journalism, Bly circumnavigated the globe in 72 days, six hours and 11 minutes, besting by more than a week the seemingly unapproachable mark established by the fictional Fileas Fogg in Jules Verne's *Around the World in 80 Days.*

I f John L. Sullivan isn't able to whip any pugilist in the world I would like to see the man who is. I went to Belfast, N.Y., to see him last week and I was surprised. Why? Well, I will tell you.

I have often thought that the sparring instinct is inborn—in everything—except women and flowers, of course. I have seen funny little spring roosters, without one feather's sprout to crow about, fight like real men. And then the boys! Isn't it funny how proud they are of their muscle, and how quiet the boy is who hasn't any? Almost as soon as a boy learns to walk he learns to jump into position of defense and double up his fists.

We reached Belfast about 7:30 o'clock in the morning and were the only passengers for that place. Mr. William Muldoon's house, where Mr. Sullivan is training, is in the prettiest part of the town and only a short distance from the hotel. Fearing that Mr. Sullivan would go out for a walk and that I would miss him, I went immediately to the Muldoon cottage.

One would never imagine from the surroundings that a prizefighter was being trained there. The house is a very pretty little two-story building, surrounded by the smoothest and greenest of green lawns, which helps to intensify the spotless whiteness of the cottage. A wide veranda surrounds the three sides of the cottage, and the easy chairs and hammocks give it a most enticing look of comfort. Large maple trees shade the house from the glare of the sun.

I rang the bell, and when a colored man came in answer I sent my letter of introduction to Mr. Muldoon. A handsome young man, whose broad shoulders were neatly fitted with a gray corduroy coat, came into the room, holding a light gray cap in his hand. His face was youthful, his eyes blue, his expression pleasing, his smile brought two dimples to punctuate his rosy cheeks, his bearing was easy and most graceful, and this was the champion wrestler and athlete, William Muldoon.

"We have just returned from our two-mile walk," he said, when I told him I had come to see Mr. Sullivan, "and Mr. Sullivan is just being rubbed down. If you will excuse me one moment I will tell him."

In a few moments Mr. Muldoon returned, followed by a man whom I would never have taken for the great and only Sullivan. He was a tall man, with enormous shoulders, and wore dark trousers, a light cheviot coat and vest and slippers. In his hand he held a light cloth cap. He paused almost as he entered the room in a half-bashful way, and twisted his cap in a very boyish but not ungraceful manner.

"Miss Bly, Mr. Sullivan," said Mr. Muldoon, and I looked into the great fighter's dark, bright eyes as he bent his broad shoulders before me.

"Mr. Sullivan, I would like to shake hands with you," I said, and he took my hand with a firm, hearty grasp, and with a hand that felt small and soft. Mr. Muldoon excused himself, and I was left to interview the great John L.

"I came here to learn all about you, Mr. Sullivan, so will you please begin by telling me at what time you get up in the morning," I said.

"Well, I get up about 6 o'clock and get rubbed down," he began, in a matter-of-fact way. "Then Muldoon and I walk and run a mile or a mile and a half away and then back. Just as soon as we get in I am given a showerbath, and after being thoroughly rubbed down again I put on an entire fresh outfit."

"What kind of clothing do you wear for your walk? Heavy?" I asked.

"Yes, I wear a heavy sweater and a suit of heavy corduroy buttoned tightly. I also wear gloves. After my walk I put on a fresh sweater, so that I won't take cold."

"What's a sweater?" I asked.

"I'll show you," he said, with a smile, and, excusing himself, he went out. In a moment he returned with a garment in his hand. It was a very heavy knit garment, with long sleeves and a standing collar. It was all in one piece and, I imagine, weighed several pounds. "Well, what do you wear a sweater for, and why do you take such violent walks?" I asked, my curiosity being satisfied as to the strange "sweater."

"I wear a sweater to make me warm, and I walk to reduce my fat and to harden my muscles. Last Friday I lost six pounds and last Saturday I lost six and a half pounds. When I came here I weighed 237 pounds, and now I weigh 218. Before I leave here I will weigh only 195 pounds."

"Do you take a cold showerbath when your walk is finished?"

"No, never. I don't believe in cold water. It chills the blood. I always have my showerbath of a medium temperature."

"How are you rubbed down, then, as you term it?"

"I have two men give me a brisk rubbing with their hands. Then they rub me down with a mixture of ammonia, camphor, and alcohol."

"What do you eat?"

"I eat nothing fattening. I have oatmeal for breakfast and meat and bread for dinner, and cold meat and stale bread for supper. I eat no sweets nor potatoes. I used to smoke all the day, but since I came here I haven't seen a cigar. Occasionally Mr. Muldoon gives me a glass of ale, but it doesn't average one a day."

"Then training is not very pleasant work?"

"It's the worst thing going. A fellow would rather fight twelve dozen times than train once, but it's got to be done," and he leaned back in the easy chair with an air of weariness. "After breakfast I rest awhile," he continued, "and then putting on our heaviest clothes again we start out at 10:30 for our twelve-mile run and walk, which we do in two hours. We generally go across the fields to Mr. Muldoon's farm because it is all uphill work and makes us warm. When we get back I am rubbed down again and at one we have dinner. In the afternoon we wrestle, punch a bag, throw footballs, swing Indian clubs and dumbbells, practice the chest movement and such things until suppertime. It's all right to be here when the sun is out, but after dark it's the dreariest place I ever struck. I wouldn't live here if they gave me the whole country."

The 'Champion Rest,' the name by which Mr. Muldoon's home is known, is surrounded by two graveyards, a church, the priest's home and a little cottage occupied by two old maids.

"I couldn't sleep after 5 o'clock this morning on account of Mr. Muldoon's cow. It kept up a hymn all the morning and the birds joined in the chorus. It's no use to try to sleep here after daybreak. The noise would knock out anything."

"Do you like prizefighting?" I asked Mr. Sullivan, after he had laid his complaint about the "singing cow" before Mrs. Muldoon.

"I don't," he replied. "Of course I did once, or rather I was fond of traveling about and the excitement of the crowds, but this is my last fight."

"Why?"

"Well, I am tired and I want to settle down. I am getting old," and he leaned back wearily.

"What is your age?"

"I was born the 15th of October, 1858. I began prizefighting when I was only nineteen years old. How did I start? Well, I had a match with a prize man who had never been downed, and I was the winner. This got me lots of notice, so I went through the country giving exhibitions. I have made plenty of money in my day, but I have been a fool and today I have nothing. It came easy and went easy. I have provided well for my father and mother, and they are in comfortable circumstances."

"What will you do if you stop fighting?"

"If I win this fight I will travel for a year giving sparring exhibitions, and then I will settle down. I have always wanted to run a hotel in New York, and if I am successful I think I shall spend the rest of my life as a hotel proprietor."

"How much money have you made during your career as a prize fighter?"

"I have made $500,000 or $600,000 in boxing. I made $125,000 from September 26, 1883, to May 26, 1884, when I traveled through the country offering $1,000 to anyone I couldn't knock out in four rounds, which takes twelve minutes."

"How do you dress when you go in a prize ring?"

"I wear knee breeches, stockings and shoes, and no shirt."

"Why no shirt?"

"Because a man perspires so freely that if he wears a shirt he is liable to chill, and a chill is always fatal in a prize ring. I took a chill when I fought with Mitchell, but it didn't last long."

"What kind of shoes do you wear?"

"Regular spike shoes. They have three big spikes to prevent slipping."

"How will you fight Kilrain, with or without gloves?"

"I will fight Kilrain according to the London prize-ring rules. That's without gloves and allows wrestling and throwing a man down. We get a rest every thirty seconds. Under the Marquis of Queensberry rules we wear gloves, anything under eleven ounces. They give us three minutes to a round under the Queensberry, and when the three minutes are up you have to rest whether you could whip your man the next instant or not."

"Your hands look very soft and small for a fighter."

"Do they?" and he held one out to me for inspection. "My friends tell me they look like hams," and he laughed. "I wear number nine gloves."

I examined his hand, he watching me with an amused expression. It looks a small hand to bear the record of so many "knockout" blows. The fingers were straight and shapely. The closely trimmed nails were a lovely oval and pink. The only apparent difference was the great thickness through.

"Feel my arm," he said, with a bright smile, as he doubled it up. I tried to feel the muscle, but it was like a rock. With both my hands I tried to span it, but I couldn't. Meanwhile the great fellow sat there watching me with a most boyish expression of amusement.

"By the time I am ready to fight there won't be any fat on my hands or face. They will be as hard as a bone. Do I harden them? Certainly. If I didn't I would have pieces knocked off of me. I have a mixture of rock salt and white wine and vinegar and several other ingredients which I wash my hands and face with."

"Do you hit a man on the face and neck and anywhere you can?" I asked.

"Certainly, any place above the belt that I get a chance," and he smiled.

"Don't you hate to hit a man so?"

"I don't think about it," still smiling.

"When you see that you have hurt him don't you feel sorry?"

"I never feel sorry until the fight is over."

"How do you feel when you get hit very hard?"

The dark, bright eyes glanced at me lazily and the deep, deep voice said with feeling: "I only want a chance to hit back."

"Did you ever see a man killed in the ring?"

"No, I never did, and I only knew of one fellow who died in the ring, and that was Walker, who died at Philadelphia from neglect after the fight was over."

Although I had my breakfast before reaching Mr. Muldoon's cottage I accepted his proposal to break bread with him and his guests. At a nearer view the dining room did not lose any of its prettiness and the daintiness of everything—the artistic surroundings, the noiseless and efficient colored waiter, the open windows on both sides, giving pretty views of green lawns and shady trees; the canary birds swelling their yellow throats occasionally with sweet little thrills, the green parrot climbing up its brass cage and talking about "crackers," the white table linen and beautiful dishes, down to the large bunch of fragrant lilacs and another of beautifully shaped and colored wild flowers, separated by a slipper filled with velvety pansies—was all entirely foreign to any idea I had ever conceived of prizefighters and their surroundings.

Yes, and they were all perfectly at ease and happy. At one end of the table sat Mrs. Muldoon and facing her was Mr. Muldoon. Next to Mrs. Muldoon sat my companion, then came myself, and next Mr. Sullivan. On the opposite side were the assistant trainers, Mr. Barnitt, a well-bred, scholarly-looking man, and Mr. Cleary, a smooth-faced, mischievous man who doesn't look much past boyhood. Mr. Sullivan's brother, who is anxious to knock out somebody, sat opposite Mr. Sullivan. And the wild flowers which graced the table were gathered by these great, strong men while taking their morning walk through the country.

About a mile from Champion Rest, his town home, is Mr. Muldoon's beautiful farm of seventy acres, which is well stocked with fine cattle. In the rear of Champion Rest are the barn and the training quarters. On the first floor are three stalls, fitted out after the latest improved method, where Mr. Muldoon keeps his favorite horses. Everything is as clean and pleasant as in a dwelling house.

In the next room, suspended from the ceiling, is a Rugby football, which Mr. Sullivan pounds regularly every day in a manner which foretells hard times for Kilrain's head. The big football with which they play ball daily is also kept here. It is enormous and so heavy that when Mr. Muldoon dropped it into my arms I almost toppled over. Upstairs the floor is covered with a white wrestling pad, where the two champions wrestle every afternoon. In one corner is a collection of dumbbells, from medium weight to the heaviest, and several sizes of Indian clubs. Fastened to one side of the wall is a chest expander, which also comes in for daily use.

Downstairs is Champion Muldoon's den. Everything about it, as about the barn, is of a hardwood finish. There is no plaster nor paper anywhere. In one corner of the den is a glass case, where hang a fur-lined overcoat and several other garments. Along the top of the case is suspended a gold-headed cane. In the center of the room is a writing table, with every-thing ready for use. Along one side of the hall is a rattan lounge, at the foot of which is spread a yellow fur rug. The floor is neatly carpeted, and several rocking chairs prove that the den is for comfort.

The walls are covered with photographs of well-known people and among them several of Modjeska, with whom Mr. Muldoon at one time traveled. Ther are also a number of photographs of Mr. Muldoon in positions assumed in posing as Greek statues. On a corner table are albums filled with photographs of prominent athletes, and scrapbooks containing hundreds of notices of Champion Muldoon's athletic conquests. Then there are a number of well-bound standard works and the photographs of Mr. Muldoon's fa-vorite authors—Bryant, Longfellow and, I believe, Shakespeare.

"I don't make any money by this," said Mr. Muldoon, in speaking about turning his home into training quarters, "but I was anxious to see Mr. Sullivan do justice to himself in this coming fight. It was a case of a fallen giant, so I thought to get him away from all bad influences and to get him in good trim. This is the healthiest place in the country and one of the most dif-ficult to reach—two desirable things. On the way here we had a special car, but there were more people in our car than in any other. When we go to New Orleans we will keep our car locked and none but Mr. Sullivan's back-ers and representatives of the press will be admitted. Mr. Sullivan is the most obedient man I ever saw. He hasn't asked for a drink or a smoke since he came here and takes what I allow him without a murmur. It is a pleasure to train him."

"Does Mr. Sullivan never get angry?" I asked.

"If you would hear him and Mr. Barnitt sometimes, you would think they were going to eat one another," said Mrs. Muldoon.

"When he does get angry he runs over the fields until his good humor returns," said Mr. Barnitt, while Mr. Muldoon said that Mr. Sullivan was as docile as a lamb. They all spoke in praise of his strong will power and his childlike obedience.

"You are the first woman who ever interviewed me," said Mr. Sulli-van in the afternoon, "and I have given you more than I ever gave any re-porter in my life. They generally manufacture things and credit them to me, although some are mighty good fellows."

"When reporters act all right we will give them all they want," said Mr. Muldoon. "The other day a fresh reporter came here, and he thought because he was going to interview prizefighters he would have to be tough, so he said, 'Where's old Sullivan?' That queered him. We wouldn't give him a line."

"Yes, he came up to me first and said, 'Where's old Sullivan?'" said Mr. Sullivan. "And I told him, 'In the barn.' And he soon got put out of there for his toughness."

At suppertime Mr. Cleary had a great story to tell about his Irish bird trap. He had caught one robin, which Mrs. Muldoon released, and another had left his tail behind him. Then Mr. Barnitt and Mr. Sullivan's brother told how they had put some bird feathers in the cage to cheat the bird trapper.

And then the carriage came to take us to the train, and after I bade them all goodbye I shook hands with John L. Sullivan and wished him success in the coming fight, and I believe he will have it, too, don't you?

Sport for Art's Sake

Sportswriter, drama critic, columnist, essayist, and activist, Heywood Broun (1888–1939) was an enormous force in American journalism in the first third of the 20th century. Never afraid to champion his causes, he turned his "It Seems to Me" column—begun at the *Tribune* and then transferred, with its creator, to *The World* in 1921—into a booming mouthpiece against what he saw as social and political injustice. In 1930, he ran unsuccessfully for Congress as a Socialist. In 1933, he founded the American Newspaper Guild and served as its first president until his death, when New York's colorful Mayor Fiorello LaGuardia observed, "The forces of reaction did not hate Broun because he was a radical, nor did they dislike him because he was liberal; but how they feared him because he was truthful."

Still, Broun was not above having fun. One of the Algonquin Round Table wits, he wrote and starred in two musical revues on Broadway, and loved covering sports whenever he could; he began his career as a baseball writer. Given his politics, it's not surprising that Broun had such a soft spot—as he makes clear here—for Georges Carpentier in his 1921 challenge to Jack Dempsey. Underdogs never had a better friend.

     🥊   🥊   🥊   🥊

For years we had been hearing about moral victories and at last we saw one. This is not intended as an excuse for the fact that we said before the fight that Carpentier would beat Dempsey. We erred with Bernard Shaw. The surprising revelation which came to us on this July afternoon was that a thing may be done well enough to make victory

8 1

entirely secondary. We have all heard, of course, of sport for sport's sake but Georges Carpentier established a still more glamorous ideal. Sport for art's sake was what he showed us in the big wooden saucer over on Boyle's dirty acres.

It was the finest tragic performance in the lives of ninety-thousand persons. We hope that Professor George Pierce Baker sent his class in dramatic composition. We will be disappointed if Eugene O'Neill, the white hope of the American drama, was not there. Here for once was a laboratory demonstration of life. None of the crowds in Greece who went to somewhat more beautiful stadia in search of Euripides ever saw the spirit of tragedy more truly presented. And we will wager that Euripides was not able to lift his crowd up upon its hind legs into a concerted shout of "Medea! Medea! Medea!" as Carpentier moved the fight fans over in Jersey City in the second round. In fact it is our contention that the fight between Dempsey and Carpentier was the most inspiring spectacle which America has seen in a generation.

Personally we would go further back than that. We would not accept a ticket for David and Goliath as a substitute. We remember that in that instance the little man won, but it was a spectacle less fine in artistry from the fact that it was less true to life. The tradition that Jack goes up the beanstalk and kills his giant, and that Little Red Ridinghood has the better of the wolf, and many other stories are limited in their inspirational quality by the fact that they are not true. They are stories that man has invented to console himself on winter's evenings for the fact that he is small and the universe is large. Carpentier showed us something far more thrilling. All of us who watched him know now that man cannot beat down Fate, no matter how much his will may flame, but he can rock it back upon its heels when he puts all his heart and his shoulders into a blow.

That is what happened in the second round. Carpentier landed his straight right upon Dempsey's jaw and the champion, who was edging in toward him, shot back and then swayed forward. Dempsey's hands dropped to his side. He was an open target. Carpentier swung a terrific right-hand uppercut and missed. Dempsey fell into a clinch and held on until his head cleared. He kept close to Carpentier during the rest of the fight and wore him down with body blows during the infighting. We know of course that when the first prehistoric creature crawled out of the ooze up to the beaches (see *The Outline of History* by H. G. Wells, some place in the first volume, just a couple of pages after that picture of the big lizard) it was already settled that Carpentier was going to miss that uppercut. And naturally it was inevitable that he should have the worst of it at infighting. Fate gets us all in the clinches, but Eugene O'Neill and all our young writers of tragedy make a great mistake if they think that the poignancy of the fate of man lies in the fact that he is weak, pitiful, and helpless. The tragedy of life is not that man loses but that he almost wins. Or, if you are intent on pointing out that his downfall is inevitable, that at least he completes the gesture of being on the eve of victory.

For just eleven seconds on the afternoon of July 2 we felt that we were at the threshold of a miracle. There was such flash and power in that right-hand thrust of Carpentier's that we believed Dempsey would go down, and that fate would go with him and all the plans laid out in the days of the oozy friends of Mr. Wells. No sooner were the men in the ring together than it seemed just as certain that Dempsey would win as that the sun would come up on the morning of July 3. By and by we were not so sure about the sun. It might be down, we thought, and also out. It was included in the scope of Carpentier's punch, we feared. No, we did not exactly fear it. We respect the regularity of the universe by which we live, but we do not love it. If the blow had been as devastating as we first believed, we should have counted the world well lost.

Great circumstances produce great actors. History is largely concerned with arranging good entrances for people; and later exits not always quite as good. Carpentier played his part perfectly down to the last side. People who saw him just as he came before the crowd reported that he was pitifully nervous, drawn, haggard. It was the traditional and becoming nervousness of the actor just before a great performance. It was gone the instant Carpentier came in sight of his ninety thousand. His head was back and his eyes and his smile flamed as he crawled through the ropes. And he gave some curious flick to his bathrobe as he turned to meet the applause. Until that very moment we had been for Dempsey, but suddenly we found ourself up on our feet making silly noises. We shouted, "Carpentier! Carpentier! Carpentier!" and forgot even to be ashamed of our pronunciation. He held his hands up over his head and turned until the whole arena, including the five-dollar seats, had come within the scope of his smile.

Dempsey came in a minute later and we could not cheer, although we liked him. It would have been like cheering for Niagara Falls at the moment somebody was about to go over in a barrel. Actually there is a difference of sixteen pounds between the two men, which is large enough, but it seemed that afternoon as if it might have been a hundred. And we knew for the first time that a man may smile and smile and be an underdog.

We resented at once the law of gravity, the Malthusian theory and the fact that a straight line is the shortest distance between two points. Everything scientific, exact, and inevitable was distasteful. We wanted the man with the curves to win. It seemed impossible throughout the first round. Carpentier was first out of his corner and landed the first blow, a light but stinging left to the face. Then Dempsey closed in and even the people who paid only thirty dollars for their seats could hear the thump, thump of his short hooks as they beat upon the narrow stomach of Carpentier. The challenger was only too evidently tired when the round ended.

Then came the second and, after a moment of fiddling about, he shot his right hand to the jaw. Carpentier did it again, a second time, and this was the blow perfected by a lifetime of training. The time was perfect, the aim was perfect, every ounce of strength was in it. It was the blow which had downed Bombardier Wells, and Joe Beckett. It rocked Dempsey to his heels, but it broke Carpentier's hand. His best was not enough. There was an earthquake in Philistia but then out came the signs "Business as usual!" and Dempsey began to pound Carpentier in the stomach.

The challenger faded quickly in the third round, and in the fourth the end came. We all suffered when he went down the first time, but he was up again, and the second time was much worse. It was in this knockdown that his head sagged suddenly, after he struck the floor, and fell back upon the canvas. He was conscious and his legs moved a little, but they would not obey him. A gorgeous human will had been beaten down to a point where it would no longer function.

If you choose, that can stand as the last moment in a completed piece of art. We are sentimental enough to wish to add the tag that after a few minutes Carpentier came out to the center of the ring and shook hands with Dempsey and at that moment he smiled again the same smile which we had seen at the beginning of the fight when he stood with his hands above his head. Nor is it altogether sentimental. We feel that one of the elements of tragedy lies in the fact that Fate gets nothing but the victories and the championships. Gesture and glamor remain with Man. No infighting can take that away from him.

Jack Dempsey won fairly and squarely. He is a great fighter, perhaps the most efficient the world has ever known, but everybody came away from the arena talking about Carpentier. He wasn't very efficient. The experts say he fought an ill-considered fight and should not have forced it. In using such a plan, they say, he might have lasted the whole twelve rounds. That was not the idea. As somebody has said, "Better four rounds of—" but we can't remember the rest of the quotation.

Dempsey won and Carpentier got all the glory. Perhaps we will have to enlarge our conception of tragedy, for that too is tragic.

Ringside (Formal)

ROBERT BENCHLEY

About the last place you'd ever have expected to find Robert Benchley (1889–1945) would have been at the fights, and, if truth be told, it's about the last place at which he'd have ever expected to be looked for. Humorist nonpareil and one of the resident wits of the famed Algonquin Round Table, his metier was exploring a more genteel world—the nagging problems of domestic life. He was also known for packing a punch when it came to poking fun at High Society. A regular in *The New Yorker,* he collected his archly whimsical sketches and acerbic observations into enormously popular volumes with titles like *From Bed to Worse* and *Benchley Beside Himself.* In time, his personality—and popularity—grew so large the page alone could no longer hold it; when movies began to talk, he lent them his voice, writing and starring in some two-dozen shorts, one of which won an Academy Award. He also acquitted himself admirably in such feature films as *Foreign Correspondent, The Major and the Minor,* and *I Married a Witch.*

Ever quotable, often irascible, and always readable, Benchley once observed that, "It took me fifteen years to discover that I had no talent for writing, but I couldn't give it up because by then I was too famous." This rare ringside excursion, chronicled for *The New Yorker* in 1927, offers clear evidence why.

    🥊   🥊   🥊   🥊

There seems to be a widespread belief that New York prizefights are patronized extensively by the *haut monde.* I have gathered in my reading that the ringside of each important metropolitan fistic encounter (prizefight) is jammed with society folk in only slightly less formal attire than that worn at court presentations. The gentlemen do not wear their swords, and the ladies are not obliged to curtsy to Mr. Rickard, but otherwise the two occasions are much the same in aspect.

Accordingly, when Mr. Charles MacGreggor came to me with two ringside seats for the fights at the Yankee Stadium, I was in considerable of a flutter. Ringside seats at a New York prizefight meant but one thing—going out in society. Now, I hadn't been out in society since I started growing my mustache, and I hardly knew where my silk hat was. The last time I had tried it on I was cheered for Stephen A. Douglas.

"We shall have to dress," I said to Mr. MacGreggor.

"Dress?" he answered, dully.

"Evening dress," I explained. "These fights are very dressy affairs. All the best people go, right from dinner, and unless you are dressed you are quite likely to be refused admission to the ringside."

This frightened Mr. MacGreggor; so from six-thirty until nine was put in on grooming. I may say that as we started out for the Stadium, we presented a rather *chic* spectacle. I had seen a picture of the Prince of Wales at a prizefight and, in addition to my faultless (or practically faultless—my shirt bosom bulges) evening attire, I carried along an eye-shade. I didn't read why it was that the Prince wore an eye-shade at fights, but there he was in the picture, anyway.

Mr. MacGreggor started to hail a cab, but I suggested that we go over to the Packard place and get a limousine.

"These cabs are pretty jouncy," I said, "and by the time we get way uptown we would probably be unpresentable, what with the grimy seats and all. And besides, you never know whom we might meet."

So we got a nice limousine with pearl gray upholstery and sat very straight, leaning on our sticks, in order not to mess our shirtfronts all up before we even got there.

On the way up through the Park we ran into a crowd of taxis, each one crowded with men.

"Quite a crowd for the fight," said Mr. MacGreggor.

"They can't be going to the fight," I said. "Look at them."

And one look was enough. They were a common lot, wearing straw hats with bands which evidently were not club bands of any sort, and dressed much in the manner of a baseball crowd. And you could tell from their faces that they were not people whom you would like to take home to dinner.

"A lodge outing of some sort," I said to Mr. MacGreggor, and he shuddered.

But as we drew near the Stadium it was evident that the *canaille* were headed for the fights, so the only explanation was that some seats had got into the hands of speculators. It is awfully hard to keep people out, once the seats get out of the right hands.

It was not until we had passed through the gates, amid considerable comment from the boys who were selling programs, that I began to wonder where the *haut monde* was. The crowd in the runways of the giant Stadium and as far as the eye could reach was much the same in appearance as the men in the taxis had been. And it was becoming more and more apparent that we were objects of derision. I thought at first that it was some drunken men behind us who were calling forth the amused glances from passersby, until I heard some one say: "They're advertising something. Let's wait and see." I felt that the sooner we reached the ringside and our own set, the better it would be.

But although our seats were well up front at the ringside, I could find no *haut monde;* at least, they were not distinguishable by their dress. And if you can't tell the *haut monde* by its dress, what can you tell it by?

On the contrary, our neighbors were all—shall we say?—of the peasant class, or at any rate, in trade. One gentleman, sitting next to Mr. MacGreggor, had trouble with the amalgam filling in one bicuspid, and made no bones about it. The one at my left was frankly more interested in the manner in which Mr. MacGreggor and I had seen fit to fix ourselves up than he was in the preliminary bout which was on when we entered. Several men whom I had known in my college days recognized me and hazarded the guess that I had been up all night and all day and was using the Stadium as a bivouac. One asked me if I was doing it for charity and another threw me into a panic by saying that I had forgotten my trousers (which turned out to be a canard).

At last the fighters in the ring became interested and stopped wrestling with each other and came over to the ropes to look. The shorter of the two offered to take Mr. MacGreggor on for four rounds—finders keepers. We were finally hoisted up on the ring and forced to take a bow, amid the plaudits of thirty thousand fight fans.

As we reached the gates, on the shoulders of frenzied partisans, Mr. MacGreggor looked across at me and said:

"I didn't see any of the Vanderbilts. I wonder where they were."

"Oh," I said, lighting a cigarette as I was tossed into an Eighth Avenue trolley car, "they go to the country in May and won't be dragged in town for love nor money."

The Sack of Shelby

When it comes to father-son seedings, the smart money puts the Lardners at the top of the draw. As a columnist for *Newsweek* and a regular contributor to *The New Yorker*, Ring's youngest son John (1912–1960) was without peer in working the shady side of the sporting street, especially if he could wring a few drips of well-formed satire from it. What he found in the way Jack Kearns, Jack Dempsey's manager, picked clean the burg of Shelby, Montana, was—and remains—a true work of genius and a sight to behold.

Lardner loved his account of the event—penned for *The New Yorker* in 1948—so much so that he volunteered it as his offering to a late '50s collection of favorite sports stories chosen by their own writers. Here was his rationale: "The story, which I merely pulled together, is an epic of the picaresque; it describes what may have been one of the last stands of the independent, romantic hustler against the 'state.' Kearns looted the state of Montana, to the best of his ability. In doing so, he also acted out a conscious burlesque of the Lewis & Clarke tradition, of the winning of the west. He produced a hell of a story, and I've never had more fun in sportswriting than in writing this one."

And it shows.

🥊   🥊   🥊   🥊

Jack Kearns became almost legendary in the prizefight business between the two world wars because of his ability to make money in large, bold scoops without recourse to day labor. After the second war, to show that his hand—green thumb, prehensile fingers, and all—was still in, he repeated an old trick by steering still another fighter to a championship. The fighter, Joey Maxim, who became world's light-heavyweight champion under Kearns, will not shine brightly in history books. He is just a footnote sort of fighter—cute but pedestrian, the critics agree, and practically punchless. I remember that there was something like boredom in Kearns' voice, one day in the late nineteen-forties, as he sat on a desk in Madison Square Garden, shortly before Maxim's bout with the Swedish heavyweight champion, Olle Tandberg, and delivered a routine hallelujah to his latest means of support.

"This kid is better than Dempsey," said Kearns. His soft blue eyes stared vacantly at the floor. "He don't hit quite as hard as Dempsey, but otherwise he's better."

Since Kearns managed Jack Dempsey when the latter was heavyweight champion, it may be that he thought he held a lifetime dispensation from some celestial chamber of commerce to misuse Dempsey's name for advertising purposes. It may be that he was right; at any rate, no thunderbolt split the ceiling to strike him down for his blasphemous words. His audience, composed of managers, trainers, reporters, and press agents, shifted its feet and withheld comment. There was nothing to be said—nothing polite. Then one of the managers, an old-time boxing man, began to warm to the recollection of the team of Dempsey and Kearns. He turned the talk to happier times.

"Remember Shelby, Doc?" he asked. "You and Dempsey broke three banks in Montana."

Kearns' eyes came to life.

"We broke four banks," he said. With rising enthusiasm, he went on to describe his withdrawal after the sack of Shelby, Montana, in 1923, with two bags of silver in a railroad caboose. His listeners drew closer. The career and prospects of Joey Maxim were, for the time being and without regrets, tabled.

To boxing people who have heard of the place, the memory of Shelby is precious for many reasons, one of them being that it brought a man of their own profession—namely, Kearns—into singlehanded combat with a state 147,138 square miles in area, producing copper, gold, silver, zinc, lead, manganese, oil, coal, grain, and livestock. No one who was involved in the Shelby affair, including Kearns and Dempsey, is any longer a perfectly reliable authority on the facts of the story, owing to the blurring influence of the autobiographical instinct on boxing memoirs. However, investigation shows that Kearns' performance compared favorably—for tenacity, at least—with those of the predatory railroad barons Jay Gould, Daniel Drew, Commodore Vanderbilt, and James J. Hill. As it happened, it was on Hill's Great Northern Railway, which opened up the north of Montana in the eighteen-eighties, that Kearns rode into the state, with a fiery purpose, and out of it again, with great haste, in 1923. The scope of Kearns' raid has been exaggerated somewhat by his admirers, himself among them, but there is no doubt that it had a profound effect on no fewer than two Montana counties, Toole and Cascade. Furthermore, the name, spirit, and wealth of the whole state were invoked by those Montanans who struggled with Kearns firsthand. They stated more than once at the time that "the honor of all Montana" was at stake. Montana today is perhaps in a sounder financial condition than Kearns, but that only goes to show the extent of its natural resources. It took an oil strike to draw Kearns to Shelby, in Toole County, in the first place, and it took another oil strike, years later, to complete Toole County's recovery from Kearns.

The raider, who was born John L. McKernan, is now sixty-five years old. He is still a dapper figure, when dressed for pleasure, but his hair is thin and a paunch shows at the conjunction of his pants and sweater when he climbs into the ring on business, as he did at the meeting of his man Maxim with Tandberg, in which Maxim won a close decision. That bout netted Kearns and his fighter approximately fifteen hundred dollars. The loser, by the terms of an arrangement based on his drawing power, got fifteen thousand dollars. Later, finding good soil in London, Kearns and Maxim did better. But the spark will never burn as high in this team as it did in Dempsey and Kearns. The bout between Dempsey and Tom Gibbons in Shelby, on July 4, 1923, brought Kearns and Dempsey nearly three hundred thousand dollars. The loser got nothing whatever. In those days, Kearns was forty years old and at the height of his genius.

A good many people in 1923, including writers of newspaper editorials, likened Shelby after the fight to a Belgian village ravaged by the Huns. They ignored or overlooked the fact that Shelby, like no Belgian village on record, had opened the relationship by begging to be taken. Kearns and Dempsey had never heard of Shelby before its citizens went to the trouble of raising a hundred thousand dollars to entice them there. In the popular view, Dempsey was the archfiend of the episode. His reputation as a draft dodger in the First World War, carefully cultivated by managers of rival fighters like Fighting Bob Martin, the A.E.F. heavyweight champion, made a strong impression on the public; during the Shelby crisis, people were quite willing to consider him a profiteer as well as a slacker. They lost sight of Kearns in

Dempsey's shadow. It was only the men directly concerned with financing the Dempsey-Gibbons match who realized that Kearns was the brains and backbone of the visiting party. In language that will not bear repeating, these men marvelled at Kearns' almost religious attachment to the principle of collecting all the cash in Montana that was not nailed down.

It was a booster spirit that got Shelby into trouble—the frontier booster spirit, which seems to have been a particularly red-blooded and chuckleheaded variety. Up to 1922, Shelby had been a village populated by four or five hundred cowhands, sheepherders, and dry-dirt farmers. In 1922, oil was struck in the Kevin-Sunburst field, just north of town. The population rose to over a thousand. It was not much of a jump superficially; the significant difference was that all the new citizens had money. Some of them were oil speculators, some of them were real-estate men from the West Coast buying up land to sell to oil speculators. A few were merchants selling standard boomtown merchandise, much of it liquid, to the oilmen and the real-estate men. Kearns had not yet seen Shelby with his own eyes when he first tried to describe it to skeptics in the East a year later, but his description was not far wrong.

"It's one of those wide-open towns," he said spaciously. "Red Dog saloon, gambling halls—you know, like you see in the movies."

It was old Blackfoot country. South of Shelby, the Marias River wound toward the site of a vanished fur-trading post on the Missouri. Not far north was the Canadian border. The Great Northern Railway ran west from Shelby to Glacier Park and the Pacific, east to Duluth and the Twin Cities, south a hundred miles to the nearest real town, Great Falls. In Shelby proper, there were the railroad depot, a few stores, a few houses, a couple of new banks, the Silver Grill Hotel, where fifty extra beds filled the lobby at the height of the boom, and half a dozen saloons.

In one of the saloons, on an evening in January, 1923, a bunch of the boys were whooping it up in a civic-minded way. The party was headed by Mayor James A. Johnson, a large man of fifty-eight who had made a comfortable fortune ranching, and had added to it in the boom through oil leases and the ownership of the First State Bank of Shelby. Sitting around him were men named Zimmerman, Sampson, Dwyer, and Schwartz. It was Sam Sampson, a storekeeper and landowner, who first suggested that the best way to make the nation and the world Shelby-conscious—that being the object of everyone in town who owned property—would be to stage a fight there for the heavyweight championship of the world. Dempsey was champion. The two most talked-of contenders for his title at that time were Harry Wills, a Negro, and

Tom Gibbons, a white man from St. Paul. The barroom committee skipped lightly over Wills. Gibbons was its choice on two counts: the color of his pelt and the fact that he was a Northwestern man, from a state with which Montana had close commercial connections. The committee toasted Gibbons, Shelby, and itself. Then Sampson began to send telegrams in all directions. He wired Dempsey and Gibbons and their managers, and received no replies, which was not surprising, in view of Shelby's overwhelming anonymity. He also sent a telegram to Mike Collins, a journalist and boxing matchmaker in Minneapolis. Collins, a friend of Gibbons, agreed to come to Shelby at the committee's expense and study the possibilities.

His reaction on stepping off the train at the Shelby depot was recorded by himself at a later date. "I was startled," he said. Shelby was small and raw beyond the power of a city man's imagination. Mayor Johnson and Sampson led Collins across a few rods of the Great Plains to a saloon, where the Mayor gave Collins the impression that Mose Zimmerman, another committeeman who owned land, was ready to finance the championship fight out of his own pocket. To substantiate this, the Mayor rounded up Zimmerman, who denied indignantly that he was ready to contribute anything but a small, decent, proportionate piece of the total. The Mayor looked sad. Collins walked back to the depot to catch the eight P.M. train for Minneapolis. As things turned out, he was the first of a series of people who started to wash their hands of Shelby by catching a train. They were all called back at the last minute. A Fate straight out of Sophocles had matters in her grip.

Before the eight-o'clock train arrived, Mayor Johnson arranged a mass meeting of citizens in a saloon. Collins was persuaded to address it. He said starkly that Shelby had no boxing arena, no population, and, as far as he could see, no money.

"You would need a hundred thousand dollars before you even talk to Dempsey and Gibbons," he added.

At this point, Shelby startled him for the second time. The Mayor and his friends raised twenty-six thousand dollars on the spot, the contributors receiving vouchers for ringside seats to the fight in exchange. Collins noted that the vouchers were marked July Fourth. The phantom battle already had a date and ticket sale. This show of *sang-froid* won him over. A short time afterward, he set out, in the company of a gentleman named Loy J. Molumby, state commander of the American Legion, to stump Montana for the balance of the money. Traveling from town to town in Molumby's private airplane, they brought the total of cash on hand to a hundred and ten thousand dollars in a little more than a week's time. The moment had come, Collins freely admitted, to let Dempsey and Gibbons in on the secret. It was now, he said, just a matter of convincing them that there was such a place as Shelby and showing them the money.

The two things were achieved in reverse order. It was after seeing the money that Dempsey and Gibbons—or, rather, their managers, Kearns and Eddie Kane—brought themselves to believe in Shelby. The rest of the country, having seen no money, did not believe in Shelby for some time to come. At the beginning of May, the boxing critic of the New York *Tribune,* Jack Lawrence, spoke of a meeting that would take place soon at Madison Square Garden between the Dempsey and Gibbons parties. "There," he wrote scornfully, "they will probably bear a counter-proposition from the lips of Tex Rickard that will waft Shelby, Montana, back to the pastoral obscurity from which it emerged so suddenly."

Lawrence was wrong. Kearns and Kane bypassed New York and Rickard and went to Chicago to inspect the cash and negotiate the Shelby deal with Molumby and Collins, who were now the accredited agents of Mayor Johnson's town. It is apparent that both managers were remarkable for the grandeur of their vision. Kane showed it by agreeing to let Dempsey and Kearns have everything the bout drew, up to three hundred thousand dollars, at the box-office in Shelby, if there was a Shelby, before taking a percentage for Gibbons. The Gibbons share was to be 50 per cent of the receipts from three hundred thousand dollars to six hundred thousand dollars, and 25 per cent of everything above that. Three hundred thousand dollars was exactly what Kearns and Dempsey had made from the spectacular million-dollar-gate fight with Georges Carpentier, which Rickard had promoted two years before on the threshold of New York City. Kearns was now counting on gouging the same sum from an infinitesimal cowtown that had no boxing ring, no professional promoter, and no large city within five hundred miles. At least, he said he was counting on that. Almost no one in New York believed there would be a fight. Kearns' friends suspected, with characteristic misanthropy, that Doc was up to some sort of practice ruse to keep his hand in and his brain lean and sharp for coming campaigns. Rickard, who did not think much of either Gibbons or Wills as an opponent for Dempsey, having sped Kearns west with a tolerant wink, went on with plans for his own notion of a Dempsey match, with the Argentine Luis Firpo, for autumn delivery.

Kearns, however, was in earnest. It pleased his fancy to undertake this Western adventure on his own. He wanted for once to be free from Eastern entanglements, free from his professional peers. Gibbons and Kane, the parties of the second part, would be amateurs at Shelby in everything but name. At Shelby, every power, privilege, and bargaining weapon would belong to Kearns. If he could carry three hundred thousand dollars out of a town of one thousand population, he would become immortal in his profession. If he couldn't he had dictated terms that said firmly that all money paid to him and Dempsey in advance was theirs to keep. If they got three hundred thousand dollars, there would be a fight; if they didn't, there would be no fight, and no rebate. Molumby agreed, on behalf of Mayor Johnson, to deliver a second installment of a hundred thousand dollars to Kearns on June 15th, and a third, and last, on July 2nd, two days before the fight. This was Molumby's last major gesture in connection with the Dempsey-Gibbons match. Like half a dozen other Montanans, who tried to learn the boxing business in the next few weeks, he flunked the course.

A slight difficulty occurred in the secondary negotiations between Kearns and Kane. The difficulty was that they had not spoken to each other for four years and had no wish to start speaking now. Kearns said much later that he could not remember the reason for the breach, which may or may not be true; boxing men usually are shy about revealing the causes of their Grade A feuds—the ones that last anywhere from a year to life. Quartered two floors apart in the Morrison Hotel in Chicago, Kane and Kearns conferred by messenger. The messenger was Collins. One question was who was to referee the fight. It was purely nominal, for Kearns had already decided on his good friend Jim Dougherty, sometimes known as the Baron of Leiperville, Pennsylvania. After four trips by Collins up and down the hotel's emergency stairway, Kane accepted Dougherty. He had no choice. Kearns, as the champion's manager, was in command. Kane, managing the challenger, and a poorly recommended challenger, at that, in the opinion of most critics—could consider himself lucky to have gained a chance at the title for Gibbons. That chance was something, although Gibbons was older and smaller than Dempsey. Beyond it, there was a possibility of making some money if the fight was highly successful, which was the dream that Mayor Johnson had sold to Collins and Collins to Kane. Kane and Gibbons were gambling, like the men of Shelby and the men of the rest of Montana who backed them. That explains, in part, the deep affection Montana came to feel for Gibbons as the time of the fight drew near.

A few days after the terms were signed, Collins, as "matchmaker," or supervisor of arrangements, announced the ticket price scale: from fifty dollars ringside, to twenty dollars, for the rear seats. There were no seats at the moment, but Mayor Johnson had persuaded Major J. E. Lane, a local lumber merchant, to build an arena at the edge of town to accommodate forty thousand people. There was no money for Major Lane, but the Mayor got him to take a seventy-thousand-dollar chattel mortgage on the arena. Training camps were staked out for both fighters. On May 16th, Kearns entrained for Montana with a staff of sparring partners for Dempsey, who made his own way there from his home in Salt Lake City. Kearns was glad to leave the decadent cities of the East, where the newspapers, when they mentioned Shelby at all, still questioned the reality of the fight and half questioned the reality of Shelby. He found Shelby in a holiday mood. The Mayor and his friends had recovered from the strain of getting up the first hundred thousand dollars, and had not yet begun to worry about finding the remaining two hundred thousand. The ticket sale would take care of that.

Kearns beamed upon these unsophisticated burghers with boots on their feet and guns in their belts. He addressed them at a Chamber of Commerce luncheon at the Silver Grill. With all the sincerity he could muster on short notice, he told them that Gibbons was a great fighter, "the best boxer in the world.

"I would not be surprised," Kearns told the meeting lovingly, "if the winner of this contest fought Harry Wills right here in Shelby on Labor Day. You will be the fight capital of the nation. We have come here," he added, "at something of a sacrifice, since we were offered half a million dollars for the same fight in New York. However, Shelby spoke first, and Shelby wins out."

Then Kearns took a rapid look at Shelby, whose facilities could all be seen at a glance with the naked eye, and caught the six o'clock train to Great Falls. All Montana, and Shelby, in particular, was well pleased with itself at this point. It is hard to say at just what hour between then and June 15th, the first day of open crisis, misgivings began to set in. They must have come soonest to Johnson and Molumby, who were in charge of the ticket sale and the cashbox. Kearns ostensibly had no notion of how things were going. When he was told, Montana was stunned by the change in the manner of the free-and-easy stranger.

Kearns had made his base in Great Falls, partly because it was a town of thirty thousand that offered some freedom of movement, and partly because Dempsey was training there, at Great Falls Park, a mile or so outside the city limits. Before June 15th, Dempsey trained well and seemed happy. The park, in a hollow in the hills of Cascade County, just east of the Missouri River and in sight of the Little and Big Belt Mountains and the Birdtail Divide, was a pleasant place, surrounded by cottonwood trees, that had formerly been a scene of revelry. Dempsey lived and sparred in a roadhouse that prohibition and repeated government raids had closed down. Sometimes the champion fished in the Missouri. He had a pet cow, a Hereford bull, a wolf cub, and a bulldog in camp, as well as two of his brothers, Johnny and Bernie; his trainer, Jerry (the Greek) Luvadis; and his stooge, Joe Benjamin, with whom he played pinochle. His sparring partners ranged from giants like Big Ben Wray, seven feet two inches tall, to small, clever middleweights who could simulate Gibbons' style. Gibbons trained in Shelby. He lived with his wife and children in a house on the great, treeless plain, not far from the arena. If anything more was needed to make Gibbons a favorite and Dempsey unpopular in Shelby after June 15th, Gibbons' choice of training quarters did it. The town saw him and his family every day. Gibbons at that time was thirty-four, six years older than Dempsey. He had had a long and fairly successful career among middleweights and light-heavyweights, though the gifted little Harry Greb had beaten him just the year before. He was a polite and colorless man, with a slim waist, a big chest, and a high shock of pompadoured hair.

On June 15th, the day appointed for the payment of the second hundred thousand dollars to Kearns and Dempsey, Kearns went to the Great Falls station to take a train to Shelby. He said later that he was going in all innocence to ask Mayor Johnson for the money, that he did not know that the Mayor and Molumby were at that moment wretchedly chewing cigars in a room in the Park Hotel in Great Falls, having just confessed to George H. Stanton, the leading banker of Great Falls, that the day of reckoning found them approximately 98 percent short. They asked him what to do. Stanton, like all Montanans, had followed the Shelby adventure closely. As the principal capitalist of that part of the state, he had followed it more closely than most, and he probably had a fair notion of the truth before he heard it from the unhappy promoters. However, he told them it was a hell of a note, and he sent someone to get Kearns off the train. Kearns came to the hotel room, looking hopeful. It was his first business contact with Stanton; it would have been better for Stanton if it had been his last. The promoters explained the situation, or what they could understand of it. They admitted frankly that it confused them. It seemed that a great many tickets that had been mailed out, unbonded, to various parts of the state and country were not yet paid for. It seemed that expenses were unexpectedly large. It appeared that there were sixteen hundred dollars cash on hand for Kearns and Dempsey. Whatever suspicions Kearns may have had before this, the cold facts undoubtedly shocked him. He flew into a rage.

"Why don't *you* take over the promotion and the sale?" suggested Stanton. "From all I can see, you own the fight right now."

"I won't promote!" screamed Kearns. "These guys are the promoters. I'm trying to train a fighter. Let them get our money up or there won't be any fight."

Kearns left the room in a black mood. He went back to the hotel that evening, at Stanton's invitation, and found that most of the money in Great Falls was represented there: Stanton, president of the Stanton Trust & Savings Bank; Dan Tracey, hotel owner; Russell and Arthur Strain, department-store owners; J. W. Speer, lawyer and former judge; and Shirley Ford, vice-president of the Great Falls National Bank. From there on, Kearns was told, the honor of Montana was at stake. The fight would have new promoters. The money would be raised. It *was* raised, within twenty-four hours. At five-fifteen P.M. the next day, June 16th, the press was summoned to see Stanton present Kearns with a check for a hundred thousand dollars, seventeen hours and a quarter after the deadline of midnight, June 15th. Kearns put the check in his pocket and congratulated Montana. "A dead-game state," he said. Stanton accepted his kind words modestly, though it must be said that he gave newspapermen present the impression that he himself had put up seventy-three thousand dollars of the money, which was not strictly true. He had supplied cash in that amount, but it was underwritten almost entirely by Mayor Jim Johnson, of Shelby, with land and oil leases from his own estate. The Strain brothers and the O'Neill brothers, Lou and John, who were oilmen, made up the balance.

While Molumby and Mayor Johnson sat humbly by—the latter quite silent about his contribution to the salvation of Montana's honor—Dan Tracey delivered a tough speech. The Great Falls committee had appointed Tracey head man of the fight. The old promoters, he said, were through as head men. He would protect the interest of his Great Falls friends. He would see that they got every nickel back. He would countersign all checks from now on. He paused, and Kearns advanced to shake him by the hand.

"This reassures me," said Kearns. "I will stick to Shelby and ignore the countless offers I have got from other states for this fight. I am sure," he added thoughtfully, "that we won't have any trouble about the last hundred thousand dollars—due midnight, July 2nd."

Mayor Johnson mopped his brow with a handkerchief.

"This is a great relief," he told the press. "I wasn't cut out to be a boxing promoter."

Molumby had nothing to say. Earlier that day, he had been de-
nounced by an American Legion post in St. Louis for involving the Legion in
Dempsey's affairs.

The reign of Tracey as head man lasted eleven days. It was a time of
stress and brooding. The backers of the fight knew that since raising the second hundred thousand dollars had been like pulling teeth, the collection of
the third hundred thousand would be on the order of a major amputation.
The advance sale of tickets brought in no money to speak of. People could
not be expected to buy tickets unless they were sure the fight would take
place, and the promoters could not persuade the strong-minded Kearns to
guarantee a fight before he was sure of the money. The Great Northern can-
celed a plan to run special trains from the East and the Pacific Coast. The promoters and their friends snarled at Kearns whenever they saw him, and nervously fondled the butts of their guns. Frank Walker, of Butte, Montana, a
lawyer and later Postmaster General under Franklin Roosevelt, came to Great
Falls to add weight to the heckling of Kearns. Kearns, however, rode his
choppy course serenely and nonchalantly, true to his lofty principle of three
hundred thousand dollars or no contest.

The strain was much harder on Dempsey than on Dempsey's manager. If Kearns was Public Enemy No. 1 to the financiers of Montana,
Dempsey was the people's choice for the part. He was sharply aware of it and
of the artillery on the hip of nearly everyone he saw. He said later that he
pleaded with Kearns, to no avail, at this time to waive the final payment, to
promise a fight, and to take over the box-office management. The champion's
state of mind showed in his work. He looked slow and easy to hit in training,
and his sparring partners complained of his viciousness when he hit them.
On his twenty-eighth birthday, June 24th, seemingly angry at his failure to
catch Jack Burke, a middleweight, he knocked down another sparring partner
seven times in five rounds, and broke the jaw of the giant Wray, who subsequently took his meals through a tube.

The crises came fast now. On June 26th, Stanton, conferring in
Shelby with Tracey nd Mayor Johnson, who had been reduced to assistant
promoter, was told that the lumber merchant and the contractors were about
to foreclose their mortgage on the arena. Stanton stalked angrily to the railroad station, but he was called back into conference, inevitably, at the last
minute. Half an hour later, he announced that the creditors had agreed to

accept payment on a pro-rata basis from the gate receipts. He said that all was well. Tracey, the tough talker of June 16th, could not bring himself to share this view. The mortgage crisis had broken his spirit. On June 27th, he resigned his job.

"The money that my people put up is nowhere in sight that I can see," he said. "I can't be sure they'll get it back, and I'm through."

Shelby was excited the next day by a telegram received by Mayor Johnson from Minneapolis signed "Louis W. Till," which it assumed to be from Louis Hill, board chairman of the Great Northern, assuring the Mayor that he was "on way with cash and securities so Tom can have chance to put profiteering Dempsey in hospital." The wire turned out to be a hoax. On June 29th, Stanton made a final, desperate move. After consulting with Great Falls leaders on a list of names, and sending telegrams to all parts of the state, he proclaimed that "twenty lifelong friends" had pledged five thousand dollars each to meet the final payment to Kearns and "save the honor of Montana." The announcement was given out now, Stanton said, to dispel doubts that the fight would be held. But the payment to Kearns would not be made until the agreed date of July 2nd, because, he went on sulkily, some of the new sponsors "are disposed to follow the lead taken by the champion's manager and adhere rigidly to the conditions of the contract." It was their opinion, he said, that Kearns "would get out of the fight if he could." Enlarging on the patriotism of his twenty lifelong friends, Stanton said that cancellation of the bout "would have cast reflections on the state that would have been far-reaching in effect." The Northwest, he added, would now save the fight; the Dakotas, Wyoming, Idaho, Washington, Oregon, and Western Canada would send at least fifteen thousand people. The members of the committee would take a loss but "are game enough to see this thing through."

Kearns, ignoring the slurs on his good faith in this manifesto, expressed satisfaction. Dempsey forced a smile and acknowledged the gameness of all Montanans. But on July 2nd, facing the press, with Kearns present, in Great Falls, Stanton revealed that he had been unable to cash the pledges of his lifelong friends. Eight of them had come through as advertised, he said, but in the circumstances he did not feel like keeping their money. He looked defiantly at Kearns. Kearns shrugged. He retired to discuss things with his lieutenant from New York, Dan McKetrick. Then he told Stanton that he would make the "gamble" that had been forced on him. He would take over the fight and the gate receipts with it. From that moment, concern about paying Kearns was outweighed by a vivid fear that

Kearns and Dempsey would slip across the border before July Fourth with the money they had already collected, leaving Shelby to whistle for its world-championship fight. There is no evidence that either man contemplated doing this, but practically everyone in Montana was convinced that both of them did contemplate it. Kearns later recalled that Frank Walker, in a state of deep emotion, shook his fist beneath Kearns' nose on July 3rd and warned him not to try to escape.

Shelby had built up to the fight, within its limits. There were concession booths and stands all the way from Main Street to the arena. Entertainers had come from every corner of the state. A tent show called the Hyland-Welty Comedians was playing the town; it starred a certain Patricia Salmon, the toast of the out-of-town reporters, who for fifty dollars a week did three song spots a day, yodeled in front of the curtain, and played the lead in *Which One Shall I Marry?, Thorns and Orange Blossoms, The Tie that Binds,* and *The Sweetest Girl in Dixie.* An acquaintance of mine from Billings, Montana, drove to Shelby for the fight with his father, an early patriotic ticket-buyer. The sign he remembers set on Main Street was "Aunt Kate's Cathouse." All tourists slept in their automobiles the night of July 3rd. The great Northwestern migration to Shelby had not materialized, but there were enough cars parked on the plain by the arena to show that there was an interest in the fight. Part of the interest was speculative; many people had not bought tickets, but counted on getting in anyway.

Dempsey came from Great Falls in a private railroad car on July Fourth, arriving in the early afternoon. A switch engine pulled his car to a siding near the arena, where a crowd of men instantly surrounded it. "There were no cheers," according to Dempsey. His party, which included a Chicago detective named Mike Trent, and a celebrated hanger-on of the time, "Senator" Wild Bill Lyons, both strongly and ostentatiously armed, took counsel. Some of the crowd were trying to climb aboard. Lyons told the engineer to keep the engine hooked on and to run the car up and down the siding till it was time for Dempsey to get off. When that time came, the crowd pressed close around the champion, but there were no gunshots or blows. "Trying to run out, were you?" called some of the men. A messenger from the ringside reported that it was still too early for Dempsey's entrance, since the program had been delayed. The crowd, however, got solidly behind Dempsey in a physical sense and pushed him firmly to the arena doors, where he waited with half a dozen retainers by a soft-drink stand, listening to comments on his character and lineage.

The reason for the delay was the public's reluctance to pay the official prices for tickets. Kearns had opened the gates in the morning, after surrendering five hundred dollars from the advance sale for the privilege to a crew of federal revenue men who were on hand looking hungrily after their country's interests. At noon, however, there were only fifteen hundred people in the grandstand to watch the first preliminary bout. Thousands milled around outside the gates, many of them shouting, "We'll come in for ten dollars!" These were the aristocrats of the mob. Kearns began to accommodate them at two-thirty, while people inside pushed down from high seats to empty ringside seats, the working press sweltered over typewriters almost too hot to touch, and two bands—the Montana State Elks band on one side of the ring and the Scottish Highlanders of Calgary on the other—alternately administered soothing music. A blind war veteran was singing a ballad in the ring when Kearns finally was overrun by the rest of the crowd outside, which came in free. Dempsey entered at three-thirty-six, thirty-six minutes late. "It was the most hostile crowd a heavyweight champion ever faced," he said a few years later, through a ghost writer, and he was probably right. There was some hissing, he recalled, but mostly "sullen silence." Gibbons made it harder for him by delaying his arrival till three-forty-five and taking ten minutes to have his hands taped in the ring. A few empty bottles came down near Dempsey's corner, tossed by spectators who blamed the champion for the delay. Dodging glassware in the corner with Dempsey were Kearns and Bill Lyons, who wore chaps and a sombrero as well as his arsenal. A number of what Kearns called "my Chicago hard guys" sat watchfully at the ringside just below.

It was a very bad fight. Dempsey, outweighing Gibbons, a hundred and eighty-eight pounds to a hundred and seventy-four, but stale and nervous, could not land his punches squarely. It was widely said later that he would not, out of fear for his safety, but that theory conflicts with the testimony of Dempsey and the opinion of expert eyewitnesses. Gibbons won a few of the early rounds. He opened a cut over Dempsey's eye in the second. Dempsey complained afterward that Kearns, never the most sure-handed of seconds, poured cut medicine inside the eye between rounds, making him half blind until the seventh. From the sixth round on, it was Dempsey's fight, easily. The crowd stopped crying, "Kill him, Tommy!" and cried, "Hang on!" That was all Gibbons tried to do—he had every reason to know he was working for nothing, and Dempsey's strength soon made him sure he couldn't win. Gibbons scored one moral triumph when he survived the twelfth round, a new record against Dempsey, and another when he survived the fifteenth and last, and forced the bout to a decision. The last round was one long clinch; Gibbons wrapped his arms around Dempsey, and the onlookers shouted derisively at the champion and threw cushions. Gibbons made no objection to referee Dougherty's decision for Dempsey. Neither did the crowd. Dempsey got out with the utmost dispatch when the verdict had been given. The Chicago hard guys, led by Detective Trent, hustled him aboard the private car on the siding. At the Shelby station, his car was hooked to a train for Great Falls. He spent the night at the Park Hotel in Great Falls and caught a regular train the next day for Salt Lake City. Both of Dempsey's eyes were discolored when he boarded the Salt Lake train and exchanged a few last words with residents of Great Falls who had come to see him off.

"Don't hurry back!" called his well-wishers.

"I won't, boys," said Dempsey sincerely.

Kearns' departure from Montana was a little more complicated. To this day, he holds to the colorful view that he narrowly escaped injury or death from the guns of the West in getting out with the money. The money, the proceeds of the last day's ticket sale, amounted to about eighty thousand dollars in silver and bills. Kearns and McKetrick counted it in the presence of the federal tax men and stuffed it into a couple of canvas sacks. It is altogether possible that if Kearns had then honored an earlier promise to meet with certain fight fans and Shelby citizens in a saloon to talk things over before saying good-bye, he and the cash would not have left the state intact. The temper of Shelby needed only a sprinkling of ninety-proof rye to boil over. But Kearns, holding to his higher purpose, which was to keep all the money, less tax, broke the date. He and McKetrick made straight from the boxoffice for a caboose attached to a locomotive that stood waiting in the twilight at the station. The getaway transportation had been chartered with the help of the federal men. As Kearns and McKetrick boarded the caboose, they observed in the street nearby the shadowy figure of a small man with a ukulele. This was the late Hype Igoe, a New York sportswriter with a turn for minstrelsy who, having written his fight piece and lingered in Shelby to take on fuel, was delicately strumming chords for his own entertainment. "This is the New York special, Hype," called Kearns. Igoe accepted the invitation and got aboard, and the special rolled out of Shelby.

Still playing a cautious game, the Kearns party spent the rest of the night in the cellar of a barbershop in Great Falls. Kearns passed up the Salt Lake City express next day, and for five hundred dollars, out of one of the canvas bags, hired a locomotive and coach from the Great Northern's Great Falls agent. He and his friends joined Dempsey the next day.

On July 9th began a series of events that canonized Kearns in the boxing business. The Stanton Trust & Savings Bank of Great Falls closed its doors that day. Stanton insisted that the closing had no connection with the Dempsey-Gibbons fight; he blamed it on post-war conditions in general. However, all other reports from Montana then and later agreed that the public knowledge of Stanton's association with the fight caused a run on the bank, which the banker could not meet because of the temporary withdrawal of seventy-three thousand dollars in cash from his own account to pay Kearns on June 16th. The state bank examiner, L. Q. Skelton, came to Great Falls to take over the bank. He saved himself an extra trip to the neighborhood by taking over Mayor Johnson's First State Bank of Shelby as well, Johnson having stopped payment to depositors on the morning of July 10th.

It was now revealed for the first time that much of the cash paid by Stanton to Kearns had been secured by Johnson with his personal property, which he began making over to Stanton after the fight. On July 11th, the First State Bank of Joplin, Montana, an affiliate of Stanton's bank, closed down. Newspaper reports from Joplin stated that all closings to date were "generally accredited" to the championship bout in Shelby. Boxing people never doubted this for a moment. Kearns and Dempsey have been pointed out ever since as winners over three Montana banks. The better-informed students of the situation, like Kearns, feel that the score should be four, for on August 16th of the same year, almost unnoticed by the press, the First National Bank of Shelby was closed by order of its board of directors, following withdrawals of something like a hundred thousand dollars in the first month after the fight. This left Shelby with, for the time being, no banks at all and practically no assets. The oil boom subsided not long afterward. The arena was torn down and the lumber salvaged by the mortgage holders.

Kearns has related that Mayor Johnson wrote to Dempsey and himself that summer asking for a loan of twenty-five thousand dollars, and that it was granted and repaid within a year. It is certain that the Mayor was comfortably off when he died in 1938, thanks mainly to another strike in the Kevin-Sunburst oil field, a few years after the first one, which reanimated the town. The career of Patricia Salmon, the tent-show actress, took an opposite course. Her New York press reviews from Shelby in 1923 won her a contract with Florenz Ziegfeld and a season in the *Follies*. It was thought for a time that she, Dempsey, and Kearns (and the U.S. government) were the beneficiaries of the Shelby fight. But Miss Salmon was a one-year wonder. Her star declined as Johnson's rose, and in 1928 she was towed off the floor of Madison Square Garden with a set of swollen feet, after performing consecutively for a hundred and thirty-five hours and forty minutes in a dance marathon that she had hoped would bring her publicity and another job in the theater.

A word should be said about the early unpopularity of Dempsey, for it contributed much to his discomfort at Shelby and to the public's reaction in Montana and elsewhere. Like other entertainers in both world wars, Dempsey, in 1918, did a certain amount of morale-building among war workers. There is evidence that he was popular with sports followers, including Army and Navy men, in 1919, when he won the championship (Willard, the champion, who had also failed to see service, was much less so). The change in Dempsey's case did not set in until after the managers of heavyweights with war records, all of them outclassed as prizefighters by Dempsey, began to play up their wartime service in interviews and advertisements. Dempsey did not speak to Jimmy Bronson, who managed Fighting Bob Martin, for more than twenty-five years after this campaign, though Bronson actually had nothing to do with the wide circulation of a 1918 photograph of Dempsey striking a pose in a shipyard with a workman's tool in his hands and patent leather shoes on his feet.

Dempsey was formally acquitted of draft evasion in 1920. From the time he lost the championship to Gene Tunney, in 1926, he was immensely popular in America and abroad. However, it was plain to anyone who knew him that he never forgot certain aspects of his public life between 1919 and 1926. He was commissioned, as a physical director, in the Coast Guard in the last war. I saw him during preparations for the Okinawa landing in 1945. He had obtained leave to go to Okinawa on a Coast Guard ship, and could hardly control his excitement; in fact, it was almost necessary to gag him to maintain security before the operation began. He went ashore on the Marines' sector of the front shortly after D (or L) Day. He did not stay long, since he served no military purpose there, but it probably helped to compensate him for an hour spent with a sharp-tongued crowd outside the wooden arena at Shelby in 1923. Shelby paid as it went for its attitude toward Dempsey, but, like Kearns, he was not an easy man to satisfy.

The Long Count

GENE TUNNEY

If the night in 1926 that Gene Tunney (1897–1978) took the heavyweight title from Jack Dempsey is best remembered for Dempsey's quick reply to his wife's post-fight question "What happened?" with "Honey, I forgot to duck," their rematch, a year later, has been fixed in stone by the events of the seventh round. Who better to weigh in on boxing's famed "Long Count" than its beneficiary, in this excerpt from *Arms for Living*, Tunney's second volume of memoirs, published in 1941. A stylist both in and out of the ring, Tunney was the only reigning world champ in any weight class ever to lecture on Shakespeare at Yale.

The height of getting hit, being surprised and thinking it out occurred in that famous knockdown during my second battle with Dempsey. The getting hit part of it was amply visible to all the world. The surprise was known only to me in its rich amazement. I never saw the punch, never glimpsed that savage left hook which Jack swung on my jaw. Getting hit is a commonplace, but not seeing it coming really injured my pride. I was always cocksure about my eyesight in the ring.

The blow was the second in that series of seven that put me on the canvas for the first time in my life. I remember clearly Jack crossing a vicious right over my left lead for the first of the series. An obvious blow, and I thought: "Tunney, what a sucker you are to be nailed by that." Then a fearful left hand wallop on the jaw. I didn't see the punch start, didn't see it in flight, but I certainly felt it. It was the hardest of seven, and made me hazy about ones that followed. I had to look at the motion pictures the next day to find out how often Dempsey had hit me. Seven punches in all. I never even felt the last three.

My blindness to the dramatic punch was caused, I believe, by a traumatic astigmatism—a severe eye injury sustained in a training bout several days before the contest. A sparring partner hit me a blow in the eye with his thumb extended. It broke several small blood vessels and injured the retina. The pain for half a minute was the most acute in my whole life. Two eye specialists were rushed out from Chicago to my camp. After the first treatment, I began to see a little out of the injured eye. That glimpse of light was one of the great moments of my life. I was not going to lose the sight of the eye. The treatment continued until the day of the contest, and I believe that the injury, still imperfectly healed, left a blind spot. Into this blind spot came what should have been the glimpse of the Dempsey left hook, the ace wallop of that tempest of wallops.

I was oblivious of the long count aspects, which caused so much debate. There has been plenty of myth and confusion about that. On the floor I first became aware of the count when I heard the referee say "two." Eight seconds to go, eight seconds in which to do the most critical thinking in my life. I had never been knocked down before, but had often thought about what I'd do if I were. Every professional boxer knows he must take advantage of the respite of nine seconds. But upon arising—what? According to previous reasoning, it would be either of two things—clinch to gain a few more seconds, or put everything in a punch as my opponent came charging in for the kill. Which course depended on the type of opponent.

But as I sat on the floor in the Dempsey fight I reflected that neither alternative would do. Trying to clinch with Dempsey, the way he was hitting, I might get knocked out then and there. Trying to slam him with one desperate punch was not promising, either. Jack's way of keeping his chin down on his chest made his jaw a difficult mark to shoot at. In twenty rounds in the ring with him I don't think I ever hit him once fairly on the jaw. The blows always landed high, on the cheeks and around the eyes and forehead. So I had to make a complete change of all I had planned, revise strategy during those seconds on the floor.

I had noted earlier in the fight that Dempsey at times would flounder toward me. This confirmed information I had; that in training his handlers had put him through special roadwork to strengthen his legs, so that a new type of footwork could be taught him. They made him get down off his toes—a mistake in my estimation.

But what about my own legs? It is a prizering commonplace that when a boxer is badly hit the first things to be affected are his legs. Still mine felt all right. I had always based my ring technique on my speed and sureness of foot and now it seemed that my best bet was to match my legs against Dempsey's legs, until I had completely recovered from the effects of the knockdown.

That was the decision I had arrived at when at the count of nine I got to one knee and then arose. I circled Dempsey to the right to keep away from his left hook. The strategy was correct. My legs were okay. My footwork was faster than his. It kept me out of danger until I was my normal self, fighting my normal fight, stepping in and hitting. Jack was almost helpless at the end.

I was bedeviled by the long count controversy that ensued, the referee having made Jack abide by the rules and having begun the count only when Jack had gone to his corner as he had been required to do. I grew tired of repeating that I knew nothing about it as I sat on the canvas; was busy with other thoughts. I suspected that when they said I had been down for fourteen seconds, they were stretching it a bit, but what was the use? I got up when the age-old rule required it, after the referee tolled nine.

I could console myself by recalling a previous long count controversy concerning Corbett and Fitzsimmons. Corbett claimed, and told me with still burning wrath, that when he knocked Fitzsimmons down in the sixth round of their championship fight the referee gave Fitz a long count. He really had Fitz knocked out, vowed Jim. Not only that—Corbett himself had a short count. Jim insisted to me repeatedly that when Fitzsimmons put him down with the solar plexus punch, the referee counted him out with a short count, less than nine. All of which makes me sigh with relief. It's dreary business being mixed up in a combined long-count-short-count argument.

You can learn best about championship from champions, in boxing as in all of life. The better to master your profession, trade, art or sport, study the performances of those who are acknowledged to do it the best. I learned from Fitzsimmons and Corbett and Dempsey. From the other heavyweight title holders, not much. Not from the legend of John L. Sullivan, for example, though earliest recollection was of my father extolling the prowess of the great man. From all I could gather about the ring technique of the Boston Strong Boy, he was merely loud and angry, courageous and strong.

I never knew Jeffries well, never had much chance to see him. I am aware that there are first-rate judges of boxing who hold the big fellow to have been the greatest of them all, and will talk with persuasion and enthusiasm to prove it. I can't agree, but that perhaps is because of my lifelong preoccupation with championship as a state of mind. Of Jeffries you might perhaps say that sometimes championship can be a state of somebody else's mind.

The ring strategy of Boilermaker Jim was the thinking of the man who trained him for the championship fight with Fitzsimmons, Tommy Ryan, the great old-time middleweight champion, and one of the cagiest of them all. Tommy Ryan created the pattern of Jeffries' actions in the ring, taught him the famous crouch, body hunched away over and left hand stuck out. Just go plodding ahead like that, pushing the left out straight. It was one of the most uninteresting of ring styles, but it had its pertinent logic in the mind of Tommy Ryan.

Jeffries' decisive quality was his tremendous physical toughness and endurance. The brawny giant could hardly be hurt. The Tommy Ryan system was for Jeffries to take all the beating the other fellow could give him, just go plodding on in a crouch and absorb all the punches that came his way—until his opponent wore himself out. It was a sublimation of the familiar "he can't hurt us" philosophy. It is said that Jeffries, the ponderous giant, often displayed little love for battle; sometimes wanted to quit. There are stories of how his tough manager, Delaney, had to use threats to make him go on fighting, or Jeff would have quit cold. Well, you could hardly blame him, with that Tommy Ryan strategy of having Jeffries take all the beating the other fellow could hand out. The Ryan mentality was an uncomfortable thing for the Jeffries physique, even though it meant the championship.

In a way you can say that Joe Louis' championship is a state of Jack Blackburn's mind. Joe has been taught everything he knows by his trainer, who was one of the greatest of the cagey old-time Negro fighters. Louis battles according to a pattern set by Blackburn. He reminds me of a schoolboy who has learned his lesson and repeats it by rote. Sometimes in the ring events do not quite fit the lesson. Then Joe Louis can be like a black boy in a canebrake, lashing out on his own with primeval fury, or sometimes floundering and bewildered like a schoolboy who has forgotten his lesson.

The Louis-Blackburn combination of matter and mind is illustrated in a story told of the recent Louis-Conn bout for the heavyweight championship. An explanation is given of the why and wherefore of the sudden and unexpected knockout in the thirteenth. The fast stepping Billy Conn was far ahead on points, baffling the champion with his speed, smartness, and clever boxing. He had only to play safe for three rounds more, continuing to outmaneuver the devastating bomber and keep out of range of the heavy artillery, and the decision and championship would have been his—at least so they say. But brilliant

Billy Conn was too pugnacious. The street corner fighting spirit got the best of him—Irish thickness, as he himself has explained. The following version of what happened was written by the sports reporter of the United Press:

> The irony of the ending was that Conn, the smart guy, was outsmarted. Maybe not by Louis, but certainly by canny old Jack Blackburn, Joe's trainer, who hung his razor-scarred face over the apron of the ring and saw things not visible to the eyes of men who were standing on their seats yelling and telling one another that the heavyweight championship of the world was about to pass hands. Blackburn saw that Conn was getting too confident and too eager, that he was missing with his left now and then and leaving his jaw as wide open as a mining camp on Saturday night. Between the 12th and 13th rounds Blackburn whispered the words. Louis nodded.
>
> Came the 13th and Conn threw a left hook that was six inches wide. Then the lightning flashed and the thunder rolled. Louis crashed a right to the jaw and Conn wobbled backward.
>
> "Now, now," somebody yelled in Louis' corner.
>
> Seven punches, rights and lefts, fell on Conn's jaw faster than these words can be written. And there, all of a sudden and to the stunned surprise of everyone except Joe Louis and Jack Blackburn, lay Conn. His great heart told him to get up, but his legs said no and kept saying no until a man in gray shouted "Ten."

I have often thought what a terrifying phenomenon it would be if some pugilistic magic were to combine the two Negro heavyweights that have won the championship, Joe Louis and Jack Johnson. Jack Johnson with his flawless perfection of defense, the cunning old master who in a prizefight used his brain as much as he did his hands. Johnson ranks up there with Fitzsimmons and Corbett as a consciously calculating mentality in the swift hurly-burly of a prize ring brawl. Imagine a combination of Louis and Johnson shuffling out at you in a ring. The prospect would be black in more than one way.

I know that in talking of champions my judgment perhaps is governed by an excessive regard for the mental side of boxing. To me the men are interesting and important in proportion to the amount of thinking they put in the conflict of boxing gloves. This is an echo of the lesson gained in military service—championship is a state of mind.

Champion

RING LARDNER

When we think of Ring Lardner (1885–1933), we think of the satiric wit behind the classic baseball stories *You Know Me, Al* and *Alibi Ike*. In *Champion*, originally published in *Metropolitan* magazine in 1916, he gives us something different. The satirist is still punching away, but the lightness of the earlier stories never makes it out of the gym. This is a darker Lardner at work; Midge Kelly, the story's title character, and the ferocious underbelly of the game itself have backed Lardner's usual drollery into a corner. Like a champ, he makes use of it with all the mastery of his growing craft. It was the very darkness at the heart of the tale that made the 1949 screen adaptation, starring Kirk Douglas, seem so uncompromisingly real for its time.

M idge Kelly scored his first knockout when he was seventeen. The knockee was his brother Connie, three years his junior and a cripple. The purse was a half dollar given to the younger Kelly by a lady whose electric had just missed bumping his soul from his frail little body.

Connie did not know Midge was in the house, else he never would have risked laying the prize on the arm of the least comfortable chair in the room, the better to observe its shining beauty. As Midge entered from the kitchen, the crippled boy covered the coin with his hand, but the movement lacked the speed requisite to escape his brother's quick eye.

"Watcha got there?" demanded Midge.

"Nothin'," said Connie.

"You're a one legged liar!" said Midge.

He strode over to his brother's chair and grasped the hand that con-cealed the coin.

"Let loose!" he ordered.

Connie began to cry.

"Let loose and shut up your noise," said the elder, and jerked his brother's hand from the chair arm.

The coin fell onto the bare floor. Midge pounced on it. His weak mouth widened in a triumphant smile.

"Nothin', huh?" he said. "All right, if it's nothin' you don't want it."

"Give that back," sobbed the younger.

"I'll give you a red nose, you little sneak! Where'd you steal it?"

"I didn't steal it. It's mine. A lady give it to me after she pretty near hit me with a car."

"It's a crime she missed you," said Midge.

Midge started for the front door. The cripple picked up his crutch, rose from his chair with difficulty, and, still sobbing, came toward Midge. The latter heard him and stopped.

"You better stay where you're at," he said.

"I want my money," cried the boy.

"I know what you want," said Midge.

Doubling up the fist that held the half dollar, he landed with all his strength on his brother's mouth. Connie fell to the floor with a thud, the crutch tumbling on top of him. Midge stood beside the prostrate form.

"Is that enough?" he said. "Or do you want this, too?"

And he kicked him in the crippled leg.

"I guess that'll hold you," he said.

There was no response from the boy on the floor. Midge looked at him a moment, then at the coin in his hand, and then went out into the street, whistling.

An hour later, when Mrs. Kelly came home from her day's work at Faulkner's Steam Laundry, she found Connie on the floor, moaning. Drop-ping on her knees beside him, she called him by name a score of times. Then she got up and, pale as a ghost, dashed from the house. Dr. Ryan left the Kelly abode about dusk and walked toward Halsted Street. Mrs. Dorgan spied him as he passed her gate.

"Who's sick, Doctor?" she called.

"Poor little Connie," he replied. "He had a bad fall."

"How did it happen?"

"I can't say for sure, Margaret, but I'd almost bet he was knocked down."

"Knocked down!" exclaimed Mrs. Dorgan.

"Why, who—?"

"Have you seen the other one lately?"

"Michael? No, not since mornin'. You can't be thinkin'—"

"I wouldn't put it past him, Margaret," said the doctor gravely. "The lad's mouth is swollen and cut, and his poor, skinny little leg is bruised. He surely didn't do it to himself and I think Helen suspects the other one."

"Lord save us!" said Mrs. Dorgan. "I'll run over and see if I can help."

"That's a good woman," said Doctor Ryan, and went on down the street.

Near midnight, when Midge came home, his mother was sitting at Connie's bedside. She did not look up.

"Well," said Midge, "what's the matter?"

She remained silent. Midge repeated his question.

"Michael, you know what's the matter," she said at length.

"I don't know nothin'," said Midge.

"Don't lie to me, Michael. What did you do to your brother?"

"Nothin'."

"You hit him."

"Well, then, I hit him. What of it? It ain't the first time."

Her lips pressed tightly together, her face like chalk, Ellen Kelly rose from her chair and made straight for him. Midge backed against the door.

"Lay off'n me, Ma. I don't want to fight no woman."

Still she came on breathing heavily.

"Stop where you're at, Ma," he warned.

There was a brief struggle and Midge's mother lay on the floor before him.

"You ain't hurt, Ma. You're lucky I didn't land good. And I told you to lay off'n me."

"God forgive you, Michael!"

Midge found Hap Collins in the showdown game at the Royal.

"Come on out a minute," he said.

Hap followed him out on the walk.

"I'm leavin' town for a w'ile," said Midge.

"What for?"

"Well, we had a little run-in up to the house. The kid stole a half buck off'n me, and when I went after it he cracked me with his crutch. So I nailed him. And the old lady came at me with a chair and I took it off'n her and she fell down."

"How is Connie hurt?"

"Not bad."

"What are you runnin' away for?"

"Who the hell said I was runnin' away? I'm sick and tired o' gettin' picked on; that's all. So I'm leavin' for a w'ile and I want a piece o' money."

"I ain't only got six bits," said Happy.

"You're in bad shape, ain't you? Well, come through with it."

Happy came through.

"You oughtn't to hit the kid," he said.

"I ain't astin' you who can I hit," snarled Midge. "You try to put somethin' over on me and you'll get the same dose. I'm goin' now."

"Go as far as you like," said Happy, but not until he was sure that Kelly was out of hearing.

Early the following morning, Midge boarded a train for Milwaukee. He had no ticket, but no one knew the difference. The conductor remained in the caboose.

On a night six months later, Midge hurried out of the "stage door" of the Star Boxing Club and made for Duane's saloon, two blocks away. In his pocket were twelve dollars, his reward for having battered up one Demon Dempsey through the six rounds of the first preliminary.

It was Midge's first professional engagement in the manly art. Also it was the first time in weeks that he had earned twelve dollars.

On the way to Duane's he had to pass Niemann's. He pulled his cap over his eyes and increased his pace until he had gone by. Inside Niemann's stood a trusting bartender, who for ten days had staked Midge to drinks and allowed him to ravage the lunch on a promise to come in and settle the moment he was paid for the "prelim."

Midge strode into Duane's and aroused the napping bartender by slapping a silver dollar on the festive board.

"Gimme a shot," said Midge.

The shooting continued until the wind-up at the Star was over and part of the fight crowd joined Midge in front of Duane's bar. A youth in the early twenties, standing next to young Kelly, finally summoned sufficient courage to address him.

"Wasn't you in the first bout?" he ventured.

"Yeh," Midge replied.

"My name's Hersch," said the other.

Midge received the startling information in silence.

"I don't want to butt in," continued Mr. Hersch, "but I'd like to buy you a drink."

"All right," said Midge, "but don't overstrain yourself."

Mr. Hersch laughed uproariously and beckoned to the bartender.

"You certainly gave that wop a trimmin' tonight," said the buyer of the drink, when they had been served. "I thought you'd kill him."

"I would if I hadn't let up," Midge replied. "I'll kill 'em all."

"You got the wallop all right," the other said admiringly.

"Have I got the wallop?" said Midge. "Say, I can kick like a mule. Did you notice them muscles in my shoulders?"

"Notice 'em? I couldn't help from noticin' 'em," said Hersch. "I says to the fella settin' alongside o' me, I says: 'Look at them shoulders! No wonder he can hit,' I says to him."

"Just let me land and it's good-by, baby," said Midge. "I'll kill 'em all."

The oral manslaughter continued until Duane's closed for the night. At parting, Midge and his new friend shook hands and arranged for a meeting the following evening.

For nearly a week the two were together almost constantly. It was Hersch's pleasant role to listen to Midge's modest revelations concerning himself, and to buy every time Midge's glass was empty. But there came an evening when Hersch regretfully announced that he must go home to supper.

"I got a date for eight bells," he confided. "I could stick till then, only I must clean up and put on the Sunday clo'es, 'cause she's the prettiest little thing in Milwaukee."

"Can't you fix it for two?" asked Midge.

"I don't know who to get," Hersch replied. "Wait, though. I got a sister and if she ain't busy, it'll be O.K. She's no bum for looks herself."

So it came about that Midge and Emma Hersch and Emma's brother and the prettiest little thing in Milwaukee foregathered at Wall's and danced half the night away. And Midge and Emma danced every dance together, for though every little onestep seemed to induce a new thirst of its own, Lou Hersch stayed too sober to dance with his own sister.

The next day, penniless at last in spite of his phenomenal ability to make someone else settle, Midge Kelly sought out Doc Hammond, matchmaker for the Star, and asked to be booked for the next show.

"I could put you on with Tracy for the next bout," said Doc.

"What's they in it?" asked Midge.

"Twenty if you cop," Doc told him.

"Have a heart," protested Midge. "Didn't I look good the other night?"

"You looked all right. But you aren't Freddie Welsh yet by a consid-'able margin."

"I ain't scared of Freddie Welsh or none of 'em," said Midge.

"Well, we don't pay our boxers by the size of their chests," Doc said. "I'm offerin' you this Tracy bout. Take it or leave it."

"All right; I'm on," said Midge, and he passed a pleasant afternoon at Duane's on the strength of his booking.

Young Tracy's manager came to Midge the night before the show.

"How do you feel about this go?" he asked.

"Me?" asked Midge, "I feel all right. What do you mean, how do I feel?"

"I mean," said Tracy's manager, "that we're mighty anxious to win, 'cause the boy's got a chance in Philly if he cops this one."

"What's your proposition?" asked Midge.

"Fifty bucks," said Tracy's manager.

"What do you think I am, a crook? Me lay down for fifty bucks. Not me!"

"Seventy-five, then," said Tracy's manager.

The market closed on eighty and the details were agreed on in short order. And the next night Midge was stopped in the second round by a terrific slap on the forearm.

This time Midge passed up both Niemann's and Duane's, having a sizable account at each place, and sought his refreshment at Stein's farther down the street.

When the profits of his deal with Tracy were gone, he learned, by firsthand information from Doc Hammond and the matchmakers at other "clubs," that he was no longer desired for even the cheapest of preliminaries. There was no danger of his starving or dying of thirst while Emma and Lou Hersch lived. But he made up his mind, four months after his defeat by Young Tracy, that Milwaukee was not the ideal place for him to live.

"I can lick the best of 'em," he reasoned, "but there ain't no more chanct for me here. I can maybe go east and get on somewheres. And besides—"

But just after Midge had purchased a ticket to Chicago with the money he had "borrowed" from Emma Hersch "to buy shoes," a heavy hand was laid on his shoulders and he turned to face two strangers.

"Where are you goin', Kelly?" inquired the owner of the heavy hand.

"Nowheres," said Midge. "What the hell do you care?"

The other stranger spoke:

"Kelly, I'm employed by Emma Hersch's mother to see that you do right by her. And we want you to stay here till you've done it."

"You won't get nothin' but the worst of it, monkeying with me," said Midge.

Nevertheless he did not depart for Chicago that night. Two days later, Emma Hersch became Mrs. Kelly, and the gift of the groom, when once they were alone, was a crushing blow on the bride's pale cheek.

Next morning, Midge left Milwaukee as he had entered it—by fast freight.

"They's no use kiddin' ourself any more," said Tommy Haley. "He might get down to thirty-seven in a pinch, but if he done below that a mouse could stop him. He's a welter; that's what he is and he knows it as well as I do. He's growed like a weed in the last six mont's. I told him, I says, 'If you don't quit growin' they won't be nobody for you to box, only Willard and them.' He says, 'Well, I wouldn't run away from Willard if I weighed twenty pounds more.'"

"He must hate himself," said Tommy's brother.

"I never seen a good one that didn't," said Tommy. "And Midge is a good one; don't make no mistake about that. I wisht we could of got Welsh before the kid growed so big. But it's too late now. I won't make no holler, though, if we can match him up with the Dutchman."

"Who do you mean?"

"Young Goetz, the welter champ. We mightn't not get so much dough for the bout itself, but it'd roll in afterward. What a drawin' card we'd be, 'cause the people pays their money to see the fella with the wallop, and that's Midge. And we'd keep the title just as long as Midge could make the weight."

"Can't you land no match with Goetz?"

"Sure, 'cause he needs the money. But I've went careful with the kid so far and look at the results I got! So what's the use of takin' a chanct? The kid's comin' every minute and Goetz is goin' back faster'n big Johnson did. I think we could lick him now; I'd bet my life on it. But six mont's from now they won't be no risk. He'll of licked hisself before that time. Then all as we'll have to do is sign up with him and wait for the referee to stop it. But Midge is so crazy to get at him now that I can't hardly hold him back."

The brothers Haley were lunching in a Boston hotel. Dan had come down from Holyoke to visit with Tommy and to watch the latter's protégé go twelve rounds, or less, with Bud Cross. The bout promised little in the way of a contest, for Midge had twice stopped the Baltimore youth and Bud's reputation for gameness was all that had earned him the date. The fans were willing to pay the price to see Midge's haymaking left, but they wanted to see it used on an opponent who would not jump out of the ring the first time he felt its crushing force. But Cross was such an opponent, and his willingness to stop boxing-gloves with his eyes, ears, nose, and throat had long enabled him to escape the horrors of honest labor. A game boy was Bud, and he showed it in his battered, swollen, discolored face.

"I should think," said Dan Haley, "that the kid'd do whatever you tell him after all you done for him."

"Well," said Tommy, "he's took my dope pretty straight so far, but he's so sure of hisself that he can't see no reason for waitin'. He'll do what I say, though; he'd be a sucker not to."

"You got a contrac' with him?"

"No, I don't need no contrac'. He knows it was me that drug him out o' the gutter and he ain't goin' to turn me down now, when he's got the dough and bound to get more. Where'd he of been at if I hadn't listened to him when he first come to me? That's pretty near two years ago now, but it seems like last week. I was settin' in the s'loon acrost from the Pleasant Club in Philly, waitin' for McCann to count the dough and come over, when this little bum blowed in and tried to stand the house off for a drink. They told him nothin' doin' and to beat it out o' there, and then he seen me and come over to where I was settin' and ast me wasn't I a boxin' man and I told him who I was. Then he ast me for money to buy a shot and I told him to set down and I'd buy it for him.

"Then we got talkin' things over and he told me his name and told me about fightin' a couple o' prelims out to Milwaukee. So I says, 'Well, boy, I don't know how good or how rotten you are, but you won't never get nowheres trainin' on that stuff.' So he says he'd cut it out if he could get on in a bout and I says I would give him a chanct if he played square with me and didn't touch no more to drink. So we shook hands and I took him up to the hotel with me and give him a bath and the next day I bought him some clo'es. And I staked him to eats and sleeps for over six weeks. He had a hard time breakin' away from the polish, but finally I thought he was fit and I give him his chanct. He went on with Smiley Sayer and stopped him so quick that Smiley thought sure he was poisoned.

"Well, you know what he's did since. The only beatin' in his record was by Tracy in Milwaukee before I got hold of him, and he's licked Tracy three times in the last year.

"I've gave him all the best of it in a money way and he's got seven thousand bucks in cold storage. How's that for a kid that was in the gutter two years ago? And he'd have still more yet if he wasn't so nuts over clo'es and got to stop at the good hotels and so forth."

"Where's his home at?"

"Well, he ain't really got no home. He came from Chicago and his mother canned him out o' the house for bein' no good. She give him a raw deal, I guess, and he says he won't have nothin' to do with her unless she comes to him first. She's got a pile o' money, he says, so he ain't worryin' about her."

The gentleman under discussion entered the café and swaggered to Tommy's table, while the whole room turned to look.

Midge was the picture of health despite a slightly colored eye and an ear that seemed to have no opening. But perhaps it was not his healthiness that drew all eyes. His diamond horse-shoe tie pin, his purple cross-striped shirt, his orange shoes and his light blue suit fairly screamed for attention.

"Where you been?" he asked Tommy. "I been lookin' all over for you."

"Set down," said his manager.

"No time," said Midge. "I'm goin' down to the w'arf and see 'em unload the fish."

"Shake hands with my brother Dan," said Tommy.

Midge shook hands with the Holyoke Haley.

"If you're Tommy's brother, you're O.K. with me," said Midge, and the brothers beamed with pleasure.

Dan moistened his lips and murmured an embarrassed reply, but it was lost on the young gladiator.

"Leave me take twenty," Midge was saying. "I prob'ly won't need it, but I don't like to be caught short."

Tommy parted with a twenty dollar bill and recorded the transaction in a small black book the insurance company had given him for Christmas.

"But," he said, "it won't cost you no twenty to look at them fish. Want me to go along?"

"No," said Midge hastily. "You and your brother here prob'ly got a lot to say to each other."

"Well," said Tommy, "don't take no bad money and don't get lost. And you better be back at four o'clock and lay down a w'ile."

"I don't need no rest to beat this guy, said Midge. "He'll do enough layin' down for the both of us."

And laughing even more than the jest called for, he strode out through the fire of admiring and startled glances.

The corner of Boylston and Tremont was the nearest Midge got to the wharf, but the lady awaiting him was doubtless a more dazzling sight than the catch of the luckiest Massachusetts fisherman. She could talk, too—probably better than the fish.

"O you Kid!" she said, flashing a few silver teeth among the gold. "O you fighting man!"

Midge smiled up at her.

"We'll go somewheres and get a drink," he said. "One won't hurt."

In New Orleans, five months after he had rearranged the map of Bud Cross for the third time, Midge finished training for his championship bout with the Dutchman.

Back in his hotel after the final workout, Midge stopped to chat with some of the boys from up north, who had made the long trip to see a champion dethroned, for the result of this bout was so nearly a foregone conclusion that even the experts had guessed it.

Tommy Haley secured the key and the mail and ascended to the Kelly suite. He was bathing when Midge came in, half an hour later.

"Any mail?" asked Midge.

"There on the bed," replied Tommy from the tub.

Midge picked up the stack of letters and postcards and glanced them over. From the pile he sorted out three letters and laid them on the table. The rest he tossed into the waste-basket. Then he picked up the three and sat for a few moments holding them, while his eyes gazed off into space. At length he looked again at the three unopened letters in his hand; then he put one in his pocket and tossed the other two at the basket. They missed their target and fell on the floor.

"Hell!" said Midge, and stooping over picked them up.

He opened one postmarked Milwaukee and read:

Dear Husband:

    I have wrote to you so manny times and got no anser and dont know if you ever got them, so I am writeing again in the hopes you will get this letter and anser. I dont like to bother you with my trubles and I would not only for the baby and I am not asking you should write to me but only send a little money and I am not asking for myself but the baby has not been well a day sence last Aug. and the dr. told me she cant live much longer unless I give her better food and thats impossible the ways things are. Lou has not been working for a year and what I make dont hardley pay for the rent. I am not asking for you to give me any money, but only you should send what I loaned when convenient and I think it amts. to about $36.00. Please try and send that amt. and it will help me, but if you cant send the whole amt. try and send me something.

Your wife,

Emma.

    Midge tore the letter into a hundred pieces and scattered them over the floor.
    "Money, money, money!" he said. "They must think I'm made o' money. I s'pose the old woman's after it too."
    He opened his mother's letter:

dear Michael Connie wonted me to rite and say you must beet the dutchman and he is sur you will and wonted me to say we wont you to rite and tell us about it, but I gess you havent no time to rite or we herd from you long beffore this but I wish you would rite jest a line or 2 boy becaus it wuld be better for Connie then a barl of medisin. It wuld help me to keep things going if you send me money now and then when you can spair it but if you cant send no money try and fine time to rite a letter onley a few lines and it will please Connie, jest think boy he hasent got out of bed in over 3 yrs. Connie says good luck.

Your Mother.

Ellen F. Kelly

"I thought so," said Midge. "They're all alike."

The third letter was from New York. It read:

Hon:—This is the last letter you will get from me before your champ, but I will send you a telegram Saturday, but I can't say as much in a telegram as in a letter and I am writing this to let you know I am thinking of you and praying for good luck.

Lick him good hon and don't wait no longer than you have to and don't forget to wire me as soon as its over. Give him that little old left of yours on the nose hon and don't be afraid of spoiling his good looks because he couldn't be no homlier than he is. But don't let him spoil my baby's pretty face. You won't will you hon.

Well hon I would give anything to be there and see it, but I guess you love Haley better than me or you wouldn't let him keep me away. But when your champ hon we can do as we please and tell Haley to go to the devil.

Well hon I will send you a telegram Saturday and I almost forgot to tell you I will need some more money, a couple hundred say and you will have to wire it to me as soon as you get this. You will won't you hon.

I will send you a telegram Saturday and remember hon I am pulling for you.

Well good-by sweetheart and good luck.

Grace.

"They're all alike," said Midge. "Money, money, money."

Tommy Haley, shining from his ablutions, came in from the adjoining room.

"Thought you'd be layn' down," he said.

"I'm goin' to," said Midge, unbuttoning his orange shoes.

"I'll call you at six and you can eat up here without no bugs to pester you. I got to go down and give them birds their tickets."

"Did you hear from Goldberg?" asked Midge.

"Didn't I tell you? Sure; fifteen weeks at five hundred, if we win. And we can get a guarantee o' twelve thousand, with privileges either in New York or Milwaukee."

"Who with?"

"Anybody that'll stand up in front of you. You don't care who it is, do
you?"

"Not me. I'll make 'em all look like a monkey."

"Well you better lay down aw'ile."

"Oh, say, wire two hundred to Grace for me, will you? Right away;
the New York address."

"Two hundred! You just sent her three hundred last Sunday."

"Well, what the hell do you care?"

"All right, all right. Don't get sore about it. Anything else?"

"That's all," said Midge, and dropped onto the bed.

"And I want the deed done before I come back," said Grace as she rose from
the table. "You won't fall down on me, will you, hon?"

"Leave it to me," said Midge. "And don't spend no more than you
have to."

Grace smiled a farewell and left the café. Midge continued to sip his
coffee and read his paper.

They were in Chicago and they were in the middle of Midge's first
week in vaudeville. He had come straight north to reap the rewards of his
glorious victory over the broken down Dutchman. A fortnight had been
spent in learning his act, which consisted of a gymnastic exhibition and a ten
minutes' monologue on the various excellences of Midge Kelly. And now he
was twice daily turning 'em away from the Madison Theater.

His breakfast over and his paper read, Midge sauntered into the lobby
and asked for his key. He then beckoned to a bellboy, who had been hoping
for that very honor.

"Find Haley, Tommy Haley," said Midge. "Tell him to come up to my
room."

"Yes, sir, Mr. Kelly," said the boy, and proceeded to break all his former records for diligence.

Midge was looking out of his seventh-story window when Tommy
answered the summons.

"What'll it be?" inquired his manager.

There was a pause before Midge replied.

"Haley," he said, "twenty-five per cent's a whole lot o' money."

"I guess I got it comin', ain't I?" said Tommy.

"I don't see how you figger it. I don't see where you're worth it to me."

"Well," said Tommy, "I didn't expect nothin' like this. I thought you
was satisfied with the bargain. I don't want to beat nobody out o' nothin', but

I don't see where you could have got anybody else that would of did all I done for you."

"Sure, that's all right," said the champion. "You done a lot for me in Philly. And you got good money for it, didn't you?"

"I ain't makin' no holler. Still and all, the big money's still ahead of us yet. And if it hadn't of been for me, you wouldn't of never got within grabbin' distance."

"Oh, I guess I could of went along all right," said Midge. "Who was it that hung that left on the Dutchman's jaw, me or you?"

"Yes, but you wouldn't been in the ring with the Dutchman if it wasn't for how I handled you."

"Well, this won't get us nowheres. The idear is that you ain't worth no twenty-five per cent now and it don't make no diff'rence what come off a year or two ago."

"Don't it?" said Tommy. "I'd say it made a whole lot of difference."

"Well, I say it don't and I guess that settles it."

"Look here, Midge," Tommy said, "I thought I was fair with you, but if you don't think so, I'm willin' to hear what you think is fair. I don't want nobody callin' me a Sherlock. Let's go down to business and sign up a contrac'. What's your figger?"

"I ain't namin' no figger," Midge replied. "I'm sayin' that twenty-five's too much. Now what are you willin' to take?"

"How about twenty?"

"Twenty's too much," said Kelly.

"What ain't too much?" asked Tommy.

"Well, Haley, I might as well give it to you straight. They ain't nothin' that ain't too much."

"You mean you don't want me at no figger?"

"That's the idear."

There was a minute's silence. Then Tommy Haley walked toward the door.

"Midge," he sad, in a choking voice, "you're makin' a big mistake, boy. You can't throw down your best friends and get away with it. That damn woman will ruin you."

Midge sprang from his seat.

"You shut your mouth!" he stormed. "Get out o' here before they have to carry you out. You been spongin' off o' me long enough. Say one more word about the girl or about anything else and you'll get what the Dutchman got. Now get out!"

And Tommy Haley, having a very vivid memory of the Dutchman's face as he fell, got out.

Grace came in later, dropped her numerous bundles on the lounge and perched herself on the arm of Midge's chair.

"Well?" she said.

"Well," said Midge, "I got rid of him."

"Good boy!" said Grace. "And now I think you might give me that twenty-five per cent."

"Besides the seventy-five you're already gettin'?" said Midge.

"Don't be no grouch, hon. You don't look pretty when you're grouchy."

"It ain't my business to look pretty," Midge replied.

"Wait till you see how I look with the stuff I bought this mornin'!"

Midge glanced at the bundles on the lounge.

"There's Haley's twenty-five per cent," he said, "and then some."

The champion did not remain long without a manager. Haley's successor was none other than Jerome Harris, who saw in Midge a better meal ticket than his popular-priced musical show had been.

The contract, giving Mr. Harris twenty-five per cent of Midge's earnings, was signed in Detroit the week after Tommy Haley had heard his dismissal read. It had taken Midge just six days to learn that a popular actor cannot get on without the ministrations of a man who thinks, talks, and means business. At first Grace objected to the new member of the firm, but when Mr. Harris had demanded and secured from the vaudeville people a one-hundred dollar increase in Midge's weekly stipend, she was convinced that the champion had acted for the best.

"You and my missus will have some great old times," Harris told Grace. "I'd of wired her to join us here, only I seen the Kid's bookin' takes us to Milwaukee next week, and that's where she is."

But when they were introduced in the Milwaukee hotel, Grace admitted to herself that her feeling for Mrs. Harris could hardly be called love at first sight. Midge, on the contrary, gave his new manager's wife the many times over and seemed loath to end the feast of his eyes.

"Some doll," he said to Grace when they were alone.

"Doll is right," the lady replied, "and sawdust where her brains ought to be."

"I'm li'ble to steal that baby," said Midge, and he smiled as he noted the effect of his words on his audience's face.

On Tuesday of the Milwaukee week the champion successfully defended his title in a bout that the newspapers never reported. Midge was alone in his room that morning when a visitor entered without knocking. The visitor was Lou Hersch.

Midge turned white at sight of him.

"What do you want?" he demanded.

"I guess you know," said Lou Hersch. "Your wife's starvin' to death and your baby's starvin' to death and I'm starvin' to death. And you're dirty with money."

"Listen," said Midge, "if it wasn't for you, I wouldn't never saw your sister. And, if you ain't man enough to hold a job, what's that to me? The best thing you can do is keep away from me."

"You give me a piece o' money and I'll go."

Midge's reply to the ultimatum was a straight right to his brother-in-law's narrow chest.

"Take that home to your sister."

And after Lou Hersch picked himself up and slunk away, Midge thought: "It's lucky I didn't give him my left or I'd of croaked him. And if I'd hit him in the stomach, I'd of broke his spine."

There was a party after each evening performance during the Milwaukee engagement. The wine flowed freely and Midge had more of it than Tommy Haley ever would have permitted him. Mr. Harris offered no objection, which was possibly just as well for his own physical comfort.

In the dancing between drinks, Midge had his new manager's wife for a partner as often as Grace. The latter's face as she floundered round in the arms of the portly Harris, belied her frequent protestations that she was having the time of her life.

Several times that week, Midge thought Grace was on the point of starting the quarrel he hoped to have. But it was not until Friday night that she accommodated. He and Mrs. Harris had disappeared after the matinee and when Grace saw him again at the close of the night show, she came to the point at once.

"What are you tryin' to pull off?" she demanded.

"It's none o' your business, is it?" said Midge.

"You bet it's my business; mine and Harris'. You cut it short or you'll find out."

"Listen," said Midge, "have you got a mortgage on me or somethin'? You talk like we was married."

"We're goin' to be, too. And tomorrow's as good a time as any."

"Just about," Midge said. "You got as much chanct o' marryin' me tomorrow as the next day or next year and that ain't no chanct at all."

"We'll find out," said Grace.

"You're the one that's got somethin' to find out."

"What do you mean?"

"I mean I'm married already."

"You lie!"

"You think so, do you? Well, s'pose you go to this here address and get acquainted with my missus."

Midge scrawled a number of a piece of paper and handed it to her. She stared at it unseeingly.

"Well," said Midge, "I ain't kiddin' you. You go there and ask for Mrs. Michael Kelly, and if you don't find her, I'll marry you tomorrow before breakfast."

Still Grace stared at the scrap of paper. To Midge it seemed an age before she spoke again.

"You lied to me all this w'ile."

"You never ast me was I married. What's more, what the hell dif-f'rence did it make to you? You got a split, didn't you? Better'n fifty-fifty."

He started away.

"Where you goin'?"

"I'm goin' to meet Harris and his wife."

"I'm goin' with you. You're not goin' to shake me now."

"Yes, I am, too," said Midge quietly. "When I leave town tomorrow night, you're going to stay here. And if I see where you're goin' to make a fuss, I'll put you in a hospital where they'll keep you quiet. You can get your stuff tomorrow mornin' and I'll slip you a hundred bucks. And then I don't want to see no more o' you. And don't try and tag along now or I'll have to add another K. O. to the old record."

When Grace returned to the hotel that night, she discovered that Midge and the Harrises had moved to another. And when Midge left town the following night, he was again without a manager, and Mr. Harris was without a wife.

Three days prior to Midge Kelly's ten-round bout with Young Milton in New York City, the sporting editor of *The News* assigned Joe Morgan to write two or three thousand words about the champion to run with a picture layout for Sunday.

Joe Morgan dropped in at Midge's training quarters Friday afternoon. Midge, he learned, was doing road work, but Midge's manager, Wallie Adams, stood ready and willing to supply reams of dope about the greatest fighter of the age.

"Let's hear what you've got," said Joe, "and then I'll try to fix up something."

So Wallie stepped on the accelerator of his imagination and shot away.

"Just a kid; that's all he is; a regular boy. Get what I mean? Don't know the meanin' o' bad habits. Never tasted liquor in his life and would prob'ly get sick if he smelled it. Clean livin' put him up where he's at. Get what I mean? And modest and unassumin' as a schoolgirl. He's so quiet you wouldn't never know he was round. And he'd go to jail before he'd talk about himself.

"No job at all to get him in shape, 'cause he's always that way. The only trouble we have with him is gettin' him to light into these poor bums they match him up with. He's scared he'll hurt somebody. Get what I mean? He's tickled to death over this match with Milton, 'cause everybody says Milton can stand the gaff. Midge'll maybe be able to cut loose a little this time. But the last two bouts he had, the guys hadn't no business in the ring with him, and he was holdin' back all the w'ile for the fear he'd kill somebody. Get what I mean?"

"Is he married?" inquired Joe.

"Say, you'd think he was married to hear him rave about them kiddies he's got. His fam'ly's up in Canada to their summer home and Midge is wild to get up there with 'em. He thinks more o' that wife and them kiddies than all the money in the world. Get what I mean?"

"How many children has he?"

"I don't know, four or five, I guess. All boys and every one of 'em a dead ringer for their dad."

"Is his father living?"

"No, the old man died when he was a kid. But he's got a grand old mother and a kid brother out in Chi. They're the first ones he thinks about after a match, them and his wife and kiddies. And he don't forget to send the old woman a thousand bucks after every bout. He's goin' to buy her a new home as soon as they pay him off for this match."

"How about his brother? Is he gong to tackle the game?"

"Sure, and Midge says he'll be a champion before he's twenty years old. They're a fightin' fam'ly and all of 'em honest and straight as a die. Get what I mean? A fella that I can't tell you his name come to Midge in Milwau-

kee onct and wanted him to throw a fight and Midge give him such a trimmin' in the street that he couldn't go on that night. That's the kind he is. Get
what I mean?"

Joe Morgan hung around the camp until Midge and his trainers
returned.

"One o' the boys from *The News*" said Wallie by way of introduction.
"I been givin' him your fam'ly hist'ry."

"Did he give you good dope?" he inquired.

"He's some historian," said Joe.

"Don't call me no names," said Wallie smiling. "Call us up if they's
anything more you want. And keep your eyes on us Monday night. Get what
I mean?"

The story in Sunday's *News* was read by thousands of lovers of the
manly art. It was well written and full of human interest. Its slight inaccuracies went unchallenged, though three readers, besides Wallie Adams and
Midge Kelly, saw and recognized them. The three were Grace, Tommy Haley,
and Jerome Harris and the comments they made were not for publication.

Neither the Mrs. Kelly in Chicago nor the Mrs. Kelly in Milwaukee
knew that there was such a paper as the New York *News*. And even if they had
known of it and that it contained two columns of reading matter about
Midge, neither mother nor wife could have bought it. For *The News* on Sunday is a nickel a copy.

Joe Morgan could have written more accurately, no doubt, if instead
of Wallie Adams, he had interviewed Ellen Kelly and Connie Kelly and
Emma Kelly and Lou Hersch and Grace and Jerome Harris and Tommy
Haley and Hap Collins and two or three Milwaukee bartenders.

But a story built on their evidence would never have passed the
sporting editor.

"Suppose you can prove it," that gentleman would have said. "It
wouldn't get us anything but abuse to print it. The people don't want to see
him knocked. He's champion."

The Croxley Master

SIR ARTHUR CONAN DOYLE

You don't need to be a Sherlock Holmes to solve this mystery: What did Sir Arthur Conan Doyle (1859–1930) do for a living before creating the most famed detective in all literature? The answer: He was a doctor.

That fact certainly plays an important part in the creation of this long non-Holmesian story, first published in 1900. And so does this: Doyle himself was not only an aficionado of the fights, he happened to be a superb boxer and an enthusiastic sponsor of its health benefits as an exercise.

Indeed, when Doyle signed on for a stint as ship's surgeon on a vessel sailing the Arctic for seal and whales in 1880, he even brought his boxing gloves along. As the story goes, when the ship's steward noticed them, he challenged Doyle, officially still a medical student, to a match. The steward was clearly impressed—and stung. "So help me," he announced, "he's the best ship's surgeon we've had! He's blackened my eye!"

Doyle never blackened the eye of the sport that's taken its fair and unfair share of body blows, though, and he often returned to it in his writings. His 1896 novel, "Rodney Stone," was one of the first to be set in the milieu, and in 1912, his play about the sport, "The House of Temperley," ran for three months in London. He even gave Holmes a boxing jones; in "The Glorie Scott," the great detective tells Dr. Watson that boxing was one of his few athletic tastes.

His creator, on the other hand, had several. In addition to boxing, Doyle was a fine cricketeer and rugby player, shot a mean game of billiards, raced cars and skied avidly. He was also an excellent golfer, even giving his good friend, Rudyard Kipling, a fair duffer himself, a series of golf lessons on a visit to Kipling's Vermont estate in the summer of 1894.

I

M
r. Robert Montgomery was seated at his desk, his head upon his hands, in a state of the blackest despondency. Before him was the open ledger with the long columns of Dr. Oldacre's prescriptions. At his elbow lay the wooden tray with the labels in various partitions, the cork box, the lumps of twisted sealing-wax, while in front a rank of empty bottles waited to be filled. But his spirits were too low for work. He sat in silence, with his fine shoulders bowed and his head upon his hands.

Outside, through the grimy surgery window over a foreground of blackened brick and slate, a line of enormous chimneys like Cyclopean pillars upheld the lowering, dun-colored cloudbank. For six days in the week they spouted smoke, but to-day the furnace fires were banked, for it was Sunday. Sordid and polluting gloom hung over a district blighted and blasted by the greed of man. There was nothing in the surroundings to cheer a desponding soul, but it was more than his dismal environment which weighed upon the medical assistant.

His trouble was deeper and more personal. The winter session was approaching. He should be back again at the University completing the last year which would give him his medical degree; but alas! he had not the money with which to pay his class fees, nor could he imagine how he could procure it. Sixty pounds were wanted to make his career, and it might have been as many thousands for any chance there seemed to be of his obtaining it.

He was roused from his black meditation by the entrance of Dr. Oldacre himself, a large, clean-shaven, respectable man, with a prim manner and an austere face. He had prospered exceedingly by the support of the local Church interest, and the rule of his life was never by word or action to run a risk of offending the sentiment which had made him. His standard of respectability and of dignity was exceedingly high, and he expected the same from his assistants. His appearance and words were always vaguely benevolent. A sudden impulse came over the despondent student. He would test the reality of this philanthropy.

"I beg your pardon, Dr. Oldacre," said he, rising from his chair; "I have a great favour to ask of you."

The doctor's appearance was not encouraging. His mouth suddenly tightened, and his eyes fell.

"Yes, Mr. Montgomery?"

"You are aware, sir, that I need only one more session to complete my course."

"So you have told me."

"It is very important to me, sir."

"Naturally."

"The fees, Dr. Oldacre, would amount to about sixty pounds."

"I am afraid that my duties call me elsewhere, Mr. Montgomery."

"One moment, sir! I had hoped, sir, that perhaps, if I signed a paper promising you interest upon your money, you would advance this sum to me. I will pay you back, sir, I really will. Or, if you like, I will work it off after I am qualified."

The doctor's lips had thinned into a narrow line. His eyes were raised again, and sparkled indignantly.

"Your request is unreasonable, Mr. Montgomery. I am surprised that you should have made it. Consider, sir, how many thousands of medical students there are in this country. No doubt there are many of them who have a difficulty in finding their fees. Am I to provide for them all? Or why should I make an exception in your favour? I am grieved and disappointed, Mr. Montgomery, that you should have put me into the painful position of having to refuse you." He turned upon his heel, and walked with offended dignity out of the surgery.

The student smiled bitterly, and turned to his work of making up the morning prescriptions. It was poor and unworthy work—work which any weakling might have done as well, and this was a man of exceptional nerve and sinew. But, such as it was, it brought him his board and £1 a week, enough to help him during the summer months and let him save a few pounds towards his winter keep. But those class fees! Where were they to come from? He could not save them out of his scanty wage. Dr. Oldacre would not advance them. He saw no way of earning them. His brains were fairly good, but brains of that quality were a drug in the market. He only excelled in his strength; and where was he to find a customer for that? But the ways of Fate are strange, and his customer was at hand.

"Look y'ere!" said a voice at the door.

Montgomery looked up, for the voice was a loud and rasping one. A young man stood at the entrance—a stocky, bull-necked young miner, in tweed Sunday clothes and an aggressive necktie. He was a sinister-looking figure, with dark, insolent eyes, and the jaw and throat of a bulldog.

"Look y'ere!" said he again. "Why hast thou not sent t' medicine oop as thy master ordered?"

Montgomery had become accustomed to the brutal frankness of the Northern worker. At first it had enraged him, but after a time he had grown callous to it, and accepted it as it was meant. But this was something different. It was insolence—brutal, overbearing insolence, with physical menace behind it.

"What name?" he asked coldly.

"Barton. Happen I may give thee cause to mind that name, yoong man. Mak' oop t' wife's medicine this very moment, look ye, or it will be the worse for thee."

Montgomery smiled. A pleasant sense of relief thrilled softly through him. What blessed safety-valve was this through which his jangled nerves might find some outlet. The provocation was so gross, the insult so unprovoked, that he could have none of those qualms which take the edge off a man's mettle. He finished sealing the bottle upon which he was occupied, and he addressed it and placed it carefully in the rack.

"Look here!" said he turning round to the miner, "your medicine will be made up in its turn and sent down to you. I don't allow folk in the surgery. Wait outside in the waiting-room, if you wish to wait at all."

"Yoong man," said the miner, "thou's got to mak' t' wife's medicine here, and now, and quick, while I wait and watch thee, or else happen thou might need some medicine thysel' before all is over."

"I shouldn't advise you to fasten a quarrel upon me." Montgomery was speaking in the hard, staccato voice of a man who is holding himself in with difficulty. "You'll save trouble if you'll go quietly. If you don't you'll be hurt. Ah, you would? Take it, then!"

The blows were almost simultaneous—a savage swing which whistled past Montgomery's ear, and a straight drive which took the workman on the chin. Luck was with the assistant. That single whizzing uppercut, and the way in which it was delivered, warned him that he had a formidable man to deal with. But if he had underrated his antagonist, his antagonist had also underrated him, and had laid himself open to a fatal blow.

The miner's head had come with a crash against the corner of the surgery shelves, and he had dropped heavily onto the ground. There he lay with his bandy legs drawn up and his hands thrown abroad, the blood trickling over the surgery tiles.

"Had enough?" asked the assistant, breathing fiercely through his nose.

But no answer came. The man was insensible. And then the danger of his position came upon Montgomery, and he turned as white as his antagonist. A Sunday, the immaculate Dr. Oldacre with his pious connection, a savage brawl with a patient; he would irretrievably lose his situation if the facts came out. It was not much of a situation, but he could not get another without a reference, and Oldacre might refuse him one. Without money for his classes, and without a situation—what was to become of him? It was absolute ruin.

But perhaps he could escape exposure after all. He seized his insensible adversary, dragged him out into the centre of the room, loosened his collar, and squeezed the surgery sponge over his face. He sat up at last with a gasp and a scowl.

"Domn thee, thou's spoilt my necktie," said he, mopping up the water from his breast.

"I'm sorry I hit you so hard," said Montgomery apologetically.

"Thou hit me hard! I could stan' such fly-flappin' all day. 'Twas this here press that cracked my pate for me, and thou art a looky man to be able to boast as thou hast outed me. And now I'd be obliged to thee if though wilt give me t' wife's medicine."

Montgomery gladly made it up and handed it to the miner.

"You are weak still," said he. "Won't you stay awhile and rest?"

"T' wife wants her medicine," said the man, and lurched out at the door.

The assistant, looking after him, saw him rolling with an uncertain step down the street, until a friend met him, and they walked on arm-in-arm. The man seemed in his rough Northern fashion to bear no grudge, and so Montgomery's fears left him. There was no reason why the doctor should know anything about it. He wiped the blood from the floor, put the surgery in order, and went on with his interrupted task, hoping that he had come scathless out of a very dangerous business.

Yet all day he was aware of a sense of vague uneasiness, which sharpened into dismay when, late in the afternoon, he was informed that three gentlemen had called and were waiting for him in the surgery. A coroner's inquest, a descent of detectives, an invasion of angry relatives—all sorts of possibilities rose to scare him. With tense nerves and rigid face he went to meet his visitors.

They were a very singular trio. Each was known to him by sight; but what on earth the three could be doing together, and above all, what they could expect from *him,* was a most inexplicable problem.

The first was Sorley Wilson, the son of the owner of the Nonpareil Coal-pit. He was a young blood of twenty, heir to a fortune, a keen sportsman, and down for the Easter Vacation from Magdalene College. He sat now upon the edge of the surgery table, looking in thoughtful silence at Montgomery, and twisting the ends of his small, black, waxed moustache.

The second was Purvis, the publican, owner of the chief beershop, and well known as the local bookmaker. He was a coarse, clean-shaven man, whose fiery face made a singular contrast with his ivory-white bald head. He had shrewd, light-blue eyes with foxy lashes, and he also leaned forward in silence from his chair, a fat, red hand upon either knee, and stared critically at the young assistant.

So did the third visitor, Fawcett, the horsebreaker, who leaned back, his long, thin legs, with their box-cloth riding-gaiters, thrust out in front of him, tapping his protruding teeth with his riding-whip, with anxious thought in every line of his rugged, bony face. Publican, exquisite, and horsebreaker were all three equally silent, equally earnest, and equally critical. Montgomery, seated in the midst of them, looked from one to the other.

"Well, gentlemen?" he observed, but no answer came.

The position was embarrassing.

"No," said the horsebreaker, at last. "No. It's off. It's nowt."

"Stand oop, lad; let's see thee standin'." It was the publican who spoke.

Montgomery obeyed. He would learn all about it, no doubt, if he were patient. He stood up and turned slowly round, as if in front of his tailor.

"It's off! It's off!" cried the horsebreaker. "Why, mon, the Master would break him over his knee."

"Oh, that behanged for a yarn!" said the young Cantab. "You can drop out if you like, Fawcett, but I'll see this thing through, if I have to do it alone. I don't hedge a penny. I like the cut of him a great deal better than I liked Ted Barton."

"Look at Barton's shoulders, Mr. Wilson."

"Lumpiness isn't always strength. Give me nerve and fire and breed. That's what wins."

"Ay, sir, you have it theer—you have it theer!" said the fat, red-faced publican, in a thick, suety voice. "It's the same wi' poops. Get 'em clean-bred an' fine, and they'll yark the thick 'uns—yark 'em out o' their skins."

"He's ten good pund on the light side," growled the horsebreaker.

"He's a welter weight, anyhow."

"A hundred and thirty."

"A hundred and fifty, if he's an ounce."

"Well, the master doesn't scale much more than that."

"A hundred and seventy-five."

"That was when he was hog-fat and living high. Work the grease out of him, and I lay there's no great difference between them. Have you been weighed lately, Mr. Montgomery?"

It was the first direct question which had been asked him. He had stood in the midst of them, like a horse at a fair, and he was just beginning to wonder whether he was more angry or amused.

"I am just eleven stone," said he.

"I said that he was a welter weight."

"But suppose you was trained?" said the publican. "Wot then?"

"I am always in training."

"In a manner of speakin', no doubt, he *is* always in trainin'," remarked the horsebreaker. "But trainin' for everyday work ain't the same as trainin' with a trainer; and I dare bet, with all respec' to your opinion, Mr. Wilson, that there's half a stone of tallow on him at this minute."

The young Cantab put his fingers on the assistant's upper arm. Then with his other hand on his wrist he bent the forearm sharply, and felt the biceps, as round and hard as a cricket-ball, spring up under his fingers.

"Feel that!" said he.

The publican and horsebreaker felt it with an air of reverence.

"Good lad! He'll do yet!" cried Purvis.

"Gentlemen," said Montgomery, "I think that you will acknowledge that I have been very patient with you. I have listened to all that you have to say about my personal appearance, and now I must really beg that you will have the goodness to tell me what is the matter."

They all sat down in their serious, business-like way.

"That's easy done, Mr. Montgomery," said the fat-voiced publican. "But before sayin' anything, we had to wait and see whether, in a way of speakin', there was any need for us to say anything at all. Mr. Wilson thinks there is. Mr. Fawcett, who has the same right to his opinion, bein' also a backer and one o' the committee, thinks the other way."

"I thought him too light built, and I think so now," said the horse-breaker, still tapping his prominent teeth with the metal head of his riding-whip. "But happen he may pull through; and he's a fine-made, buirdly young chap, so if you mean to back him, Mr. Wilson—"

"Which I do."

"And you, Purvis?"

"I ain't one to go back, Fawcett."

"Well, I'll stan' to my share of the purse."

"And well I knew you would," said Purvis, "for it would be somethin' new to find Isaac Fawcett as a spoil-sport. Well, then, we make up the hundred for the stake among us, and the fight stands—always supposin' the young man is willin'."

"Excuse all this rot, Mr. Montgomery," said the University man, in a genial voice. "We've begun at the wrong end, I know, but we'll soon straighten it out, and I hope that you will see your way to falling in with our views. In the first place, you remember the man whom you knocked out this morning? He is Barton—the famous Ted Barton."

"I'm sure, sir, you may well be proud to have outed him in one round," said the publican. "Why, it took Morris, the ten-stone-six champion, a deal more trouble than that before he put Barton to sleep. You've done a fine performance, sir, and happen you'll do a finer, if you give yourself the chance."

"I never heard of Ted Barton, beyond seeing the name on a medicine label," said the assistant.

"Well, you may take it from me that he's a slaughterer," said the horsebreaker. "You've taught him a lesson that he needed, for it was always a word and a blow with him, and the word alone was worth five shillin' in a public court. He won't be so ready now to shake his nief in the face of everyone he meets. However, that's neither here nor there."

Montgomery looked at them in bewilderment.

"For goodness sake, gentlemen, tell me what it is you want me to do!" he cried.

"We want you to fight Silas Craggs, better known as the Master of Croxley."

"But why?"

"Because Ted Barton was to have fought him next Saturday. He was the champion of the Wilson coal-pits, and the other was the Master of the iron-folk down at the Croxley smelters. We'd matched our man for a purse of a hundred against the Master. But you've queered our man, and he can't face such a battle with a two-inch cut at the back of his head. There's only one thing to be done, sir, and that is for you to take his place. If you can lick Ted Barton you may lick the Master of Croxley; but if you don't we're done, for there's no one else who is in the same street with him in this district. It's twenty rounds, two-ounce gloves, Queensberry rules, and a decision on points if you fight to the finish."

For a moment the absurdity of the thing drove every other thought out of Montgomery's head. But then there came a sudden revulsion. A hundred pounds!—all he wanted to complete his education was lying there ready to his hand, if only that hand were strong enough to pick it up. He had thought bitterly that morning that there was no market for his strength, but here was one where his muscle might earn more in an hour than his brains in a year. But a chill of doubt came over him.

"How can I fight for the coal-pits?" said he. "I am not connected with them"

"Eh, lad, but thou art!" cried old Purvis. "We've got it down in writin', and it's clear enough. 'Any one connected with the coalpits.' Doctor Oldacre is the coal-pit club doctor; thou art his assistant. What more can they want?"

"Yes, that's right enough," said the Cantab. "It would be a very sporting thing of you, Mr. Montgomery, if you would come to our help when we are in such a hole. Of course, you might not like to take the hundred pounds; but I have no doubt that, in the case of your winning, we could arrange that it should take the form of a watch or piece of plate, or any other shape which might suggest itself to you. You see, you are responsible for our having lost our champion, so we really feel that we have a claim upon you."

"Give me a moment, gentlemen. It is very unexpected. I am afraid the doctor would never consent to my going—in fact, I am sure that he would not."

"But he need never know—not before the fight, at any rate. We are not bound to give the name of our man. So long as he is within the weight limits on the day of the fight, that is all that concerns any one."

The adventure and the profit would either of them have attracted Montgomery. The two combined were irresistible.

"Gentlemen," said he, "I'll do it!"

The three sprang from their seats. The publican had seized his right hand, the horsedealer his left, and the Cantab slapped him on the back.

"Good lad! good lad!" croaked the publican. "Eh, mon, but if thou yark him, thou'll rise in one day from being just a common doctor to the best-known mon 'twixt here and Bradford. Thou art a witherin' tyke, thou art, and no mistake; and if thou beat the Master of Croxley, thou'll find all the beer thou want for the rest of thy life waiting for three at the Four Sacks."

"It is the most sporting thing I ever heard of in my life," said young Wilson. "By George, sir, if you pull it off, you've got the constituency in your pocket, if you care to stand. You know the outhouse in my garden?"

"Next the road?"

"Exactly. I turned it into a gymnasium for Ted Barton. You'll find all you want there: clubs, punching ball, bars, dumb-bells, everything. Then you'll want a sparring partner. Ogilvy has been acting for Barton, but we don't think that he is class enough. Barton bears you no grudge. He's a good-hearted fellow, though cross-grained with strangers. He looked upon you as a stranger this morning, but he says he knows you now. He is quite ready to spar with you for practice, and he will come at any hour you will name."

"Thank you; I will let you know the hour," said Montgomery; and so the committee departed jubilant upon their way.

The medical assistant sat for a little time in the surgery turning it over in his mind. He had been trained originally at the University by the man who had been middle-weight champion in his day. It was true that his teacher was long past his prime, slow upon his feet and stiff in his joints, but even so he was still a tough antagonist; but Montgomery had found at last that he could more than hold his own with him. He had won the University medal, and his teacher, who had trained so many students, was emphatic in his opinion that he had never had one who was in the same class with him. He had been ex-horted to go in for the Amateur Championships, but he had no particular am-bition in that direction. Once he had put on the gloves with Hammer Tunstall in a booth at a fair, and had fought three rattling rounds, in which he had the worst of it, but had made the prize-fighter stretch himself to the uttermost. There was his whole record, and was it enough to encourage him to stand up to the Master of Croxley? He had never heard of the Master before, but then he had lost touch of the ring during the last few years of hard work. After all, what did it matter? If he won, there was the money, which meant so much to him. If he lost, it would only mean a thrashing. He could take punishment without flinching, of that he was certain. If there were only one chance in a hundred of pulling it off, then it was worth his while to attempt it.

Dr. Oldacre, new come from church, with an ostentatious Prayer-book in his kid-gloved hand, broke in upon his meditation.

"You don't go to service, I observe, Mr. Montgomery," said he, coldly.

"No sir; I have had some business to detain me."

"It is very near to my heart that my household should set a good example. There are so few educated people in this district that a great respon-sibility devolves upon us. If we do not live up to the highest, how can we ex-pect these poor workers to do so? It is a dreadful thing to reflect that the parish takes a great deal more interest in an approaching glove-fight than in their religious duties."

"A glove-fight, sir?" said Montgomery, guiltily.

"I believe that to be the correct term. One of my patients tells me that it is the talk of the district. A local ruffian, a patient of ours, by the way, is matched against a pugilist over at Croxley. I cannot understand why the law does not step in and stop so degrading an exhibition. It is really a prize-fight."

"A glove fight, you said."

"I am informed that a two-ounce glove is an evasion by which they dodge the law, and make it difficult for the police to interfere. They contend for a sum of money. It seems dreadful and almost incredible—does it not?—to think that such scenes can be enacted within a few miles of our peaceful home. But you will realize, Mr. Montgomery, that while there are such influences for us to counteract, it is very necessary that we should live up to our highest."

The doctor's sermon would have had more effect if the assistant had not once or twice had occasion to test his highest and come upon it at unexpectedly humble elevations. It is always so particularly easy to "compound for sins we're most inclined to by damning those we have no mind to." In any case, Montgomery felt that of all the men concerned in such a fight—promoters, backers, spectators—it is the actual fighter who holds the strongest and most honourable position. His conscience gave him no concern upon the subject. Endurance and courage are virtues, not vices, and brutality is, at last, better than effeminacy.

There was a little tobacco-shop at the corner of the street, where Montgomery got his birds-eye and also his local information, for the shopman was a garrulous soul, who knew everything about the affairs of the district. The assistant strolled down there after tea and asked, in a casual way, whether the tobacconist had ever heard of the Master of Croxley.

"Heard of him! Heard of him!" the little man could hardly articulate in his astonishment. "Why, sir, he's the first mon o' the district, an' his name's as well known in the West Riding as the winner o' t' Derby. But Lor', sir"— here he stopped and rummaged among a heap of papers. "They are makin' a fuss about him on account o' his fight wi' Ted Barton, and so the *Croxley Herald* has his life an' record, an' here it is, an' thou canst read it for thysel'."

The sheet of the paper which he held up was a lake of print around an islet of illustration. The latter was a coarse wood-cut of a pugilist's head and neck set in a cross-barred jersey. It was a sinister but powerful face, the face of a debauched hero, clean-shaven, strongly eyebrowed, keen-eyed, with a huge aggressive jaw and an animal dewlap beneath it. The long, obstinate cheeks ran flush up to the narrow, sinister eyes. The mighty neck came down square from the ear and curved outwards into shoulders, which had lost nothing at the hands of the local artist. Above was written "Silas Craggs," and beneath, "The Master of Croxley."

"Thou'll find all about him there, sir," said the tobacconist. "He's a witherin' tyke, he is, and we're proud to have him in the county. If he hadn't broke his leg he'd have been champion of England."

"Broke his leg, has he?"

"Yes, and it set badly. They ca' him owd K behind his bock, for thot is how his two legs look. But his arms—well, if they was both stropped to a bench, as the sayin' is, I wonder where the champion of England would be then."

"I'll take this with me," said Montgomery; and putting the paper into his pocket he returned home.

It was not a cheering record which he read there. The whole history of the Croxley Master was given in full, his many victories, his few defeats.

"Born in 1857," said the provincial biographer, "Silas Craggs, better known in sporting circles as The Master of Croxley, is now in his fortieth year."

"Hang it, I'm only twenty-three," said Montgomery to himself, and read on more cheerfully.

"Having in his youth shown a surprising aptitude for the game, he fought his way up among his comrades, until he became the recognized champion of the district and won the proud title which he still holds. Ambitious of a more than local fame, he secured a patron, and fought his first fight against Jack Barton, of Birmingham, in May, 1880, at the old Loiterers' Club. Craggs, who fought at ten-stone-two at the time, had the better of fifteen rattling rounds, and gained an award on points against the Midlander. Having disposed of James Dunn, of Rotherhithe, Cameron, of Glasgow, and a youth named Fernie, he was thought so highly of by the fancy that he was matched against Ernest Willox, at that time middle-weight champion of the North of England, and defeated him in a hard-fought battle, knocking him out in the tenth round after a punishing contest. At this period it looked as if the very highest honours of the ring were within the reach of the young Yorkshireman, but he was laid upon the shelf by a most unfortunate accident. The kick of a horse broke his thigh, and for a year he was compelled to rest himself. When he returned to his work the fracture had set badly, and his activity was much impaired. It was owing to this that he was defeated in seven rounds by Willox, the man whom he had previously beaten, and afterwards by James Shaw, of London, though the latter acknowledged that he had found the toughest customer of his career. Undismayed by his reverses, the Master adapted the style of his fighting to his physical disabilities and resumed his career of victory—defeating Norton (the black), Bobby Wilson, and Levy Cohen, the latter a heavy-weight. Conceding two stone, he fought a draw with the famous Billy McQuire, and afterwards, for a purse of fifty pounds, he defeated Sam Hare at the Pelican Club, London. In 1891 a decision was given against him upon a foul when fighting a winning fight against Jim Taylor, the Australian middle-weight, and so mortified was he by the decision, that he withdrew from the ring. Since then he has hardly fought at all save to accommodate any local aspirant who may wish to learn the difference between a bar-room scramble and a scientific contest. The latest of these ambitious souls comes from the Wilson coal-pits, which have undertaken to put up a stake of £100 and back their local champion. There are various rumours afloat as to who their representative is to be, the name of Ted Barton being freely mentioned; but the betting, which is seven to one on the Master against any untried man, is a fair reflection of the feeling of the community."

Montgomery read it over twice, and it left him with a very serious face. No light matter this which he had undertaken; no battle with a rough-and-tumble fighter who presumed upon a local reputation. This man's record showed that he was first-class—or nearly so. There were a few points in his favour, and he must make the most of them. There was age—twenty-three against forty. There was an old ring proverb that "Youth will be served," but the annals of the ring offer a great number of exceptions. A hard veteran, full of cool valour and ring-craft, could give ten or fifteen years and a beating to most striplings. He could not rely too much upon his advantage in age. But then there was the lameness; that must surely count for a great deal. And, lastly, there was the chance that the Master might underrate his opponent, that he might be remiss in his training, and refuse to abandon his usual way of life, if he thought that he had an easy task before him. In a man of his age and habits this seemed very possible. Montgomery prayed that it might be so. Meanwhile, if his opponent were the best man who ever jumped the ropes into a ring, his own duty was clear. He must prepare himself carefully, throw away no chance, and do the very best that he could. But he knew enough to appreciate the difference which exists in boxing, as in every sport, between the amateur and the professional. The coolness, the power of hitting, above all the capability of taking punishment, count for so much. Those specially developed, gutta-percha-like abdominal muscles of the hardened pugilist will take without flinching a blow which would leave another man writhing on the ground. Such things are not to be acquired in a week, but all that could be done in a week should be done.

The medical assistant had a good basis to start from. He was 5 feet 11 inches—tall enough for anything on two legs, as the old ring men used to say—lithe and spare, with the activity of a panther, and a strength which had hardly yet ever found its limitations. His muscular development was finely hard, but his power came rather from that higher nerve-energy which counts for nothing upon a measuring tape. He had the well-curved nose and the widely-opened eye which never yet were seen upon the face of a craven, and behind everything he had the driving force, which came from the knowledge that his whole career was at stake upon the contest. The three backers rubbed their hands when they saw him at work punching the ball in the gymnasium next morning; and Fawcett, the horsebreaker, who had written to Leeds to hedge his bets, sent a wire to cancel the letter, and to lay another fifty at the market price of seven to one.

Montgomery's chief difficulty was to find time for his training without any interference from the doctor. His work took him a large part of the day, but as the visiting was done on foot, and considerable distances had to be traversed, it was a training in itself. For the rest, he punched the swinging ball and worked with the dumb-bells for an hour every morning and evening, and boxed twice a day with Ted Barton in the gymnasium, gaining as much profit as could be got from a rushing, two-handed slogger. Barton was full of admiration for his cleverness and quickness, but doubtful about his strength. Hard hitting was the feature of his own style, and he exacted it from others.

"Lord, sir, that's a turble poor poonch for an eleven-stone man!" he would cry. "Thou wilt have to hit harder than that afore t' Master will know that thou art theer. Ah, thot's better, mon, thot's fine!" he would add, as his opponent lifted him across the room on the end of a right counter. "Thot's how I likes to feel 'em. Happen thou'lt pull through yet." He chuckled with joy when Montgomery knocked him into a corner. "Eh, mon, thou art comin' along grand. Thou hast fair yarked me off my legs. Do it again, lad, do it again!"

The only part of Montgomery's training which came within the doctor's observation was his diet, and that puzzled him considerably.

"You will excuse my remarking, Mr. Montgomery, that you are becoming rather particular in your tastes. Such fads are not to be encouraged in one's youth. Why do you eat toast with every meal?"

"I find that it suits me better than bread, sir."

"It entails unnecessary work upon the cook. I observe, also, that you have turned against potatoes."

"Yes, sir; I think that I am better without them."

"And you no longer drink your beer?"

"No, sir."

"These causeless whims and fancies are very much to be deprecated, Mr. Montgomery. Consider how many there are to whom these very potatoes and this very beer would be most acceptable."

"No doubt, sir. But at present I prefer to do without them."

They were sitting alone at lunch, and the assistant thought it would be a good opportunity of asking leave for the day of the fight.

"I should be glad if you could let me have leave for Saturday, Doctor Oldacre."

"It is very inconvenient upon so busy a day."

"I should do a double day's work on Friday so as to leave everything in order. I should hope to be back in the evening."

"I am afraid I cannot spare you, Mr. Montgomery."

This was a facer. If he could not get leave he would go without it.

"You will remember, Doctor Oldacre, that when I came to you it was understood that I should have a clear day every month. I have never claimed one. But now there are reasons why I wish to have a holiday upon Saturday."

Doctor Oldacre gave in with a very bad grace.

"Of course, if you insist upon your formal rights, there is no more to be said, Mr. Montgomery, though I feel that it shows a certain indifference to my comfort and the welfare of the practice. Do you still insist?"

"Yes, sir."

"Very good. Have your way."

The doctor was boiling over with anger, but Montgomery was a valuable assistant—steady, capable, and hard-working—and he could not afford to lose him. Even if he had been prompted to advance those class fees, for which his assistant had appealed, it would have been against his interests to do so, for he did not wish him to qualify, and he desired him to remain in his subordinate position, in which he worked so hard for so small a wage. There was something in the cool insistence of the young man, a quiet resolution in his voice as he claimed his Saturday, which aroused his curiosity.

"I have no desire to interfere unduly with your affairs, Mr. Montgomery, but were you thinking of having a day in Leeds upon Saturday?"

"No, sir."

"In the country?"

"Yes, sir."

"You are very wise. You will find a quiet day among the wild flowers a very valuable restorative. Had you thought of any particular direction?"

"I am going over Croxley way."

"Well, there is no prettier country when once you are past the ironworks. What could be more delightful than to lie upon the Fells, basking in the sunshine, with perhaps some instructive and elevating book as your companion? I should recommend a visit to the ruins of St. Bridget's Church, a very interesting relic of the early Norman era. By the way, there is one objection which I see to your going to Croxley on Saturday. It is upon that date, as I am informed, that that ruffianly glove-fight takes place. You may find yourself molested by the blackguards whom it will attract."

"I will take my chance of that, sir," said the assistant.

On the Friday night, which was the last before the fight, Montgomery's three backers assembled in the gymnasium and inspected their man as he went through some light exercise to keep his muscles supple. He was certainly in splendid condition, his skin shining with health, and his eyes with energy and confidence. The three walked round him and exulted.

"He's simply ripping!" said the undergraduate. "By gad, you've come out of it splendidly. You're hard as a pebble, and fit to fight for your life."

"Happen he's a trifle on the fine side," said the publican. "Runs a bit light at the loins, to my way of thinkin'."

"What weight to-day?"

"Ten stone eleven," the assistant answered.

"That's only three pund off in a week's trainin'," said the horse-breaker. "He said right when he said that he was in condition. Well, it's fine stuff all there is of it, but I'm none so sure as there is enough." He kept poking his finger into Montgomery, as if he were one of his horses. "I hear that the Master will scale a hundred and sixty odd at the ring-side."

"But there's some of that which he'd like well to pull off and leave behind wi' his shirt," said Purvis. "I hear they've had a rare job to get him to drop his beer, and if it had not been for that great red-headed wench of his they'd never ha' done it. She fair scratted the face off a potman that had brought him a gallon from t' Chequers. They say the hussy is his sparrin' partner, as well as his sweetheart, and that his poor wife is just breakin' her heart over it. Hullo, young 'un, what do you want?"

The door of the gymnasium had opened, and a lad about sixteen, grimy and black with soot and iron, stepped into the yellow glare of the oil-lamp. Ted Barton seized him by the collar.

"See here, thou yoong whelp, this is private, and we want noan o' thy spyin'!"

"But I maun speak to Mr. Wilson."

The young Cantab stepped forward.

"Well, my lad, what is it?"

"It's aboot t' fight, Mr. Wilson, sir. I wanted to tell your mon somethin' aboot t' Maister."

"We've no time to listen to gossip, my boy. We know all about the Master."

"But thou doant, sir. Nobody knows but me and mother, and we thought as we'd like thy mon to know, sir, for we want him to fair bray him."

"Oh, you want the Master fair brayed, do you? So do we. Well, what have you to say?"

"Is this your mon, sir?"

"Well, suppose it is?"

"Then it's him I want to tell aboot it. T' Maister is blind o' the left eye."

"Nonsense!"

"It's true, sir. Not stone blind, but rarely fogged. He keeps it secret, but mother knows, and so do I. If thou slip him on the left side he can't cop thee. Thou'll find it right as I tell thee. And mark him when he sinks his right. 'Tis his best blow, his right upper-cut. T' Maister's finisher, they ca' it at t' works. It's a turble blow, when it do come home."

"Thank you, my boy. This is information worth having about his sight," said Wilson. "How came you to know so much? Who are you?"

"I'm his son, sir."

Wilson whistled.

"And who sent you to us?"

"My mother. I maun get back to her again."

"Take this half-crown."

"No, sir, I don't seek money in coming' here. I do it—"

"For love?" suggested the publican.

"For hate!" said the boy, and darted off into the darkness.

"Seems to me t' red-headed wench may do him more harm than good, after all," remarked the publican. "And now, Mr. Montgomery, sir, you've done enough for this evenin', an' a nine hours' sleep is the best trainin' before a battle. Happen this time to-morrow night you'll be safe back again with your £100 in your pocket."

II

Work was struck at one o'clock at the coal-pits and the iron-works, and the fight was arranged for three. From the Croxley Furnaces, from Wilson's Coal-pits, from the Heartease Mine, from the Dodd Mills, from the Leverworth Smelters the workmen came trooping, each with his fox-terrier or his lurcher at his heels. Warped with labour and twisted by toil, bent double by week-long work in the cramped coal galleries, or half-blinded with years spent in front of white-hot fluid metal, these men still gilded their harsh and hopeless lives by their devotion to sport. It was their one relief, the only thing which could distract their mind from sordid surroundings, and give them an interest beyond the blackened circle which inclosed them. Literature, art, science, all these things were beyond the horizon; but the race, the football match, the cricket, the fight, these were things which they could understand, which they could speculate upon in advance and comment upon afterwards. Sometimes brutal, sometimes grotesque, the love of sport is still one of the great agencies which make for the happiness of our people. It lies very deeply in the springs of our nature, and when it has been educated out, a higher, more refined nature may be left, but it will not be of that robust British type which has left its mark so deeply on the world. Every one one of these ruddled workers, slouching with his dog at his heels to see something of the fight, was a true unit of his race.

It was a squally May day, with bright sunbursts and driving showers. Montgomery worked all morning in the surgery getting his medicine made up.

"The weather seems so very unsettled, Mr. Montgomery," remarked the doctor, "that I am inclined to think that you had better postpone your little country excursion until a later date."

"I am afraid that I must go to-day, sir."

"I have just had an intimation that Mrs. Potter, at the other side of Angleton, wishes to see me. It is probably that I shall be there all day. It will be extremely inconvenient to leave the house empty so long."

"I am very sorry, sir, but I must go," said the assistant, doggedly.

The doctor saw that it would be useless to argue, and departed in the worst of bad tempers upon his mission. Montgomery felt easier now that he was gone. He went up to his room, and packed his running-shoes, his fighting-drawers, and his cricket-sash into a handbag. When he came down Mr. Wilson was waiting for him in the surgery.

"I hear the doctor has gone."

"Yes; he is likely to be away all day."

"I don't see that it matters much. It's bound to come to his ears by tonight."

"Yes; it's serious with me, Mr. Wilson. If I win, it's all right. I don't mind telling you that the hundred pounds will make all the difference to me. But if I lose, I shall lose my situation, for, as you say, I can't keep it secret."

"Never mind. We'll see you through among us. I only wonder the doctor has not heard, for it's all over the country that you are to fight the Croxley Champion. We've had Armitage up about it already. He's the Master's backer, you know. He wasn't sure that you were eligible. The Master said he wanted you whether you were eligible or not. Armitage has money on, and would have made trouble if he could. But I showed him that you came within the conditions of the challenge, and he agreed that it was all right. They think they have a soft thing on."

"Well, I can only do my best," said Montgomery.

They lunched together; a silent and rather nervous repast, for Montgomery's mind was full of what was before him, and Wilson had himself more money at stake than he cared to lose.

Wilson's carriage and pair were at the door, the horses with blue-and-white rosettes at their ears, which were the colours of the Wilson Coal-pits, well known on many a football field. At the avenue gate a crowd of some hundred pitmen and their wives gave a cheer as the carriage passed. To the assistant it all seemed dream-like and extraordinary—the strangest experience of his life, but with a thrill of human action and interest in it which made it passionately absorbing. He lay back in the open carriage and saw the fluttering handkerchiefs from the doors and windows of the miners' cottages. Wilson had pinned a blue-and-white rosette upon his coat, and every one knew him as their champion. "Good luck, sir! good luck to thee!" they shouted from the roadside. He felt that it was like some unromantic knight riding down to sordid lists, but there was something of chivalry in it all the same. He fought for others as well as for himself. He might fail from want of skill or strength, but deep in his sombre soul he vowed that it should never be for want of heart.

Mr. Fawcett was just mounting into his high-wheeled, spidery dogcart, with his little bit of blood between the shafts. He waved his whip and fell in behind the carriage. They overtook Purvis, the tomato-faced publican, upon the road, with his wife in her Sunday bonnet. They also dropped into the procession, and then, as they traversed the seven miles of the high-road to Croxley, their two-horsed, rosetted carriage became gradually the nucleus of a comet with a loosely radiating tail. From every side-road came the miners' carts, the humble, ramshackle traps, black and bulging, with their loads of noisy, foul-tongued, open-hearted partisans. They trailed for a long quarter of a mile behind them—cracking, whipping, shouting, galloping, swearing. Horsemen and runners were mixed with the vehicles. And then suddenly a squad of the Sheffield Yeomanry, who were having their annual training in those parts, clattered and jingled out of a field, and rode as an escort to the carriage. Through the dust-clouds round him Montgomery saw the gleaming brass helmets, the bright coats, and the tossing heads of the chargers, the delighted brown faces of the troopers. It was more dream-like than ever.

And then, as they approached the monstrous, uncouth line of bottle-shaped buildings which marked the smelting-works of Croxley, their long, writhing snake of dust was headed off by another but longer one which wound across their path. The main-road onto which their own opened was filled by the rushing current of traps. The Wilson contingent halted until the others should get past. The ironmen cheered and groaned, according to their humour, as they whirled past their antagonist. Rough chaff flew back and forwards like iron nuts and splinters of coal. "Brought him up, then!" "Got t' hearse for to fetch him back?" "Where's t' owd K-legs?" "Mon, mon, have thy photograph took—'twill mind thee of what thou used to look!" "He fight?—he's now't but a half-baked doctor!" "Happen he'll doctor thy Croxley Champion afore he's through wi't."

So they flashed at each other as the one side waited and the other passed. Then there came a rolling murmur swelling into a shout, and a great break with four horses came clattering along, all streaming with salmon-pink ribbons. The driver wore a white hat with pink rosette, and beside him, on the high seat, were a man and a woman—she with her arm round his waist. Montgomery had one glimpse of them as they flashed past: he with a furry cap drawn low over his brown, a great frieze coat, and a pink comforter round his throat; she brazen, red-headed, bright-coloured, laughing excitedly. The Master, for it was he, turned as he passed, gazed hard at Montgomery, and gave him a menacing, gap-toothed grin. It was a hard, wicked face, blue-jowled and craggy, with long, obstinate cheeks and inexorable eyes. The break behind was full of patrons of the sport—flushed iron-foreman, heads of departments, managers. One was drinking from a metal flask, and raised it to Montgomery as he passed; and then the crowd thinned, and the Wilson *cortège* with their dragoons swept in at the rear of the others.

The road led away from Croxley, between curving green hills, gashed and polluted by the searchers for coal and iron. The whole country had been gutted, and vast piles of refuse and mountains of slag suggested the mighty chambers which the labor of man had burrowed beneath. On the left the road curved up to where a huge building, roofless, and dismantled, stood crumbling and forlorn, with the light shining through the windowless squares.

"That's the old Arrowsmith's factory. That's where the fight is to be," said Wilson. "How are you feeling now?"

"Thank you. I was never better in my life," Montgomery answered.

"By Gad, I like your nerve!" said Wilson, who was himself flushed and uneasy. "You'll give us a fight for our money, come what may. That place on the right is the office, and that has been set aside as the dressing and weighing-room."

The carriage drove up to it amidst the shouts of the folk upon the hill-side. Lines of empty carriages and traps curved down upon the winding road, and a black crowd surged round the door of the ruined factory. The seats, as a huge placard announced, were five shillings, three shillings, and a shilling, with half-price for dogs. The takings, deducting expenses, were to go to the winner, and it was already evident that a larger stake than a hundred pounds was in question. A babel of voices rose from the door. The workers wished to bring their dogs in free. The men scuffled. The dogs barked. The crowd was a whirling, eddying pool surging with a roar up to the narrow cleft which was its only outlet.

The break, with is salmon-coloured streamers and four reeking horses, stood empty before the door of the office; Wilson, Purvis, Fawcett, and Montgomery passed in.

There was a large, bare room inside with square, clean patches upon the grimy walls, where pictures and almanacs had once hung. Worn linoleum covered the floor, but there was no furniture save some benches and a deal table with a ewer and a basin upon it. Two of the corners were curtained off. In the middle of the room was a weighing-chair. A hugely fat man, with a salmon tie and a blue waistcoat with bird's-eye spots, came bustling up to them. It was Armitage, the butcher and grazier, well known for miles around as a warm man, and the most liberal patron of sport in the Riding.

"Well, well," he grunted, in a thick, fussy, wheezy voice, "you have come, then. Got your man? Got your man?"

"Here he is, fit and well. Mr. Montgomery, let me present you to Mr. Armitage."

"Glad to meet you, sir. Happy to make your acquaintance. I make bold to say, sir, that we of Croxley admire your courage, Mr. Montgomery, and that our only hope is a fair fight and no favour and the best man win. That's our sentiment at Croxley."

"And it is my sentiment also," said the assistant.

"Well, you can't say fairer than that, Mr. Montgomery. You've taken a large contrac' in hand, but a large contrac' may be carried through, sir, as any one that knows my dealings could testify. The Master is ready to weigh in!"

"So am I."

"You must weigh in the buff."

Montgomery looked askance at the tall, red-headed woman who was standing gazing out of the window.

"That's all right," said Wilson. "Get behind the curtain and put on your fighting-kit."

He did so, and came out the picture of an athlete, in white, loose drawers, canvas shoes, and the sash of a well-known cricket club round his waist. He was trained to a hair, his skin gleaming like silk, and every muscle rippling down his broad shoulders and along his beautiful arms as he moved them. They bunched into ivory knobs, or slid into long, sinuous curves, as he raised or lowered his hands.

"What thinkest thou o' that?" asked Ted Barton, his second, of the woman in the window.

She glanced contemptuously at the young athlete.

"It's but a poor kindness thou dost him to put a thread-paper yoong gentleman like yon against a mon as is a mon. Why, my Jock would throttle him wi' one hond lashed behind him."

"Happen he may—happen not," said Barton. "I have but twa pund in the world, but it's on him, every penny, and no hedgin'. But here's t' Maister, and rarely fine he do look."

The prize-fighter had come out from his curtain, a squat, formidable figure, monstrous in chest and arms, limping slightly on his distorted leg. His skin had none of the freshness and clearness of Montgomery's, but was dusky and mottled, with one huge mole amid the mat of tangled black hair which thatched his mighty breast. His weight bore no relation to his strength, for those huge shoulders and great arms, with brown, sledge-hammer fists, would have fitted the heaviest man that ever threw his cap into a ring. But his loins and legs were slight in proportion. Montgomery, on the other hand, was as symmetrical as a Greek statue. It would be an encounter between a man who was specially fitted for one sport, and one who was equally capable of any. The two looked curiously at each other: a bulldog, and a high-bred, clean-limbed terrier, each full of spirit.

"How do you do?"

"How do?" The Master grinned again, and his three jagged front teeth gleamed for an instant. The rest had been beaten out of him in twenty years of battle. He spat upon the floor. "We have a rare fine day for't."

"Capital," said Montgomery.

"That's the good feelin' I like," wheezed the fat butcher. "Good lads, both of them!—prime lads!—hard meat an' good bone. There's no ill-feelin'."

"If he downs me, Gawd bless him!" said the Master.

"An' if we down him, Gawd help him!" interrupted the woman.

"Haud thy tongue, wench!" said the Master, impatiently. "Who art thou to put in thy word? Happen I might draw my hand across thy face."

The woman did not take the threat amiss.

"Wilt have enough for thy hand to do, Jock," said she. "Get quit o' this gradely man afore thou turn on me."

The lovers' quarrel was interrupted by the entrance of a new comer, a gentleman with a fur-collared overcoat and a very shiny top-hat—a top-hat of a degree of glossiness which is seldom seen five miles from Hyde Park. This hat he wore at the extreme back of his head, so that the lower surface of the brim made a kind of frame for his high, bald forehead, his keen eyes, his rugged and yet kindly face. He bustled in with the quiet air of possession with which the ringmaster enters the circus.

"It's Mr. Stapleton, the referee from London," said Wilson.

"How do you do, Mr. Stapleton? I was introduced to you at the big fight at the Corinthian Club, in Piccadilly."

"Ah, I dare say," said the other, shaking hands. "Fact is, I'm introduced to so many that I can't undertake to carry their names. Wilson, is it? Well, Mr. Wilson, glad to see you. Couldn't get a fly at the station, and that's why I'm late."

"I'm sure, sir," said Armitage, "we should be proud that any one so well known in the boxing world should come down to our little exhibition."

"Not at all. Not at all. Anything in the interests of boxin'. All ready? Men weighed?"

"Weighing now, sir."

"Ah, just as well I should see it done. Seen you before, Craggs. Saw you fight your second battle against Willox. You had beaten him once, but he came back on you. What does the indicator say?—one hundred and sixty-three pounds—two off for the kit—one hundred and sixty-one. Now, my lad, you jump. My goodness, what colours are you wearing?"

"The Anonymi Cricket Club."

"What right have you to wear them? I belong to the club myself."

"So do I."

"You an amateur?"

"Yes, sir."

"And you are fighting for a money prize?"

"Yes."

"I suppose you know what you are doing? You realize that you're a professional pug from this onwards, and that if ever you fight again—"

"Happen you won't," said the woman, and the Master turned a terrible eye upon her.

"Well, I suppose you know your own business best. Up you jump. One hundred and fifty-one, minus two, one hundred and forty-nine—twelve pounds difference, but youth and condition on the other scale. Well, the sooner we get to work the better, for I wish to catch the seven o'clock express at Hellifield. Twenty three-minute rounds, with one-minute intervals, and Queensberry rules. Those are the conditions, are they not?"

"Yes, sir."

"Very good, then, we may go across."

The two combatants had overcoats thrown over their shoulders, and the whole party, backers, fighters, seconds, and the referee, filed out of the room. A police inspector was waiting for them in the road. He had a notebook in his hand—that terrible weapon which awes even the London cabman.

"I must take your names, gentlemen, in case it should be necessary to proceed for breach of peace."

"You don't mean to stop the fight?" cried Armitage, in a passion of indignation. "I'm Mr. Armitage, of Croxley, and this is Mr. Wilson, and we'll be responsible that all is fair and as it should be."

"I'll take the names in case it should be necessary to proceed," said the inspector, impassively.

"But you know me well."

"If you was a dook or even a judge it would be all the same," said the inspector. "It's the law, and there's an end. I'll not take upon myself to stop the fight, seeing that gloves are to be used, but I'll take the names of all concerned. Silas Craggs, Robert Montgomery, Edward Barton, James Stapleton, of London. Who seconds Silas Craggs?"

"I do," said the woman. "Yes, you can stare, but it's my job, and no one else's. Anastasia's the name—four a's."

"Craggs?"

"Johnson. Anastasia Johnson. If you jug him, you can jug me."

"Who talked of juggin', ye fool?" growled the Master. "Coom on, Mr. Armitage, for I'm fair sick o' this loiterin'."

The inspector fell in with the procession, and proceeded, as they walked up the hill, to bargain in his official capacity for a front seat, where he could safeguard the interests of the law, and in his private capacity to lay out thirty shillings at seven to one with Mr. Armitage. Through the door they passed, down a narrow lane walled with a dense bank of humanity, up a wooden ladder to a platform, over a rope which was slung waist-high from four corner stakes, and then Montgomery realized that he was in that ring in which his immediate destiny was to be worked out. On the stake at one corner there hung a blue-and-white streamer. Barton led him across, the over-coat dangling loosely from his shoulders, and he sat down on a wooden stool. Barton and another man, both wearing white sweaters, stood beside him. The so-called ring was a square, twenty feet each way. At the opposite angle was the sinister figure of the Master, with his red-headed woman and a rough-faced friend to look after him. At each corner were metal basins, pitchers of water, and sponges.

During the hubbub and uproar of the entrance Montgomery was too bewildered to take things in. But now there was a few minutes' delay, for the referee had lingered behind, and so he looked quietly about him. It was a sight to haunt him for a lifetime. Wooden seats had been built in, sloping upwards to the tops of the walls. Above, instead of a ceiling, a great flight of crows passed slowly across a square of grey cloud. Right up to the topmost benches the folk were banked—broadcloth in front, corduroys and fustian behind; faces turned everywhere upon him. The grey reek of the pipes filled the building, and the air was pungent with the acrid smell of cheap, strong tobacco. Everywhere among the human faces were to be seen the heads of the dogs. They growled and yapped from the back benches. In that dense mass of humanity one could hardly pick out individuals, but Montgomery's eyes caught the brazen gleam of the helmets held upon the knees of the ten yeoman of his escort. At the very edge of the platform sat the reporters, five of them: three locals, and two all the way from London. But where was the all-important referee? There was no sign of him, unless he were in the centre of that angry swirl of men near the door.

Mr. Stapleton had stopped to examine the gloves which were to be used, and entered the building after the combatants. He had started to come down that narrow lane with the human walls which led to the ring. But already it had gone abroad that the Wilson champion was a gentleman, and that another gentleman had been appointed as referee. A wave of suspicion passed through the Croxley folk. They would have one of their own people for a referee. They would not have a stranger. His path was stopped as he made for the ring. Excited men flung themselves in front of him; they waved their fists in his face and cursed him. A woman howled vile names in his ear. Somebody struck at him with an umbrella. "Go thou back to Lunnon. We want noan o' thee. Go thou back!" they yelled.

Stapleton, with his shiny hat cocked backwards, and his large, bulging forehead swelling from under it, looked round him from beneath his bushy brows. He was in the centre of a savage and dangerous mob. Then he drew his watch from his pocket and held it dial upwards in his palm.

"In three minutes," said he, "I will declare the fight off."

They raged round him. His cool face and that aggressive top-hat irritated them. Grimy hands were raised. But it was difficult, somehow, to strike a man who was so absolutely indifferent.

"In two minutes I declare the fight off."

They exploded into blasphemy. The breath of angry men smoked into his placid face. A gnarled, grimy fist vibrated at the end of his nose. "We tell thee we want noan o' thee. Get though back where thou com'st from"

"In one minute I declare the fight off."

Then the calm persistence of the man conquered the swaying, mutable, passionate crowd.

"Let him through, mon. Happen there'll be no fight after a'."

"Let him through."

"Bill, thou loomp, let him pass. Dost want the fight declared off?"

"Make room for the referee!—room for the Lunnon referee!"

And half pushed, half carried, he was swept up to the ring. There were two chairs by the side of it, one for him and one for the timekeeper. He sat down, his hands on his knees, his hat at a more wonderful angle than ever, impassive but solemn, with the aspect of one who appreciates his responsibilities.

Mr. Armitage, the portly butcher, made his way into the ring and held up two fat hands, sparkling with rings, as a signal for silence.

"Gentlemen!" he yelled. And then in a crescendo shriek, "Gentlemen!"

"And ladies!" cried somebody, for indeed there was a fair sprinkling of women among the crowd. "Speak up, owd man!" shouted another. "What price pork chops?" cried somebody at the back. Everybody laughed and the dogs began to bark. Armitage waved his hands amidst the uproar as if he were conducting an orchestra. At last the babel thinned into silence.

"Gentlemen," he yelled, "the match is between Silas Craggs, whom we call the Master of Croxley, and Robert Montgomery, of the Wilson Coalpits. The match was to be under eleven-eight. When they were weighed just now Craggs weighed eleven-seven, and Montgomery ten-nine. The conditions of the contest are—the best of twenty three-minute rounds with two-ounce gloves. Should the fight run to its full length it will, of course, be decided upon points. Mr. Stapleton, the well-known London referee, has kindly consented to see fair play. I wish to say that Mr. Wilson and I, the chief backers of the two men, have every confidence in Mr. Stapleton, and that we beg that you will accept his rulings without dispute."

He then turned from one combatant to the other, with a wave of his hand.

III

"Montgomery—Craggs!" said he.

A great hush fell over the huge assembly. Even the dogs stopped yapping; one might have thought that the monstrous room was empty. The two men had stood up, the small white gloves over their hands. They advanced from their corners and shook hands: Montgomery gravely, Craggs with a smile. Then they fell into position. The crowd gave a long sigh—the intake of a thousand excited breaths. The referee tilted his chair on to its back legs, and looked moodily critical from the one to the other.

It was strength against activity—that was evident from the first. The Master stood solidly upon his K-leg. It gave him a tremendous pedestal; one could hardly imagine his being knocked down. And he could pivot round upon it with extraordinary quickness; but his advance or retreat was ungainly. His fame, however, was so much larger and broader than that of the student, and his brown, massive face looked so resolute and menacing, that the hearts of the Wilson party sank within them. There was one heart, however, which had not done so. It was that of Robert Montgomery.

Any nervousness which he may have had completely passed away now that he had his work before him. Here was something definite—this hard-faced, deformed Hercules to beat, with a career as the price of beating him. He glowed with the joy of action; it thrilled through his nerves. He faced his man with little in-and-out steps, breaking to the left, breaking to the right, feeling his way, while Craggs, with a dull, malignant eye, pivoted slowly upon his weak leg, his left arm half extended, his right sunk low across the mark. Montgomery led with his left, and then led again, getting lightly home each time. He tried again, but the Master had his counter ready, and Montgomery reeled back from a harder blow than he had given. Anastasia, the woman, gave a shrill cry of encouragement, and her man let fly his right. Montgomery ducked under it, and in an instant the two were in each other's arms.

"Break away! Break away!" said the referee.

The Master struck upwards on the break, and shook Montgomery with the blow. Then it was "time." It had been a spirited opening round. The people buzzed into comment and applause. Montgomery was quite fresh, but the hairy chest of the Master was rising and falling. The man passed a sponge over his head, while Anastasia flapped the towel before him. "Good lass! Good lass!" cried the crowd, and cheered her.

The men were up again, the Master grimly watchful, Montgomery as alert as a kitten. The Master tried a sudden rush, squattering along with his awkward gain, but coming faster than one would think. The student slipped aside and avoided him. The Master stopped, grinned, and shook his head. Then he motioned with his hand as an invitation to Montgomery to come to him. The student did so and led with his left, but got a swinging right counter in the ribs in exchange. The heavy blow staggered him, and the Master came scrambling in to complete his advantage; but Montgomery, with his greater activity, kept out of danger until the call of "time." A tame round, and the advantage with the Master.

"'T' Maister's too strong for him," said a smelter to his neighbour.

"Ay; but t' other's a likely lad. Happen we'll see some sport yet. He can joomp rarely."

"But t' Maister can stop and hit rarely. Happen he'll mak' him joomp when he gets his nief upon him."

They were up again, the water glistening upon their faces. Montgomery led instantly and got his right home with a sounding smack upon the Master's forehead. There was a shout from the colliers, and "Silence! Order!" from the referee. Montgomery avoided the counter and scored with his left. Fresh applause, and the referee upon his feet in indignation. "No comments, gentlemen, if *you* please, during the rounds."

"Just bide a bit!" growled the Master.

"Don't talk—fight!" said the referee, angrily.

Montgomery rubbed in the point by a flush hit upon the mouth, and the Master shambled back to his corner like an angry bear, having had all the worst of the round.

"Where's thot seven to one?" shouted Purvis, the publican. "I'll take six to one!"

There were no answers.

"Five to one!" There were givers at that. Purvis booked them in a tattered notebook.

Montgomery began to feel happy. He lay back with his legs outstretched, his back against the corner-post, and one gloved hand upon each rope. What a delicious minute it was between each round. If he could only keep out of harm's way, he must surely wear this man out before the end of twenty rounds. He was so slow that all his strength went for nothing. "You're fightin' a winnin' fight—a winnin' fight," Ted Barton whispered in his ear. "Go canny, tak' no chances; you have him proper."

But the Master was crafty. He had fought so many battles with his maimed limb that he knew how to make the best of it. Warily and slowly he manoeuvered round Montgomery, stepping forward and yet again forward until he had imperceptibly backed him into his corner. The student suddenly saw a flash of triumph upon the grim face, and a gleam in the dull, malignant eyes. The Master was upon him. He sprang aside and was on the ropes. The Master smashed in one of his terrible upper-cuts, and Montgomery half broke it with his guard. The student sprang the other way and was against the other converging rope. He was trapped in the angle. The Master sent in another, with a hoggish grunt which spoke of the energy behind it. Montgomery ducked, but got a jab from the left upon the mark. He closed with his man. "Break away! Break away!" cried the referee. Montgomery disengaged, and got a swinging blow on the ear as he did so. It had been a damaging round for him, and the Croxley people were shouting their delight.

"Gentlemen, I will *not* have this noise!" Stapleton roared. "I have been accustomed to preside at a well-conducted club, and not at a beer-garden." This little man, with the tilted hat and the bulging forehead, dominated the whole assembly. He was like a headmaster among his boys. He glared round him, and nobody cared to meet his eye.

Anastasia had kissed the Master when he resumed his seat. "Good lass. Do't again!" cried the laughing crowd, and the angry Master shook his glove at her, as she flapped her towel in front of him. Montgomery was weary and a little sore, but not depressed. He had learned something. He would not again be tempted into danger.

For three rounds the honours were fairly equal. The student's hitting was the quicker, the Master's the harder. Profiting by his lesson, Montgomery kept himself in the open, and refused to be herded into a corner. Sometimes the Master succeeded in rushing him to the sideropes, but the younger man slipped away, or closed and then disengaged. The monotonous "Break away! Break away!" of the referee broke in upon the quick, low patter of rubber-soled shoes, the dull thud of the blows, and the sharp, hissing breath of two tired men.

The ninth round found both of them in fairly good condition. Montgomery's head was still singing from the blow that he had in the corner, and one of his thumbs pained him acutely and seemed to be dislocated. The Master showed no sign of a touch, but his breathing was the more laboured, and a long line of ticks upon the referee's paper showed that the student had a good show of points. But one of this iron-man's blows was worth three of his, and he knew that without the gloves he could not have stood for three rounds against him. All the amateur work that he had done was the merest tapping and flapping when compared to those frightful blows, from arms toughened by the shovel and the crowbar.

It was the tenth round, and the fight was half over. The betting now was only three to one, for the Wilson champion had held his own much better than had been expected. But those who knew the ringcraft as well as the staying power of the old prize-fighter knew that the odds were still a long way in his favour.

"Have a care of him!" whispered Barton, as he sent his man up to the scratch. "Have a care! He'll play thee a trick, if he can."

But Montgomery saw, or imagined he saw, that his antagonist was tiring. He looked jaded and listless, and his hands drooped a little from their position. His own youth and condition were beginning to tell. He sprang in and brought off a fine left-handed lead. The Master's return lacked his usual fire. Again Montgomery led, and again he got home. Then he tried his right upon the mark, and the Master guarded it downwards.

"Too low! Too low! A foul! A foul!" yelled a thousand voices.

The referee rolled his sardonic eyes slowly round. "Seems to me this buildin' is chock-full of referees," said he.

The people laughed and applauded, but their favor was as immaterial to him as their anger.

"No applause, please! This is not a theatre!" he yelled.

Montgomery was very pleased with himself. His adversary was evidently in a bad way. He was piling on his points and establishing a lead. He might as well make hay while the sun shone. The Master was looking all abroad. Montgomery popped one upon his blue jowl and got away without a return. And then the Master suddenly dropped both his hands and began rubbing his thigh. Ah! that was it, was it? He had muscular cramp.

"Go in! Go in!" cried Teddy Barton.

Montgomery sprang wildly forward, and the next instant was lying half senseless, with his neck nearly broken, in the middle of the ring.

The whole round had been a long conspiracy to tempt him within reach of one of those terrible right-hand upper-cuts for which the Master was famous. For this the listless, weary bearing, for this the cramp in the thigh. When Montgomery had sprang in so hotly he had exposed himself to such a blow as neither flesh nor blood could stand. Whizzing up from below with a rigid arm, which put the Master's eleven stone into its force, it struck him under the jaw: he whirled half round, and fell a helpless and half-paralyzed mass. A vague groan and murmur, inarticulate, too excited for words, rose from the great audience. With open mouths and staring eyes they gazed at the twitching and quivering figure.

"Stand back! Stand right back!" shrieked the referee, for the Master was standing over his man ready to give him the *coup-de-grâce* as he rose.

"Stand back, Craggs, this instant!" Stapleton repeated.

The Master sank his hands sulkily and walked backwards to the rope with his ferocious eyes fixed upon his fallen antagonist. The timekeeper called the seconds. If ten of them passed before Montgomery rose to his feet, the fight was ended. Ted Barton wrung his hand and danced about in an agony in his corner.

As if in a dream—a terrible nightmare—the student could hear the voice of the timekeeper—three-four-five—he got up on his hand—six-seven—he was on his knee, sick, swimming, faint, but resolute to rise. Eight—he was up, and the Master was on him like a tiger, lashing savagely at him with both hands. Folk held their breath as they watched those terrible blows, and anticipated the pitiful end—so much more pitiful where a game but helpless man refuses to accept defeat.

Strangely automatic is the human brain. Without volition, without effort, there shot into the memory of this bewildered, staggering, half-stupefied man the one thing which would have saved him—that blind eye of which the Master's son had spoken. It was the same as the other to look at, but Montgomery remembered that he had said that it was the left. He reeled to the left side, half felled by a drive which lit upon his shoulder. The Master pivoted round upon his leg and was at him in an instant.

"Yark him, lad! yark him!" screamed the woman.

"Hold your tongue!" said the referee.

Montgomery slipped to the left again and yet again; but the Master was too quick and clever for him. He struck round and got him full on the face as he tried once more to break away. Montgomery's knees weakened under him, and he fell with a groan to the floor. This time he knew that he was done. With bitter agony he realized, as he groped blindly with his hands, that he could not possibly raise himself. Far away and muffled he heard, amid the murmurs of the multitude, the fateful voice of the timekeeper counting off the seconds.

"One-two-three-four-five-six-"

"Time!" said the referee.

Then the pent-up passion of the great assembly broke loose. Croxley gave a deep groan of disappointment. The Wilsons were on their feet, yelling with delight. There was still a chance for them. In four more seconds their man would have been solemnly counted out. But now he had a minute in which to recover. The referee looked round with relaxed features and laughing eyes. He loved this rough game, this school for humble heroes, and it was pleasant to him to intervene as a *Deux ex machinâ* at so dramatic a moment. His chair and his hat were both tilted at an extreme angle; he and the timekeeper smiled at each other. Ted Barton and the other second had rushed out and thrust an arm each under Montgomery's knee, the other behind his loins, and so carried him back to his stool. His head lolled upon his shoulder, but a douche of cold water sent a shiver through him, and he started and looked round him.

"He's a' right!" cried the people round. "He's a rare brave lad. Good lad! Good lad!" Barton poured some brandy into his mouth. The mists cleared a little, and he realized where he was and what he had to do. But he was still very weak, and he hardly dared to hope that he could survive another round.

"Seconds out of the ring!" cried the referee. "Time!"

The Croxley Master sprang eagerly off his stool.

"Keep clear of him! Go easy for a bit," said Barton, and Montgomery walked out to meet his man once more.

He had had two lessons—the one when the Master got him into his corner, the other when he had been lured into mixing it up with so powerful an antagonist. Now he would be wary. Another blow would finish him; he could afford to run no risks. The Master was determined to follow up his advantage, and rushed at him, slogging furiously right and left. But Montgomery was too young and active to be caught. He was strong upon his legs once more, and his wits had all come back to him. It was a gallant sight—the line-of-battleship trying to pour its overwhelming broadside into the frigate, and the frigate manoeuvering always so as to avoid it. The Master tried all his ring-craft. He coaxed the student up by pretended inactivity; he rushed at him with furious rushes towards the ropes. For three rounds he exhausted every wile in trying to get at him. Montgomery during all this time was conscious that his strength was minute by minute coming back to him. The spinal jar from an upper-cut is overwhelming, but evanescent. He was losing all sense of it beyond a great stiffness of the neck. For the first round after his downfall he had been content to be entirely on the defensive, only too happy if he could stall off the furious attacks of the Master. In the second he occasionally ventured upon a light counter. In the third he was smacking back merrily where he saw an opening. His people yelled their approval of him at the end of every round. Even the iron-workers cheered him with that fine unselfishness which true sport engenders. To most of them, unspiritual and unimaginative, the sight of this clean-limbed young Apollo, rising above disaster and holding on while consciousness was in him to his appointed task, was the greatest thing their experience had ever known.

But the Master's naturally morose temper became more and more murderous at this postponement of his hopes. Three rounds ago the battle had been in his hands; now it was all to do over again. Round by round his man was recovering his strength. By the fifteenth he was strong again in wind and limb. But the vigilant Anastasia saw something which encouraged her.

"That bash in t' ribs is telling on him, Jock," she whispered. "Why else should he be gulping t' brandy? Go in, lad, and thou hast him yet."

Montgomery had suddenly taken the flask from Barton's hand, and had a deep pull at the contents. Then, with his face a little flushed, and with a curious look of purpose, which made the referee stare hard at him, in his eyes, he rose for the sixteenth round.

"Game as a pairtridge!" cried the publican, as he looked at the hard-set face.

"Mix it oop, lad; mix it oop!" cried the iron-men to their Master.

And then a hum of exultation ran through their ranks as they realized that their tougher, harder, stronger man held the vantage, after all.

Neither of the men showed much sign of punishment. Small gloves crush and numb, but they do not cut. One of the Master's eyes was even more flush with his cheek than Nature had made it. Montgomery had two or three livid marks upon his body, and his face was haggard, save for that pink spot which the brandy had brought into either cheek. He rocked a little as he stood opposite his man, and his hands drooped as if he felt the gloves to be an unutterable weight. It was evident that he was spent and desperately weary. If he received one other blow it must surely be fatal to him. If he brought one home, what power could there be behind it, and what chance was there of its harming the colossus in front of him? It was the crisis of the fight. This round must decide it. "Mix it oop, lad; mix it oop!" the ironmen whooped. Even the savage eyes of the referee were unable to restrain the excited crowd.

"Mix it oop, lad; mix it oop!" cried the iron-men to their Master.

Now, at last, the chance had come for Montgomery. He had learned a lesson from his more experienced rival. Why should he not play his own game upon him? He was spent, but not nearly so spent as he pretended. That brandy was to call up his reserves, to let him have strength to take full advantage of the opening when it came. It was thrilling and tingling through his veins, at the very moment when he was lurching and rocking like a beaten man. He acted his part admirably. The Master felt that there was an easy task before him, and rushed in with ungainly activity to finish it once for all. He slap-banged away left and right, boring Montgomery up against the ropes, swinging in his ferocious blows with those animal grunts which told of the vicious energy behind them.

But Montgomery was too cool to fall a victim to any of those murderous upper-cuts. He kept out of harm's way with a rigid guard, an active foot, and a head which was swift to duck. And yet he contrived to present the same appearance of a man who is hopelessly done. The Master, weary from his own shower of blows, and fearing nothing from so weak a man, dropped his hand for an instant, and at that instant Montgomery's right came home.

It was a magnificent blow, straight, clean, crisp, with the force of the loins and the back behind it. And it landed where he had meant it to—upon the exact point of that blue-grained chin. Flesh and blood could not stand such a blow in such a place. Neither valour nor hardihood can save the man to whom it comes. The Master fell backwards, flat, prostrate, striking the ground with so simultaneous a clap that it was like a shutter falling from a wall. A yell which no referee could control broke from the crowded benches as the giant went down. He lay upon his back, his knees a little drawn up, his huge chest panting. He twitched and shook, but could not move. His feet pawed convulsively once or twice. It was no use. He was done. "Eight-nine-ten!" said the timekeeper, and the roar of a thousand voices, with a deafening clap like the broadside of a ship, told that the Master of Croxley was the Master no more.

Montgomery stood half dazed, looking down at the huge, prostrate figure. He could hardly realize that it was indeed all over. He saw the referee motion towards him with his hand. He heard his name bellowed in triumph from every side. And then he was aware of some one rushing towards him; he caught a glimpse of a flushed face and an aureole of flying red hair, a gloveless fist struck him between the eyes, and he was on his back in the ring beside his antagonist, while a dozen of his supporters were endeavouring to secure the frantic Anastasia. He heard the angry shouting of the referee, the screaming of the furious woman, and the cries of the mob. Then something seemed to break like an over-stretched banjo-string, and he sank into the deep, deep, mist-girt abyss of unconsciousness.

The dressing was like a thing in a dream, and so was a vision of the Master with the grin of a bulldog upon his face, and his three teeth amicably protruded. He shook Montgomery heartily by the hand.

"I would have been rare pleased to shake thee by the throttle, lad, a short while syne," said he. "But I bear no ill-feelin' again' thee. It was a rare poonch that brought me down—I have not had a better since my second fight wi' Billy Edwards in '89. Happen thou might think o' goin' further wi' this business. If thou dost, and want a trainer, there's not much inside t' ropes as I don't know. Or happen thou might like to try it wi' me old style and bare knuckles. Thou hast but to write to t' iron-works to find me.

But Montgomery disclaimed any such ambition. A canvas bag with his share—one hundred and ninety sovereigns—was handed to him, of which he gave ten to the Master, who also received some share of the gate-money.

Then, with young Wilson escorting him on one side, Purvis on the other, and Fawcett carrying his bag behind, he went in triumph to his carriage, and drove amid a long road, which lined the highway like a hedge for the seven miles, back to his starting-point.

"It's the greatest thing I ever saw in my life. By George, it's ripping!" cried Wilson, who had been left in a kind of ecstasy by the events of the day. "There's a chap over Barnsley way who fancies himself a bit. Let us spring you on him, and let him see what he can make of you. We'll put up a purse—won't we, Purvis? You shall never want a backer."

"At his weight," said the publican, "I'm behind him, I am, for twenty rounds, and no age, country, or color barred."

"So am I!" cried Fawcett; "middle-weight champion of the world, that's what he is—here, in the same carriage with us."

But Montgomery was not to be beguiled.

"No; I have my own work to do now."

"And what may that be?"

"I'll use this money to get my medical degree."

"Well, we've plenty of doctors, but you're the only man in the Riding that could smack the Croxley Master off his legs. However, I suppose you know your own business best. When you're a doctor, you'd best come down into these parts, and you'll always a job waiting for you at the Wilson Coal-pits."

Montgomery had returned by devious ways to the surgery. The horses were smoking at the door, and the doctor was just back from his long journey. Several patients had called in his absence, and he was in the worst of tempers.

"I suppose I should be glad that you have come back at all, Mr. Montgomery!" He snarled. "When next you elect to take a holiday, I trust it will not be at so busy a time."

"I am sorry, sir, that you should have been inconvenienced."

"Yes, sir, I have been exceedingly inconvenienced." Here, for the first time, he looked hard at the assistant. "Good heavens, Mr. Montgomery, what have you been doing with your left eye?"

It was where Anastasia had lodged her protest.

Montgomery laughed. "It is nothing, sir," said he.

"And you have a livid mark under your jaw. It is, indeed, terrible that my representative should be going about in so disreputable a condition. How did you receive these injuries?"

"Well, sir, as you know, there was a little glove-fight to-day over at Croxley."

"And you got mixed up with that brutal crowd?"

"I *was* rather mixed up with them."

"And who assaulted you?"

"One of the fighters."

"Which of them?"

"The Master of Croxley."

"Good heavens! Perhaps you interfered with him?"

"Well, to tell the truth, I did a little."

"Mr. Montgomery, in such a practice as mine, intimately associated as it is with the highest and most progressive elements of our small community, it is impossible—"

But just then the tentative bray of a cornet-player searching for his keynote jarred upon their ears, and an instant later the Wilson Colliery brass band was in full cry with, "See the Conquering Hero Comes," outside the surgery window. There was a banner waving, and a shouting crowd of miners.

"What is it? What does it mean?" cried the angry doctor.

"It means, sir, that I have, in the only way which was open to me, earned the money which is necessary for my education. It is my duty, Doctor Oldacre, to warn you that I am about to return to the University, and that you should lose no time in appointing my successor."

from Requiem for a Heavyweight

ROD SERLING

How's this for a *Twilight Zone* episode?

It's the early '70s, and you're paying for college by driving a taxicab in New York on summer break. One blistering afternoon, a well-dressed gentleman hails you as you're driving south on 5th Avenue just above 59th Street. He asks, in a thick accent, "Are you air conditioned?" You look at his face, see that it's film director Otto Preminger, and wonder if he's joking. Air conditioning? You tell him, in all honesty, that the free *schvitz* comes with the ride. He slams the door, dismissing you with an insouciant wave. But, before you can hit the gas, you hear the door open again. At first, you don't look back . . . until you hear a gravelly, familiar voice ask if you want to go to Kennedy Airport. Sure, you answer, and for the next hour or so, you've got Rod Serling in the flesh behind you to listen to your breathless rants about your favorite *Twilight Zone* episodes.

Doo-doo-doo-doo . . .

It's true, and it happened. I only wish I had by then seen—and read—the original *Playhouse 90* production of *Requiem for a Heavyweight* so I could have talked to this majestic craftsman of television's Golden Age about that masterpiece, as well. The 1956 broadcast of Serling's searing voyage into the musty underside of the boxing game was deemed a landmark of the medium right from the opening bell.

The *New York Times* called the production "a play of overwhelming force and tenderness, and *Requiem* won a slew of awards, including a Peabody and five Emmys—notably for the year's best program, for Serling's teleplay, and for Jack Palance's wrenching turn as Mountain McClintock, the washed-up requiemee. Keenan Wynn starred as Maish Resnick, Mountain's conniving

169

manager. His father, comic Ed Wynn, earned an Emmy nomination in his first dramatic turn as the soft-hearted cornerman Army Hakes. And in a nod to cinema verite—or perhaps just a bit of type casting—"Slapsie" Maxie Rosenbloom, the former light-heavyweight who had almost as many movie roles as he did fights, acquitted himself admirably as an ex-pug in a trio of saloon scenes. (Anthony Quinn, Jackie Gleason, and Mickey Rooney reprised those roles a few years later in an inferior silver-screen rendition perhaps best remembered now for the brief movie debut of a precocious personality then known as Cassius Clay.)

This scene, near the beginning of the first act, takes place in the dressing room following Mountain's last fight. The doctor has just walked in to examine him. The rest tells itself.

Oh, yeah. I'm happy to report Mr. Serling graciously sparred with the writer-in-training I then was, in the end knocking me out with his concurrence that my favorite *Twilight Zone* of all time—*The Eye of the Beholder*—was one of his, as well. I'm also happy to report that he not only left me with a good memory, he left me with a 30 percent tip.

🥊 🥊 🥊 🥊

ARMY (concerned)

It's his eye, Doc.

DOCTOR

I know. I was watching. *(He opens his bag.)*
Look at it this way, boys, I wouldn't have let it go eight, that's for sure—if he hadn't quit when he did—

ARMY *(belligerently)*

What do you mean quit? This boy never quit in his life!

DOCTOR

God, what loyalty, Army! You should have been a solicitor for the United Jewish Appeal.

(He bends over MOUNTAIN, peering into his eye with a small flashlight. MAISH leans over, puffing on his cigar stub.)

Christ, let me breathe, will ya? Where do you get your cigars, Maish? I'll see that they condemn the store.

(He continues to work on the eye with some gauze, cotton swabs, and some medicine that he has taken from his bag.)

I got three more nights, boys. And I'm off for fishing in Florida.

ARMY

Vacation?

DOCTOR

Vacation, hell. Retirement! I'm the one man in the fight business who walks away without a wobble. Thirty-eight years, Maish. Retirement.

MAISH

You've seen some good ones.

DOCTOR

Good ones. Bad ones. Fast ones and slow ones. Live ones and a couple of dead ones.

(He points to MOUNTAIN with his swab.)

And *almost* dead ones. *(a pause)*

He's got no business in there, Maish. You hungry, is that it?

MAISH
(picking up MOUNTAIN's hand and absently massaging it)

What do you mean hungry? In 1948 we were number five.

DOCTOR

Only 1948? When *was* that, Maish? The day before yesterday? *(He looks down at MOUNTAIN. This time he touches him with a gentleness not unlike a caress.)* Now if they were all just machines, we wouldn't have any problems at all. Parts get worn—replace 'em. And when they're past peak, just chuck 'em.

When I first came, they used to lay them out in front of me. They were human beings then. *(He continues his work.)*

Now it's like a guy who grades meat in a packing plant. They roll the carcasses down in front of him and he stamps them. Beef. Understand? Look here, Maish, I want to show you something. *(MAISH looks in.)*

Look at his pupil. See? See around the eye there? Known as sclerotic damage. Look at the tissue there. Couple of good, solid rights to that eye and you can buy him a tin cup and some pencils.

(The doctor straightens up and begins to put his things back into his bag.)

Or . . . maybe that won't have to happen. Maybe some day he'll bang his head on the bathroom door and bleed to death. Either way, Maish. It could happen either way.

(Then there's a long pause and he takes a deep breath.)

No more. This is it. Mountain and I will *both* retire this week.

MAISH
(Looks from MOUNTAIN to the doctor. His eyes narrow and his voice comes out strained and tight.)

What do you mean?

DOCTOR
No more.

MAISH
He can rest up. I've got nothing scheduled for him—

DOCTOR *(interrupting)*
He can rest up for the rest of his life.

MAISH *(pause)*
What're you talkin' about? He's fourteen years in this business. Suddenly he gets a cut and we put him out to pasture?

DOCTOR

Suddenly he gets a cut? It isn't one cut. It's fourteen years of cuts.

(He looks at MAISH inquisitively, sharply.)

How long did you *think* he'd go on?

MAISH

Forget it—

DOCTOR

I mean how long did you figure, Maish? Forever?

MAISH

No. I knew he was gettin' there. I was just hoping that—

DOCTOR

Hoping what?

MAISH

Hoping that maybe he had . . . well . . . a few more in him. He still looks plenty sharp. He knows his way around in there. This boy's a pro.

DOCTOR

You bet your life he is. That's probably why he's alive now. Oh, he'll look sharp at times. They always do, Maish. There was middleweight, name of Corwin. Used to fight over at St. Nick's. Remember? Had an embolism. He fought Billy Sharkey one night and by the middle of the fourth round he was a maniac. By the end of the fifth he was a corpse. They look sharp all right. Halfway to the grave they're still dancing. But it's instinct or reflex. And the one function they're still efficient at is bleeding.

MAISH

You're a real joker, Doc.

DOCTOR

Yeah?

(He looks at MOUNTAIN.)

Who's laughing?

(*He exits. MAISH and ARMY stare at one another for a moment as MOUNTAIN begins to come around.*)

McCLINTOCK

Doc here?

ARM

He left.

McCLINTOCK

It hurts, Maish.

MAISH (*Turns his back deliberately.*)

Of this I have no doubt.

McCLINTOCK

It hurts like hell. God, after that eighth round—

MAISH

It didn't go eight.

McCLINTOCK (*Nods slowly.*)

I remember. I got mixed up. I remember now. I couldn't get up. Jesus that's an . . . an awful feeling. Not being able to get up.

(*Shakes his head, reacts with sharp pain, and touches the bandage over his eye.*)

Deep, huh, Maish?

MAISH

Enough. I got a clear view into your head.

(*a pause*)

You'd better take a shower, Mountain. Make you feel better.

McCLINTOCK
(Pushes his feet around heavily as they hang over the table, then he balances himself on his hands. His head goes up and down and he begins to breathe rhythmically, deeply.)

I'm coming around now. God, I caught it tonight, Maish. I really did. . . . What did I do wrong?

MAISH (with a half smile)
You aged. That was the big trouble. You aged.

McCLINTOCK (not understanding)
What do you mean, Maish? I aged. Don't everybody age?

MAISH
Yeah. Everybody ages. Everybody grows old, kid. I think a shower will do you good.

(pause)

Try not to get that bandage wet.

(MOUNTAIN exits.)

ARMY
(Starts to pick up the dirty towels. He waits until MOUNTAIN has disappeared and at the sound of the shower water, he looks up at MAISH.)

Hey, Maish—Who were you rooting for out there?

MAISH (sloughing it off)
Stop it, will ya? Maybe you can tell me when there was a good moment to cheer? Did he land a punch? Did he land an honest-to-God punch? If he did, it must have been a fast one because I sure as hell didn't see it.

ARMY
That's my point. Did you want him to?

                              MAISH
(Studies ARMY for a long moment.)

Spit it out, Army.

                              ARMY
You made a bet tonight.

                              MAISH
That I did.

                              ARMY
Who'd you bet on, Maish?

                              MAISH
The wrong man.

                              ARMY
Just for a favor, Maish, don't side-step me tonight, huh?

                              MAISH
You want it clearer, huh?

                              ARMY
A little bit.

                              MAISH
I said the Mountain wouldn't go four.

                              ARMY
(There is a dead silence as his face whitens. He whirls around abruptly, takes a little unsteady walk over to the locker, opens it, takes out MOUNTAIN's clothes, and then suddenly slams it shut.)

Helluva big disappointment, huh?

MAISH

Where you been? You knew he was over the hill. When Maxie showed us the new kid—I didn't see you look away. Well, Maxie's kid was good. And he cost. I needed dough and I figured this was the one way to get it.

ARMY

By betting against your own boy? God, what a prince of a guy you are, Maish.

MAISH *(defensively)*

They match him against Gibbons! We have to spot him eleven years.

ARMY

Who told you to bet?

MAISH

Who told me I had to eat?

ARMY

You picked the sport—

MAISH

Sport? Look around, Army—this isn't any sport. If there was head room, they'd hold them in sewers. You ought to know that. You had a few fights of your own. I was in the corner for at least half. You walked away with something. You got a name out of it at least.

ARMY

And the Mountain? That's what he walks away with, too, huh? A name.

MAISH

He's got more than most, let me tell you!

ARMY

What?

MAISH

He's got his brains, don't he?

ARMY (quietly)

Yeah. He's got his brains. Fourteen years and that's what he's got to show for it. His brains. So what's to do, Maish? Cheer?

(He looks at MAISH.)

The Mountain was good.

MAISH (Nods, his voice is soft now.)

He was the best. . . . And I thought I had another boy just like him.

(MOUNTAIN enters. He shadow boxes a bit as if to show MAISH and ARMY that he's got his wits.)

McCLINTOCK

Feel better, Maish. Lots better. Eye kind of feels funny—but I'll be okay now. Got a lot of spring yet, huh, Army?

(He continues to shadow box.)

How about it, Army? Still there, huh?

(ARMY nods, not being able to say anything. He exchanges a look with MAISH.)

MAISH (after a moment)

Mountain, sit down, huh?

McCLINTOCK

(Stops his dancing, looks from one to the other, and goes over to the rubbing table and sits down.)

Sure, Maish, sure.

MAISH

The Doctor looked you over.

McCLINTOCK (grins)

Yeah, I thought he was in here. I wasn't sure, though. A little groggy yet, you know?

MAISH

Yeah. Well, anyway he looked you over good this time.

McCLINTOCK

Yeah?

MAISH *(half turning away)*

He figures you've had it.

McCLINTOCK *(quietly)*

What did you say, Maish?

MAISH

The Doctor says you've had it. No more. He says you've got to leave now.

McCLINTOCK

(Looks at ARMY for a moment and then back to MAISH.) Leave? Leave where?

MAISH

Army! Lay it out for him, will ya? Mountain, no more fights. This is where you get off. You leave.

McCLINTOCK

(Another pause. He walks over to MAISH and pokes him with a forefinger.)

Leave? Maish, that's . . . that's crazy. Leave. I swear to God that's crazy—

MAISH *(Turns away from him)*

So it's crazy. Go fight the Commission.

(He deliberately turns his back on MOUNTAIN.)

McCLINTOCK

Maish, what'll I do?

MAISH *(impatiently)*

Anything you like. It's as easy as that.

McCLINTOCK

I mean . . . I mean a guy's got to do something.

MAISH

So you do something.

McCLINTOCK *(the words coming out hard)*

Maish, you know it's a funny thing, but . . . but I don't know anything but fighting. You know, Maish, it's fourteen years . . . I've been a pro. I've been with you fourteen years.

ARMY

And before that?

McCLINTOCK *(Smiles and shrugs.)*

Before that what? Who remembers before that?

ARMY

You can go back home, kid. You used to talk about it enough. The green hills of Tennessee. Isn't that what you called it? Why don't you try it back there?

McCLINTOCK

Home? What's back there? I haven't been home in all those years. I don't know anybody, and nobody'd know me.

(then suddenly, as if struck by an afterthought)

Maish, we could try another state, maybe?

MAISH

You don't pass muster in New York State, you don't pass muster anyplace else. You know that.

McCLINTOCK

Maybe some club fights. You know—unofficial—

MAISH

Mountain, you're not gonna be able to fight any more. Got to get yourself another business. Army, you want to get him dressed.

ARMY
You want me to help you get dressed, Mountain?

McCLINTOCK
No. No, I can dress myself. *(quietly)* Hey, Maish?

MAISH
Yeah, Mountain?

McCLINTOCK
I'm . . . I'm sorry about tonight. I'm sorry I lost.

MAISH
(For just a single moment his features work and then instinctively he reaches out to touch MOUNTAIN's face. The gesture is sudden, but there is much unsaid that goes with it. MAISH finally has to turn his face away. He coughs, wheezes, shoves the cigar back in his mouth, and shrugs.)

Don't be sorry, Mountain. You tried. You always tried.

(He turns away.)

You were the number one. That's what you were. So don't give it another thought.

(His hand slides down to grip MOUNTAIN's arm and then as if embarrassed by the realization that it's there, he drops it awkwardly and turns away.)

Anyone want a cup of coffee? You, Army?

(ARMY shakes his head. MAISH shrugs.)

Well . . . get him dressed, Army.

(He exits.)

Bred for Battle

DAMON RUNYON

Of all the sports that Damon Runyon (1880–1946) wrote about—and he pretty much wrote about all of them—boxing was the one he was most attached to, in part because his interests in the game were more than literary. Runyon promoted fights and owned pieces of several fighters. Still, of all the tomato cans that came through his stable, none, we can presume, were quite as hapless as the hapless heavyweight at the center of this delightfully Runyonesque souffle.

🥊　🥊　🥊　🥊

One night a guy by the name of Bill Corum, who is one of these sport scribes, gives me a Chinee for a fight at Madison Square Garden, a Chinee being a ducket with holes punched in it like old-fashioned Chink money, to show that it is a free ducket, and the reason I am explaining to you how I get this ducket is because I do not wish anybody to think I am ever simple enough to pay out my own potatoes for a ducket to a fight, even if I have any potatoes.

Personally, I will not give you a bad two-bit piece to see a fight anywhere, because the way I look at it, half the time the guys who are supposed to do the fighting go in there and put on the old do-se-do, and I consider this a great fraud upon the public, and I do not believe in encouraging dishonesty.

But of course I never refuse a Chinee to such events, because the way I figure it, what can I lose except my time, and my time is not worth more than a bob a week the way things are. So on the night in question I am standing in the lobby of the Garden with many other citizens, and I am trying to find out if there is any skullduggery doing in connection with the fight, because any time there is any skullduggery doing I love to know it, as it is something worth knowing in case a guy wishes to get a small wager down.

Well, while I am standing there, somebody comes up behind me and hits me an awful belt on the back, knocking my wind plumb out of me, and making me very indignant indeed. As soon as I get a little of my wind back again, I turn around figuring to put a large blast on the guy who slaps me, but who is it but a guy by the name of Spider McCoy, who is known far and wide as a manager of fighters.

Well, of course I do not put the blast on Spider McCoy, because he is an old friend of mine, and furthermore, Spider McCoy is such a guy as is apt to let a left hook go at anybody who puts the blast on him, and I do not believe in getting in trouble, especially with good left-hookers.

So I say hello to Spider, and am willing to let it go at that, but Spider seems glad to see me, and says to me like this:

"Well, well, well, well, well!" Spider says.

"Well," I say to Spider McCoy, "how many wells does it take to make a river?"

"One, if it is big enough," Spider says, so I can see he knows the answer all right. "Listen," he says, "I just think up the greatest proposition I ever think of in my whole life, and who knows but what I can interest you in same."

"Well, Spider," I say, "I do not care to hear any propositions at this time, because it may be a long story, and I wish to step inside and see the impending battle. Anyway," I say, "if it is a proposition involving financial support, I wish to state that I do not have any resources whatever at this time."

"Never mind the battle inside," Spider says. "It is nothing but a tank job, anyway. And as for financial support," Spider says, "this does not require more than a pound note, tops, and I know you have a pound note because I know you put the bite on Overcoat Obie for this amount not an hour ago. Listen," Spider McCoy says, "I know where I can place my hands on the greatest heavyweight prospect in the world today, and all I need is the price of carfare to where he is."

Well, off and on, I know Spider McCoy twenty years, and in all this time I never know him when he is not looking for the greatest heavyweight prospect in the world. And as long as Spider knows I have the pound note, I know there is no use trying to play the duck for him, so I stand there wondering who the stool pigeon can be who informs him of my financial status.

"Listen," Spider says, "I just discover that I am all out of line in the way I am looking for heavyweight prospects in the past. I am always looking for nothing but plenty of size," he says. "Where I make my mistake is not looking for bloodlines. Professor D just smartens me up," Spider says.

Well, when he mentions the name of Professor D, I commence taking a little interest, because it is well-known to one and all that Professor D is one of the smartest old guys in the world. He is once a professor in a college out in Ohio, but quits this dodge to handicap the horses, and he is a first-rate handicapper, at that. But besides knowing how to handicap the horses, Professor D knows many other things, and is highly respected in all walks of life, especially on Broadway.

"Now then," Spider says, "Professor D calls my attention this afternoon to the fact that when a guy is looking for a racehorse, he does not take just any horse that comes along, but he finds out if the horse's papa is able to run in his day, and if the horse's mamma can get out of her own way when she is young. Professor D shows me how a guy looks for speed in a horse's breeding away back to its great-great-great-great-grandpa and grandmamma," Spider McCoy says.

"Well," I say, "anybody knows this without asking Professor D. In fact," I say, "you can look up a horse's parents to see if they can mud before betting on a plug to win in heavy going."

"All right," Spider says, "I know all this myself, but I never think much about it before Professor D mentions it. Professor D says if a guy is looking for a hunting dog he does not pick a Pekingese pooch, but he gets a dog that is bred to hunt from away back yonder, and if he is after a game chicken he does not take a Plymouth Rock out of the backyard.

"So then," Spider says, "Professor D wishes to know why, when I am looking for a fighter, I do not look for one who comes of fighting stock. Professor D wishes to know," Spider says, "why I do not look for some guy who is bred to fight, and when I think this over, I can see the professor is right.

"And then all of a sudden," Spider says, "I get the largest idea I ever have in all my life. Do you remember a guy I have about twenty years back by the name of Shamus Mulrooney, the Fighting Harp?" Spider says. "A big, rough, tough heavyweight out of Newark?"

"Yes," I say, "I remember Shamus very well indeed. The last time I see him is the night Pounder Pat O'Shea almost murders him in the old Garden," I say. "I never see a guy with more ticker than Shamus, unless maybe it is Pat."

"Yes," Spider says, "Shamus has plenty of ticker. He is about through the night of the fight you speak of, otherwise Pat will never lay a glove on him. It is not long after this fight that Shamus packs in and goes back to bricklaying in Newark, and it is also about this same time," Spider says, "that he marries Pat O'Shea's sister, Bridget.

"Well, now," Spider says, "I remember they have a boy who must be around nineteen years old now, and if ever a guy is bred to fight it is a boy by Shamus Mulrooney out of Bridget O'Shea, because," Spider says, "Bridget herself can lick half the heavyweights I see around nowadays if she is half as good as she is the last time see her. So now you have my wonderful idea. We will go to Newark and get this boy and make him heavyweight champion of the world."

"What you state is very interesting indeed, Spider," I say. "But," I say, "how do you know this boy is a heavyweight?"

"Why," Spider says, "how can he be anything else but a heavyweight, what with his papa as big as a house, and his mamma weighing maybe a hundred and seventy pounds in her step-ins? Although of course," Spider says, "I never see Bridget weigh in in such manner.

"But," Spider says, "even if she does carry more weight than I will personally care to spot a doll, Bridget is by no means a pelican when she marries Shamus. In fact," he says, "she is pretty good-looking. I remember their wedding well, because it comes out that Bridget is in love with some other guy at the time, and this guy comes to see the nuptials, and Shamus runs him all the way from Newark to Elizabeth, figuring to break a couple of legs for the guy if he catches him. But," Spider says, "the guy is too speedy for Shamus, who never has much foot anyway."

Well, all that Spider says appeals to me as a very sound business proposition, so the upshot of it is, I give him my pound note to finance his trip to Newark.

Then I do not see Spider McCoy again for a week, but one day he calls me up and tells me to hurry over to the Pioneer gymnasium to see the next heavyweight champion of the world, Thunderbolt Mulrooney.

I am personally somewhat disappointed when I see Thunderbolt Mulrooney, and especially when I find out his first name is Raymond and not Thunderbolt at all, because I am expecting to see a big, fierce guy with red hair and a chest like a barrel, such as Shamus Mulrooney has when he is in his prime. But who do I see but a tall, pale looking young guy with blond hair and thin legs.

Furthermore, he has pale blue eyes, and a faraway look in them, and he speaks in a low voice, which is nothing like the voice of Shamus Mulrooney. But Spider seems satisfied with Thunderbolt, and when I tell him Thunderbolt does not look to me like the next heavyweight champion of the world, Spider says like this:

"Why," he says, "the guy is nothing but a baby, and you must give him time to fill out. He may grow to be bigger than his papa. But you know," Spider says, getting indignant as he thinks about it, "Bridget Mulrooney does not wish to let this guy be the next heavyweight champion of the world. In fact," Spider says, "she kicks up an awful row when I go to get him, and Shamus finally has to speak to her severely. Shamus says he does not know if I can ever make a fighter of this guy because Bridget coddles him until he is nothing but a mush-head, and Shamus says he is sick and tired of seeing the guy sitting around the house doing nothing but reading and playing the zither."

"Does he play the zither yet?" I ask Spider McCoy.

"No," Spider says, "I do not allow my fighters to play zithers. I figure it softens them up. This guy does not play anything at present. He seems to be in a daze most of the time, but of course everything is new to him. He is bound to come out okay, because," Spider says, "he is certainly bred right. I find out from Shamus that all the Mulrooneys are great fighters back in the old country," Spider says, "and furthermore he tells me Bridget's mother once licks four Newark cops who try to stop her from pasting her old man, so," Spider says, "this lad is just naturally steaming with fighting blood."

Well, I drop around to the Pioneer once or twice a week after this, and Spider McCoy is certainly working hard with Thunderbolt Mulrooney. Furthermore, the guy seems to be improving right along, and gets so he can box fairly well and punch the bag, and all this and that, but he always has that faraway look in his eyes, and personally I do not care for fighters with far faraway looks.

Finally one day Spider calls me up and tells me he has Thunderbolt Mulrooney matched in a four-round preliminary bout at the St. Nick with a guy by the name of Bubbles Browning, who is fighting almost as far back as the first battle of Bull Run, so I can see Spider is being very careful in matching Thunderbolt. In fact, I congratulate Spider on his carefulness.

"Well," Spider says, "I am taking this match just to give Thunderbolt the feel of the ring. I am taking Bubbles because he is an old friend of mine and very deserving, and furthermore," Spider says, "he gives me his word he will not hit Thunderbolt very hard and will become unconscious the instant

Thunderbolt hits him. You know," Spider says, "you must encourage a young heavyweight, and there is nothing that encourages one so much as knocking somebody unconscious."

Now of course it is nothing for Bubbles to promise not to hit anybody very hard because even when he is a young guy, Bubbles cannot punch his way out of a paper bag, but I am glad to learn that he also promises to become unconscious very soon, as naturally I am greatly interested in Thunderbolt's career, what with owning a piece of him, and having an investment of one pound in him already.

So the night of the fight, I am at the St. Nick very early, and many other citizens are there ahead of me, because by this time Spider McCoy gets plenty of publicity for Thunderbolt by telling the boxing scribes about his wonderful fighting bloodlines, and everybody wishes to see a guy who is bred for battle, like Thunderbolt.

I take a guest with me to the fight by the name of Harry the Horse, who comes from Brooklyn, and as I am anxious to help Spider McCoy all I can, as well as to protect my investment in Thunderbolt, I request Harry to call on Bubbles Browning in his dressing room and remind him of his promise about hitting Thunderbolt.

Harry the Horse does this for me, and furthermore he shows Bubbles a large revolver and tells Bubbles that he will be compelled to shoot his ears off if Bubbles forgets his promise, but Bubbles says all this is most unnecessary, as his eyesight is so bad he cannot see to hit anybody, anyway.

Well, I know a party who is a friend of the guy who is going to referee the preliminary bouts, and I am looking for this party to get him to tell the referee to disqualify Bubbles in case it looks as if he is forgetting his promise and is liable to hit Thunderbolt, but before I can locate the party, they are announcing the opening bout, and there is Thunderbolt in the ring looking very far away indeed, with Spider McCoy behind him.

It seems to me I never see a guy who is so pale all over as Thunderbolt Mulrooney, but Spider looks down at me and tips me a large wink, so I can see that everything is as right as rain, especially when Harry the Horse makes motions at Bubbles Browning like a guy firing a large revolver at somebody, and Bubbles smiles, and also winks.

Well, when the bell rings, Spider gives Thunderbolt a shove toward the center, and Thunderbolt comes out with his hands up, but looking more far away than somewhat, and something tells me that Thunderbolt by no means feels the killer instinct such as I love to see in fighters. In fact, something tells me that Thunderbolt is not feeling enthusiastic about this proposition in any way, shape, manner, or form.

Old Bubbles almost falls over his own feet coming out of his corner, and he starts bouncing around making passes at Thunderbolt, and waiting for Thunderbolt to hit him so he can become unconscious. Naturally, Bubbles does not wish to become unconscious without getting hit, as this may look suspicious to the public.

Well, instead of hitting Bubbles, what does Thunderbolt Mulrooney do but turn around and walk over to a neutral corner, and lean over the ropes with his face in his gloves, and bust out crying. Naturally, this is a most surprising incident to one and all, and especially to Bubbles Browning.

The referee walks over to Thunderbolt Mulrooney and tries to turn him around, but Thunderbolt keeps his face in his gloves and sobs so loud that the referee is deeply touched, and starts sobbing with him. Between sobs he asks Thunderbolt if he wishes to continue the fight, and Thunderbolt shakes his head, although as a matter of fact no fight whatever starts so far, so the referee declares Bubbles Browning the winner, which is a terrible surprise to Bubbles.

Then the referee puts his arm around Thunderbolt and leads him over to Spider McCoy, who is standing in his corner with a very strange expression on his face. Personally, I consider the entire spectacle so revolting that I go out into the air, and stand around awhile expecting to hear any minute that Spider McCoy is in the hands of the gendarmes on a charge of mayhem.

But it seems that nothing happens, and when Spider finally comes out of the St. Nick, he is only looking sorrowful because he just hears that the promoter declines to pay him the fifty bobs he is supposed to receive for Thunderbolt's services, the promoter claiming that Thunderbolt renders no service.

"Well," Spider says, "I fear this is not the next heavyweight champion of the world after all. There is nothing in Professor D's idea about bloodlines as far as fighters are concerned, although," he says, "it may work out all right with horses and dogs, and one thing and another. I am greatly disappointed," Spider says, "but then I am always being disappointed in heavyweights. There is nothing we can do but take this guy back home, because," Spider says, "the last thing I promised Bridget Mulrooney is that I will personally return him to her in case I am not able to make him heavyweight champion, as she is afraid he will get lost if he tries to find his way home alone."

So the next day, Spider McCoy and I take Thunderbolt Mulrooney over to Newark and to his home, which turns out to be a nice little house in a side street with a yard all around and about, and Spider and I are just as well pleased that old Shamus Mulrooney is absent when we arrive, because Spider says that Shamus is just such a guy as will be asking a lot of questions about the fifty bobbos that Thunderbolt does not get.

Well, when we reach the front door of the house, out comes a big, fine-looking doll with red cheeks, all excited, and she takes Thunderbolt in her arms and kisses him, so I know this is Bridget Mulrooney, and I can see she knows what happens, and in fact I afterwards learn that Thunderbolt telephones her the night before.

After a while she pushes Thunderbolt into the house and stands at the door as if she is guarding it against us entering to get him again which of course is very unnecessary. And all this time Thunderbolt is sobbing no little, although by and by the sobs die away, and from somewhere in the house comes the sound of music I seem to recognize as the music of a zither.

Well, Bridget Mulrooney never says a word to us as she stands in the door, and Spider McCoy keeps staring at her in a way that I consider very rude indeed. I am wondering if he is waiting for a receipt for Thunderbolt, but finally he speaks as follows:

"Bridget," Spider says, "I hope and trust that you will not consider me too fresh, but I wish to learn the name of the guy you are going around with just before you marry Shamus. I remember him well," Spider says, "but I cannot think of his name, and it bothers me not being able to think of names. He is a tall, skinny, stoop-shouldered guy," Spider says, "with a hollow chest and a soft voice, and he loves music."

Well, Bridget Mulrooney stands there in the doorway, staring back at Spider, and it seems to me that the red suddenly fades out of her cheeks, and just then we hear a lot of yelling, and around the corner of the house comes a bunch of five or six kids, who seem to be running from another kid.

This kid is not very big, and is maybe fifteen or sixteen years old, and he has red hair and many freckles, and he seems very mad at the other kids. In fact, when he catches up with them, he starts belting away at them with his fists, and before anybody can as much as say boo, he has three of them on the ground as flat as pancakes, while the others are yelling bloody murder.

Personally, I never see such wonderful punching by a kid, especially with his left hand, and Spider McCoy is also much impressed, and is watching the kid with great interest. Then Bridget Mulrooney runs out and grabs the frecklefaced kid with one hand and smacks him with the other hand, and hauls him, squirming and kicking, over to Spider McCoy and says to Spider like this:

"Mr. McCoy," Bridget says, "this is my youngest son, Terence, and though he is not a heavyweight, and will never be a heavyweight, perhaps he will answer your purpose. Suppose you see his father about him sometime," she says, "and hoping you will learn to mind your own business, I wish you a very good day."

Then she takes the kid into the house under her arm and slams the door in our kissers, and there is nothing for us to do but walk away. And as we are walking away, all of a sudden Spider McCoy snaps his fingers as guys will do when they get an unexpected thought, and says like this:

"I remember the guy's name," he says. "It is Cedric Tilbury, and he is a floorwalker in Hamburgher's department store, and," Spider says, "how he can play the zither!"

I see in the papers the other day where Jimmy Johnston, the matchmaker at the Garden, matches Tearing Terry Mulrooney, the new sensation in the light-weight division, to fight for the championship, but it seems from what Spider McCoy tells me that my investment with him does not cover any fighters in his stable except maybe heavyweights.

And it also seems that Spider McCoy is not monkeying with heavy-weights since he gets Tearing Terry.

You're Joe Louis

Jimmy Cannon (1910–1973) couldn't have been better named. As a sports columnist for the *New York Post* and the *Journal-American,* he was a big gun who shot from the lip. His fast-paced, rat-a-tat *Nobody Asked Me But . . .* columns were veritable fusillades of opinion, information, observations, and bias. Yet, there was another side of Cannon—appreciative and even sentimental—expressed with often chilling beauty in columns, like this one from 1951, that he dispensed in the second person. It was a conceit that led him deeper under the skin—of his subjects and of his readers.

🥊   🥊   🥊   🥊

You're Joe Louis, aged thirty-seven, a main-event heavyweight. You were the greatest champion of your time. But now you're trapped by the fight racket which you conquered. You're absolutely through but you can't declare yourself. You're still making a living the only way you know. You always fought for money. It was there, all you needed, a fortune for a night's work. You signed a marker and a promoter advanced you what you asked for. The sum didn't matter. The signature on the paper got it by the ton. What you did with it is no one's business but your own.

You know you're finished. You knew it first. You understand what happened to you better than anyone. You're the guy taking the punches. You share everything in the fight racket but the punches. You have no partners in pain. They don't sue you to be in with the beatings. They never give you a contract which entitles them to a percentage of the blows. They allow you

193

that. You don't have to hire an attorney to guarantee you the right to take a licking all by yourself.

The dream is gone forever. It's not only getting knocked out by a kid who wouldn't have lasted a round with you ten years ago. It's the subtle differences you feel. You aren't disturbed by the small matters. They inform you what's liable to happen. You're holding on, watching it slip away. But there's still some of it left.

You tried to soften it up for Jimmy Braddock. You became what Braddock used to be. You became the champion of the world by beating him. So whenever you met him you made it a point to call him champ. He wasn't the champ. You were. There are many ex-champions. There is only one champion. You knew that. So did Braddock.

You must have noticed that the night Rocky Marciano knocked you out. Neither of you is the champion. But he's coming. You're going. They stuck close to the winner. You know how they came piling into your dressing room when you were standing guys on their head.

You looked around the dressing room, and who was there? The corner guys had to be there. It's the newspaperman's job. There were a few old friends. But was Jim Norris there? Was Art Wirtz hanging around? Was Harry Markson? Was Al Weill? They're the International Boxing Club. They were sitting on a bench in Marciano's place. They were talking about Marciano. Explaining what a great fight he had made. You know what they said. They said it to you after every fight you won.

You look back and the past belongs to you. There never was one like you. You were born a man, not a champion. You are a fighter, not a symbol. But always, because you are what you are, you will be a symbol and a champion to a lot of people as long as you live. You meant more to people than any fighter in any time. That includes Dempsey and John L.

You were born in poverty. You worked as a factory hand. But once you were twenty you were like a guy who had inherited a million dollars. You were never alone except when the bell rang. There were guys who ran your errands. You never handled the money. They told you the proposition. You fought. They showed you an expense account. They kept books like you were a big corporation, instead of a kid fighting with his hands.

You took down more than four million but that was cut many ways. It's all in statements where it went. It's down in the ledgers. The neat figures explaining what became of it. The bookkeepers can account for it all. Do you ever wonder what four million looks like? Four million is what a CPA writes in a book.

You fought twice for charity. You did a hitch in the army. You were generous with your friends. You played golf and bet on yourself. You staked guys. You put some in business. You lifted tabs. Champions always get the check. But four million? Where could it go? Taxes didn't take it all. The dude ranch didn't and the chicken shack in Detroit. Where are the annuities and the real estate? The books say more than four million. The books are right.

You quit when you were winning. You finished with the title. You were in with the I.B.C. It wasn't enough. There were the back taxes. You fought Ezzard Charles and you lost. People who never met you wept that night. It embarrassed Charles because he was the one who did it.

You never thought you squandered money. It was just the way a champion traveled. You went first class but it never seemed like four million dollars' worth.

You can still make a lot of money letting guys punch you around. What else does a guy fight for? But it always seemed it was for more than money. That's why you affected people so. You can't help it if a whole lot of people feel lousy every time you fight. But they do. They do.

The Boxer and the Blonde

FRANK DEFORD

His voice is on NPR's *Morning Edition,* his face is on *RealSports* with Bryant Gumbel, and, with the exception of a few years where they went wandering off to other publications, his words have been an anchor at *Sports Illustrated* since 1962. He's written 13 books—seven of them novels—and a screenplay. With six Sportswriter of the Year Awards and two national Magazine Writer of the Year nods, Frank Deford possesses one of the most honored bylines around. And if he's not exactly known for his boxing writing, his story-telling transcends stadiums and arenas, as it does in this multi-dimensional saga of Billy Conn and his wife, Mary Louise, from the 1985 pages of *Sports Illustrated.*

🥊   🥊   🥊   🥊

The boxer and the blonde are together, downstairs in the club cellar. At some point, club cellars went out, and they became family rooms instead. This is, however, very definitely a club cellar. Why, the grandchildren of the boxer and the blonde could sleep soundly upstairs, clear through the big Christmas party they gave when everybody came and stayed late and loud down here. The boxer and the blonde are sitting next to each other, laughing about the old times, about when they fell hopelessly in love almost half a century ago in New Jersey, at the beach. *Down the shore* is the way everyone in Pennsylvania says it. This club cellar is in Pittsburgh.

The boxer is going on 67, except in *The Ring* record book, where he is going on 68. But he has all his marbles; and he has his looks (except for the fighter's mashed nose); and he has the blonde; and they have the same house, the one with the club cellar, that they bought in the summer of 1941. A great deal of this is about that bright ripe summer, the last one before the forlorn simplicity of a Depression was buried in the thick-braided rubble of blood and Spam. What a fight the boxer had that June! It might have been the best in the history of the ring. Certainly, it was the most dramatic, all-time, any way you look at it. The boxer lost, though. Probably he would have won, except for the blonde—whom he loved so much, and wanted so much to make proud of him. And later, it was the blonde's old man, the boxer's father-in-law (if you can believe this), who cost him a rematch for the heavyweight championship of the world. Those were some kind of times.

The boxer and the blonde laugh again, together, remembering how they fell in love. "Actually, you sort of forced me into it," she says.

"I did you a favor," he snaps back, smirking at his comeback. After a couple of belts, he has been known to confess that although he fought twenty-one times against world champions, he has never yet won a decision over the blonde—never yet, as they say in boxing, *outpointed* her. But you can sure see why he keeps on trying. He still has his looks? Hey, you should see her. The blonde is past 60 now, and she's still cute as a button. Not merely beautiful, you understand, but schoolgirl cute, just like she was when the boxer first flirted with her down the shore in Jersey. There is a picture of them on the wall. Pictures cover the walls of the club cellar. This particular picture was featured in a magazine, the boxer and the blonde running, hand in hand, out of the surf. Never in your life did you see two better-looking kids. She was Miss Ocean City, and Alfred Lunt called him "a Celtic god," and Hollywood had a part for him that Errol Flynn himself wound up with after the boxer said no thanks and went back to Pittsburgh.

The other pictures on the walls of the club cellar are mostly of fighters. Posed. Weighing in. Toe to toe. Bandaged. And ex-fighters. Mostly in Las Vegas, it seems, the poor bastards. And celebrities. Sinatra, Hope, Bishop Sheen. Politicians. Various Kennedys. Mayor Daley. President Reagan. Vice-President Bush. More fighters. Joe Louis, whom the boxer loved so much, is in a lot of the pictures, but the largest single photograph belongs to Harry Greb, the Pittsburgh Windmill, the middleweight champeen, the only man ever to beat Gene Tunney. When the boxer's mother died that summer of '41, one of the things that mattered most then was to get her the closest possible plot in Calvary Cemetery to where Harry Greb already lay in peace.

But then, down on the far wall, around the corner from Greb, behind the bar, there's another big photograph, and it's altogether different from the others, because this one is a horizontal. Boxing pictures are either square, like the ring itself, or vertical, the fighter standing tall, fists cocked high. If you see a horizontal, it's almost surely not a boxing photograph. More than likely it's from another sport; it's a team picture, all the players spread out in rows. And sure enough, the photograph on the far wall is of the 1917 New York Giants, winners of the National League pennant, and there in the middle of the back row, with a cocky grin hung on his face, is Greenfield Jimmy Smith. The story really starts with him. He was the one who introduced the boxer and the blonde down the shore.

The book on Greenfield Jimmy Smith as a ballplayer was good mouth, no hit (.219 lifetime). His major talent earned him another nickname up in the bigs, Serpent Tongue. Muggsy McGraw, the Giants' manager, kept Smith around pretty much as a bench jockey. But after the Giants lost to the White Sox in the '17 Series, four games to two, McGraw traded him. That broke Smith's heart. He loved McGraw. They were both tough cookies.

"Ah, rub it with a brick," Greenfield Jimmy would say whenever anybody complained of an injury. He was just a little guy, maybe 5'9", a banty rooster, but one time he went over to the Dodger dugout and yelled, "All right, you so-and-sos, I'll fight you one at a time or in groups of five." Not a single Dodger took up the offer.

Greenfield Jimmy's grandchildren remember a day in Jimmy's sixties when he took them out for a drive. A truck got behind him coming up Forbes Avenue and sat on his tail, and Greenfield Jimmy slowed down. The truck driver rested on his horn until finally the grandfather pulled his car over and got out. Livid, the big truck driver came over and started hollering down at the little old guy. Softly Greenfield Jimmy cut in, "Oh, I'm so sorry, but my neighbor over there saw the whole thing."

"What neighbor?" the big truck driver asked, twisting his head to catch a glimpse of this witness. That was his mistake. As soon as he turned to the side, Greenfield Jimmy reared back and popped him flush on the chin. The old man wasn't anything but a banjo hitter on the diamond, but he could sure slug off it.

Greenfield Jimmy played in the bigs as late as '22, but by then the Eighteenth Amendment was the law of the land, and he was discovering that his playing baseball was getting in the way of a more lucrative new career, which was providing alcoholic beverages to those who desired them, notwithstanding their legal unavailability. Sometimes, he would even carry the hooch about in the big trunks that held the team's uniforms and equipment.

Back in Pittsburgh, where he hailed from—the Greenfield section, as you might imagine—Greenfield Jimmy Smith became a man of substance and power. He consorted with everybody, priests and pugs and politicians alike. He ran some speakeasies and, ultimately, the Bachelor's Club, which was the classiest joint in town—a "city club," so-called, as opposed to the numerous neighborhood clubs, which would let in anybody with a couple of bucks' annual dues and the particularly correct European heritage. But the Bachelor's Club was a plush place, and some of Pittsburgh's finest made a great deal of walking-around money by overlooking its existence. Even after repeal, the Bachelor's Club offered games of chance for those so inclined. It helped that, like so much of the Steel City constabulary, Greenfield Jimmy Smith was Irish.

The Bachelor's Club was located in the East Liberty section of Pittsburgh—or 'Sliberty, as it's pronounced in the slurred argot of the community. In a city of neighborhoods, before automobiles begat suburbs, 'Sliberty was known as a very busy place; people came to shop there. For action, though, it was probably not the match of Oakland, a couple of miles away. Most neighborhoods in Pittsburgh were parochial, with a single ethnic legacy, but Oakland had more of a mix and stronger outside influences as well, inasmuch as it embraced the University of Pittsburgh and Forbes Field (where the Pirates played), and the Duquesne Gardens, which must surely be the only boxing arena that was ever set right across the street from a cathedral, which, in this particular case, was St. Paul's.

The Gardens was an old converted carbarn—which, once upon a time, was a place where streetcars were kept when they were sleeping. Pittsburgh was strictly a streetcar town. That was how everybody got to the steel mills. Only in Pittsburgh, nobody ever said "carbarn." They said "coreborn." In Pittsburgh, even now, they don't know how to correctly pronounce any of the vowels and several of the consonants. Even more than the *a*'s, they mess up the *o*'s. A cawledge, for example, is what Pitt is; a dawler is legal tender; and, at that time, the most popular bawxer at the Duquesne Gardens was a skinny Irish contender from 'Sliberty named Billy Cawn, which, despite the way everybody said it, was, curiously, spelled Conn.

Greenfield Jimmy took a real liking to the kid. They had a lot in common. Somebody asked Conn once if he had learned to fight in the streets; no, he replied, it was a long time before he got to the streets from the alleys. Early in '39, after fifty fights around Pittsburgh and West Virginia and two in San Francisco, Conn finally got a shot in New York. "Uncle" Mike Jacobs, the promoter, brought him to Gotham in order to get beat up by a popular Italian fighter, a bellhop out of San Francisco named Freddie Apostoli. Only it was Conn who beat Apostoli in ten, and then, in a rematch a month later, with 19,000 fans packed to the rafters of the old Madison Square Garden on Eighth Avenue, he beat Apostoli in a fifteen-round bloodbath. As much as possible, then, the idea was to match the ethnic groups, so after Conn had beat the Italian twice, Uncle Mike sent him up against a Jew named Solly Krieger. And when the Irish boy beat Krieger in twelve, he was signed to fight Melio Bettina for the world light-heavyweight title the following July.

Suddenly, Conn was the hottest thing in the ring. "Matinee-idol looks," they all said, curly-haired, quick with a quip, full of fun, free, white, and (almost) 21. Money was burning a hole in his pocket, and the dames were chasing him. Right at the time, he took up with an older woman, a divorcée, and remember, this was back in the days when divorcée meant Look Out. He left her for a couple of days and came to Greenfield Jimmy's summer place down the shore in a Cadillac driven by a chauffeur.

Billy Conn was the cat's meow, and Smith was anxious for his wife and kids to meet him, too. Greenfield Jimmy wasn't just a provider, you understand, but also a great family man, and, they said, he never missed Mass. He thought it was really swell when Billy volunteered to take Mary Louise, his little daughter, out to dinner that evening. She was only 15, and for her to be able to go over to Somers Point and have a meal out with Sweet William, the Flower of the Monongahela, would sure be something she could tell the other girls back at Our Lady of Mercy Academy.

How would Greenfield Jimmy ever know that before the evening was over, Billy Conn would turn to the pretty little 15-year-old kid and say right out, "I'm going to marry you."

Mary Louise managed to stammer back, "You're crazy." She remembered what her father had advised her—that all prizefighters were punchy—only it surprised her that one so young and good-looking could be that way. Only, of course, he wasn't punchy. He had just fallen for the kid doll like a ton of bricks.

So now you see. It is Billy Conn who is the boxer in the club cellar and Mary Louise who is the blonde. By the time Greenfield Jimmy Smith (who prided himself on knowing everything) found out what was going on right under his nose, it was too late.

The Conn house is in the Squirrel Hill district. It has long been mostly a Jewish area, but the house was a good bargain at $17,500 when Billy bought it forty-four years ago because he wanted to stay in the city. Billy is a city guy, a Pittsburgh guy. Billy says, "Pittsburgh is the town you can't wait to leave, and the town you can't wait to get back to." They loved him in Gotham, and they brought him to Tinseltown to play the title role in *The Pittsburgh Kid,* and later he spent a couple of years in Vegas, working the Stardust's lounge as a greeter, like Joe Louis at the Dunes down the Strip. His son Timmy remembers the time a high roller gave the boxer $9,000, just for standing around and being Billy Conn. But soon the boxer grew tired of that act and came back to the house in Squirrel Hill, where, in the vernacular, he "loafs with" old pals like Joey Diven, who was recognized as the World's Greatest Street Fighter.

Pittsburgh may be a metropolitan area of better than two million souls, but it still has the sense of a small town. "Everybody's closely knitted," Diven explains. "A guy hits a guy in 'Sliberty, everybody knows about it right away, all over." Or it's like this: One time the boxer was trying to get a patronage job with the county for a guy he loafs with. But everybody was onto the guy's act. "Billy," the politician said, "I'd like to help you. I really would. But everybody knows, he just don't ever come to work."

Conn considered that fact. "Look at it this way," he said at last. "Do you *want* him around?" The guy got the job.

Pittsburgh, of course, like everyplace else, has changed . . . only more so. The mills are closed, the skies are clear, and Rand McNally has decreed that it is the very best place to live in the United States. Oakland is just another cawledge town; the warm saloons of Forbes Avenue have become fast-food "outlets." Where Forbes Field once stood is Pitt's Graduate School of Business, and in place of Duquesne Gardens is an apartment house.

It was so different when Conn was growing up. Then it was the best of capitalism, it was the worst of capitalism. The steel came in after the Civil War—Bessemer and his blasts—and then came the immigrants to do the hard, dirty work of making ore into endless rolls of metal. Then the skies were so black with smoke that the office workers had to change their white shirts by lunchtime, and the streetlights seldom went off during the day, emitting an eerie glow that turned downtown Pittsburgh into a stygian nightmare. At the time Conn was a kid, taking up space at Sacred Heart School, H. L. Mencken wrote of Pittsburgh that it was "so dreadfully hideous, so intolerably bleak and forlorn that it reduced the whole aspiration of a man to a macabre and depressing joke."

The people coughed and wheezed, and those who eschewed the respiratory nostrums advertised daily in the newspapers would, instead, repair to the taprooms of Pittsburgh, there to try to cut the grime and soot that had collected in their dusty throats. The Steel City was also known as "the wettest spot in the United States," and even at seven in the morning the bars would be packed three deep, as the night-shift workers headed home in the gloom of another graying dawn, pausing to toss down the favored local boilermaker—a shot of Imperial whiskey chased by an Iron City beer. An Iron and an Imp.

And then another. Can't expect someone to fly on one wing.

Conn's father, Billy, Sr., was such a man. He toiled at Westinghouse for forty years. Eventually, Billy would come to call his old man Westinghouse instead of Dad. But even in the worst of the Depression, Billy Sr., kept his job as a steam fitter, and he was proud of it, and one day he took his oldest boy down to the plant, and he pointed to it and said, "Here's where you're gonna work, son."

Billy, Jr., was aghast. "That scared the shit out of me," he says. Shortly thereafter he began to apprentice as a prizefighter, and when he got to New York and began to charm the press, he could honestly boast that his greatest achievement in life was never having worked a day.

The mills meant work, but it was a cruel living, and even so recently as the time when Conn was growing up, two-thirds of the work force in Pittsburgh was foreign-born. "People think you gotta be nuts to be a fighter," he says now.

Well?

"Yeah, they're right. I *was* nuts. But it beats working in those mills."

The immigrants who were shipped in from Europe to work in the mills mostly stayed with their own—the Galway Irish on the North Side, the Italians in the Bloomfield section, the Poles and Balkans on the South Side, the Irish in 'Sliberty, the Germans on Troy Hill. Harry Greb was German, but his mother was Irish, which mattered at the gate. Promoters liked Irishers. A good little lightweight named Harry Pitler, Jewish boy, brother of Jake Pitler, who would play for the Pirates and later become a Brooklyn Dodger coach, took the Irish handle of Johnny Ray to fight under. Jawnie Ray, one of Erin's own.

Everybody fought some in Pittsburgh. It was a regular activity, like dancing or drinking. It wasn't just that the men were tough and the skies were mean; it was also a way of representing your parish or your people. It wasn't just that Mr. Art Rooney, promoter, or Mr. Jake Mintz, matchmaker, would pit an Irishman against a Jew or a Pole versus an Italian, or bring in a colored boy the white crowds could root against at Duquesne Gardens. No, it was every mother's son scuffling, on the streets or at the bar rail. It was a way of life. It was also cheap entertainment.

Greenfield Jimmy Smith, as we know, enjoyed fighting all his life. So did Billy Conn, Sr., Westinghouse. Nearing 50, he was arrested and fined a five-spot for street-fighting only a few weeks before his son fought for the heavyweight title. Just for kicks, Westinghouse used to fight Billy all the time. When Westinghouse came to New York to watch his boy in the ring one time, Billy told the press, "My old man is a fighting mick. Give him a day or two here, and he'll find some guys to slug it out with."

Billy fought even more with his younger brother Jackie, who was an absolutely terrific street fighter. One time Jimmy Cannon wrote that "if the ring in Madison Square Garden were made of cobblestones," it would be Jackie Conn, not Billy, who would be the champion of the world. A night or so after Cannon's tribute appeared in the paper, Jackie came strolling into Toots Shor's. He was dressed to the nines, as usual. Jackie fancied himself a fashion plate, and he regularly rifled his brother's wardrobe. So Jackie took a prominent seat at the bar, and he was sitting there, accepting compliments and what-have-you from the other patrons, when a stranger came over to him and asked if he was Jackie Conn, the street-fighting champion of the world.

Jackie puffed up and replied that indeed he was, whereupon the stranger coldcocked him, sending Jackie clattering to the floor of Toots Shor's Saloon. "Now I'm the champion," the guy said.

Still, everybody says that Joey Diven was the best street fighter who ever lived. There are stories that he would, for amusement, take on and beat up the entire Pitt football team. Joey is a decade younger than Billy, in his fifties now, working as an assistant to the Allegheny County commissioner. He is a big, red-faced Irishman. That's unusual because most ace street fighters are little guys. Does Billy Martin come to mind? Big guys grow up figuring nobody will challenge them, so they don't learn how to fight. Big guys break up fights. Little guys are the ones who learn to fight because they figure they had better. Billy always told his three sons, "Don't fight on the streets, because you'll only find out who's good when it's too late."

But Joey Diven was good and big. So first the other Irish pretenders in the neighborhood—the champion of this street or that bar—would come by to find him at the Oakland Cafe, where he loafed, and when he was done beating all those comers, the champs from the other neighborhoods would come over and insult him, so as to get into an inter-ethnic fight.

Insults were automatic. People routinely referred to one another, face to face, with the racial epithets we find so offensive today. For fighting, it was the dagos and the Polacks, the micks and the jigs, and so forth. Sticks and stones. Before a fight with Gus Dorazio, when Dorazio was carrying on at the weigh-in about what color trunks he would wear, Conn cut the argument short by snapping, "Listen, dago, all you're going to need is a catcher's mitt and a chest protector." It was late in Conn's career before he took to using a mouthpiece, because, like his hero Greb, he got a kick out of insulting the people he fought.

On the street, stereotypes prevailed all the more. Usually that meant that everybody (your own group included) was dim-witted, everybody else practiced poor hygiene, everybody else's women were sluts, and everybody but the Jews drank too much and had the most fun. Were the Irish the best fighters? Joey Diven says, "Ah, they just stayed drunk more and stayed louder about it."

One time Joey Diven was working as a doorman over at the AOH on Oakland Avenue. The AOH is the Ancient Order of Hibernians. You needed a card to get into the place, which was located on the third floor, or, as Joey explains it, "Up twenty-eight steps if you accidentally fell down them." This particular night, a guy showed up, but he didn't have a card, so Joey told him to take off. "Come on, let me in, I'm Irish," the guy said. Joey said no card, no admittance, and when the guy persisted, Joey threw him down the steps.

Pretty soon there was a knock on the door again. Joey opened it. Same guy. Same thing; no card. "Come on, let me in, I'm Irish." Joey threw him down the steps again.

A few more minutes and another knock. And get this: It was the same guy. What did Joey do? He ushered him in, and said, "You're right. You must be Irish."

What made Joey Diven such a good street fighter was that he held no illusions. Poor Jackie Conn (who is dead now) was different. He thought he could be as good as his brother in the prize ring. Jackie was on the undercard a night in '39 when Billy defended against Gus Lesnevich, but the kid brother lost a four-rounder. The failure ate him up so, he came apart afterward in the locker room. Just before Billy went off to fight Lesnevich, he had to soothe Jackie and make sure the brother would be taken to the hospital and sedated. Diven was different. "Ah, I didn't ever have the killer instinct like Billy in the ring," he says. "You see, even though Billy's such a God-fearing man, he could be ruthless in the ring. That's why Billy was so good."

Still, Joey will razz Billy good. For example, he says that Conn always was a rotten drinker—"Three drinks, and he's talking about the Blessed Mother or Thomas Aquinas." He also kids Conn that, when he travels, he still sleeps with all his valuables tucked into his pillowcase. Once when they were staying together in Vegas, Billy got up in the middle of the night to take a leak, and Joey was awakened by the sound of change rattling in the pillow-case. Billy was taking his nickels and dimes with him to the bathroom.

"Hey, Billy," Joey said. "You didn't have to take the pillow to the toi-let. There's nobody here."

Conn stopped. *"You're* here," he said.

Joey had a lot of fun with Billy. They had a lot of fun street-fighting. It wasn't ever vicious. In those days, nobody ever drew guns or knives or even clubs. Nobody was loco with drugs. You could do all the same stuff Billy did in the ring—gouging and biting and that type of thing, plus the friendly name-calling—all the things that made up what used to be known as *a fair fight.* "No booting, though," says Joey.

"And it never took more than four or five minutes. Somebody would get in one good shot, and that would wear you out pretty quick, and after that there'd be a lot of mauling and rassling, and then it was history." It wasn't at all like in the movies, where the fights go on forever no matter how many times people get clobbered. "As soon as a guy said he'd had enough, that was it. No more," Joey says. That was the code. "Then you'd go back into the joint together and buy each other a drink, maybe even end up getting fractured together." An Iron and an Imp, twice. Do this again for both of us. One more time.

That was the sort of environment young Billy grew up in in 'Slib-erty—scrapping with everyone in the neighborhood, running errands for the bootleggers over on Station Street, filching pastries from the bakery wagon to put a little something extra on the family table. There were four younger brothers and sisters. To help make ends meet, Billy's father didn't altogether shy away from working with the bootleggers; the authorities estimated there were 10,000 stills in the Pittsburgh area during Prohibition. Westinghouse some-times brewed beer in the family bathtub. For Mrs. Conn, the former Mar-guerite McFarland, the most devout of Catholic women, this made it nearly impossible to ensure that cleanliness would take its assigned runner-up spot to godliness. "Be patient, woman, the beer'll be ready in a few days," Westing-house would chide his wife as she fretted over her dirty-necked tykes.

Billy adored his mother. He was the one who named her Maggie, and it was that—not Mother or Mom—he called her as he grew older. He al-ways gives nicknames to the people he loves the most. Maggie had come over in steerage from County Cork when she was a young girl, and she never did lose all of her brogue. She grew plump, but with her magnificent skin and blue eyes in a beautiful face framed by black hair, she was a colleen to the day she died. She lavished all that she could upon her oldest, and she was not frightened when he told her he wanted to be a boxer. She knew how hard it was in the mills, and when Westinghouse gave the boy gloves one Christmas, Maggie made him some fine, Celtic green trunks.

Billy Conn leans back in his chair in the club cellar and takes a deep drag on his cigarette, and this is what he says: "Your mother should be your best friend."

Maggie's boy did have one other talent besides boxing and loafing, and that was art. He could draw, and if he were growing up in Pittsburgh today, when Irish boys stay in school and don't lace on gloves, no doubt he would become an artist or a draftsman of some sort. But he never pursued drawing, never even played team sports. His children—Timmy, Billy, Susan, and Mike—all had to learn games from their granddad Greenfield Jimmy, and they still like to laugh at their old man, the former champion of the world, because he throws like a girl.

He stayed two years in the eighth grade at Sacred Heart before one of the sisters suggested that he give up his seat to someone who might use it to greater advantage. He departed school then, but it didn't matter because already, as he puts it, "I was going to cawledge at Jawnie Ray's." That was in 'Sliberty. Ray had retired from fighting, but he ran a gym so he could keep himself in bootleg whiskey. It came in milk bottles and cost 15 cents a pint.

The first time Billy ventured into the gym, Ray was amazed at how tiny and smooth the boy's face was. And Billy couldn't have weighed more than 80, maybe 85, pounds. But Jawnie let him audition in the ring, and he saw the instincts and the courage right off. So he let Billy work around the gym, tidying the place up, fetching him his booze, earning the occasional chance to spar.

One day a bunch of older neighborhood toughs confronted Billy as he came back to the gym toting a pint of moonshine. "What are you, a messenger boy for the rummy?" one of them said, and they jostled and taunted Billy.

He pulled himself up as tall as he could, and he hollered back, "You bums! Someday, I'm gonna be a champeen!"

They laughed, and he went on inside and gave Ray the moonshine. Billy came to call him Moonie for his addiction, and Moonie called him Junior. "All right now, Junior," Moonie would say, swilling the rotgut, "keep your hands up and punch straight." This was the shell defense Jawnie Ray taught. "Moonie was quiet, but he was a Michelangelo as a teacher. Hell, I didn't know he drank until one day I saw him sober. You know how it is—no Jews drink. I get the one who does. Only I tell you one thing, Jawnie Ray knew more about bawxing drunk than anybody else did sober."

Conn stayed with Ray in the gym three years but never was allowed to engage in an official fight. That was because Ray didn't believe in amateur fisticuffs. If you were going to chance being busted in the kisser, then you should make a dawler off it. Also, what could you learn from some amateur? During one period in the late thirties and early forties, the Pittsburgh area gave the world five champions, and Conn got to practice against a lot of talent in the gym. When Joe Louis came to town to fight Hans Birkie, Conn made a buck holding the spit box for the Brown Bomber. It was the first time he ever saw the man with whom he would be linked forever in boxing history.

Finally, when he was 17 years old, Ray drove him down to Fairmont, West Virginia, where he went four rounds against an experienced 24-year-old named Dick Woodwer. There were probably 300 fans at the armory, and Woodwer outpointed the novice. Conn's share was $2.50.

Ray gave him four bits. "Hey, Moon, what is this?" Billy said. "I get two and a half."

"We gotta eat," Ray said.

"Yeah, but how come we're both eating out of my share?"

"You were the one who lost," said Ray.

They never had a contract, but no other man ever managed Billy Conn. He even told the mob to back off when it tried to muscle in.

In the beginning, Ray had Billy fighting somebody somewhere every two weeks or so. Fairmont, Charleston, Wheeling, Johnstown. It was nickel hamburgers, 15-cent moonshine, and 16-cent-a-gallon gas that kept them going. "You tell kids that nowadays, they're sure you ran into too many of Joe Louis' blows," Billy says. And nowadays it's not just the prices that are different. A prospect is brought along against handpicked roundheels on Sunday afternoon TV. After ten bouts everybody gets to fight for the championship of something or other. Conn was barely out of West Virginia after ten fights, and even after fourteen he was hardly .500; then he had to win or draw thirteen in a row before he was allowed a ten-rounder. It was against Honeyboy Jones.

But he was learning. Always, he learned. Even when he fought for championships, he seldom won any of the early rounds. "They don't matter," he says. They counted, but they didn't matter, because that was the time you picked up the other guy's style. And Ray put him in against everybody, every style.

Near the end of 1936, when Conn was still only 18, Ray threw the boy in against the older Fritzie Zivic. "He put an awful face on me," Billy says, and he still honors Zivic, a Pittsburgh guy, by calling him the dirtiest fighter he ever met. But Billy outpointed Zivic and moved out of the welter-weight.

A few months later, he won his twenty-third in a row over a red-haired black powerhouse named Oscar Rankins, who knocked Billy down in the eighth with such a stiff blow that, says Conn, "I didn't know I'd won till I read it the next day in the paper." Years later, when Joe Louis heard that Conn had fought Rankins, he said to Billy, "The people who managed you must not have liked you very much. Nobody would let *me* fight that sonuvabitch."

Conn's favorite photograph in the club cellar is a wirephoto of him-self bandaged and stitched after he won the rematch with Freddie Apostoli. The headline reads: IF THIS IS THE WINNER, WHAT DOES THE LOSER LOOK LIKE? Conn howls at that, and to this day he speaks with greatest affection about the fighters who did him the most damage.

Damn, it was fun. After he beat Zivic and made big money, $2,180, Conn bought himself a brand new Chevy for $600. When he whipped Bet-tina for the title, he said, "Gee, I'm champion. Now I can eat regular." Then he went back home to Pittsburgh and out to 'Sliberty. "I hadn't been around the corner for a long time," he says. But now he made a point of going back, and he found the guys who had ridiculed him when he had just been starting out, running errands for Jawnie Ray. They were loafing in a bar. "Remember the messenger boy you laughed at?" he asked, and they nodded, cowering. Billy brought his hands up fast, and they ducked away, but all he did was lay a lot of big bills on the hardwood. "Well, all right," Billy said, "stay drunk a long time on the light-heavyweight champeen of the world."

He bought Maggie anything she wanted. He gave her champagne, the real stuff. She loved champagne. He bought presents for his younger brothers and sisters, and for the dames he found and who found him. He was even interviewed by a New York fashion editor on the subject of how a woman should be turned out.

"I guess these women's fashions are O.K.," Conn declared. "That is, except those dizzy hats and the shoes some of them wear. . . . I wouldn't wear a boxing glove for a hat, but some girls do. . . . Plaid dresses are pips. I think plaid looks swell on any woman, and I like any color as long as it's red. . . . Some evening dresses are pretty nice, if they're lacy and frilly and with swoopy skirts. But most girls look too much like China dolls when they're dressed in evening dresses. But what the hell! They're going to dress up the slightest chance you give 'em. And I'm for giving 'em every chance."

"We're just a bunch of plain, ordinary bums having a good time," Jawnie Ray explained. He and Billy would scream at each other and carry on constantly. "I'm glad we ain't got a contract, you dumb mick sonuvabitch," Jawnie would holler, "because maybe I'll get lucky and somebody even dumber than you will steal you from me." "Yeah, you rummy Jew bastard," Billy would coo back. It was like that, right to the end. The last time Billy saw him, Jawnie was at death's door in the hospital, and Joey Diven and Billy were visiting him.

"C'mon you guys, sneak me outta here for some drinks," Jawnie Ray pleaded from the hospital bed.

"Moonie," Billy replied, "the only way you're gettin' outta this place is with a tag tied on your big toe."

Sometimes Westinghouse joined the traveling party, too, and on one occasion, coming back from Erie, he and Jawnie Ray got into a first-class fight. As Conn described it in a contemporary account, "My old man swung, Jawnie swung. When it was finished, Pop had a broken nose and Jawnie had lost a tooth. That made them pals."

Yes, sir, it was a barrelful of monkeys. They all loved to throw water on one another, too, and to play practical jokes with the telephone and whatnot. Eventually, when Jackie had grown up enough to come on board, it made it even more fun because then Billy had a partner to scuffle with. Billy would always go after Jackie when he caught him wearing his cloths. One time Billy was voted Best-Dressed Sportsman of the Year, so, Billy chuckled, that must have made Jackie the Second-Best-Dressed Sportsman of the Year.

The day before Conn defended his crown in Forbes Field against Bettina in September of '39, Billy found out that Jackie had been joyriding with his pals in Billy's new black Cadillac, so he put out a $300 bounty on his brother, and when he caught up with him he thrashed him bare-knuckled in the garage. "OK, get it over," Jackie said when he had positively had enough, and he laid out his chin for Billy to paste him square on it. Billy popped him a right, and Jackie was sliding down the wall clear across the garage when Jawnie Ray and Uncle Mike Jacobs and the cops burst in, all of them in disbelief that Billy would get into a fraternal dustup right before a championship fight. They were much relieved to discover that the blood all over Billy was only Jackie's.

Billy wiped himself clean and outpointed Bettina in fifteen. He was the toast of Pittsburgh and the world, as well. The *New York Daily News* rhapsodized: "The Irishman is indeed a beauteous boxer who could probably collect coinage by joining the ballet league if he chose to flee the egg-eared and flattened-nose fraternity." When Conn fought in New York, Owney McManus, who ran a saloon in Pittsburgh, would charter trains, and hundreds of the Irish faithful would follow Conn to Gotham—the Ham and Cabbage Special, they called it—and loaf on Broadway, even if it meant that maybe when they went back to the mills in Pittsburgh they'd be handed a DCM.

A DCM is a Don't Come Monday, the pink slip.

When Conn fought in Oakland, at the Gardens, the streetcars would disgorge fans from all over the Steel City. Pittsburgh's streetcar lines were almost all laid out east-west, except for one, which ran north from the mills along the river. It was called the Flying Fraction because it was number 77/54—a combination of two east-west lines, the 77 and the 54—and it went right past both the Gardens and Forbes Field. Three rides to a quarter, and if you were getting off for the fights you got a transfer anyhow and sold it for a nickel to the people waiting, so they could save 3 cents on their ride home.

Photos of Conn went up in all the bars where those of Greb and Zivic were to be seen, and in a lot of other places where the Irish wanted strictly their own hero. And now that Billy had grown into a light heavyweight and had beaten all of them, it seemed like the only one left for him to fight was the heavyweight champion, the Brown Bomber himself. There wasn't anybody Irish in the country who wasn't looking forward to that. And by this point, there probably wasn't anybody Irish in Pittsburgh who hadn't seen Billy Conn fight, except for Mary Louise Smith.

"I've never seen a prizefight in my life," she said just the other day. Mary Louise just never cared very much for Billy's business, even when he was earning a living at it.

"You didn't miss anything," Billy replied.

But even if she hadn't seen him work, she was in love with him. She had fallen in love with the boxer. He gave her a nickname, too: Matt—for the way her hair became matted on her brow when she went swimming down the Jersey shore. She was still only a kid, still at Our Lady of Mercy, but she had become even more beautiful than she had been at that first dinner, and the sheltered life Greenfield Jimmy had imposed upon her was backfiring some. Billy had the lure of forbidden fruit. "I was mature for my age," Mary

Louise says, "something of a spitfire. And I guess you'd have to say that when my father didn't want me to see Billy, I turned out to be a good prevaricator, too." She sighs. "Billy just appealed to me so."

"Ah, I told her a lot of lies," he says.

They would sneak off, mostly for dinners, usually at out-of-town roadhouses, hideaways where they could be alone, intimate in their fashion, staring into each other's blue eyes. It was so very innocent. He was always in training, and she was too young to drink, and kisses are what they shared. That and their song, "A Pretty Girl Is Like a Melody." Well, Billy made it their song, and he would request it from the big band on Saturdays when they would get all gussied up and go dancing downtown at the William Penn Hotel, which was the fanciest spot in Pittsburgh. And he was the champion of the world, and she was the prettiest girl, dressed all *lacy and frilly and with swoopy skirts.*

Even if Greenfield Jimmy didn't know the half of it, he could sense that it was getting out of hand. Mary Louise played Jo in *Little Women* at Our Lady of Mercy, and he liked that; he wanted her to be an actress, to be something, to move up. He liked Billy, he really did, and he thought he was as good a boxer as he had ever seen, but he didn't want his daughter, his firstborn, marrying a pug. So Greenfield Jimmy sent Mary Louise to Philadelphia, to a classy, cloistered college called Rosemont, and he told the mother superior never to let his daughter see the likes of Mr. Billy Conn.

So Billy had to be content sending letters and presents. When he came into Philly for a fight, he had twenty ringside tickets delivered to Rosemont so that Mary Louise could bring her friends. The mother superior wouldn't let any of the young ladies go, though, and when Billy climbed into the ring and looked down and saw empty seats, he was crestfallen. His opponent that night was Gus Dorazio, and despite Billy's lipping off at the weigh-in, Billy was even slower than usual to warm up, and the fight went eight rounds before Billy won on a KO.

Greenfield Jimmy was pleased to learn about these events and that Mary Louise was going out with nice young men from the Main Line, who went to St. Joseph's and Villanova, who called for her properly and addressed her as Mary Louise, and not anything common like Matt. Greenfield Jimmy sent her off to Nassau for spring vacation with a bunch of her girlfriends, demure young ladies all.

As for Billy, he went into the heavies, going after Louis. "We're in this racket to make money," Jawnie Ray said. Billy had some now. He rented

Maggie and the family a house on Fifth Avenue, an address that means as much in Pittsburgh as it does in New York. One of the Mellons had a mansion on Fifth with sixty-five rooms and eleven baths. "The days of no money are over, Maggie," Billy told his mother. She said fine, but she didn't know anybody on Fifth Avenue. Couldn't he find something in 'Sliberty? "Bring your friends over every day," Billy told her.

Maggie was 40 that summer, a young woman with a son who was a renowned champion of the world. But she began to feel a little poorly and went for some tests. The results were not good. Not at all. So now, even if Billy Conn was a champion, what did it mean? Of the two women he loved, one he almost never got to hold, and now the other was dying of cancer.

Conn's first fight against a heavyweight was with Bob Pastor in September of 1940. Pastor irritated him. "I hit him low one time," Billy recalls. "All right, all right. But he just kept on bitching. So now, I'm *really* gonna hit him low. You know, you were supposed to do everything to win." He knocked Pastor out in thirteen, then he outpointed Al McCoy in ten and Lee Savold in twelve, even after Savold busted his nose in the eighth.

All too often now, though, Conn wasn't himself. He couldn't get to see Mary Louise, and worse, Maggie was becoming sicker and weaker, and almost every cent he made in the ring went to pay for the treatment and the doctors and the round-the-clock nurses he ordered. "His mother's illness has Billy near crazy at times," Jawnie Ray explained after one especially lackluster bout. Between fights Billy would head back to Pittsburgh and slip up to see Maggie, and, against doctor's orders, he would bring her champagne, the finest, and the two of them would sit there on an afternoon, best friends, and get quietly smashed together. They were the happiest moments Maggie had left.

June 18, 1941, was the night set for the Louis fight at the Polo Grounds, and Uncle Mike Jacobs began to beat the biggest drums for Conn, even as Louis kept trooping the land, beating up on what became known as the Bums-of-the-Month. Incredibly, 27,000 people—most of them coming off the Flying Fraction—showed up at Forbes Field to watch Conn's final tune-up in May, against a nobody named Buddy Knox.

Everywhere, the world was swirling, and that seemed to make even everyday events larger and better and more full of ardor. Even if Americans didn't know what lay ahead, even if they told themselves it couldn't happen here, that foreign wars wouldn't engage us, there may have been deeper and truer instincts that inspired and drove them as the year of 1941 rushed on. It was the last summer that a boy hit .400. It was the only summer that anyone hit safely in fifty-six straight games. A great beast named Whirlaway, whipped by Eddie Arcaro, the little genius they called Banana Nose, ran a Derby so fast that the record would stand for more than twenty years, and he finished up with the Triple Crown in June. That was when the Irishman and the Brown Bomber were poised to do battle in what might have been the most wonderful heavyweight final there ever was. And all this as the Nazis began their move toward Russia and Yamamoto was okaying the attack on Pearl Harbor.

The pace was quickening. Mary Louise was as impetuous now as the boy she loved. It couldn't go on this way anymore. On May 28, a couple of days after he beat Knox, Billy drove her to Brookville, way north out of Pittsburgh, and took out a marriage license. DiMaggio got a triple in Washington that day, at Griffith Stadium, to raise his streak to thirteen. Mary Louise was 18 now, and Greenfield Jimmy couldn't change her plans any more than he could her heart, but she and Billy were good Catholic kids, and they wanted to be married in the Church, and that meant the banns had to be posted.

So Greenfield Jimmy heard, and he fulminated, "I'm just trying to raise a decent family, and I know where these boxers end up." He said he would punch Billy's lights out, and Westinghouse said he would rattle Greenfield Jimmy's cage first. Greenfield Jimmy went directly to the rectory where the bishop lived in Pittsburgh. He banged on the door and said there had better not be any priest anywhere in Pennsylvania who would marry his flesh and blood to the pug.

It worked, too. The next Saturday, Billy left his training camp and went to a nearby parish named St. Philomena's. He and Mary Louise had someone who had promised to marry them at the altar by 9:30 A.M., and an exited crowd had gathered. But the priests wouldn't buck Greenfield Jimmy, and, after a couple of hours of bickering, somebody came out and told the people there wouldn't be any June wedding this day.

Billy went back to prepare to fight the heavyweight champion. DiMaggio got three singles against the Brownies that afternoon.

The next time Billy left camp, a few days before the bout, he flew to Pittsburgh to see his mother. He probably didn't realize how close to the end she was, because she kept the news from him. "Listen, I've got to live a little longer," Maggie told everyone else in the family. "I can't worry Billy."

He couldn't bring her champagne this time. Instead, he brought her a beautiful diamond bracelet, and he gave it to her. "Maggie," he said, "this is for you." She was so sick, so weak, so in pain that she could barely work up a smile, but she thanked him the best she could. And then she pushed it back.

"Oh, it's so beautiful, Billy," she said. "But don't give it to me. Give it to Mary Louise." And Maggie told him then that he was to marry her, no matter what Greenfield Jimmy said, because he was her boy and a good boy and as good as any boy, and because he loved Mary Louise more than anyone else in the world.

Billy nodded. He kept his hand wrapped around the bracelet. He couldn't stay much longer. Just these few minutes had tired Maggie so. He kissed her and got ready to leave. "Maggie," Billy said, "I gotta go now, but the next time you see me, I'll be the heavyweight champion of the world."

Maggie smiled one more time. "No, son," she said, "the next time I see you will be in Paradise."

Tuesday, the seventeenth, the day before the fight, DiMaggio made it an even thirty in a row, going 1 for 4 against the Chisox across the river in the Bronx. That night, Billy slept hardly at all. And he always slept. Sometimes he would even lie down in the locker room while the undercard bouts were being fought and doze right off just minutes before he had to go into the ring. But this whole night he barely got forty winks. And he wasn't even worrying about getting in the ring with Joe Louis. He was worrying about Maggie and Matt.

At the weigh-in the next morning Louis, who had trained down because of Conn's speed, came in at 200. Conn tipped 169. That made Uncle Mike a bit nervous. It was already 17 to 5 for the champion in the betting, and this weight spread was making the bout look like homicide. Uncle Mike announced Conn's weight at a more cosmetic 174 and Louis at $199\frac{1}{2}$.

Conn went back to his hotel to rest, but the Ham and Cabbage Special had just got in, and all the fans, wearing leprechaun hats and carrying paper shamrocks and clay pipes, came over to see him, and when a bunch of them barged right into his room, Billy went outside and loafed with them.

Finally, Jawnie got him back to his room, but who should come storming in, wearing a zoot suit and smoking a big cigar, but Jackie. Naturally, he and Billy started wrestling each other all over the suite, driving the trainer, Freddie Fierro, nuts. People can get hurt wrestling. At last Fierro was able to separate them, but Billy still couldn't sleep, so he looked in on Jackie and saw him snoring with his mouth open. He called down to room service, ordered a seltzer bottle, and squirted it right into Jackie's mouth. You can bet that woke Jackie up.

Jackie chased Billy into the hall. Billy was laughing, and he wasn't wearing anything but his shorts. That was how Billy spent the day getting ready for the Brown Bomber. Just a few miles away, at the Stadium, DiMaggio went 1 for 3 to stretch it to thirty-one.

Back in Pittsburgh the Pirates had scheduled one of their few night games for this evening, June 18. They knew everybody wanted to stay home to listen to the fight on the radio, so the Pirates announced that when the fight began, the game would be suspended and the radio broadcast would go out over the PA. Baseball came to a halt. Most of America did. Maybe the only person not listening was Maggie. She was so sick the doctors wouldn't let her.

Billy crossed himself when he climbed into the ring that night.

And then the Pirates stopped, and America stopped, and the fight began, Louis's eighteenth defense, his seventh in seven months.

Conn started slower than even he was accustomed to. Louis, the slugger, was the one who moved better. Conn ducked a long right so awkwardly that he slipped and fell to one knee. The second round was worse, Louis pummeling Conn's body, trying to wear the smaller man down. He had thirty pounds on him, after all. Unless you knew the first rounds didn't matter, it was a rout. This month's bum.

In his corner, Conn sat down, spit, and said, "All right, Moon, here we go." He came out faster, bicycled for a while, feinted with a left, and drove home a hard right. By the end of the round he was grinning at the champ, and he winked to Jawnie Ray when he returned to the corner. The spectators were up on their feet, especially the ones who had bet Conn.

The fourth was even more of a revelation, for now Conn chose to slug a little with the slugger, and he came away the better for the exchange. When the bell rang, he was flat out laughing as he came back to his corner. "This is a cinch," he told Jawnie.

But Louis got back on track in the fifth, and the fight went his way for the next two rounds as blood flowed from a nasty cut over the challenger's right eye. At Forbes Field in Pittsburgh the crowd grew still, and relatives and friends listening downstairs from where Maggie lay worried that Billy's downfall was near.

But Conn regained command in the eighth, moving back and away from Louis's left, then ripping into the body or the head. The ninth was all the more Conn, and he grew cocky again. "Joe, I got you," he popped off as he flicked a good one square on the champ's mouth, and then, as Billy strode back to his corner at the bell, he said, "Joe, you're in a fight tonight."

"I knows it," Louis replied, confused and clearly troubled now.

The tenth was something of a lull for Conn, but it was a strategic respite. During the eleventh, Conn worked Louis high and low, hurt the champ, building to the crescendo of the twelfth, when the *New York Herald Tribune* reported in the casual racial vernacular of the time that Conn "rained left hooks on Joe's dusky face." He was a clear winner in this round, which put him up 7–5 on one card and 7–4–1 on another; the third was 6–6. To cap off his best round, Conn scored with a crushing left that would have done in any man who didn't outweigh him by thirty pounds. And it certainly rattled the crown of the world's heavyweight champion. The crowd was gong berserk. Even Maggie was given the report that her Billy was on the verge of taking the title.

Only later would Conn realize the irony of striking that last great blow. "I miss that, I beat him," he says. It was that simple. He was nine minutes from victory, and now he couldn't wait. "He wanted to finish the thing as Irishmen love to," the *Herald Tribune* wrote.

Louis was slumped in his corner. Jack Blackburn, his trainer, shook his head and rubbed him hard. "Chappie," he said, using his nickname for the champ, "you're *losing*. You gotta knock him out." Louis didn't have to be told. Everyone understood. Everyone in the Polo Grounds. Everyone listening through the magic of radio. Everyone. There was bedlam. It was wonderful. Men had been slugging it out for eons, and there had been 220 years of prizefighting, and there would yet be Marciano and the two Sugar Rays and Ali, but this was it. This was the best it had ever been and ever would be, the twelfth and thirteenth rounds of Louis and Conn on a warm night in New York just before the world went to hell. The people were standing and cheering for Conn, but it was really for the sport and for the moment and for themselves that they cheered. They could be a part of it, and every now and then, for an instant, *that* is it, and it can't ever get any better. This was such a time in the history of games.

Only Billy Conn could see clearly—the trouble was, what he saw was different from what everybody else saw. What he saw was himself walking with Mary Louise on the boardwalk at Atlantic City, down the shore, and they were the handsomest couple who ever lived, and people were staring, and he could hear what they were saying. What they were saying was: "There goes Billy Conn with his bride. He just beat Joe Louis." And he didn't want to hear just that. What he wanted to hear was: "There goes Billy Conn with his bride. He's the guy who just *knocked out* Joe Louis." Not for himself: That was what Mary Louise deserved.

Billy had a big smile on his face. "This is easy, Moonie," he said. "I can take this sonovabitch out this round."

Jawnie blanched. "No, no, Billy," he said. "Stick and run. You got the fight won. Stay away, kiddo. Just stick and run, stick and run. . . ." There was the bell for the thirteenth.

And then it happened. Billy tried to bust the champ, but it was Louis who got through the defenses, and then he pasted a monster right on the challenger's jaw. "Fall! Fall!" Billy said to himself. He knew if he could just go down, clear his head, he would lose the round, but he could still save the day. "But for some reason, I couldn't fall. I kept saying, 'Fall, fall,' but there I was, still standing up. So Joe hit me again and again, and when I finally did fall, it was a slow, funny fall. I remember that." Billy lay flush out on the canvas. There were two seconds left in the round, 2:58 of the thirteenth, when he was counted out. *The winnah and still champeen. . . .*

"It was nationality that cost Conn the title," the *Herald Tribune* wrote. "He wound up on his wounded left side, trying to make Irish legs answer an Irish brain."

On the radio, Billy said, "I just want to tell my mother I'm all right."

Back in the locker room, Jawnie Ray said not to cry because bawxers don't cry. And Billy delivered the classic: "What's the sense of being Irish if you can't be dumb?"

Maggie lasted a few more days. "She held on to see me leading Joe Louis in the stretch," Billy says.

He and Mary Louise got married the day after the funeral. The last time they had met with Greenfield Jimmy, he said that Billy had to "prove he could be a gentleman," but what did a father-in-law's blessing matter anymore after the twelfth and thirteenth rounds and after Maggie's going?

They found a priest in Philly, a Father Schwindlein, and he didn't care from Greenfield Jimmy or the bishop or whoever. As Mary Louise says, "He just saw two young people very much in love." They had a friend with them who was the best man, and the cleaning lady at the church stood in as the maid of honor. DiMaggio got up to forty-five that day in Fenway, going 2 for 4 and then 1 for 3 in a twin bill. Greenfield Jimmy alerted the state police and all the newspapers when he heard what was going on, but Billy and Mary Louise were on their honeymoon in Jersey, man and wife, by the time anybody caught up with them.

"They're more in love than ever today, forty-four years later," Michael Conn says. He is their youngest child. The Conns raised three boys and a girl at the house they bought that summer in Squirrel Hill.

That was it, really. DiMaggio's streak ended the night of July 17 in Cleveland. Churchill and Roosevelt signed the Atlantic Charter four weeks later, and on November 26 the first subs pulled away from Japan on the long haul to Pearl Harbor. By then Billy was shooting a movie. It was called *The Pittsburgh Kid,* and in it he played (in an inspired bit of casting) an Irish fighter from the Steel City. Mary Louise was so pretty the producers wanted at least to give her a bit part as a cigarette girl, but she was too bashful, and Billy wasn't crazy about the idea himself. Billy did so well that the moguls asked him to stay around and star in the life story of Gentleman Jim Corbett, but the house in Squirrel Hill was calling. And Mary Louise was pregnant. "We were just a couple of naive young kids from Pittsburgh, and we didn't like Hawllywood," she says.

Joey Diven says that if Billy doesn't care for somebody a whole lot, he'll have them over to the house, take them down to the club cellar, and make them watch *The Pittsburgh Kid.*

After Pearl Harbor, Conn fought three more times. Nobody knew it then, but he was done. Everything ended when he hit Louis that last big left. The best he beat after that was Tony Zale, but even the fans in the Garden booed his effort, and he only outpointed the middleweight. It didn't matter, though, because all anybody cared about was a rematch with Louis—even if both fighters were going into the service.

The return was in the works for the summer, a year after the first meeting. It was looked upon as a great morale builder and diversion for a rattled America. The victories at Midway and Guadalcanal were yet to come.

Then, in the middle of May, Private First Class Conn got a three-day pass to come home to the christening of his firstborn, Timmy. Art Rooney was the godfather, and he thought it would be the right time to patch things up between Greenfield Jimmy and his son-in-law; and so he and Milton Jaffe, Conn's business adviser, arranged a christening party at Smith's house and they told Billy that his father-in-law was ready to smoke the peace pipe.

On Sunday, at the party, Greenfield Jimmy and Conn were in the kitchen with some of the other guests. That is where people often congregated in those days, the kitchen. Billy was sitting up on the stove, his legs dangling, when it started. "My father liked to argue," Mary Louise says, "but you can't drag Billy into an argument." Greenfield Jimmy gave it his best, though. Art Rooney says, "He was always the boss, telling Conn that if he was going to be married to his daughter and be the father of his grandson, he damn sight better attend church more regularly. Then, for good measure, he also told Billy he could beat him up. Finally, Greenfield Jimmy said too much.

"I can still see Billy come off that stove," Rooney says.

Just because it was family, Billy didn't hold back. He went after his father-in-law with his best, a left hook, but he was mad, he had his Irish up, and the little guy ducked like he was getting away from a brushback pitch, and Conn caught him square on the top of his skull. As soon as he did it, Billy knew he had broken his hand. He had hurt himself worse against his own father-in-law than he ever had against any bona fide professional in the prize ring.

Not only that, but when the big guys and everybody rushed in to break it up, Milton Jaffe fractured an ankle and Mary Louise got herself all cut and bruised. Greenfield Jimmy took advantage of the diversion to inflict on Conn additional scratches and welts—around the neck, wrists, and eyes. Billy was so furious about blowing the rematch with Louis that he busted a window with his good hand on the way out and cut himself more. The *New York Times,* ever understated, described Conn's appearance the next day "as if he had tangled with a half-dozen alley cats."

Greenfield Jimmy didn't have a single mark on him.

Years later, whenever Louis saw Conn, he would usually begin, "Is your old father-in-law still beating the shit out of you?"

In June, Secretary of War Henry Stimson announced there would be no more public commercial appearances for Louis, and the champ began a series of morale-boosting tours. The fight at the christening had cost Louis and Conn hundreds of thousands of dollars and, it turned out, any real chance Conn had for victory. Every day the war dragged on diminished his skills.

The legs go first.

Conn was overseas in Europe for much of the war, pulling punches in exhibition matches against regimental champs. One time, the plane he was on developed engine trouble over France, and Billy told God he would do two things if the plane landed safely.

It did, and he did. Number one, he gave $5,000 to Dan Rooney, Art's brother, who was a missionary in the Far East. And number two, he gave $5,000 to Sacred Heart, his old parish in 'Sliberty, to build a statue of the Blessed Virgin. It is still there, standing prominently by the entrance.

Conn was with Bob Hope at Nuremberg when V-E day came. There is a picture of that in the club cellar.

Then he came home and patched up with Greenfield Jimmy and prepared for the long-awaited rematch with Louis. It was on June 19, 1946, and such was the excitement that, for the first time, ringside seats went for $100, and a $2 million gate was realized. This was the fight—not the first one—when Louis observed, "He can run, but he can't hide." And Joe was absolutely right. Mercifully, the champion ended the slaughter in the eighth. In the locker room Conn himself called it a "stinkeroo," and it was Jawnie Ray who cried, because, he said, "Billy's finished."

As Conn would tell his kids, boxing is bad unless you happen to be very, very good at it. It's not like other sports, where you can get by. If you're not very, very good, you can get killed or made over into a vegetable or what-have-you. Now Billy Conn, he had been very, very good. Almost one-third of his seventy-five fights had been against champions of the worlds, and he had beaten all those guys except Louis, and that was as good a fight as there ever was. Some people still say there never has been a better fighter, a stylist, than Sweet William, the Flower of the Monongahela. But, of course, all anybody remembers is the fight that warm June night in the year of '41 and especially that one round, the thirteenth.

One time, a few years ago, Art Rooney brought the boxer into the Steelers' locker room and introduced him around to a bunch of white players standing there. They obviously didn't have the foggiest idea who Billy Conn was. Conn saw some black players across the way. "Hey, blackies, you know who Joe Louis was?" They all looked up at the stranger and nodded. Conn turned back to the whites and shook his head. "And you sonsofbitches don't know me," he said.

But really he didn't care. "Everything works out for the best," he says in the club cellar. "I believe that." He's very content. They can't ever get him to go to sports dinners so they can give him awards and stuff. "Ah, I just like being another bum here," he says. "I just loaf around, on the corner, different places." Then Mary Louise comes around, and he falls into line. He never moved around much, Billy Conn. Same town, same house, same wife, same manager, same fun. "All the guys who know me are dead now, but, let me tell you, if I drop dead tomorrow, I didn't miss anything."

He's standing over by the photograph of Louis and him, right after their first fight. He still adores Louis, they became fast friends, and he loves to tell stories about Louis and money. Some guys have problems with money. Some guys have, say, problems with fathers-in-law. Nobody gets off scot-free. Anyway, in the picture Louis has a towel wrapped around a puzzled, mournful countenance. Conn, next to him, is smiling to beat the band. He was the loser?

Billy says, "I told Joe later, 'Hey, Joe, why didn't you just let me have the title for six months?' All I ever wanted was to be able to go around the corner where the guys are loafing and say, 'Hey, I'm the heavyweight champeen of the world.'

"And you know what Joe said back to me? He said, 'I let you have it for twelve rounds, and you couldn't keep it. How could I let you have it for six months?'"

A few years ago Louis came to Pittsburgh, and he and Conn made an appearance together at a union hall. Roy McHugh, the columnist for the *Pittsburgh Press,* was there. Billy brought the film of the '41 fight over from Squirrel Hill in a shopping bag. As soon as the fight started, Louis left the room and went into the bar to drink brandy. Every now and then Louis would come to the door and holler out, "Hey, Billy, have we got to the thirteenth yet?" Conn just laughed and watched himself punch the bigger man around, until finally, when they did come to the thirteenth, Joe called out, "Good-bye, Billy."

Louis knocked out Conn at 2:58, just like always, but when the lights went on, Billy wasn't there. He had left when the thirteenth round started. He had gone into another room, to where the buffet was, after he had watched the twelve rounds when he was the heavyweight champeen of the world, back in that last indelible summer when America dared yet dream that it could run and hide from the world, when the handsomest boy loved the prettiest girl, when streetcars still clanged and fistfights were fun, and the smoke hung low when Maggie went off to Paradise.

The Fight: Patterson vs. Liston

JAMES BALDWIN

When novelist *(Go Tell It On the Mountain, Another Country, Giovanni's Room)* and essayist *(Nobody Knows My Name, The Fire Next Time)* James Baldwin (1924–1987) was asked by *Nugget* magazine to weigh in on the first Liston-Patterson fight, he had never written about sports before. It didn't matter. What Baldwin may not have known about sports in general—or boxing in particular—he more than made up for with what he knew about character, conflict, drama, and race.

🥊　🥊　🥊　🥊

We, the writers—a word I am using in its most primitive sense—arrived in Chicago about ten days before the baffling, bruising, an unbelievable two minutes and six seconds at Comiskey Park. We will get to all that later. I know nothing whatever about the Sweet Science or the Cruel Profession or the Poor Boy's Game. But I know a lot about pride, the poor boy's pride, since that's my story and will, in some way, probably, be my end.

There was something vastly unreal about the entire bit, as though we had all come to Chicago to make various movies and then spent all our time visiting the other fellow's set—on which no cameras were rolling. Dispatches went out every day, typewriters clattered, phones rang; each day, carloads of journalists invaded the Patterson or Liston camps, hung around until Patterson or Liston appeared; asked lame, inane questions, always the same questions, went away again, back to those telephones and typewriters; and informed a waiting, anxious world, or at least a waiting, anxious editor, what

223

Patterson and Liston had said or done that day. It was insane and desperate, since neither of them ever really *did* anything. There wasn't anything for them *to* do, except train for the fight. But there aren't many ways to describe a fighter in training—it's muscle and sweat and grace, it's the same thing over and over—and since neither Patterson nor Liston were doing much boxing, there couldn't be any interesting thumbnail sketches of their sparring partners. The "feud" between Patterson and Liston was as limp and tasteless as British roast lamb. Patterson is really far too much of a gentleman to descend to feuding with anyone, and I simply never believed, especially after talking with Liston, that he had the remotest grudge against Patterson. So there we were, hanging around, twiddling our thumbs, drinking Scotch, and telling stories, and trying to make copy out of nothing. And waiting, of course, for the Big Event, which would justify the monumental amounts of time, money, and energy which were being expended in Chicago.

Neither Patterson nor Liston have the *color,* or the instinct for drama which is possessed to such a superlative degree by the marvelous Archie Moore, and the perhaps less marvelous, but certainly vocal, and rather charming Cassius Clay. In the matter of color, a word which I am not now using in its racial sense, the Press Room far outdid the training camps. There were not only the sportswriters, who had come, as I say, from all over the world: there were also the boxing greats, scrubbed and sharp and easygoing, Rocky Marciano, Barney Ross, Ezzard Charles, and the King, Joe Louis, and Ingemar Johansson, who arrived just a little before the fight and did not impress me as being easygoing at all. Archie Moore's word for him is "desperate," and he did not say this with any affection. There were the ruined boxers, stopped by an unlucky glove too early in their careers, who seemed to be treated with the tense and embarrassed affection reserved for faintly unsavory relatives, who were being used, some of them, as sparring partners. There were the managers and trainers, who, in public anyway, and with the exception of Cus D'Amato, seemed to have taken, many years ago, the vow of silence. There were people whose functions were mysterious indeed, certainly unnamed, possibly unnamable, and, one felt, probably, if undefinably, criminal. There were hangers-on and protégés, a singer somewhere around, whom I didn't meet, owned by Patterson, and another singer owned by someone else—who couldn't sing, everyone agreed, but who didn't have to, being so loaded with personality—and there were some improbable-looking women, turned out, it would seem, by a machine shop, who didn't seem, really, to walk or talk, but rather to gleam, click and glide, with an almost soundless meshing of gears. There were some pretty incredible girls, too, at the parties, impeccably blank and beautiful and rather incredibly vulnerable. There were the parties and the post mortems and the gossip and speculations and recollections and the liquor and the anecdotes, and dawn coming up to find you leaving somebody else's house or somebody else's room or the Playboy Club; and Jimmy Cannon, Red Smith, Milton Gross, Sandy Grady, and A. J. Liebling; and Norman Mailer, Gerald Kersh, Budd Schulberg, and Ben Hecht—who arrived, however, only for the fight and must have been left with a great deal of time on his hands—and Gay Talese (of the *Times*), and myself. Hanging around in Chicago, hanging on the lightest word, or action, of Floyd Patterson and Sonny Liston.

I am not an *aficionado* of the ring, and haven't been since Joe Louis lost his crown—*he* was the last great fighter for me—and so I can't really make comparisons with previous events of this kind. But neither, it soon struck me, could anybody else. Patterson was, in effect, the *moral* favorite—people *wanted* him to win, either because they liked him, though many people didn't, or because they felt that his victory would be salutary for boxing and that Liston's victory would be a disaster. But no one could be said to be enthusiastic about either man's record in the ring. The general feeling seemed to be that Patterson had never been tested, that he was the champion, in effect, by default; though, on the other hand, everyone attempted to avoid the conclusion that boxing had fallen on evil days and that Patterson had fought no worthy fighters because there were none. The desire to avoid speculating too deeply on the present state and the probable future of boxing was responsible, I think, for some very odd and stammering talk about Patterson's personality. (This led Red Smith to declare that he didn't feel that sportswriters had any business trying to be psychiatrists, and that he was just going to write down who hit whom, how hard, and where, and the hell with why.) And there was very sharp disapproval of the way he has handled his career, since he has taken over most of D'Amato's functions as a manager, and is clearly under no one's orders but his own. "In the old days," someone complained, "the manager told the fighter what to do, and he did it. You didn't have to futz around with the guy's *temperament,* for Christ's sake." Never before had any of the sportswriters been compelled to deal directly with the fighter instead of with his manager, and all of them seemed baffled by this necessity and many were resentful. I don't know how they got along with D'Amato when he was running the entire show—D'Amato can certainly not be described as either simple or direct—but at least the figure of D'Amato was familiar and operated to protect them from the oddly compelling and touching figure of Floyd

Patterson, who is quite probably the least likely fighter in the history of the sport. And I think that part of the resentment he arouses is due to the fact that he brings to what is thought of—quite erroneously—as a simple activity a terrible note of complexity. This is his personal style, a style which strongly suggests that most un-American of attributes, privacy, the will to privacy; and my own guess is that he is still relentlessly, painfully shy—he lives gallantly with his scars, but not all of them have healed—and while he has found a way to master this, he has fond no way to hide it; as, for example, another miraculously tough and tender man, Miles Davis, has managed to do. Miles' disguise would certainly never fool anybody with sense, but it keeps a lot of people away, and that's the point. But Patterson, tough and proud and beautiful, is also terribly vulnerable, and looks it.

I met him, luckily for me, with Gay Talese, whom he admires and trusts, I say luckily because I'm not a very aggressive journalist, don't know enough about boxing to know which questions to ask, and am simply not able to ask a man questions about his private life. If Gay had not been there, I am not certain how I would ever have worked up my courage to say anything to Floyd Patterson—especially after having sat through, or suffered, the first, for me, of many press conferences. I only sat through two with Patterson, silently, and in the back—he, poor man, had to go through it every day, sometimes twice a day. And if I don't know enough about boxing to know which questions to ask, I must say that the boxing experts are not one whit more imaginative, though they were, I thought, sometimes rather more insolent. It was a curious insolence, though, veiled, tentative, uncertain—they couldn't be sure that Floyd wouldn't give them as good as he got. And this led, again, to that curious resentment I mentioned earlier, for they were forced, perpetually, to speculate about the man instead of the boxer. It doesn't appear to have occurred yet to many members of the press that one of the reasons their relations with Floyd are so frequently strained is that he has no reason, on any level, to trust them, and no reason to believe that they would be capable of hearing what he had to say, even if he could say it. Life's far from being as simple as most sportswriters would like to have it. The world of sports, in fact, is far from being as simple as the sports pages often make it sound.

Gay and I drove out, ahead of all the other journalists, in a Hertz car, and got to the camp at Elgin while Floyd was still lying down. The camp was very quiet, bucolic, really, when we arrived; set in the middle of small, rolling hills; four or five buildings, a tethered goat—the camp mascot; a small green tent containing a Spartan cot; lots of cars. "They's very car-conscious here," someone said of Floyd's small staff of trainers and helpers. "Most of them have two cars." We ran into some of them standing around and talking on the grounds, and Buster Watson, a close friend of Floyd's, stocky, dark, and able, led us into the Press Room. Floyd's camp was actually Marycrest Farm, the twin of a Chicago settlement house, which works, on a smaller scale but in somewhat the same way, with disturbed and deprived children, as does Floyd's New York alma mater, the Wiltwyck School for Boys. It is a Catholic institution—Patterson is a converted Catholic—and the interior walls of the building in which the press conferences took place were decorated with vivid mosaics, executed by the children in colored beans, of various biblical events. There was an extraordinarily effective crooked cross, executed in charred wood, hanging high on one of the walls. There were two doors to the building in which the two press agents worked, one saying *Caritas,* the other saying *Veritas.* It seemed an incongruous setting for the life being lived there, and the event being prepared, but Ted Carroll, the Negro press agent, a tall man with white hair and a knowledgeable, weary, gentle face, told me that the camp was like the man. "The man lives a secluded life. He's like this place— peaceful and far away." It was not all that peaceful, of course, except naturally; it was otherwise menaced and inundated by hordes of human beings, from small boys, who wanted to be boxers, to old men who remembered Jack Dempsey as a kid. The signs on the road, pointing the way to Floyd Patterson's training camp, were perpetually carried away by souvenir hunters. ("At first," Ted Carroll said, "we were worried that maybe they were carrying them away for another reason—you know, the usual hassle—but no, they just want to put them in the rumpus room.") We walked about with Ted Carroll for a while and he pointed out to us the house, white, with green shutters, somewhat removed from the camp and on a hill, in which Floyd Patterson lived. He was resting now, and the press conference had been called for three o'clock, which was nearly three hours away. But he would be working out before the conference. Gay and I left Ted and wandered close to the house. I looked at the ring, which had been set up on another hill near the house, and examined the tent. Gay knocked lightly on Floyd's door. There was no answer, but Gay said that the radio was on. We sat down in the sun, near the ring, and speculated on Floyd's training habits, which kept him away from his family for such long periods of time.

Presently, here he came across the grass, loping, rather, head down, with a small, tight smile on his lips. This smile seems always to be there when he is facing people and disappears only when he begins to be comfortable.

Then he can laugh, as I never heard him laugh at a press conference, and the face which he watches so carefully in public is then, as it were, permitted to be its boyish and rather surprisingly zestful self. He greeted Gay, and took sharp, covert notice of me, seeming to decide that if I were with Gay, I was probably all right. We followed him into the gym, in which a large sign faced us, saying *So we being many are one body in Christ.* He went through his work-out, methodically, rigorously, pausing every now and again to disagree with his trainer, Dan Florio, about the time—he insisted that Dan's stopwatch was unreliable—or to tell Buster that there weren't enough towels, to ask that the windows be closed. "You threw a good right-hand that time," Dan Florio said; and, later, "Keep the right hand *up. Up!*" "We got a floor scale that's no good," Floyd said, cheerfully. "Sometimes I weigh two hundred, sometimes I weigh 'eighty-eight." And we watched him jump rope, which he must do according to some music in his head, very beautiful and gleaming and far away, like a boy saint helplessly dancing and seen through the steaming windows of a storefront church.

We followed him into the house when the workout was over, and sat in the kitchen and drank tea; he drank chocolate. Gay knew that I was somewhat tense as to how to make contact with Patterson—my own feeling was that he had a tough enough row to hoe, and that everybody should just leave him alone; how would *I* like it if I were forced to answer inane questions every day concerning the progress of my work?—and told Patterson about some of the things I'd written. But Patterson hadn't heard of me, or read anything of mine. Gay's explanation, though, caused him to look directly at me, and he said, "I've seen you someplace before. I don't know where, but I know I've seen you." I hadn't seen him before, except once, with Liston, in the Commissioner's office, when there had been a spirited fight concerning the construction of Liston's boxing gloves, which were "just about as flat as the back of my hand," according to a sportswriter, "just like wearing no gloves at all." I felt certain, considering the number of people and the tension in that room, that he could not have seen me *then*—but we do know some of the same people, and have walked very often on the same streets. Gay suggested that he had seen me on TV. I had hoped that the contact would have turned out to be more personal, like a mutual friend or some activity connected with the Wiltwyck School, but Floyd now remembered the subject of the TV debate he had seen—the race problem, of course—and his face lit up. "I *knew* I'd seen you somewhere!" he said, triumphantly, and looked at me for a moment with the same brotherly pride I felt—and feel—in him.

By now he was, with good grace but a certain tense resignation, preparing himself for the press conference. I gather that there are many people who enjoy meeting the press—and most of them, in fact, were presently in Chicago—but Floyd Patterson is not one of them. I think he hates being put on exhibition, he doesn't believe it is real; while he is terribly conscious of the responsibility imposed on him by the title which he held, he is also afflicted with enough imagination to be baffled by his position. And he is far from having acquired the stony and ruthless perception which will allow him to stand at once within and without his fearful notoriety. Anyway, we trailed over to the building in which the press waited, and Floyd's small, tight, shy smile was back.

But he has learned, though it must have cost him a great deal, how to handle himself. He was asked about his weight, his food, his measurements, his morale. He had been in training for nearly six months ("Is that necessary?" "I just like to do it that way"), had boxed, at this point, about 162 rounds. This was compared to his condition at the time of the first fight with Ingemar Johansson. "Do you believe that you were overtrained for that fight?" "Anything I say now would sound like an excuse." But, later, "I was careless—not overconfident, but careless." He had allowed himself to be surprised by Ingemar's aggressiveness. "Did you and D'Amato fight over your decision to fight Liston?" The weary smile played at the corner of Floyd's mouth, and though he was looking directly at his interlocutors, his eyes were veiled. "No." Long pause. "Cus knows that I do what I want to do—ultimately, he accepted it." Was he surprised by Liston's hostility? No. Perhaps it had made him a bit more determined. Had he anything against Liston personally? "No. I'm the champion and I want to remain the champion." Had he and D'Amato ever disagreed before? "Not in relation to my opponents." Had he heard it said that, as a fighter, he lacked viciousness? "Whoever said that should see the fights I've won without being vicious." And why was he fighting Liston? "Well," said Patterson, "it was my decision to take the fight. You gentlemen disagreed, but you were the ones who placed him in the Number One position, so I felt that it was only right. Liston's criminal record is behind him, not before him." "Do you feel that you've been accepted as a champion?" Floyd smiled more tightly than ever and turned toward the questioner. "No," he said. Then, "Well, I have to be accepted as the champion—but maybe not a good one." "Why do you say," someone else asked, "that the opportunity to become a great champion will never arise?" "Because," said Floyd, patiently, "you gentlemen will never let it arise." Someone asked him about his experiences when boxing in Europe—what kind of reception had he enjoyed? Much greater and much warmer than here, he finally admitted, but added, with a weary and humorous caution, "I don't want to say anything derogatory about the United States. I am satisfied." The press seemed rather to flinch from the purport of this grim and vivid little joke, and switched to the subject of Liston again. Who was most in awe of whom? Floyd had no idea, he said, but, "Liston's confidence is on the surface. Mine is within."

And so it seemed to be indeed, as, later, Gay and I walked with him through the flat, midwestern landscape. It was not exactly that he was less tense—I think that he is probably always tense, and it is that, and not his glass chin, or a lack of stamina, which is his real liability as a fighter—but he was tense in a more private, more bearable way. The fight was very much on his mind, of course, and we talked of the strange battle about the boxing gloves, and the Commissioner's impenetrable and apparent bias toward Liston, though the difference in the construction of the gloves, and the possible meaning of this difference, was clear to everyone. The gloves had been made by two different firms, which was not the usual procedure, and, though they were the same standard eight-ounce weight, Floyd's gloves were the familiar, puffy shape, with most of the weight of the padding over the fist, and Liston's were extraordinarily slender, with most of the weight of the padding over the wrist. But we didn't talk only of the fight, and I can't now remember all the things we *did* talk about. I mainly remember Floyd's voice, going cheerfully on and on, and the way his face kept changing, and the way he laughed; I remember the glimpse I got of him then, a man more complex than he was yet equipped to know, a hero for many children who were still trapped where he had been, who might not have survived without the ring, and who yet, oddly, did not really seem to belong there. I dismissed my dim speculations, that afternoon, as sentimental inaccuracies, rooted in my lack of knowledge of the boxing world, and corrupted with a guilty chauvinism. But now I wonder. He told us that his wife was coming in for the fight, against his will "in order," he said, indescribably, "to *console* me if—" and he made, at last, a gesture with his hand, downward.

Liston's camp was very different, an abandoned racetrack in, or called, Aurora Downs, with wire gates and a uniformed cop, who lets you in, or doesn't. I had simply given up the press conference bit, since they didn't teach me much, and I couldn't ask those questions. Gay Talese couldn't help me with Liston, and this left me floundering on my own until Sandy Grady called up Liston's manager, Jack Nilon, and arranged for me to see Liston for a few minutes alone the next day. Liston's camp was far more outspoken concerning Liston's attitude toward the press than Patterson's. Liston didn't like most of the press and most of them didn't like him. But I didn't, myself, see any reason why he *should* like them, or pretend to—they had certainly never been very nice to him, and I was sure that he saw in them merely some more ignorant, uncaring white people, who, no matter how fine we cut it, had helped to cause him so much grief. And this impression was confirmed by reports from people who *did* get along with him—Wendell Phillips and Bob Teague, who are both Negroes, but rather rare and salty types, and Sandy Grady, who is not a Negro, but is certainly rare, and very probably salty. I got the impression from them that Liston was perfectly willing to take people as they were, if they would do the same for him. Again, I was not particularly appalled by his criminal background, believing, rightly or wrongly, that I probably knew more about the motives and even the necessity of this career than most of the white press could. The only relevance Liston's—presumably previous—associations should have been allowed to have, it seemed to me, concerned the possible effect of these on the future of boxing. Well, while the air was thick was rumor and gospel on this subject, I really cannot go into it without risking, at the very least, being sued for libel; and so, one of the most fascinating aspects of the Chicago story will have to be left in the dark. But the Sweet Science is not, in any case, really so low on shady types as to be forced to depend on Liston. The question is to what extent Liston is prepared to cooperate with whatever powers of darkness there are in boxing; and the extent of his cooperation, we must suppose, must depend, at least partly, on the extent of his awareness. So that there is nothing unique about the position in which he now finds himself and nothing unique about the speculation which now surrounds him.

I got to his camp at about two o'clock one afternoon. Time was running out, the fight was not more than three days away, and the atmosphere in the camp was, at once, listless and electric. Nilon looked as though he had not slept and would not sleep for days, and everyone else rather gave the impression that they wished they could—except for three handsome Negro ladies, related, I supposed, to Mrs. Liston, who sat, rather self-consciously, on the porch of the largest building on the grounds. They may have felt as I did, that training camps are like a theater before the curtain goes up, and if you don't have any function in it, you're probably in the way.

Liston, as we all know, is an enormous man, but surprisingly trim. I had already seen him work out, skipping rope to a record of "Night Train," and, while he wasn't nearly, for me, as moving as Patterson skipping rope in silence, it was still a wonderful sight to see. The press has really maligned Liston very cruelly, I think. He is far from stupid; is not, in fact, stupid at all. And, while there is a great deal of violence in him, I sensed no cruelty at all. On the contrary, he reminded me of big, black men I have known who acquired the reputation of being tough in order to conceal the fact that they weren't hard. Anyone who cared to could turn them into taffy.

Anyway, I liked him, liked him very much. He sat opposite me at the table, sideways, head down, waiting for the blow: for Liston knows, as only the inarticulately suffering can, just how inarticulate he is. But let me clarify that: I say suffering because it seems to me that he has suffered a great deal. It is in his face, in the silence of that face, and in the curiously distant light in the eyes—a light which rarely signals because there have been so few answering signals. And when I say inarticulate, I really do not mean to suggest that he does not know how to talk. He is inarticulate in the way we all are when more has happened to us than we know how to express; and inarticulate in a particularly Negro way—he has a long tale to tell which no one wants to hear. I said, "I can't ask you any questions because everything's been asked. Perhaps I'm only here, really, to say that I wish you well." And this was true, even though I wanted Patterson to win. Anyway, I'm glad I said it because he looked at me then, really for the first time, and he talked to me for a little while.

And what had hurt him most, somewhat to my surprise, was not the general press reaction to him, but the Negro reaction. "Colored people," he said, with great sorrow, "say they don't want their children to look up to me. Well, they ain't teaching their children to look up to Martin Luther King, either." There was a pause. "I wouldn't be no bad example if I was up there. I could tell a lot of those children what they need to know—because—I passed that way. I could make them *listen*." And he spoke a little of what he would like to do for young Negro boys and girls, trapped in those circumstances which so nearly defeated himself and Floyd, and from which neither can yet be said to have recovered. "I tell you one thing, though," he said, "if I was up there, I wouldn't bite my tongue." I could certainly believe that. And we discussed the segregation issue, and the role, in it, of those prominent Negroes who find him so distasteful. "I would never," he said, "go against my brother—we got to learn to stop fighting among our own." He lapsed into silence again. "They said they didn't want me to have the title. They didn't say that about Johansson." "They" were the Negroes. "*They* ought to know why I got some of the bum raps I got." But he was not suggesting that they were *all* bum raps. His wife came over, a very pretty woman, seemed to gather in a glance how things were going, and sat down. We talked for a little while of matters entirely unrelated to the fight, and then it was time for his workout, and I left. I felt terribly ambivalent, as many Negroes do these days, since we are all trying to decide, in one way or another, which attitude, in our terrible American dilemma, is the most effective: the disciplined sweetness of Floyd, or the outspoken intransigence of Liston. *If I was up there, I wouldn't bite my tongue.* And Liston is a man aching for respect and responsibility. Sometimes we grow into our responsibilities and sometimes, of course, we fail them.

I left for the fight full of a weird and violent depression, which I traced partly to fatigue—it had been a pretty grueling time—partly to the fact that I had bet more money than I should have—on Patterson—and partly to the fact that *I* had had a pretty definitive fight with someone with whom I had hoped to be friends. And I was depressed about Liston's bulk and force and his twenty-five-pound weight advantage. I was afraid that Patterson might lose, and I really didn't want to see that. And it wasn't that I didn't like Liston. I just felt closer to Floyd.

I was sitting between Norman Mailer and Ben Hecht. Hecht felt about the same way that I did, and we agreed that if Patterson didn't get "stopped," as Hecht put it, "by a baseball bat," in the very beginning—if he could carry Liston for five or six rounds—he might very well hold the title. We didn't pay an awful lot of attention to the preliminaries—or I didn't; Hecht did; I watched the ballpark fill with people and listened to the vendors and the jokes and the speculations; and watched the clock.

From my notes: Liston entered the ring to an almost complete silence. Someone called his name, he looked over, smiled, and winked. Floyd entered, and got a hand. But he looked terribly small next to Liston, and my depression deepened.

My notes again: Archie Moore entered the ring, wearing an opera cape. Cassius Clay, in black tie, and as insolent as ever. Mickey Allen sang "The Star-Spangled Banner." When Liston was introduced, some people boo'd—they cheered for Floyd, and I think I know how this made Liston feel. It promised, really, to be one of the worst fights in history.

Well, I was wrong, it was scarcely a fight at all, and I can't but wonder who on earth will come to see the rematch, if there is one. Floyd seemed all right to me at first. He had planned for a long fight, and seemed to be feeling out his man. But Liston got him with a few bad body blows, and a few bad blows to the head. And no one agrees with me on this, but, at one moment, when Floyd lunged for Liston's belly—looking, it must be said, like an amateur, wildly flailing—it seemed to me that some unbearable tension in him broke, that he lost his head. And, in fact, I nearly screamed, "Keep your head, baby!" but it was really too late. Liston got him with a left, and Floyd went down. I could not believe it. I couldn't hear the count and though Hecht said, "It's over," and picked up his coat, and left, I remained standing, staring at the ring, and only conceded that the fight was really over when two other boxers entered the ring. Then I wandered out of the ball park, almost in tears. I met an old colored man at one of the exits, who said to me, cheerfully, "I've been robbed," and we talked about it for a while. We started walking through the crowds and A. J. Liebling, behind us, tapped me on the shoulder and we went off to a bar, to mourn the very possible death of boxing, and to have a drink, with love, for Floyd.

The Death of Paret

NORMAN MAILER

Emile Griffith began his career in ladies' hats. Truly.

It was the late 1950s, and the future welterweight and middleweight champ was training for the Golden Gloves and earning his keep as a stockboy for a wholesale millinery salesman named Howie Albert, who would go on to manage Griffith's career. I know this because my father was in the millinery business then, and his partner and Albert were related. When my father opened his new showroom, Griffith, by then a promising professional, was the evening's guest of honor. And I got to shake his hand.

The next time I saw Griffith live was on the night of March 24, 1962, the night the events reported on here by Norman Mailer transpired. I was technically too young even to attend a prizefight, but Howie Albert had given tickets to my father, and my father decided it was time the fights took on dimension for me beyond that exhibited by the black and white television in the den. I was excited. This was, after all, Emile, whose hand I'd once shook, who knew my father and me personally, fighting to regain his rightful crown.

Looking back, I'd like to say that what I observed changed me somehow, or at least stayed with me, but the truth is I had only a vague idea of what I was witnessing. It happened quickly. It was a blur. And I really couldn't see past the shoulders—or smoke—of the cigar-chomper in front of me. What I do remember, and what I've never been able to shake, is the *Daily News* image of Paret, comatose in a hospital bed, his last link to the living, breathing world he would soon leave the tracheotomy tube shoved into an opening in his throat.

Mailer, of course, needs no introduction, nor does his longtime fascination with the fights. There is a story behind this piece, though. He inserted the Griffith-Paret interlude as a flashback into his much larger piece on the first Patterson-Liston fight, originally published in Esquire as *Ten Thousand Words a Minute*. Mailer then included it—as *Death*—in his 1963 essay collection, *The Presidential Papers*.

𝕒   𝕒   𝕒   𝕒

On the afternoon of the night Emile Griffith and Benny Paret were to fight a third time for the welterweight championship, there was murder in both camps. "I hate that kind of guy," Paret had said earlier to Pete Hamill about Griffith. "A fighter's got to look and talk and act like a man." One of the Broadway gossip columnists had run an item about Griffith a few days before. His girlfriend saw it and said to Griffith, "Emile, I didn't know about you being that way." So Griffith hit her. So he said. Now at the weigh-in that morning, Paret had insulted Griffith irrevocably, touching him on the buttocks, while making a few more remarks about his manhood. They almost had their fight on the scales.

The accusation of homosexuality arouses a major passion in many men; they spend their lives resisting it with a biological force. There is a kind of man who spends every night of his life getting drunk in a bar, he rants, he brawls, he ends in a small rumble on the street; women say, "For God's sakes, he's homosexual. Why doesn't he just turn queer and get his suffering over with." Yet men protect him. It is because he is choosing not to become homosexual. It was put best by Sartre who said that a homosexual is a man who practices homosexuality. A man who does not, is not homosexual—he is entitled to the dignity of his choice. He is entitled to the fact that he chose not to become homosexual, and is paying presumably his price.

The rage in Emile Griffith was extreme. I was at the fight that night, I had never seen a fight like it. It was scheduled for fifteen rounds, but they fought without stopping from the bell which began the round to the bell which ended it, and then they fought after the bell, sometimes for as much as fifteen seconds before the referee could force them apart.

Paret was a Cuban, a proud club fighter who had become welterweight champion because of his unusual ability to take a punch. His style of fighting was to take three punches to the head in order to give back two. At the end of ten rounds, he would still be bouncing, his opponent would have a headache. But in the last two years, over the fifteen-round fights, he had started to take some bad maulings.

This fight had its turns. Griffith won most of the early rounds, but Paret knocked Griffith down in the sixth. Griffith had trouble getting up, but made it, came alive and was dominating Paret again before the round was over. Then Paret began to wilt. In the middle of the eighth round, after a clubbing punch had turned his back to Griffith, Paret walked three disgusted steps away, showing his hindquarters. For a champion, he took much too long to turn back around. It was the first hint of weakness Paret had ever shown, and it must have inspired a particular shame, because he fought the rest of the fight as if he were seeking to demonstrate that he could take more punishment than any man alive. In the twelfth, Griffith caught him. Paret got trapped in a corner. Trying to duck away, his left arm and his head became tangled on the wrong side of the top rope. Griffith was in like a cat ready to rip the life out of a huge boxed rat. He hit him eighteen right hands in a row, an act which took perhaps three or four seconds, Griffith making a pent-up whimpering sound all the while he attacked, the right hand whipping like a piston rod which has broken through the crankcase, or like a baseball bat demolishing a pumpkin. I was sitting in the second row of that corner—they were not ten feet away from me, and like everybody else, I was hypnotized. I had never seen one man hit another so hard and so many times. Over the referee's face came a look of woe as if some spasm had passed its way through him, and then he leaped on Griffith to pull him away. It was the act of a brave man. Griffith was uncontrollable. His trainer leaped into the ring, his manager, his cut man, there were four people holding Griffith, but he was off on an orgy, he had left the Garden, he was back on a hoodlum's street. If he had been able to break loose from his handlers and the referee, he would have jumped Paret to the floor and whaled on him there.

And Paret? Paret died on his feet. As he took those eighteen punches something happened to everyone who was in psychic range of the event. Some part of his death reached out to us. One felt it hover in the air. He was still standing in the ropes, trapped as he had been before, he gave some little half-smile of regret, as if he were saying, "I didn't know I was going to die just yet," and then, his head leaning back but still erect, his death came to breathe about him. He began to pass away. As he passed, so his limbs descended beneath him, and he sank slowly to the floor. He went down more slowly than any fighter had ever gone down, he went down like a large ship which turns on end and slides second by second into its grave. As he went down, the sound of Griffith's punches echoed in the mind like a heavy ax in the distance chopping into a wet log.

Paret lay on the ground, quivering gently, a small froth on his mouth. The house doctor jumped into the ring. He knelt. He pried Paret's eyelid open. He looked at the eyeball staring out. He let the lid snap shut. He reached into his satchel, took out a needle, jabbed Paret with a stimulant. Paret's back rose in a high arch. He writhed in real agony. They were calling him back from death. One wanted to cry out, "Leave the man alone. Let him die." But they saved Paret long enough to take him to a hospital where he lingered for days. He was in coma. He never came out of it. If he lived, he would have been a vegetable. His brain was smashed. But they held him in life for a week, they fed him chemicals, and made exploratory operations into his skull, and fed details of his condition to The Goat. And The Goat kicked clods of mud all over the place, and spoke harshly of prohibiting boxing. There was shock in the land. Children had seen the fight on television. There were editorials, gloomy forecasts that the Game was dead. The managers and the prizefighters got together. Gently, in thick, depressed hypocrisies, they tried to defend their sport. They did not find it easy to explain that they shared an unstated view of life which was religious.

It was of course not that religion which is called Judeo-Christian. It was an older religion, a more primitive one—a religion of blood, a murderous and sensitive religion which mocks the effort of the understanding to approach it, and scores the lungs of men like D. H. Lawrence, and burns the brain of men like Ernest Hemingway when they explore out into the mystery, searching to discover some part of the secret. It is the view of life which looks upon death as a condition which is more alive than life or unspeakably more deadening. As such it is not a very attractive notion to the Establishment. But then the Establishment has nothing very much of even the Judeo-Christian tradition. It has a respect for legal and administrative aspects of justice, and it is devoted to the idea of compassion for the poor. But the Establishment has no idea of death, no tolerance for Heaven or Hell, no comprehension of bloodshed. It sees no logic in pain. To the Establishment these notions are a detritus from the past.

Like a patient submerged beneath the plastic cover of an oxygen tent, boxing lives on beneath the cool, bored eyes of the doctors in the Establishment. It would not take too much to finish boxing off. Shut down the oxygen, which is to say, turn that switch in the mass media which still gives sanction to organized pugilism, and the fight game would be dead.

But the patient is permitted to linger for fear the private detectives of the Establishment, the psychiatrists and psychoanalysts, might not be able to neutralize the problem of gang violence. Not so well as the Game. Of course, the moment some piece of diseased turnip capable of being synthesized cheaply might prove to have the property of tranquilizing a violent young man for a year, the Establishment would wipe out boxing. Every time a punk was arrested, the police would prescribe a pill, and violence would walk the street sheathed and numb. Of course the Mob would lose revenue, but then the Mob is also part of the Establishment, it, and the labor unions and the colleges and the newspapers and the corporations are all part of the Establishment. The Establishment is never simple. It needs the Mob to grease the chassis on its chariot. Therefore, the Mob would be placated. In a society with strong central government, it is not so difficult to turn up a new source of revenue. What is more difficult is to enter the plea that violence may be an indispensable element of life. This is not the place to have the argument: it is enough to say that if the liberal Establishment is right in its unstated credo that death is a void, and man leads out his life suspended momentarily above that void, whey then there is no argument at all. Whatever shortens life is monstrous. We have not the right to shorten life, since life is the only possession of the psyche, and in death we have only nothingness. What then can there be said in defense of sports-car racing, war, or six-ounce gloves?

But if we go from life into a death which is larger than our life has been, or into a death which is small, if death comes to nothing for one man because he swallowed his death in his life, and if for another death is alive with dimension, then the certitudes of the Establishment lose power. A drug which offers peace to a pain may dull the nerve which could have taught the mind how to carry that pain into the death which comes on the next day or on the decades that follow. A tranquilizer gives coma to an anxiety which may later smell of the dungeon, beneath the ground. If we are born into life as some living line of intent from an eternity which may have tortured us or nurtured us in death, then we may be obliged to go back to death with more courage and art than we left it. Or face the dim end of going back with less.

That is the existential venture, the unstated religious view of boxers trying to beat each other into unconsciousness or, ultimately, into death. It is the culture of the killer who sickens the air about him if he does not find some half-human way to kill a little in order not to deaden all. It is a defense against the plague, against that plague which comes from violence converted into the nausea of all that nonviolence which is void of peace. Paret's death was with horror, but not all the horror was in the beating, much was in the way his death was cheated. Which is to say that his death was twice a nightmare. I knew that something in boxing was spoiled forever for me, that there would be a fear in watching a fight now which was like the fear one felt for any *novillero* when he was having an unhappy day, the bull was dangerous, and the crowd was ugly. You knew he would get hurt. There is fascination in seeing that the first time, but it is not as enjoyable as one expects. It is like watching a novelist who has written a decent book get run over by a car.

Something in boxing was spoiled. But not the principle, not the right for one man to try to knock another out in the ring. That was perhaps not a civilized activity, but it belonged to the tradition of the humanist, it was a human activity, it showed a part of what man was like, it belonged to his ability to create art and artful movement on the edge of death or pain or danger or attack, and it had much to say about the subtleties of human style. For there are boxers whose bodies move like a fine brain, and there are others who pound the opposition down with the force of a trade-union leader, there are fools and wits and patient craftsmen among boxers, wild men full of a sense of outrage, and steady oppressive peasants, clever spoilers, dogged infantrymen who walk forward all night, hypnotists (like Liston), dancers, lovers, mothers giving a scolding, horsemen high on their legs. There is knowledge to be found about our nature, and the nature of animals, of big cats, lions, tigers, gorillas, bears, walruses (Archie Moore), birds, elephants, jackals, bulls. No, I was not down on boxing, but I loved it with freedom no longer. It was more like somebody in your family was fighting now. And the feeling one had for a big fight was no longer clear of terror in its excitement. There was awe in the suspense.

Return to Kansas City

IRWIN SHAW

Sometimes, a fighter's smoothest battles are the ones he fights *inside* the ring. Domesticity, as Irwin Shaw (1913–1984), the muscular stylist of such novels as *The Young Lions, Sailing to Byzantium,* and *Rich Man, Poor Man,* explores in this 1939 confection, can sometimes lay a boxer out flat.

A rline opened the bedroom door and softly went over between the twin beds, the silk of her dress making a slight rustle in the quiet room. The dark shades were down and the late afternoon sun came in only in one or two places along the sides of the window frames, in sharp, thin rays.

Arline looked down at her husband, sleeping under the blankets. His fighter's face with the mashed nose was very peaceful on the pillow and his hair was curled like a baby's and he snored gently because he breathed through his mouth. A light sweat stood out on his face. Eddie always sweated, any season, any place. But now, when she saw Eddie begin to sweat, it made Arline a little angry.

She stood there, watching the serene, glovemarked face. She sat down on the other bed, still watching her husband. She took a lace-bordered handkerchief out of a pocket and dabbed at her eyes. They were dry. She sniffed a little and the tears started. For a moment she cried silently, then she sobbed aloud. In a minute the tears and the sobs were regular, loud in the still room.

Eddie stirred in his bed. He closed his mouth, turned over on his side.

"Oh, my," Arline sobbed, "oh, my God."

She saw, despite the fact that Eddie's back was toward her, that he had awakened.

"Oh," Arline wept, "sweet Mother of God."

She knew that Eddie was wide awake listening to her and he knew that she knew it, but he hopefully pretended he hadn't been roused. He even snored experimentally once or twice. Arline's sobs shook her and the mascara ran down her cheeks in straight black lines.

Eddie sighed and turned around and sat up, rubbing his hair with his hands.

"What's the matter?" he asked. "What's bothering you, Arline?"

"Nothing," Arline sobbed.

"If nothing's the matter," Eddie said mildly, "what're you crying for?"

Arline didn't say anything. She stopped sobbing aloud and turned the grief inward upon herself and wept all the more bitterly, in silence. Eddie wiped his eye with the heel of his hand, looked wearily at the dark shades that shut out the slanting rays of the sun.

"There are six rooms in this house, Arline darling," he said. "If you have to cry why is it necessary to pick the exact room where I am sleeping?"

Arline's head sank low on her breast, her beautiful beauty-shop straw-colored hair falling tragically over her face. "You don't care," she murmured, "you don't care one dime's worth if I break my heart."

She squeezed the handkerchief and the tears ran down her wrist.

"I care," Eddie said, throwing back the covers neatly and putting his stockinged feet onto the floor. He had been sleeping in his pants and shirt, which were very wrinkled now. He shook his head two or three times as he sat on the edge of the bed and hit himself smartly on the cheek with the back of his hand to awaken himself. He looked unhappily across at his wife, sitting on the other bed, her hands wrung in her lap, her face covered by her careless hair, sorrow and despair in every line of her. "Honest, Arline, I care." He went over and sat next to her on the bed and put his arm around her. "Baby," he said. "Now, baby."

She just sat there crying silently, her round, soft shoulders shaking now and then under his arm. Eddie began to feel more and more uncomfortable. He squeezed her shoulder two or three times, exhausting his methods of consolation. "Well," he said finally, "I think maybe I'll put the kid in the carriage and take him for a walk. A little air. Maybe when I come back you'll feel better."

"I won't feel better," Arline promised him, without moving. "I won't feel one ounce better."

"Arline," Eddie said.

"The kid." She sat up erect now and looked at him. "If you paid as much attention to me as to the kid."

"I pay equal attention. My wife and my kid." Eddie stood up and padded around the room uneasily in his socks.

Arline watched him intently, the creased flannel trousers and the wrinkled shirt not concealing the bulky muscles.

"The male sleeping beauty," she said. "The long-distance sleeping champion. My husband."

"I don't sleep so awful much," Eddie protested.

"Fifteen hours a day," Arline said. "Is it natural?"

"I had a hard workout this morning," Eddie said, standing at the window. "I went six fast rounds. I got to get rest. I got to store up my energy. I am not so young as some people any more. I got to take care of myself. Don't I have to store up energy?"

"Store up energy!" Arline said loudly. "All day long you store up energy. What is your wife supposed to do when you are storing up energy?"

Eddie let the window shade fly up. The light shot into the room, making it harder for Arline to cry.

"You ought to have friends," Eddie suggested without hope.

"I have friends."

"Why don't you go out with them?"

"They're in Kansas City," Arline said.

There was silence in the room. Eddie sat down and began putting on his shoes.

"My mother's in Kansas City," Arline said. "My two sisters are in Kansas City. My two brothers. I went to high school in Kansas City. Here I am, in Brooklyn, New York."

"You were in Kansas City two and a half months ago," Eddie said, buttoning his collar and knotting his tie. "A mere two and a half months ago."

"Two and a half months are a long time," Arline said, clearing away the mascara lines from her cheeks, but still weeping. "A person can die in two and a half months."

"What person?" Eddie asked.

Arline ignored him. "Mamma writes she wants to see the baby again. After all, that is not unnatural, a grandmother wants to see her grandchild. Tell me is it unnatural?"

"No," said Eddie, "it is not unnatural." He combed his hair swiftly. "If Mamma wants to see the baby," he said, "explain to me why she can't come here. Kindly explain to me."

"My husband is of the opinion that they are handing out gold pieces with movie tickets in Kansas City," Arline said with cold sarcasm.

"Huh?" Eddie asked, honestly puzzled. "What did you say?"

"How can Mamma afford to come here?" Arline asked. "After all, you know, there are no great prizefighters in *our* family. I had to *marry* to bring one into the family. Oh, my God!" Once more she wept.

"Lissen, Arline," Eddie ran over to her and spoke pleadingly, his tough, battered face very gentle and sad, "I can't afford to have you to Kansas City every time I take a nap in the afternoon. We have been married a year and a half and you have gone to Kansas City five times. I feel like I am fighting for the New York Central Railroad, Arline!"

Arline shook her head obstinately. "There is nothing to do in New York," she said.

"There is nothing to do in New York!" Eddie's mouth opened in surprise. "My God! There's something to do in Kansas City?" he cried. "What the hell is there to do in Kansas City? Remember, I have been in that town myself. I married you in that town."

"I didn't know how it was going to be," Arline said flatly. "It was nice in Kansas City. I was an innocent young girl."

"Please," said Eddie. "Let us not rake up the past."

"I was surrounded by my family," Arline went on shakily. "I went to high school there."

She bent over and grief took possession once more. Eddie licked his lips uncomfortably. They were dry from the morning's workout and the lower lip was split a little and smarted when he ran his tongue over it. He searched his brain for a helpful phrase.

"The kid," he ventured timidly, "why don't you play more with the kid?"

"The kid!" Arline cried defiantly. "I take very good care of the kid. I have to stay in every night minding the kid while you are busy storing up your energy." The phrase enraged her and she stood up, waving her arms. "What a business! You fight thirty minutes a month, you got to sleep three hundred and fifty hours. Why, it's laughable. It is very laughable! You are some fighter!" She shook her fist at him in derision. "With all the energy you store up you ought to be able to beat the German army!"

"That is the business I am in," Eddie tried to explain gently. "That is the nature of my profession."

"Don't tell me that!" Arline said. "I have gone out with other fighters. They don't sleep all the time."

"I am not interested," Eddie said. "I do not want to hear anything about your life before our marriage."

"They go to night clubs," Arline went on irresistibly, "and they dance and they take a drink once in a while and they take a girl to see a musical show!"

Eddie nodded. "They are after something," he said. "That is the whole story."

"I wish to God you were after something!"

"I meet the type of fighter you mention, too," Eddie said. "The night-club boys. They knock my head off for three rounds and then they start breathing through the mouth. By the time they reach the eighth round they wish they never saw a naked lady on a dance floor. And by the time I get through with them they are storing up energy flat on their backs. With five thousand people watching them. You want me to be that kind of a fighter?"

"You're wonderful," Arline said, wrinkling her nose, sneering. "My Joe Louis. Big-Purse Eddie Megaffin. I don't notice you bringing back the million-dollar gate."

"I am progressing slowly," Eddie said, looking at the picture of Mary and Jesus over his bed. "I am planning for the future."

"I am linked for life to a goddam health-enthusiast," Arline said despairingly.

"Why do you talk like that, Arline?"

"Because I want to be in Kansas City," she wailed.

"Explain to me," Eddie said, "why in the name of God you are so crazy for Kansas City?"

"I'm lonesome," Arline wept with true bitterness. "I'm awful lonesome. I'm only twenty-one years old, Eddie."

Eddie patted her gently on the shoulder. "Look, Arline." He tried to make his voice very warm and at the same time logical. "If you would only go easy. If you would go by coach and not buy presents for everybody, maybe I can borrow a coupla bucks and swing it."

"I would rather die," Arline said. "I would rather never see Kansas City again for the rest of my life than let them know my husband has to watch pennies like a streetcar conductor. A man with his name in the papers every week. It would be shameful!"

"But, Arline, darling—" Eddie's face was tortured—"you go four times a year, you spread presents like the WPA and you always buy new clothes ..."

"I can't appear in Kansas City in rags!" Arline pulled at a stocking, righting it on her well-curved leg. "I would rather ..."

"Some day, darling," Eddie interrupted. "We're working up. Right now I can't."

"You can!" Arline said. "You're lying to me, Eddie Megaffin. Jake Blucher called up this morning and he told me he offered you a thousand dollars to fight Joe Principe."

Eddie sat down in a chair. He looked down at the floor, understanding why Arline had picked this particular afternoon.

"You would come out of that fight with seven hundred and fifty dollars." Arline's voice was soft and inviting. "I could go to Kansas ..."

"Joe Principe will knock my ears off."

Arline sighed. "I am so anxious to see my mother. She is an old woman and soon she will die."

"At this stage," Eddie said slowly, "I am not ready for Joe Principe. He is too strong and too smart for me."

"Jake Blucher told me he thought you had a wonderful chance."

"I have a wonderful chance to land in the hospital," Eddie said. "That Joe Principe is made out of springs and cement. If you gave him a pair of horns it would be legal to kill him with a sword."

"He is only a man with two fists just like you," Arline said.

"Yeah."

"You're always telling me how good you are."

"In two years," Eddie said, "taking it very easy and careful, making sure I don't get knocked apart ..."

"You could make the money easy!" Arline pointed her finger dramatically at him. "You just don't want to. You don't want me to be happy. I see through you, Eddie Megaffin!"

"I just don't want to get beaten up," Eddie said, shaking his head.

"A fine fighter!" Arline laughed. "What kind of fighter are you, anyhow? A fighter is supposed to get beaten up, isn't he? That's his business, isn't it? You don't care for me. All you wanted was somebody to give you a kid and cook your goddam steaks and lamb chops. In Brooklyn! I got to stay in a lousy little house day in and . . ."

"I'll take you to the movies tonight," Eddie promised.

"I don't want to go to the movies. I want to go to Kansas City." Arline threw herself face down on the bed and sobbed. "I'm caught! I'm caught! You don't love me! You won't let me go to people who love me! Mama! Mama!"

Eddie closed his eyes in pain. "I love you," he said, meaning it, "I swear to God."

"You say it."

Her voice was smothered in the pillow. "But you don't prove it! Prove it! I never knew a young man could be so stingy. Prove it . . ." The words trailed off in sorrow.

Eddie went over and bent down to kiss her. She shook her shoulders to send him away and cried like a heartbroken child. From the next room, where the baby had been sleeping, came the sound of his wailing.

Eddie walked over to the window and looked out at the peaceful Brooklyn street, at the trees and the little boys and girls skating.

"O.K.," he said, "I'll call Blucher."

Arline stopped crying. The baby still wailed in the next room.

"I'll try to raise him to twelve hundred," Eddie said. "You can go to Kansas City. You happy?"

Arline sat up and nodded. "I'll write Mama right away," she said.

"Take the kid out for a walk, will you?" Eddie said, as Arline started repairing her face before the mirror. "I want to take a little nap."

"Sure," Arline said, "sure, Eddie."

Eddie took off his shoes and lay down on the bed to start storing up his energy.

His Brother's Keeper

DASHIELL HAMMETT

By the time Dashiell Hammett (1894–1961) had turned 30, he'd already worked as a freight clerk, a railroad laborer, a messenger, a stevedore, and a Pinkerton; it seemed only logical that his next career path would be to create the "hard-boiled" genre of detective fiction. In his *Continental Op* stories, and his five novels—*Red Harvest, The Dain Curse, The Maltese Falcon, The Glass Key* and *The Thin Man*—Hammett dusted off some of the darker corners of human nature, unsparingly exploring themes like violence, greed, betrayal, corruption, and infidelity. The year that he wrote his final novel—1934—was also the year he chose to poke into some of the darker corners of boxing with this hard-boiled tale, published in *Collier's* magazine.

● ● ● ●

I knew what a lot of people said about Loney but he was always swell to me. Ever since I remember he was swell to me and I guess I would have liked him just as much even if he had been just somebody else instead of my brother; but I was glad he was not just somebody else.

He was not like me. He was slim and would have looked swell in any kind of clothes you put on him, only he always dressed classy and looked like he had stepped right out of the bandbox even when he was just loafing around the house, and he had slick hair and the whitest teeth you ever saw and long, thin, clean-looking fingers. He looked like the way I remembered my father, only better-looking. I took more after Ma's folks, the Malones, which was funny because Loney was the one that was named after them, Malone Bolan. He was smart as they make them, too. It was no use trying to put anything over on him and maybe that was what some people had against him, only that was kind of hard to fit in with Pete Gonzalez.

Pete Gonzalez not liking Loney used to bother me sometimes because he was a swell guy, too, and he was never trying to put anything over on anybody. He had two fighters and a wrestler named Kilchak and he always sent them in to do the best they could, just like Loney sent me in. He was the top-notch manager in our part of the country and a lot of people said there was no better anywhere, so I felt pretty good about him wanting to handle me, even if I did say no.

It was in the hall leaving Tubby White's gym that I ran into him that afternoon and he said, "Hello, Kid, how's it?" moving his cigar further over in a corner of his mouth so he could talk.

"Hello. All right."

He looked me up and down, squinting on account of the smoke from his cigar. "Going to take this guy Saturday?"

"I guess so."

He looked me up and down again like he was weighing me in. His eyes were little enough anyhow and when he squinted like that you could hardly see them at all. "How old are you, Kid?"

"Going on nineteen."

"And you'll weigh about a hundred and sixty," he said.

"Sixty-seven and a half. I'm growing pretty fast."

"Ever see this guy you're fighting Saturday?"

"No."

"He's plenty tough."

I grinned and said, "I guess he is."

"And plenty smart."

I said, "I guess he is," again.

He took his cigar out of his mouth and scowled at me and said like he was sore at me, "You know you got no business in the ring with him, don't you?" Before I could think up anything to say he stuck the cigar back in his mouth and his face and his voice changed. "Why don't you let me handle you, Kid? You got the stuff. I'll handle you right, build you up, not use you up, and you'll be good for a long trip."

"I couldn't do that," I said. "Loney taught me all I know and—"

"Taught you what?" Pete snarled. He looked mad again. "If you think you been taught anything at all you just take a look at your mug in the next looking glass you come across." He took the cigar out of his mouth and spit out a piece of tobacco that had come loose. "Only eighteen years old and ain't been fighting a year and look at the mug on him!"

I felt myself blushing. I guess I was never any beauty but, like Pete said, I had been hit in the face a lot and I guess my face showed it. I said, "Well, of course, I'm not a boxer."

"And that's the God's truth," Pete said. "And why ain't you?"

"I don't know. I guess it's just not my way of fighting."

"You could learn. You're fast and you ain't dumb. What's this stuff getting you? Every week Loney sends you in against some guy you're not ready for yet and you soak up a lot of fists and—"

"I win, don't I?" I said.

"Sure you win—so far—because you're young and tough and got the moxie and can hit, but I wouldn't want to pay for winning what you're paying, and I wouldn't want any of my boys to. I seen kids—maybe some of them as promising as you—go along the way you're going, and I seen what was left of them a couple years later. Take my word for it, Kid, you'll do better than that with me."

"Maybe you're right," I said, "and I'm grateful to you and all that, but I couldn't leave Loney. He—"

"I'll give Loney a piece of change for your contract, even if you ain't got one with him."

"No, I'm sorry, I—I couldn't."

Pete started to say something and stopped and his face began to get red. The door of Tubby's office had opened and Loney was coming out. Loney's face was white and you could hardly see his lips because they were so tight together, so I knew he had heard us talking.

He walked up close to Pete, not even looking at me once, and said, "You chiseling rat."

Pete said, "I only told him what I told you when I made you the offer last week."

Loney said, "Swell. So now you've told everybody. So now you can tell 'em about this." He smacked Pete across the mouth with the back of his hand.

I moved over a little because Pete was a lot bigger than Loney, but Pete just said, "O.K., pal, maybe you won't live forever. Maybe you won't live forever even if Big Jake don't never get hep to the missus."

Loney swung at him with a fist this time but Pete was backing away down the hall and Loney missed him by about a foot and a half, and when Loney started after him Pete turned and ran toward the gym.

Loney came back to me grinning and not looking mad any more. He could change that way quicker than anybody you ever saw. He put an arm around my shoulder and said, "The chiseling rat. Let's blow." Outside he turned me around to look at the sign advertising the fights. "There you are, Kid. I don't blame him for wanting you. There'll be a lot of 'em wanting you before you're through."

It did look swell, KID BOLAN VS. SAILOR PERELMAN, in red letters that were bigger than any of the other names and up at the top of the card. That was the first time I ever had had my name at the top. I thought, I'm going to have it there like that all the time now and maybe in New York sometime, but I just grinned at Loney without saying anything and we went on home.

Ma was away visiting my married sister in Pittsburgh and we had a Negro woman named Susan taking care of the house for us and after she washed up the supper dishes and went home Loney went to the telephone and I could hear him talking low. I wanted to say something to him when he came back but I was afraid I would say the wrong thing because Loney might think I was trying to butt into his business, and before I could find a safe way to start the doorbell rang.

Loney went to the door. It was Mrs. Schiff, like I had a hunch it would be, because she had come over the first night Ma was away.

She came in laughing, with Loney's arm around her waist, and said, "Hello, Champ," to me.

I said, "Hello," and shook hands with her.

I liked her, I guess, but I guess I was kind of afraid of her. I mean not only afraid of her on Loney's account but in a different way. You know, like sometimes when you were a kid and you found yourself all alone in a strange neighborhood on the other side of town. There was nothing you could see to be downright afraid of but you kept halfway expecting something. It was something like that. She was awful pretty but there was something kind of wild-looking about her. I don't mean wild-looking like some floozies you see; I mean almost like an animal, like she was always on the watch for something. It was like she was hungry. I mean just her eyes and maybe her mouth because you could not call her skinny or anything or fat either.

Loney got out a bottle of whisky and glasses and they had a drink. I stalled around for a few minutes just being polite and then said I guessed I was tired and I said good night to them and took my magazine upstairs to my room. Loney was beginning to tell her about his run-in with Pete Gonzalez when I went upstairs.

After I got undressed I tried to read but I kept worrying about Loney. It was this Mrs. Schiff that Pete made the crack about in the afternoon. She was the wife of Big Jake Schiff, the boss of our ward, and a lot of people must have known about her running around with Loney on the side. Anyhow Pete knew about it and he and Big Jake were pretty good friends besides him now having something to pay Loney back for. I wished Loney would cut it out. He could have had a lot of other girls and Big Jake was nobody to have trouble with, even leaving aside the pull he had down at the City Hall. Every time I tried to read I would get to thinking things like that so finally I gave it up and went to sleep pretty early even for me.

That was a Monday. Tuesday night when I got home from the movies she was waiting in the vestibule. She had on a long coat but no hat, and she looked pretty excited.

"Where's Loney?" she asked, not saying hello or anything.

"I don't know. He didn't say where he was going."

"I've got to see him," she said. "Haven't you any idea where he'd be?"

"No, I don't know where he is."

"Do you think he'll be late?"

I said, "I guess he usually is."

She frowned at me and then she said, "I've got to see him. I'll wait for a little while anyhow." So we went back to the dining room.

She kept her coat on and began to walk around the room looking at things but without paying much attention to them. I asked her if she wanted a drink and she said, "Yes," sort of absent-minded, but when I started to get it for her she took hold of the lapel of my coat and said, "Listen, Eddie, will you tell me something? Honest to God?"

I said, "Sure," feeling kind of embarrassed looking in her face like that, "if I can."

"Is Loney really in love with me?"

That was a tough one. I could feel my face getting redder and redder. I wished the door would open and Loney would come in. I wished a fire would break out or something.

She jerked my lapel. "Is he?"

I said, "I guess so. I guess he is, all right."

"Don't you know?"

I said, "Sure, I know, but Loney don't ever talk to me about things like that. Honest, he don't."

She bit her lip and turned her back on me. I was sweating. I spent as long a time as I could in the kitchen getting the whisky and things. When I went back in the dining room she had sat down and was putting lipstick on her mouth. I set the whisky down on the table beside her.

She smiled at me and said, "You're a nice boy, Eddie. I hope you win a million fights. When do you fight again?"

I had to laugh at that. I guess I had been going around thinking that everybody in the world knew I was going to fight Sailor Perelman that Saturday just because it was my first main event. I guess that is the way you get a swelled head. I said, "This Saturday."

"That's fine," she said, and looked at her wristwatch. "Oh, why doesn't he come? I've got to be home before Jake gets there." She jumped up. "Well, I can't wait any longer. I shouldn't have stayed this long. Will you tell Loney something for me?"

"Sure."

"And not another soul?"

"Sure."

She came around the table and took hold of my lapel again. "Well, listen. You tell him that somebody's been talking to Jake about—about us. You tell him we've got to be careful, Jake'll kill both of us. You tell him I don't think Jake knows for sure yet, but we've got to be careful. Tell Loney not to phone me and to wait here till I phone him tomorrow afternoon. Will you tell him that?"

"Sure."

"And don't let him do anything crazy."

I said, "I won't." I would have said anything to get it over with.

She said, "You're a nice boy, Eddie," and kissed me on the mouth and went out of the house.

I did not go to the door with her. I looked at the whisky on the table and thought maybe I ought to take the first drink of my life, but instead I sat down and thought about Loney. Maybe I dozed off a little but I was awake when he came home and that was nearly two o'clock.

He was pretty tight. "What the hell are you doing up?" he said.

I told him about Mrs. Schiff and what she told me to tell him.

He stood there in his hat and overcoat until I had told it all, then he said, "That chiseling rat," kind of half under his breath and his face began to get like it got when he was mad.

"And she said you mustn't do anything crazy."

"Crazy?" He looked at me and kind of laughed. "No, I won't do anything crazy. How about you scramming off to bed?"

I said, "All right," and went upstairs.

The next morning he was still in bed when I left for the gym and he had gone out before I got home. I waited supper for him until nearly seven o'clock and then ate it by myself. Susan was getting sore because it was going to be late before she got through. Maybe he stayed out all night but he looked all right when he came in Tubby's the next afternoon to watch me work out, and he was making jokes and kidding along with the fellows hanging around there just like he had nothing at all on his mind.

He waited for me to dress and we walked over home together. The only thing that was kind of funny, he asked me, "How do you feel, Kid?" That was kind of funny because he knew I always felt all right. I guess I never even had a cold all my life.

I said, "All right."

"You're working good," he said. "Take it easy tomorrow. You want to be rested up for this baby from Providence. Like that chiseling rat said, he's plenty tough and plenty smart."

I said, "I guess he is. Loney, do you think Pete really tipped Big Jake off about—"

"Forget it," he said. "Hell with 'em." He poked my arm. "You got nothing to worry about but how you're going to be in there Saturday night."

"I'll be all right."

"Don't be too sure," he said. "Maybe you'll be lucky to get a draw."

I stopped still in the street, I was so surprised. Loney never talked like that about any of my fights before. He was always saying, "Don't worry about how tough this mug looks, just go in and knock him apart," or something like that.

I said, "You mean—?"

He took hold of my arm to start me walking again. "Maybe I over-matched you this time, Kid. The sailor's pretty good. He can box and he hits a lot harder than anybody you been up against so far."

"Oh, I'll be all right," I said.

"Maybe," he said, scowling straight ahead. "Listen, what do you think about what Pete said about you needing more boxing?"

"I don't know. I don't ever pay any attention much to what anybody says but you."

"Well, what do you think about it now?" he asked.

"Sure, I'd like to learn to box better, I guess."

He grinned at me without moving his lips much. "You're liable to get some fine lessons from this Sailor whether you want 'em or not. But no kidding, suppose I told you to box him instead of tearing in, would you do it? I mean for the experience, even if you didn't make much of a showing that way?"

I said, "Don't I always fight the way you tell me?"

"Sure you do. But suppose it meant maybe losing this one but learning something?"

"I want to win, of course," I said, "but I'll do anything you tell me. Do you want me to fight him that way?"

"I don't know," he said. "We'll see."

Friday and Saturday I just loafed around. Friday I tried to find somebody to go out and shoot pheasants with but all I could find was Bob Kirby and I was tired of listening to him make the same jokes over and over, so I changed my mind and stayed home.

Loney came home for supper and I asked him what the odds were on our fight.

He said, "Even money. You got a lot of friends."

"Are we betting?" I asked.

"Not yet. Maybe if the price gets better. I don't know."

I wished he had not been so afraid I was going to lose but I thought it might sound kind of conceited if I said anything about it, so I just went on eating.

We had a swell house that Saturday night. The armory was packed and we got a pretty good hand when we went in the ring. I felt fine and I guess Dick Cohen, who was going to be in my corner with Loney, felt fine too, because he looked like he was trying to keep from grinning. Only Loney looked kind of worried, not enough that you would notice it unless you knew him as well as I did, but I could notice it.

"I'm all right," I told him. A lot of fighters say they feel uncomfortable waiting for their fight to start but I always feel fine.

Loney said, "Sure you are," and slapped me on my back. "Listen, Kid," he said, and cleared his throat. He put his mouth over close to my ear so nobody else would hear him. "Listen, Kid, maybe—maybe you better box him like we said. O.K.?"

I said, "O.K."

"And don't let those mugs out front yell you into anything. You're doing the fighting up there."

I said, "O.K."

The first couple of rounds were kind of fun in a way because this was new stuff to me, this moving around him on my toes and going in and out with my hands high. Of course I had done some of that with fellows in the gym but not in the ring before and not with anybody that was as good at it as he was. He was pretty good and had it all over me both of those rounds but nobody hurt anybody else.

But in the first minute of the third he got to my jaw with a honey of a right cross and then whammed me in the body twice fast with his left. Pete and Loney had not been kidding when they said he could hit. I forgot about boxing and went in pumping with both hands, driving him all the way across the ring before he tied me up in a clinch. Everybody yelled so I guess it looked pretty good but I only really hit him once; he took the rest of them on his arms. He was the smartest fighter I had ever been up against.

By the time Pop Agnew broke us I remembered I was supposed to be boxing so I went back to that, but Perelman was going faster and I spent most of the rest of the round trying to keep his left out of my face.

"Hurt you?" Loney asked when I was back in my corner.

"Not yet," I said, "but he can hit."

In the fourth I stopped another right cross with my eye and a lot of lefts with other parts of my face and the fifth round was still tougher. For one thing, the eye he had hit me in was almost shut by that time and for another thing I guess he had me pretty well figured out. He went around and around me, not letting me get set.

"How do you feel?" Loney asked when he and Dick were working on me after that round. His voice was funny, like he had a cold.

I said, "All right." It was hard to talk much because my lips were puffed out.

"Cover up more," Loney said.

I shook my head up and down to say I would.

"And don't pay any attention to those mugs out front."

I had been too busy with Sailor Perelman to pay much attention to anybody else but when we came out for the sixth round I could hear people hollering things like, "Go in and fight him, Kid," and, "Come on, Kid, go to work on this guy," and, "What are you waiting for, Kid?" so I guessed they had been hollering like that all along. Maybe that had something to do with it or maybe I just wanted to show Loney that I was still all right so he would not worry about me. Anyway, along toward the last part of the round, when Perelman jarred me with another one of those right crosses that I was having so much trouble with, I got down low and went in after him. He hit me some but not enough to keep me away and, even if he did take care of most of my punches, I got in a couple of good ones and I could tell that he felt them. And when he tied me up in a clinch I knew he could do it because he was smarter than me and not because he was stronger.

"What's the matter with you?" he growled in my ear. "Are you gone nuts?" I never liked to talk in the ring so I just grinned to myself without saying anything and kept trying to get a hand loose.

Loney scowled at me when I sat down after that round. "What's the matter with you?" he said. "Didn't I tell you to box him?" He was awful pale and his voice was hoarse.

I said, "All right, I will."

Dick Cohen began to curse over on the side I could not see out of. He did not seem to be cursing anybody or anything, just cursing in a low voice until Loney told him to shut up.

I wanted to ask Loney what I ought to do about that right cross but, with my mouth the way it was, talking was a lot of work and, besides, my nose was stopped up and I had to use my mouth for breathing, so I kept quiet. Loney and Dick worked harder on me than they had between any of the other rounds. When Loney crawled out of the ring just before the gong he slapped me on the shoulder and said in a sharp voice, "Now box."

I went out and boxed. Perelman must have got to my face thirty times that round; anyway it felt like he did, but I kept on trying to box him. It seemed like a long round.

I went back to my corner not feeling exactly sick but like I might be going to get sick, and that was funny because I could not remember being hit in the stomach to amount to anything. Mostly Perelman had been working on my head. Loney looked a lot sicker than I felt. He looked so sick I tried not to look at him and I felt kind of ashamed of making a burn out of him by letting this Perelman make a monkey out of me like he was doing.

"Can you last it out?" Loney asked.

When I tried to answer him I found that I could not move my lower lip because the inside of it was stuck on a broken tooth. I put a thumb up to it and Loney pushed my glove away and pulled the lip loose from the tooth.

Then I said, "Sure. I'll get the hang of it pretty soon."

Loney made a queer gurgling kind of noise down in his throat and all of a sudden put his face up close in front of mine so that I had to stop looking at the floor and look at him. His eyes were like you think a hophead's are. "Listen, Kid," he says, his voice sounding cruel and hard, almost like he hated me. "To hell with this stuff. Go in and get that mug. What the hell are you boxing for? You're a fighter. Get in there and fight."

I started to say something and then stopped, and I had a goofy idea that I would like to kiss him or something and then he was climbing through the ropes and the gong rang.

I did like Loney said and I guess I took that round by a pretty good edge. It was swell, fighting my own way again, going in banging away with both hands, not swinging or anything silly like that, just shooting them in short and hard, leaning from side to side to get everything from the ankles up into them. He hit me of course but I figured he was not likely to be able to hit me any harder than he had in the other rounds and I had stood up under that, so I was not worrying about it now. Just before the gong rang I threw him out of a clinch and when it rang I had him covering up in a corner.

It was swell back in my corner. Everybody was yelling all around except Loney and Dick and neither of them said a single word to me. They hardly looked at me, just at the parts they were working on and they were rougher with me than they ever were before. You would have thought I was a machine they were fixing up. Loney was not looking sick any more. I could tell he was excited because his face was set hard and still. I like to remember him that way, he was awful good-looking. Dick was whistling between his teeth very low while he doused my head with a sponge.

I got Perelman sooner than I expected, in the ninth. The first part of the round was his because he came out moving fast and left-handing me and making me look pretty silly, I guess, but he could not keep it up and I got in under one of his lefts and cracked him on the chin with a left hook, the first time I had been able to lay one on his head the way I wanted to. I knew it was a good one even before his head went back and I threw six punches at him as fast as I could get them out—left, right, left, right, left, right. He took care of four of them but I got him on the chin again with a right and just above his trunks with another, and when his knees bent a little and he tried to clinch I pushed him away and smacked him on the cheekbone with everything I had.

Then Dick Cohen was putting my bathrobe over my shoulders and hugging me and sniffling and cursing and laughing all at the same time, and across the ring they were propping Perelman up on his stool.

"Where's Loney?" I asked.

Dick looked around. "I don't know. He was here. Boy, was that a mill!"

Loney caught up to us just as we were going in the dressing room. "I had to see a fellow," he said. His eyes were bright like he was laughing at something, but he was white as a ghost and he held his lips tight against his teeth even when he grinned kind of lopsided at me and said, "It's going to be a long time before anybody beats you, Kid."

I said I hoped it was. I was awful tired now that it was all over. Usually I get awful hungry after a fight but this time I was just awful tired.

Loney went across to where he had hung his coat and put it on over his sweater, and when he put it on the tail of it caught and I saw he had a gun in his hip pocket. That was funny because I never knew him to carry a gun before and if he had had it in the ring everybody would have been sure to see it when he bent over working on me. I could not ask him about it because there were a lot of people in there talking and arguing.

Pretty soon Perelman came in with his manager and two other men who were strangers to me, so I guessed they had come down from Providence with him too. He was looking straight ahead but the others looked kind of hard at Loney and me and went up to the other end of the room without saying anything. We all dressed in one long room there.

Loney said to Dick, who was helping me, "Take your time. I don't want the Kid to go out till he's cooled off."

Perelman got dressed pretty quick and went out still looking straight ahead. His manager and the two men with him stopped in front of us. The manager was a big man with green eyes like a fish and a dark kind of flat face. He said, "Smart boys, huh?"

Loney was standing up with one hand behind him. Dick Cohen put his hands on the back of a chair and kind of leaned over it. Loney said, "I'm smart. The Kid fights the way I tell him to fight."

The manager looked at me and looked at Dick and looked at Loney again and said, "M-m-m, so that's the way it is." He thought a minute and said, "That's something to know." Then he pulled his hat down tighter on his head and turned around and went out with the other two men following.

I asked Loney, "What's the matter?"

He laughed but not like it was anything funny. "Bad losers."

"But you've got a gun in—"

He cut me off. "Uh-huh, a fellow asked me to hold it for him. I got to go give it back to him now. You and Dick go on home and I'll see you there in a little while. But don't hurry, because I want you to cool off before you go out. You two take the car, you know where we parked it. Come here, Dick."

He took Dick over in a corner and whispered to him. Dick kept nodding his head up and down and looking more and more scared, even if he did try to hide it when he turned around to me. Loney said, "Be seeing you," and went out.

"What's the matter?" I asked Dick.

He shook his head and said, "It's nothing to worry about," and that was every word I could get out of him.

Five minutes later Bob Kirby's brother Pudge ran in and yelled, "Jees, they shot Loney!"

If I was not so dumb he would still be alive any way you figure it. For a long time I blamed it on Mrs. Schiff, but I guess that was just to keep from admitting that it was my own fault. I mean I never thought she actually did the shooting, like the people who said that when he missed the train that they were supposed to go away on together she came back and waited outside the armory and when he came out he told her he had changed his mind and she shot him. I mean I blamed her for lying to him, because it came out that nobody had tipped Big Jake off about her and Loney. Loney had put the idea in her head, telling her about what Pete had said, and she had made up the lie so Loney would go away with her. But if I was not so dumb Loney would have caught that train.

Then a lot of people said Big Jake killed Loney. They said that was why the police never got very far, on account of Big Jake's pull down at the City Hall. It was a fact that he had come home earlier than Mrs. Schiff had expected and she had left a note for him saying that she was running away with Loney, and he could have made it down to the street near the armory where Loney was shot in time to do it, but he could not have got to the railroad station in time to catch their train, and if I was not so dumb Loney would have caught that train.

And the same way if that Sailor Perelman crowd did it, which is what most people including the police thought even if they did have to let them go because they could not find enough evidence against them. If I was not so dumb Loney could have said to me right out, "Listen, Kid, I've got to go away and I've got to have all the money I can scrape up and the best way to do it is to make a deal with Perelman for you to go in the tank and then bet all we got against you." Why, I would have thrown a million fights for Loney, but how could he know he could trust me, with me this dumb?

Or I could have guessed what he wanted and I could have gone down when Perelman copped me with that uppercut in the fifth. That would have been easy. Or if I was not so dumb I would have learned to box better and, even losing to Perelman like I would have anyway, I could have kept him from chopping me to pieces so bad that Loney could not stand it any more and had to throw away everything by telling me to stop boxing and go in and fight.

Or even if everything had happened like it did up to then he could still have ducked out at the last minute if I was not so dumb that he had to stick around to look out for me by telling those Providence guys that I had nothing to do with double-crossing them.

I wish I was dead instead of Loney.

"I Could've Been a Contender . . ."

BUDD SCHULBERG

In this, one of the most powerful boxing scenes in all the movies, not a single punch is thrown. The dialogue that Budd Schulberg wrote in *On the Waterfront* for pug/longshoreman Terry Malloy—played to Oscar-winning perfection by Marlon Brando—stings like a series of jabs that brilliantly set up the emotional kayo that comes with the unforgettable phrase, "I could've been a contender."

Schulberg grew up surrounded by the movies. His father ran Paramount studios when the silents evolved into talkies, and as a young writer, he nearly got himself blackballed from his hometown with his first novel, *What Makes Sammy Run?,* so ferocious in its depiction of the Hollywood hustle that contemporary young agents and producers cling to it as a training manual. But if Hollywood despised the mirror Schulberg held up to it, it couldn't deny his talent: his screenplays for *Waterfront, The Harder They Fall,* and *A Face in the Crowd* all turned into riveting dramas on screen.

Boxing transfixed Schulberg, especially the seedier side of its milieu. He wrote about it for several magazines, mined it for his plot in *The Harder They Fall,* which had its first incarnation as a novel, and wrung it to bring dimension to *Waterfront.* The movie won an Academy Award for Best Picture of 1954, as did Brando for Best Actor, and Schulberg for his screenplay.

As the scene begins, Charley, played by Rod Steiger, has just left a meeting with Johnny Friendly, the dock boss, played by Lee J. Cobb. Johnny's worried that Terry's about to expose his rackets. He's sent Charley to bring his brother in so a little sense can be knocked into him. By the end of the scene it's clear that Terry, who once took a dive at Charley's behest, has already taken one dive too many.

    🥊   🥊   🥊   🥊

TERRY

Gee, Charley, I'm sure glad you stopped by for me. I needed to talk to you. What's it they say about blood, it's—

(falters)

CHARLEY *(looking away coldly)*

Thicker than water.

DRIVER

(gravel voice, without turning around)

Where to?

CHARLEY

Four thirty-seven River Street.

TERRY

River Street? I thought we was going to the Garden.

CHARLEY

I've got to cover a bet there on the way over. Anyway, it gives us a chance to talk.

TERRY *(good-naturedly)*

Nothing ever stops you from talking, Charley.

CHARLEY

The grapevine says you picked up a subpoena.

TERRY *(Noncommittal, sullen.)*

That's right. . . .

CHARLEY *(watching for his reaction)*

Of course the boys know you too well to mark you down for a cheese-eater.

> TERRY

Mm—hmm.

> CHARLEY

You know, the boys are getting rather interested in your future.

> TERRY

Mm—hmmm.

> CHARLEY

They feel you've been sort of left out of things. They think it's time you had a few little things going for you on the docks.

> TERRY

A steady job and a few bucks extra, that's all I wanted.

> CHARLEY

Sure, that's all right when you're a kid, but you'll be pushing thirty pretty soon, slugger. It's time you got some ambition.

> TERRY

I always figured I'd live longer without it.

> CHARLEY

Maybe.

Terry looks at him.

> CHARLEY

There's a slot for a boss loader on the new pier we're opening up.

> TERRY *(interested)*

Boss loader?

> CHARLEY

Ten cents a hundred pounds on everything that moves in and out. And you don't have to lift a finger. It'll be three-four hundred a week just for openers.

> TERRY

And for all that dough I don't do nothin'?

CHARLEY

Absolutely nothing. You do nothing and you say nothing. You understand, don't you, kid?

TERRY

(struggling with an unfamiliar problem of conscience and loyalties)

Yeah—yeah—I guess I do—but there's a lot more to this whole thing than I thought, Charley.

CHARLEY

You don't mean you're thinking of testifying against—

(turns a thumb in toward himself)

TERRY

I don't know—I don't know! I tell you I ain't made up my mind yet. That's what I wanted to talk to you about.

CHARLEY

(patiently, as to a stubborn child)

Listen, Terry, these piers we handle through the local—you know what they're worth to us?

TERRY

I know, I know.

CHARLEY

Well, then, you know Cousin Johnny isn't going to jeopardize a setup like that for one rubber-lipped—

TERRY *(simultaneous)*

Don't say that!

CHARLEY *(continuing)*

—ex-tanker who's walking on his heels—?

TERRY

Don't say that!

CHARLEY

What the hell!!!

TERRY

I could have been better!

CHARLEY

Listen, that isn't the point.

TERRY

I could have been better!

CHARLEY

The point is—there isn't much time, kid.

(There is a painful pause, as they appraise each other.)

TERRY

(desperately)

I tell you, Charley, I haven't made up my mind!

CHARLEY

Make up your mind, kid, I beg you, before we get to four thirty-seven River. . . .

TERRY

(stunned)

Four thirty-seven—that isn't where Gerry G. . . .?

(Charley nods solemnly. Terry grows more agitated.)

TERRY

Charley . . . you wouldn't take me to Gerry G. . . .?

(Charley continues looking at him. He does not deny it. They stare at each other for a moment. Then suddenly Terry starts out of the cab. Charley pulls a pistol. Terry is motionless, now, looking at Charley.)

CHARLEY
Take the boss loading, kid. For God's sake. I don't want to hurt you.

TERRY
(hushed, gently guiding the gun down toward Charley's lap)

Charley . . . Charley . . . Wow. . . .

CHARLEY *(genuinely)*
I wish I didn't have to do this, Terry.

(Terry eyes him, beaten. Charley leans back and looks at Terry strangely. Terry raises his hands above his head, somewhat in the manner of a prizefighter mitting the crowd. The image nicks Charley's memory.)

TERRY *(an accusing sigh)*
Wow. . . .

CHARLEY *(gently)*
What do you weigh these days, slugger?

TERRY *(shrugs)*
—eighty-seven, eighty-eight. What's it to you?

CHARLEY *(nostalgically)*
Gee, when you tipped one seventy-five you were beautiful. You should've been another Billy Conn. That skunk I got to manage you brought you along too fast.

TERRY

It wasn't him!

(years of abuse crying out in him)

It was you, Charley. You and Johnny. Like the night the two of youse come in the dressing room and says, 'Kid, this ain't your night—we're going for the price on Wilson.' *It ain't my night.* I'd of taken Wilson apart that night! I was ready—remember the early rounds throwing them combinations. So what happens—This bum Wilson he gets the title shot—outdoors in the ballpark!—and what do I get—a couple of bucks and a one-way ticket to Palookaville.

(more and more aroused as he relives it)

It was you, Charley. You was my brother. You should of looked out for me. Instead of making me take them dives for the short-end money.

CHARLEY *(defensively)*
I always had a bet down for you. You saw some money.

TERRY *(agonized)*
See! You don't understand!

CHARLEY
I tried to keep you in good with Johnny.

TERRY
You don't understand! I could've been a contender. I could've had class and been somebody. Real class. Instead of a bum, let's face it, which is what I am. It was you, Charley.

(Charley takes a long, fond look at Terry. Then he glances quickly out the window.)

MEDIUM SHOT—WATERFRONT—NIGHT

(From Charley's angle. A gloomy light reflects the street numbers—433—435)

INT—CLOSE—CAB—ON CHARLEY AND TERRY—NIGHT

TERRY
It was you, Charley. . . .

CHARLEY

(turning back to Terry, his tone suddenly changed)

Okay—I'll tell him I couldn't bring you in. Ten to one they won't believe it, but—go ahead, blow. Jump out, quick, and keep going . . . and God help you from here on in.

LONGER ANGLE—CAB—NIGHT

(As Terry jumps out. A bus is just starting up a little further along the street.)

The Greatest, Pound for Pound

W. C. HEINZ

One of the mentors of the New Journalism that broke out in the '60s, W.C. Heinz knocked romanticization and cliche out of sportswriting and replaced it with something far more powerful—reality. A master of clean prose, crisp dialogue, and telling detail, he left the grind of daily newspapering in the early '50s to go long. *The Professional,* his first novel—set in the world of the ring—was hailed by no less an authority on boxing and fiction than Hemingway. His profiles of Pete Reiser and Red Grange are on everybody's short list of sportswriting as art; so are two of his earlier boxing pieces, *Brownsville Bum* and *The Day of the Fight.*

In the late '70s, Heinz set out on a fascinating quest, a trip across the United States in search of the sporting heroes of an earlier time. "As each new generation shoulders its way in, occasioning its own clamor and claim to greatness," Heinz observed, "a writer experiences a hesitancy to attempt to intrude with his own memories of the people who moved him and stay with him still from a time now gone." Fortunately, Heinz didn't hesitate, and the incomparable Sugar Ray Robinson is among those he reconnected with in *Once They Heard the Cheers.*

W hen I am old," I wrote more than twenty years ago, "I shall tell them about Ray Robinson. When I was young, I used to hear the old men talk of Joe Gans and Terry McGovern and Kid McCoy. They told of the original Joe Walcott and Sam Langford, of Stanley Ketchel and Mickey Walker and Benny Leonard. How

271

well any of them really knew those men I'm not sure, but it seemed to me that some of the greatness of those fighters rubbed off on these others just because they lived at the same time.

"That is the way," I wrote, "I plan to use Sugar Ray. When the young assault me with their atomic miracles and reject my Crosby records and find comical the movies that once moved me, I shall entice them into talking about fighters. Robinson will be a form of social security for me, because they will have seen nothing like him, and I am convinced that they never will."

I am still sure today that they will never be able to match Robinson because of the social changes that were altering life in this country while he fought. The prejudice that drove the black—as before him it drove the Irish, the Jew, and then the Italian—to the ring in desperation is becoming a part of our past. In an age of reason fewer men are forced to fight with their fists, the amateurs are not what they used to be, the bootleg circuit, where Robinson received his intermediate schooling, is long gone, and the professional game has been on the decline for twenty-five years.

Ray Robinson—and Archie Moore, the venerable Sage of San Diego and the greatest ring mechanic I ever saw—were the last of the old-fashioned fighters because they fought from the end of one era through the beginning of another, and because they were the products of poverty as well as prejudice. Robinson was eight years old when his mother brought him and his two older sisters from Detroit to New York, and tried to support them on the fifteen dollars a week she made working in a laundry. Robinson sold firewood he gathered in a wagon under the West Side Highway and as far south as the Bowery. On Saturdays and Sundays he shined shoes, and at night he danced for coins on the sidewalks off Broadway. For him, as for all those others of that time, the fight game was a court of last resort.

"You may find this hard to believe," he told me a couple of times, "but I've never loved fightin'. I really dislike it. I don't believe I watch more than two fights a year, and then it has to be some friend of mine fightin'.

"Fightin', to me, seems barbaric," he said. "It seems to me like the barbarous days when men fought in a pit and people threw money down to them. I really don't like it."

"But at the same time," I said, "I must believe that fighting has given you the most satisfying experiences you have ever known."

"That's right," he said. "I enjoy out-thinkin' another man and out-maneuverin' him, but I still don't like to fight."

I believed him then, and I still do, because of something else he once told me and that one of his sisters confirmed. On the streets of Detroit and New York he ran from fights.

"I would avoid fightin'," he said, "even if I had to take the short end. I'd even apologize when I knew I was right. I got to be known as a coward, and my sisters used to fight for me. They used to remark that they hoped that some day I'd be able to take care of myself."

How able he became is in the record. He began fighting when he was fifteen, and he had 160 amateur and bootleg-amateur fights before he turned pro. As a professional he not only won the welterweight championship of the world, but he won the middleweight title for the fifth time when he was thirty-seven and he went fifteen rounds trying for it again when he was forty. He was forty-five when he finally retired in 1965, and in 362 fights, amateur and pro, over thirty years, he failed to finish only once. On that June night in 1952, when he boxed Joey Maxim for the light-heavyweight title, giving away fifteen pounds, it was 104 degrees under the Yankee Stadium ring lights, so brutally hot and humid that Ruby Goldstein, the referee, had to be replaced in the eleventh round. Robinson was giving Maxim a boxing lesson, and seemed on his way to winning yet another title, when he collapsed in his corner at the end of the thirteenth.

While Willie Pep was the greatest creative artist I ever saw in a ring, Sugar Ray Robinson remains the greatest fighter, pound-for-pound and punch-for-punch, of more than a half century, or since Benny Leonard retired with the lightweight title in 1924. Perhaps it is foolish to try to compare them, for Pep was a poet, often implying, with his feints and his footwork, more than he said, as that night when he won a round without even throwing a punch. Robinson was the master of polished prose, structuring his sentences, never wasting a word, and, as he often did, taking the other out with a single punch. That was the Robinson, however, that most Americans, enthralled by him as they were but who came to follow boxing on television, never saw. His talent had peaked between 1947 and 1950, before the era of TV boxing and before it saddened me to watch him years later on the screen struggling with fighters like Gene Fullmer and Paul Pender whom once he would have handled with ease.

"The public don't know it," he told me when I brought it up as far back as 1950, fifteen years before he retired, "but I do. The fighter himself is the first one to know."

"And how does he know it?" I said.

"You find you have to think your punches," he said. "The punches you used to throw without thinkin', you now have to reason."

It is something that happens to all of us, once the instinctive inventions and discoveries have been made. Then we reach back into the library of our experience, and what was once the product of inspiration is now merely the result of reason.

"How are you, old buddy?" he said on the phone, when I called him before flying out to Los Angeles. "When are you comin' out?"

"I'm fine," I said, "and I want to come out next week if you'll be there. How about next Friday?"

"Let me check that," he said, and then, "I'll be here. I'll be lookin' for you, because you're my man."

In his 202 professional fights, he hit fifty or more towns, and I imagine that in most, if not in all, there are still writers today whom he anointed as his "man." He was as smooth outside the ring as he was in it, and under pressing interrogation he was as elusive, but until you found that out he was a charmer.

I met him first in the spring of 1946. Already unquestionably the best welterweight in the world, he was unable to get a shot at the title, and he had hired a press agent named Pete Vaccare. We were sitting, late one morning, in Vaccare's office in the old Brill Building on Broadway, waiting for Robinson as, I was to find out, one almost inevitably did, when we heard singing out in the hall. Then the door opened, and they came in, Robinson and Junius ("June") Clark, whom he called his secretary, both of them in heavy road clothes topped off by red knitted skating caps, for they had been running on the Harlem Speedway, and they finished the song. It was "The Very Thought of You," with Robinson carrying the melody and Clark improvising, and they ended it with a soft-shoe step and a hand flourish, and amid the laugher, we were introduced. We talked, with Robinson telling how he once stole so much from a grocery store that the owner gave him a job as a delivery boy to protect his stock, and how the minister who caught him in a crap game on the steps of the Salem Methodist Episcopal Church took him inside and introduced him to boxing.

"I've just met Ray Robinson," I said to Wilbur Wood when I got back to the office that afternoon. "He's quite a guy."

"Oh, no," Wilbur said. "He conned you too."

"What do you mean, conned me?" I said.

"Hang around the fight game a little longer," Wilbur said, "and you'll find out."

In the fight game they like fighters who will fight anybody anywhere at any time and leave the business end to their managers. After he won the welterweight title, with George Gainford doing the dickering, Robinson made his own deals, and I knew a New York boxing writer who had collected two dozen complaints against him from promoters around the country.

"The trouble with Robinson," another one told me one day at lunch in Lindy's, "is that every time I get ready to bomb him, he shows up at some hospital or at the bedside of some sick kid. He's always one move ahead of you."

"As he is in the ring," I said.

There was about him an air of humble superiority, a contrariety that annoyed and frustrated those who tried to come to know him. He would plead humility and reserve a pew in church for Easter Sunday. At big fights, when other notables gathered for their introductions in the ring before the main event, Robinson would wait beyond the ringside rows and receive his applause apart as he came down the aisle and, all grace, vaulted through the ropes. He was a man who was trying to find something he had lost even before he turned professional.

"The biggest thrill I ever got," he told me once, "was when I won the Golden Gloves and they streamed that light down on me in Madison Square Garden and said, 'The Golden Gloves featherweight champion, Sugar Ray Robinson!' I bought the papers. I read about it over and over. It was more of a thrill than when I won the welterweight championship of the world.

"Once I read," he said—and he even read law, fascinated by its contradictions—"something that King Solomon said. He said, 'The wiser a man gets the less beauty he finds in life.' If I try to explain that to people they don't understand. It's like the first time you go to Coney Island and you ride the chute-the-chute and you get a big thrill. The second time it isn't so much."

Few fighters have been as disliked within their profession and by its press as was Robinson while he was struggling to make his way, and the fight game was, in part, responsible for that. In this country, from the turn of the century on, boxing gave the black man, because it needed him, a better break than he received in any other sport, but it only gave him what it had to. For years, while Mike Jacobs ran big-time boxing, he refused Robinson that chance at the welterweight title.

"Mike explained that to me," Robinson told me once. "He explained that I'd kill the division. He said, 'I got to have two or three guys fightin' for the title. You'd darken the class.' I understand that. That's good business."

I am sure he understood it, but he did not have to like it. In his early days, in order to get fights, he had to take less money than the opponents he knocked out. Once, after he had trained three weeks for a fight, the promoter ran out. A couple of years later, Jacobs promised him $2,000 beyond his small purse if he would box for a Boston promoter to whom Jacobs owed a favor. When, after the fight, Robinson showed up for his money, Jacobs ridiculed him.

"You didn't think I'd go into my own kick," Mike said, "for some other guy's fight."

They tried to do it to him in the ring, too. There was the story that Duke Stefano, then a manager of fighters, was telling me one afternoon in Stillman's Gym.

"I remember Robinson one night when he was just starting out as a pro," Duke said. "Just before the fight, Robinson complained that he had a bad ear, and he didn't want to go through with the fight. It was his left ear, and they looked in it, and you could see it was red and swollen.

"The other guy's manager—he was from New Jersey—looked at it and he said, 'Look, my guy is just an opponent. Go through with the fight, and I promise you he won't touch the ear.' Robinson said, 'Okay, long as he stays away from the ear.' Well, the bell rang, and the other guy came out of his corner and winged a right hand at the ear. Robinson just turned his head and looked at the corner. The guy did it a second time, and Robinson looked at the manager again. The third time the guy tried it, Robinson stepped in with a hook and flattened him.

"The manager," Duke said, "turned right around and went back to New Jersey. He didn't even second another kid he had in the next bout."

Fritzie Zivic did it to him too, as he did to many others. He was the recently dethroned welterweight champion of the world when Robinson, in only his second year as a pro, outpointed him over ten rounds in Madison Square Garden. Ten weeks later he would knock Zivic out in ten.

"Fritzie Zivic," Robinson told me once, "taught me more than anybody I ever fought."

"What did he teach you?" I said.

"He taught me that a man can make you butt open your own eye," he said, and I appreciated the phrasing. He was one of the cleanest fighters, and what he had learned from Zivic was not something that you did to another man, but that he could do to you.

"And how does a man do that?" I said.

"He slipped one of my jabs," Robinson said, "and reached his right glove around behind my head and pulled my head down on his."

Young Otto, who boxed the best lightweights during the first two decades of this century and was a great student of the science, refereed that first fight. One day in Stillman's I asked him about it.

"In the sixth round," he said, "Robinson said to me, 'He's stickin' his thumbs in my eyes.' I said, 'You ain't no cripple.' After that he give it back to Zivic better than Zivic was givin' it to him. I said to myself then, 'This kid is gonna be a great fighter.'"

So they tried to use him and abuse him, and sometimes succeeded, in and out of the ring. When, in self-defense, he retaliated, he acquired the reputation that provoked *The Saturday Evening Post* to ask me to do a piece they were to entitle, "Why Don't They Like Ray Robinson?"

"This is a tough assignment for me," I said to him.

"How's that?" he said.

We were sitting in his office at Ray Robinson Enterprises, Inc., in Harlem, and he had his feet up on his triangular glass-topped desk. He owned most of the block on the west side of Seventh Avenue from 123rd to 124th streets, and he had $250,000 tied up in the five-story apartment house, Sugar Ray's Bar and Restaurant, Edna Mae's Lingerie Shop, and Sugar Ray's Quality Cleaners, with its five outlets.

"I have to ask you the tough questions," I said.

"That's all right," he said. "Go ahead."

"I will," I said, "but I want to explain something first. I think this piece can do you a lot of good. You're unquestionably the greatest fighter since Benny Leonard, and there are some old-timers who say you may be the best since Joe Gans, who died ten years before you were born."

"They say that?" he said, as if he hadn't known. "I appreciate that."

"My point is," I said, "that you should be the most popular fighter of your time, but you're not. There are raps against you in the fight game, and they keep bringing up your Army record and you've never made the money that you should. A fighter like Graziano, who's a beginner compared to you and has a dishonorable discharge from the Army while you have an honorable one, has made twice as much as you have."

"That's right," he said.

"Part of that is style," I said. "All his fights are wars, and that's what the public likes, but it's style outside the ring, too. He's open and frank, and you're not, really. What I want to do is explain you. I want you to tell me what it's like to have a fine mind and great physical talents, to be a great artist but to be colored and to have that used against you in the fight game and out of it. It can explain a lot about you, and I'll understand. If I understand, I can make the readers understand, and as I said, that can mean a lot to you, if you'll level with me."

"If you can do that," he said, "I'll appreciate it. Nobody's ever done that for me before. You just ask me the questions, what you want to know."

I really believed it. I believed it for about five minutes.

"All right," I said. "Let's get the Army thing out of the way first."

It wasn't any good. We went around and around, as in a ring, and when Robinson couldn't counter my leads or even slip them, he professed only astonishment that I should hold such documented assertions to be facts.

There was something to be celebrated in his Army record. He had been a member of Casual Detachment 7, known as "The Joe Louis Troupe." Joe and he and four other fighters spent seven months touring camps in this country and putting on boxing exhibitions. In Florida, Robinson refused to box unless black troops were allowed to attend, and he, an enlisted man, faced down a general. At Camp Sibert, Alabama, a white M.P. saw Louis emerge from a phone booth in so-called white territory, and he threatened to club Joe. Robinson took him on, the two rolling on the ground, and there was rioting by black troops before apologies were made to the two fighters.

It was a matter of Army record and common knowledge, however, that when the troupe sailed for Europe, from Pier 90, New York, on March 31, 1944, Robinson was not aboard. It was also in the record that he had previously declared his intention not to go, and that the Articles of War as they applied to the punishment for desertion had been explained to him.

"But why would a man say such a thing?" he said when I had read to him from the affidavit.

"He not only said it," I said, "but he swore to it."

"I can't understand that," Robinson said. "I never met that officer, and he never read me such things."

Years later, in his autobiography, he would state that he had been suffering from amnesia following a fall, and had been hospitalized for that before his honorable discharge as a sergeant on June 3, 1944. It was a book he had wanted me to write after he had retired for the first time in 1952. Because he preferred to avoid using elevators, as he also preferred not to fly, we had met late one afternoon with my agent and another, not in my agent's office on the twentieth floor of the Mutual of New York Building, but in the cocktail lounge of the Park Sheraton.

"I just can't do it, Ray," I said, after we had talked for a while, the others listening, and I had tried again. "There are those conflicting versions of those events in your life, in and out of boxing, and we tried two years ago in your office and we've tried again now, and we still can't resolve them. I'm sorry, but I just can't do the book."

"That's all right, old buddy," he said. "I understand."

I doubt that he did—why couldn't we just put it all down the way he said, and possibly even believed it had been, and ignore the conflicts? And when I would see him after that it would always be in camp before his fights and I would be with others. Now I had heard that he was heading up a youth project in Los Angeles, and at ten o'clock on that Friday morning the taxi driver and I found it, finally, on West Adams Boulevard with the sign—Sugar Ray's Youth Foundation—fronting the one-story building.

"He's in conference with Mr. Fillmore right now," the woman said across the counter, and I had missed her name when she had introduced herself. "I don't think he'll be long, though."

"That's all right," I said. "I have plenty of time."

"Maybe while you're waiting," she said, "you'd like to look at some of our material."

"That would be fine," I said.

She introduced me then to Mel Zolkover, who had arisen from behind one of the desks beyond the counter. He is a middle-aged retired mechanical engineer and the foundation's administrative director, and we shook hands.

She went back to a desk, and while I waited I could hear the even tones of Robinson's voice, still familiar after all the years, in an office on the left. When she came back she handed me the several sheets of publicity and a folder from the 1976–77 "Miss Sugar Ray Teen Pageant." From a photograph I identified her as Thelma Smith, the executive secretary, and elsewhere I noted that Bob Hope is the foundation's honorary chairman, Robinson the chairman, and Wright Fillmore the president. I read about arts and crafts projects, costume making, karate instruction, talent shows, art classes, and workshops in beauty and personal development, drama, band and combo repertory, and dance.

"Old buddy!" he said, smiling and his face fuller and shaking hands across the counter. "How's my old buddy?"

"Fine," I said. "And you?"

"Just fine," he said. "Come on in here and sit down and we'll talk."

I followed him to the middle desk at the back. He was wearing a blue leisure suit, the jacket over a dark blue-and-fuchsia sports shirt. Once I had checked his wardrobe. He owned thirty-four suits, twenty-six pairs of shoes, nine sports jackets and as many pairs of slacks, six overcoats and four topcoats, most of which apparel he said he had never worn even once.

"You've gained some weight," I said.

As a fighter he was one of the most lithe and handsome of men. He moved with such grace and rhythm, in the ring and out, that watching him made me think of rubbing silk or satin between one's hands. During his first retirement, in fact, he tried it as a dancer, opening at the French Casino in New York for $15,000 a week. After that, it was downhill.

"Robinson was a good dancer, for a fighter," a Broadway booking agent told me, after Robinson had come back to knock out Bobo Olson and win the middleweight title the second time. "Maybe no other fighter ever danced as well, but the feature of his act was his change of clothes. He looked good in everything he put on."

He was leaning back now in the high-backed desk chair. Not only was his face fuller, but at fifty-six he was a lot heavier across the shoulders and chest and at the waist.

"Yeah, I'm heavier," he said now. "You see, I sit here with something on my mind, and I don't get the exercise I should. Every day, though, I try to take a five-mile walk."

"How heavy are you?"

"Oh, 183–84," he said, and he fought best at 147. "You see, you've got a certain ego about having been a champion, and you'd like to keep like that, but it's so difficult. There are temptations, and it takes willpower. When you're fightin' you have to live by the rules, because when that bell rings condition is the name of the game. Even then, in camp, Joe Louis and I would go out in the boat and have quarts of ice cream and our trainers would get mad."

He reached into a desk drawer, and he brought out a package of Danish pastries. He tore one end off the transparent wrapper and took out one and, leaning back again, began eating.

"My breakfast," he said. "You know, the most important meal is breakfast."

"And that's your breakfast?"

"That's right," he said, "and Jack Blackburn used to get after Joe and me."

Blackburn was Louis' discoverer, teacher, and trainer. He developed Louis so precisely in the image of what he himself had been as a fighter that Louis had the same flaw that Blackburn had of dropping the left arm after a jab. It was what made Louis vulnerable to a straight right counter over the jab.

"Blackburn," Robinson was saying, "used to tell us, 'You got to eat breakfast.' Then they used to squeeze blood from the meat, and I'd drink that. From Monday through Friday I'd drink it. You have to get that from a slaughterhouse, and they put this blood in a can and I used to go down there and get it. I'll tell you, that's the most potent thing there is."

"I remember that you used to do that," I said. "Do you ever drink it now?"

"Every now and then I think I'll do it," he said, "but I don't."

He had finished the pastry and folded over the end of the package. He put the package back in the desk drawer.

"What brought you out here to California?" I said.

"My wife is from out here," he said. When he was fighting he was married to Edna Mae Holly. She had been a dancer and they had two sons, and I had not known he had remarried. "Joe Louis was goin' with a girl out here, and I met Millie through the recommendation of this other girl. You know, like a dog. You see something, and the ears go bong! We were married in 1965, and that's how I met Mr. Fillmore, and we started this foundation."

"Tell me about that."

"We went to London," he said, "and she was having her thirty-third or thirty-fourth birthday party, and . . .'"

"Who was?" I said.

"Queen Elizabeth," he said. "Millie and I, we were invited and we went to the party. It was a wonderful ceremony, and Prince Phillip and I were talkin'. You remember those strikes?"

"What strikes?"

"I think it started in Berkeley," he said.

"The student protests?"

"That's right," he said. "We were talkin', and he said, 'Sugar, I believe you could help that.' I said, 'What do you mean?' He said, 'Youngsters look up to you, and I've got an idea.' I had met Mr. Fillmore, and of all the people I've met—all the Popes and all—I never met a man who believes in God and lives it more than Mr. Fillmore. You never hear the guy say a harsh word, even a loud word, and I want you to meet him."

"I'd like to," I said.

"I came back to New York," he said, "and I was goin' with my present wife. She lived upstairs out here and Mr. Fillmore lived downstairs. I talked with him, and we went to the Council of Churches and asked them to help us, and they gave us money. The county saw the potential and funded us. Now we hope to have the State Junior Olympics, and Jimmy Carter was out and I met with him, and he's a nice guy and likes what we're doing, and we hope for Federal funding. We work with the Board of Education and the Department of Parks and Recreation, and there has never been a paid member of the board of trustees. Every dollar goes in, and I'm about the poorest cat on the board."

"What happened to all that property you owned in Harlem?"

"I sold that even at a loss," he said, "just to get out. I fell in love with my wife out here, and Harlem was goin' downhill so bad, and now if you see a white face there, you know it's a cop."

"Did you get clipped?"

One day, sitting in his office in Harlem, he had told me that he felt he was destined to make a great success in business. It was that afternoon in 1950, when he spoke of how he knew his ring skills were starting to decline.

"After a man attains all the things he likes," he had said then, "he has to find some other form of happiness. I feel I'm gonna find that in business. I'm not cocky within myself. I'm an extreme Christian within myself. I just believe. My faith is so strong that I know that someday I'm gonna be the head of some real big business. I thank God for the success I've had, and the investments I've made."

"Yeah, I got clipped," he said now. "It happened to Joe, too, but that's a part of life. I didn't get out with too much, but I didn't lose too much, either."

"As you say," I said, "it happened to Joe, too, and it happens so often. They talk about the dirty fight game, but a fighter makes a fortune in it, and when he gets out into the nice clean world of American business they take it all from him."

"You're so right," he said. "What other fighters are you seeing for the book?"

"I just saw Willie Pep last month."

"He was a great one," he said. "When I beat him in the amateurs in Connecticut, they took me to the police station."

"I remember that story," I said. "Willie's all right. He's working for the Athletic Commission in Connecticut, and he's married for the fifth time."

"You know how that is," he said, smiling. "When Joe was the champion and I used to go to the airport, they came off that plane like it was a parade."

"And I saw Billy Graham," I said. "He's doing fine, working for Seagram's."

"Billy Graham?" he said. "He's my man. He beat me in the first fight I lost."

"When you were ninety-pound kids," I said.

He had reached into the desk drawer again. He brought out the Danish, and started on another one.

"There are so many of your fights I remember," I said. "The night you won the middleweight title from Jake LaMotta in Chicago . . ."

"Jake wasn't smart," he said, "but he was in condition. He was 'The Bull.'"

"I know," I said. "I remember that, after your first fight with him, you were passing blood for days."

"That's right," he said.

"When you fought him in Chicago for the title in '51," I said, "I watched it at a neighbor's house on TV. Ted Husing was announcing the fight, and in the early rounds he was filled with LaMotta. He kept saying that we were seeing an upset, that LaMotta was running the fight."

"He said that?"

"Yes, and I said to my neighbor, 'Husing doesn't know what he's talking about. Watch what Robinson does the next time the referee breaks them, or Robinson backs off from an exchange.' You would back off so far that sometimes you went out of the camera range, right off the screen. I said, 'LaMotta had trouble making the weight, and Robinson is walking the legs off him. When he gets ready to turn it on, Jake won't have much left.' In the thirteenth round you turned it on, and the referee had to stop it."

"That's right," he said, nodding. "That's exactly what I did. You remember that?"

"Another fight I remember," I said, "was the one with 'Flash' Sebastian, and that one scared me."

"That scared me, too," he said.

On June 24, 1947, Robinson knocked out Jimmy Doyle in the eighth round in Cleveland, and the next day Doyle died of brain injury. At the coroner's inquest, Robinson was asked, "Couldn't you tell from the look on Doyle's face that he had been hurt?" Robinson said, "Mister, that's what my business is, to hurt people." Because he was absolutely frank, he caught the criticism. He set up a $10,000 trust fund for Doyle's mother, and two months later he took little more than his expenses to fight Sebastian, the welterweight champion of the Philippines, on an American Legion show in Madison Square Garden.

"It was right after that Doyle fight," I said now.

"I know," he said. "The night before the Doyle fight I dreamed what was gonna happen, and I got up the next day and I called the commission and I told them. They said that they'd sold all the tickets, and they went so far as to get a Catholic priest to talk to me."

"In that Sebastian fight," I said, "you came out of your corner for the first round and he threw a wide hook, and you brought your right glove up and blocked it. He backed off, and came in again and did the same thing. This time you threw the right hand inside the hook and followed it with a hook of your own, and he went back on his head. Then he tried to get up, and he fell forward on his face, and the photographers at ringside were hollering, 'Get this! Get this! This guy may die, too!'"

"I know," he said. "I said, 'Oh, Lord, don't let it happen again.'"

"In the dressing room later," I said, "Sebastian was hysterical. Whitey Bimstein had seconded him, and he took a towel and soaked it in ice water and snapped it in Sebastian's face to bring him out of it. I said to Whitey, 'What kind of a fighter is this they brought all the way from the Philippines to almost be killed?' Whitey said, 'I never saw him before tonight, but they asked me to work with him. After I got him taped, I told him to warm up. He threw one punch, and I stopped him. I said, "Look, fella. When you throw that hook, don't raise your head. You're fightin' Ray Robinson. You do that with him, and he'll take your head right off your shoulders."'"

"Then sometime later I was talking with Ruby Goldstein. You remember Ruby was the referee that night, and Ruby said, 'That Sebastian threw that first hook, and Robinson brushed it away. I was just thinkin' to myself that if he did that again Robinson would cross a right. The next thing I knew he did, and I was saying, 'One . . . two . . . three.'"

"I was lucky that night," Robinson said now.

"And Sebastian was, too," I said, "and I'll tell you another night when you were lucky."

"When was that?" he said.

"When you got the title back from Randy Turpin."

In August of 1950 Robinson carried Charley Fusari over fifteen rounds of what was ostensibly a fight for Robinson's welterweight title but was, on Robinson's part, just one of the greatest boxing exhibitions I have ever seen. He gave his entire purse to the Damon Runyon Cancer Fund, of which Dan Parker, the sports editor and columnist of the *New York Daily Mirror,* was president. This act of charity had the effect, however unintended, of silencing Parker, who, whenever the word got out that Robinson intended to go to Europe, would recall that he had missed that opportunity when he had failed to sail with the "Joe Louis Troupe."

The following May, Robinson left for Paris—Parker merely pointing out that it was "by boat"—and took along his fuchsia Cadillac and George Gainford's black one. Included in the party of eleven were Robinson's golf pro, and his barber, and in Paris they acquired an Arabian midget who spoke five languages. They occupied most of one floor of the Claridge, and seldom left to eat in restaurants. There was an almost constant flow of room-service waiters through the suites, and the bill at the end was staggering.

"You know how the French are," Lew Burston, who had lived for many years in Paris and ran the foreign affairs of the Mike Jacobs boxing empire, said to me one day following Robinson's return. "In the old days they used to see the maharajas arrive with their retinues, and they basically believe that another man's business is his own. At the end of Robinson's stay, though, even the French were somewhat stunned."

Robinson fought a half-dozen times in Europe, in Paris and elsewhere, and on July 10 in London he defended his middleweight title against Randy Turpin, the British and European champion. Turpin out-pointed him over the fifteen rounds in an upset so startling that in the fight game on this side of the ocean they found it hard to believe.

"You may remember," I was saying to him now, "what Lew Burston said after the first Turpin fight. He said, 'Robinson had Paris in his legs.'"

"That was one of the few fights," he said, nodding, "where I took a chance. Remember what I told you—about temptation and willpower? Then he had one of the most unorthodox styles, too. You remember the second fight?"

Two months after the London fight they met again in the Polo Grounds in New York. Robinson won the early rounds, but then Turpin, awkward, sometimes punching off the wrong foot, lunging with his jab, chopping with his right in close and eight years younger, began to come on. By the tenth round, Robinson seemed spent, and then a wide cut opened over his left eye and, obviously fearful that the fight might be stopped and with the blood gushing out of the cut, he took the big gamble. He walked in with both hands going. He shook Turpin with a right, pushed him off and dropped him in the middle of the ring with another right. When Turpin got up at nine, Robinson drove him to the ropes, and there he must have thrown forty punches. Turpin, reeling now and trying to cover, was half sitting on the middle rope, and there were 61,000 people there, and it sounded as if they were all screaming.

"Of course I remember the fight," I was saying now, "and, as I said, you were lucky that night. When you had him on the ropes and he didn't go down, you reached out with your left, put your glove behind his head and tried to pull him forward. There were only eight seconds left in the round, so if you had pulled him off the ropes and he had gone down, the count would have killed the rest of the round. You had that cut and you were exhausted, and you would never have survived the next five rounds."

"You're right," he said.

"And I'll tell you a night," I said, "when you did out-smart yourself."

"What night was that?" he said.

"That night in the Yankee Stadium when you fought Maxim and it was 104 degrees in there. You were not only licking him, but you were licking him so easily that you made a show of it, dancing around in and out, throwing unnecessary punches. That's why, in that heat, you collapsed at the end of the thirteenth."

"You're right, old buddy," he said. "That was a mistake. I was incoherent all the next day. I never remembered when Goldstein fell out. I had a premonition the night before that fight too. I had a premonition that I would die."

He had finished the pastry and reclosed the package again, and he returned it to the desk drawer.

"There's this Sugar Ray Leonard," I said, "who won a gold medal in the Olympics. There was another one—Sugar Ray Seales. How do you feel about these kids calling themselves Sugar Ray?"

"Bill, you know," he said, sitting back and smiling, "it's a good feeling to think that the kids think that much of me."

It was different when he was a fighter. There was another welterweight at that time named George Costner, and in Chicago in 1945 Robinson knocked him out in two minutes and fifty-five seconds of the first round. Five years later they were matched again, this time in Philadelphia, and in the days leading up to the fight, the other, by then known as George ("Sugar") Costner, was quoted on the sports pages as disparaging Robinson.

"Listen, boy," Robinson said to him at the weigh-in, "I've been readin' what you've been sayin' in the papers about what you're gonna do to me."

"Why, there are no hard feelings, are there, Ray?" Costner said. "I just did that to boost the gate."

"That may be all right," Robinson said, "but when I boost the gate I do it by praisin' my opponent."

The logic of publicity, revolving as it does around the build-up of the underdog, was all on Costner's side, but this time Robinson knocked him out in two minutes and forty-nine seconds. While it was succinct, this was, in its scientific precision, one of Robinson's finest performances.

"There's only one 'Sugar,'" Robinson was quoted as saying right after the fight, but I remember another aftermath. It involved still another welter-weight who was asked by his manager if he would fight Sugar Costner.

"No thanks," the fighter said.

"But you can lick Costner," the manager said. "Robinson flattened him twice inside of one round."

"I don't want to fight anybody named Sugar," the fighter said.

"I've been remembering," I said to Robinson now, "the first time I ever met you. It was in Pete Vaccare's office in the Brill Building, and we heard you singing out in the hall, and you and June Clark came in wearing road clothes and harmonizing 'The Very Thought of You.' You two did it very well."

"Yeah," Robinson said, smiling. "June Clark, he was a musician—Armstrong was in his band—and he, too, was a believer in God."

"That was a long time ago," I said. "It was in March of 1946."

"Are you sure?" Robinson said. "Didn't we meet before then?"

"I'm certain," I said, "because I didn't start to write sports until I came back from the war."

"You were in the war?" Robinson said.

"Yes," I said, "but only as a war correspondent."

"Where were you?" Robinson said.

"All through northern Europe," I said.

"In the ETO?" he said. "Then how come we didn't meet over there?"

"I don't know," I said. It was as if I had just been stunned by a sucker punch, one you never expect the other to throw, and I was sparring for time.

"We were over there," Robinson was saying now. "Joe Louis and I, we had a troupe, and we boxed in the ETO and everything."

I still didn't know what to say. There were the others at their desks—Thelma Smith and Mel Zolkover and a secretary—who could have heard us, and I didn't want to challenge it there. I am quite sure that, if we had been alone, I would have, just to try again after so many years to understand him, but as I have thought about it since, I believe it was better that I let it ride. He is a man who has his own illusions about his life, as do we all, about the way he wishes it had been, and there is little if any harm, although some sadness, in that now. I shall send him a copy of this book, however, and when he reads this chapter I hope he understands that, as a reporter, my responsibility, as pompous as this may sound, is to draw as accurate and honest a portrait as I can.

"I want you to meet Mr. Fillmore," he was saying now. "Mr. Fillmore can tell you a lot about the foundation."

"I'd like to meet him," I said, and he led me into Fillmore's office and introduced us.

Fillmore, a slim, immaculate man, bald and wearing dark glasses, said that he would be seventy-eight in a couple of months. He had worked, he said, for the Southern Pacific Railroad for forty years, as a waiter and then as an instructor, and he had been retired for seven years when Robinson and he started the foundation in 1969.

"The first time I met Ray personally," he said, "was through his present wife. She was rooming with us, and he was going with her, and then he finally married. We got to talking and got to be buddies, and one day I got a telegram from London that he wanted to see me.

"I wondered, with all the people he knew, why he wanted to see me. I waited, and he and his wife flew in and, it being hot, we sat in the backyard. I asked him what was so important, and he said he'd always wanted to do something for youth. I said, 'What do you want me to do about it, Ray? With all the people you know, you want me to put together something for children? I'm retired.' He said, 'No. You have just started working.' I told him, 'We need money, and we need children. If you can get the money, I can get the children.'

"From the back step we moved to Millie's kitchen, then to the church, and when it got too big for there, we moved here. Since 1969 there's no black mark on this organization, and I challenge anybody to go to the IRS or wherever.

"The Southern Pacific," he said, "had given me a three-year course in human relations, and what we try to do here is make good citizens, not only a Sugar Ray Robinson or a Sandy Koufax. We had these fellas here, and they called themselves 'The Young Black Panthers.' They knew every way to do wrong. There was 'One-Legged Joe' and there was 'Bluefish,' and the one was fourteen and the other was fifteen, and we gained their confidence.

"The news came out one time that a hamburger stand had been held up, and it sounded to me like 'One-Legged Joe' and 'Bluefish,' so I called in

Tony, one of the lesser lights. I said to him, 'Where were you on such-and-such a night?' He said, 'I know what you want, but I wasn't in it.' I said, 'I know, but if I could find out where it was and I could find the pistol, I could help out.'

"He told me where it was, where to find the pistol, and it was a toy. 'One-Legged Joe' went to UCLA and stayed there three years and got a job. 'Bluefish' joined the Navy, and that was what Ray Robinson had in mind, and what we try to do."

When I came out of Fillmore's office, Robinson was at his desk, finishing another Danish, and he suggested that we go over to the foundation's annex. We walked up the sidewalk, then through the blacktopped parking area of a shopping center, and at the far side, into what had been a store and was now partitioned into several rooms. He led me into a conference room, and we sat down with Zolkover, and with Richard Jackman, a then thirty-two-year-old law graduate who is the program director, and his assistant, Scott McCreary, then twenty-six and a graduate of the University of California at Santa Barbara.

"Tell Bill," Robinson said, at the head of the long table, "what we do here."

"Well, take our baseball program," Zolkover said. "We kind of take the place of the YMCA and the Little League for kids six to sixteen in the lower socioeconomic areas where they can't afford those others. The children are not allowed to pay, and when you think of it, when Ray was a kid his mother couldn't afford it."

"We're not trying to build a Sugar Ray," Jackman said.

"That's right," Robinson said, "and the last thing, that we're just goin' to start now, is the boxing. I didn't want people to think we're a boxing organization."

"At the same time," Jackman said, "it's Mr. Robinson's charisma that makes it go. He has friends all over the world, and if we get the Junior Olympics started here it could include ten to fifteen cities, and we could expand to Europe, too."

"He can open any door," Zolkover said, nodding toward Robinson. "One day the question was, where could we get readership? I said, 'The Reader's Digest.' I looked up the chairman of the board, and Ray called, and it was, 'Hey, Ray!'"

"You see," he said, "we're like a church. We pay no money, so we have to have people with dedication like Ray."

"When he was boxing," Scott said, "they called him the greatest fighter, pound-for-pound. We say that, pound-for-pound, we get the greatest distance out of our money."

When Robinson and I left them a few minutes later, we stood for a moment on the sidewalk edging the parking area, looking out over the quadrangle of parked cars. The California climate, unlike that of the Northeast, where I abide, is conducive to keeping cars clean, and I was struck by how they glistened, older models as well as new, in the sunlight.

"Are you still on the Cadillac kick?" I said to him.

"No," he said. "No more."

"I remember you turned that chartreuse one in for the fuchsia one."

"The car I drive now," he said, and then pointing, "is that little red Pinto over there."

"That's your car?"

"Yeah," he said, and then, smiling, "but I've been there."

"I'll say you have," I said.

We walked slowly across the parking area. We were dawdling in the warm sunlight.

"While you were fighting," I said, "did you take out any annuities?"

"Nope," he said.

"Did you buy any stocks?"

"A few, and I sold those."

"When you had all those investments in Harlem," I said, "I was always afraid you were going to get clipped."

"That's right," he said.

"So how do you get along now?"

"I've got friends," he said. "I borrow five grand, and I pay back three. I borrow three, and pay two. Then something drops in, and I pay everybody. People say to me about this foundation, 'What are you gettin'?' They can't understand doing something for kids. I've always been a Christian believer in God. I was gifted with a talent that helped introduce me to people, and all that was in preparation for what I'm doin' now."

"And I celebrate it," I said.

When we got back to the office I called for a cab. While I was waiting for it, he said he thought he would take his five-mile walk, and we shook hands and wished each other well. He went out the door and, through the wide front window, I saw him start up the sidewalk, the greatest fighter I ever saw, the one I wanted so much to know.

Pride of the Tiger

ROBERT M. LIPSYTE

Haunting, heart-breaking, majestic, tragic and, in the end, timeless, Robert Lipsyte's 1976 portrait for *The Atlantic* of Dick Tiger is a superb piece of writing about a superb man who happened to be a superb fighter. Lipsyte, who had recently left his post as sports columnist at *The New York Times* to freelance and write novels, has since returned to the paper as a featured sports columnist on Sundays.

* * *

The first time I saw Dick Tiger he was waiting for me in front of the old Madison Square Garden, a homburg perched on top of his head. The homburg was much too small, and I thought he looked comical. It was years before I learned that he always bought his hats a size too small, so he could share them with his brothers back home in Nigeria.

I introduced myself to Tiger and he shook my hand gravely. Then he turned and began moving down Eighth Avenue on the balls of his feet, like a big black cat. His manager and I followed.

"Nigerian fighters are very good, very tough," said his manager. "They're closer to the jungle."

Over his shoulder, Tiger said, "There is no jungle in Nigeria."

"It's just an expression, Dick, just a figure of speech," said the manager. "I mean they're hungry fighters."

Tiger stopped. "Hungry fighters." He winked at me. "We eat hoo-mon bee-inks. Medium rare."

We walked a mile and a half to the gym where he was training because Tiger would not consider a cab, even if I paid. It was said around that Tiger had the terminal cheaps. I followed him into a dressing room and watched him shed the comedy of his clothes. As the homburg, the brown sports jacket, the blue tie, and white shirt disappeared into a rusty metal locker, Tiger seemed to grow larger. The blue tribal tattoos across his chest and back rippled over knotty muscle. He seemed suddenly savage, dangerous.

But there was only gentleness in his eyes, and humor twitched at the corners of his wide mouth. I watched him tape his hands slowly and with great care, first winding the dirty gray bandages around and around, then placing the sponge across the knuckles, then wrapping on the adhesive. I asked him why he didn't have his manager or trainer perform this daily chore, now that he was middleweight champion of the world.

"I am a travelin' man, and I got to do things myself, a fighter should know these things," he said. "This is my business. I don't want to spoil myself for someday when there is no one around to help me."

He was thirty-four years old at the time and had been champion for less than a year. He was training in New York, where facilities and sparring partners were the best, for the second defense of that championship, to be held in Ibadan, Nigeria. Tiger was taking this fight very seriously. It would be Nigeria's first world title fight, and his own real homecoming. "It is very important I win," he said. "For pride. They receive me different, people, when I am champion."

This was June 1963 and I had interviewed few fighters. I watched Tiger work out for two hours, methodically, intensely, oblivious of sound and movement around him. Great silver globules of sweat formed, swelled, exploded on his forehead, and he never wiped them away. He weighed about 160 pounds then, and his 5-foot-8 body was unusually hard and fit. His calisthenics were so violent that they seemed beyond human tolerance; I was sure his eyes would pop out of his head as he twisted his neck, that his muscles and veins would burst through his skin.

We talked again after he was finished. His voice was softer now, his body more relaxed. He had been born in Amaigbo, a remote eastern Nigerian town in the rain forests of the Binin River delta, a town that appeared on few maps. He was raised on a farm and educated in English and Ibo at an Anglican mission school. At nineteen he went to the city of Aba to work in his brother's grocery store. At a local boys' club he learned to box.

He had been christened Richard Ihetu, Ibo for "what I want," but assumed the ring name Dick Tiger for his early pro fights against the likes of Easy Dynamite and Super Human Power. He kept the name when a British promoter brought him to England to fight on the Blackpool-Liverpool circuit. He was lonely and chilled in the dank foreign gyms, and he lost his first four fights. Letters from his family in Nigeria were beseeching him to give up the foolishness and return to his father's farm or his brother's grocery store. Tiger gave himself one more chance. In his fifth fight, he knocked out a Liverpool boy in 90 seconds, and Richard Ihetu, farmer and clerk, disappeared forever.

He first came to American in 1959 and lived with his pregnant wife in third-rate Manhattan hotels, cooking meals on a hot plate and running in Central Park. He slowly gained a reputation among boxing promoters as an honest workman. He was always in top condition, he always gave his best. He would never be spectacular, he did not have a great deal of boxing finesse or personal "color," but he was dependable and tough. His wife gave birth to twins, then to a third child in 1960. Tiger sent her back to Nigeria and began commuting between New York and Aba. Now he lived in fourth-rate hotels, walked whenever possible, window-shopped for entertainment, sent every penny home. After he won the title in 1962, he was able to send more money home, but he did not improve the quality of his living conditions or his clothing. I asked him if he was saving his money for something special.

"This will not always be my business. I want money," he said, rubbing his fingers together. "Six hundred thousand to start a big business. Now all I have is a house and a Peugeot, that is all."

We left the gym together and took the subway uptown. We made small talk on the ride, and he told me the only tiger he had ever seen was in a cage in the Liverpool zoo. My stop came first. I got off the train and looked back at him through the window. In his clothes again, he was just a chunky man in a too-small homburg, hanging from an overhead strap, jostled by a rush-hour crowd.

I went back to the office and wrote a tidy Sunday feature story, my specialty. A month later, I read that he had won his bout in Ibadan. I was glad of that; something about Tiger had touched me.

In December of that year, 1963, he defended his title against Joey Giardello in Atlantic City. It was my first championship fight, and my notes were unusually voluminous, including the first stanza of the Nigerian anthem, which was played before the fight began.

> Nigeria, we hail thee,
> Our own dear native land.
> Though tribe and tongue may differ
> In brotherhood we stand.

Tiger lost the 15-round fight by a decision. I knew he would be very upset. He had become a national hero in Nigeria: he had been awarded a medal, Member of the British Empire, in Lagos, and he was amassing property in Aba. In a few days he would be returning home a loser.

But the next morning he smiled at me and said amiably, "Look at my face. I don't look like I was in a fight last night. I did a bit of dancing last night with Giardello, and I am a fighter, not a dancer. I thought I did enough to win, as he kept running away."

He shrugged and sighed. "These days you get a title by running away."

We shook hands gravely and said good-bye. I would have liked to tell him that I was sorry he had lost, but the words stuck in my throat. It seemed somehow unprofessional, and Tiger was a professional.

Giardello promised Tiger a rematch within six months, but it was two years before they met again. Giardello enjoyed his championship hugely and did nothing to endanger it, like fighting someone who might take it away. Tiger, meanwhile waited patiently and rarely fought: his reputation as a head-down, hands-up, straight-ahead slugger who plodded into his opponent and beat away scared off anyone who didn't need to fight him for a payday or a shot at the title.

By the time they met again I was a regular boxing writer, veteran of the Clay-Liston spectacles, a seasoned observer who almost knew A. J. Liebling's *The Sweet Science* by heart. I even kept my own scorecard, which usually conflicted with the judges'. I was also a great deal more appreciative of Dick Tiger, now that I had interviewed many other boxers and watched them train and fight. Of all athletes, boxers are generally the friendliest and the most dedicated, and Tiger had the most heart and soul of them all.

I liked Joey Giardello, but I was secretly rooting for Tiger to win back his title the night of the rematch in Madison Square Garden. Tiger was shorter and lighter and older than Giardello, but from the opening bell, when a Nigerian *etulago* set a thumping drumbeat, Tiger doggedly followed Giardello around the ring, pressing and battering and slugging. Giardello stayed on his feet as a point of pride. At the start of the fifteenth and last round, with the decision certain for Tiger, Giardello leaned forward and whispered, "Nice fight."

Tiger did not hold the title very long this time, either. He was over thirty-six years old, and the strain of keeping his weight below the 160-pound middleweight limit sapped his strength. Emile Griffith, the welterweight champion, who could no longer keep his weight below 147 pounds, moved up in class and beat him. So, logically, Tiger decided to move up in class, too. In the winter of 1966 he beat the brilliant but erratic José Torres and became light-heavyweight champion. The morning after that fight I visited his shabby hotel room. He greeted me with the same amiable, win-or-lose smile.

"The people all said that Tiger is finished, that he looks a hundred years old, and now they come around to pat my head and tell me I'm a good boy." He shrugged. "That's life."

His investments in Nigeria were doing well, he told me, although he was concerned by the mounting violence and political instability. Many thousands of his fellow Ibo tribesmen had been slaughtered in pogroms in northern Nigeria. The Ibo, who were Christians, were civil servants and small businessmen in the Moslem north. Ibo were fleeing back to their native lands in eastern Nigeria. Tiger's holdings were in Aba, in the eastern region, where he lived in a large, air-conditioned home, owned several buildings, operated several businesses and shops, and had a chauffeur for his Mercedes-Benz limousine. He was still optimistic about the future of his six children and the many nieces and nephews that he took pride and joy in supporting.

Tiger fought Torres again the following spring, as usual giving away height and weight and age, and he beat him again. This time, when the decision was announced, fights broke out in the balcony and bottles of wine and rum smashed on the Garden floor and sprayed the crowd with shards of glass. There was blood and there were a number of injuries. I wrote most of my story crouched under the Garden ring, with my typewriter on my knees. The incident was discussed and written about for several days, and then dismissed as one of those cultural-ethnic-economic-sporting inevitabilities. Garden officials blamed "a few nuts or hoodlums" who wanted to read about themselves in the papers. Torres said he was proud of his fellow Puerto Ricans for showing their "support" of him, and Lipsyte analyzed the random violence as an expression of the class struggle. The boxing commissioner declared: "A hundred years ago Charles Dickens went to a fight with William Makepeace Thackeray and wrote about a riot in London."

It was an ironic send-off for Tiger, who flew back home into the Nigerian civil war.

The next time I saw him, in March of 1968, the smile was gone. His mouth was twisted, his voice high and tense. His square hands plucked at his baggy gray suit pants.

"I used to be a happy man, but now I have seen something I have never seen before. I read about killing and war, but I had never seen such things. Now, I have seen massacres."

He bounded from the straight-backed hotel chair and began fishing in his bureau drawers, through pamphlets and books and newspaper clippings. "Ah, here," he said, almost reverentially opening tissue paper. "This is Aba." He spread the photographs on the bed.

"The hospital. There were eight patients and a doctor when the planes came and threw bombs around. Hired pilots. The Nigerians can't fly planes. They are a thousand years behind civilization, that is why they are doing everything wrong.

"The open market, look at that. In that corner, that is a hand. A little girl's hand. What does she know of war? This woman burned. These men dead, not even soldiers. This is a woman, too. No, it is not rags, it was a woman."

He carefully repacked the photographs and sat down again. "The Nigerian radio says Dick Tiger of Nigeria will defend his light-heavyweight championship against Bob Foster in Madison Square Garden on May 24. Dick Tiger of Nigeria. They still claim me and they would kill me, they want to kill us all. I am a Biafran. And we just want to live."

I asked him about his family, which now included seven children. He said he had moved them back to Amaigbo while he tended his businesses in Aba. "I do not worry so much anymore. The children have learned to take cover quickly when they hear the planes. It is the fighter planes we worry about. The bombs fall slowly. If you see them you can run away. But you never see the bullets."

Foster knocked him cold in the fourth round of the fight. Tiger went straight down, his head smacked the canvas sickeningly. He twitched on his back like a turtle on its shell. He had to be helped up. In his dressing room he managed a smile at the crowd, which included various countrymen, boxing buffs, and Giardello. "Since I been winning I never had my fans stay in my dressing room so long. Now, I'm a loser and everybody's here. I guess I am a good man."

He left the United States without his light-heavyweight title, but with enough currency to buy a planeload of tinned meat and powdered milk in Lisbon and fly it into Biafra.

In the summer of 1968 there were reports of 6,000 Ibos a day dying of malnutrition and disease and wounds. Occasionally we would hear that Tiger was dead, too. And sometimes we would hear that he was hiding out in Brooklyn.

He reappeared in September to fight an upcoming young light heavyweight, Frankie DePaula.

I visited him in training. I was completing my first year as a columnist, and I had tried to stay away from boxing, to break the identification and establish my credentials in other sports. But Tiger had become a touchstone for me; I think I derived some symbolic nourishment from watching him tape his own hands. The honest, independent workman, a man of dignity and courage.

"If I had been a flashy fellow," he told me, "with fancy clothes and many women and big cars and nightclubs every night, I would have trouble. But I have never been a flashy fellow; I eat what is there to eat, I just dress, you know . . ."

"And still you have nothing now."

"This is true. I saved all my money and brought it home. I had apartment buildings in Lagos and Port Harcourt and Aba, and a movie and factories and shops and now, with the shelling, I guess it is all gone. Everything I have saved. But I am not sorry. If I had been a flashy fellow when I had lots of money, what would I do with myself now?"

He was training in the evening because he could no longer afford professional sparring partners; he sparred against dockers coming off work. He spent his days at the Biafra Mission, reading cables and dispatches. He disputed reports in American newspapers that the Nigerians were in complete control of almost all the cities.

"In every city they are still fighting," he said. "The Biafran fights to the end; the Nigerian will kill him anyway. The plan is to kill every Biafran over two years old. Then all the children will pray to the sun and moon instead of God, and never know who their fathers were. That is why we fight to survive."

We walked out of the dressing room to the training ring. In the hallway, a schoolboy caught his own reflection in the mirror of a vending machine and jabbed at it.

Tiger smiled. "When I was young, if I ever saw my shadow I had to fight it, I always boxed at mirrors. No more. I am just one old man."

He was thirty-nine, and he looked even older in his fight with DePaula. Tiger won, but in the late rounds he seemed to be melting like a candle.

He took his money and disappeared again.

I didn't see him for more than a year: my second year as a columnist, and probably the most interesting. The Mexico City Olympics. The Jets Super Bowl. The Aqueduct Boycott. The Mets World Series. The start of the Knicks' first championship season.

The rehabilitation of Muhammad Ali began: liberals discovered that his antiwar stand was compatible with theirs, even if his racial views were not, and sprang to defend his constitutional rights. Together they would prove that the American legal system worked perfectly for anyone with the money and the power to go all the way.

I began to wish I had more time to think and read and talk to people, to stop writing so much and with such assurance. Columnists have to write with assurance because they are paid to raise The Truth. As that second year slipped into a third year, as the column became progressively easier to write, as my work brought me greater access to people I wanted to talk with, I found I was less and less sure of what I knew absolutely. Was I growing wiser, losing my nerve, taking myself too seriously, getting bored? Was I over the hill, choking in the clutch, hearing footsteps, getting fat?

In November of 1969, Tiger sluggishly won a dreary decision over a light-heavyweight no one had heard of before, or would hear of again. A victory that had meaning only when translated into milk and salt and meat. On December 5 we sat down at a table in a publicity office of the Garden to discuss a matter that had suddenly become very urgent to Tiger. The medal he had received in Lagos in 1963 had grown too heavy in his mind to keep. When he read that John Lennon had returned his M.B.E. award for reasons that included Britain's involvement in the Nigerian civil war, Tiger decided to mail back his medal, too. But he needed help with the accompanying letter. Garden officials had not wanted to become involved in his protest and had called Dave Anderson, then covering boxing for *The New York Times*. Dave called me. I had misgivings. I had always been contemptuous of sports writers who acted as go-betweens for professional clubs and city governments, for high school athletes and college recruiters, for out-of-work coaches and potential employers. They were no longer honest journalists. I thought, they could no longer be trusted by their readers. They were supposed to cover stories, not make them happen.

But I had known and written about Tiger for more than six years; he had always been cooperative and friendly. I would be his amanuensis, no more: not a single idea or even word of mine would slip into the letter; it would make a good column for my readers, my kind of column, a famous athlete taking a principled stand on a headline issue that transcended sports. I didn't think, This is a very important cause, life, freedom, justice, I should be involved and make a worthwhile contribution as a human being. In those days I thought being an honest journalist was enough.

We wrote the letter and addressed it to the British ambassador, Washington, D.C.

"I am hereby returning the M.B.E. because every time I look at it I think of millions of men, women, and children who died and are still dying in Biafra because of the arms and ammunition the British government is sending to Nigeria and its continued moral support of this genocidal war against the people of Biafra."

He signed it "Dick Tiger Ihetu."

We walked across Eighth Avenue in the brilliant chilly afternoon and up the post-office steps. Tiger said, "If they ask me how much it's worth, what should I say?"

I shrugged. "We should try to pawn it and find out."

"I'll say a million dollars." Tiger laughed for the first time. "I'll say fifty or a hundred, just so it gets there."

The clerk behind the registry wicket hefted the package and shook his head. "No good, you got Scotch tape on it. Go around the corner, they'll give you some brown paper."

Another line. He stood very quietly, a small black hat perched on his head, his body muffled in a fur-lined coat. I would always remember him for being overdressed and patient. He was always cold, and he was always willing to wait, for a bout, for a return bout, for a shot at a title. He was forty then, picking up fights wherever he could, waiting for one more big payday. If there had been no war, he would be retired in Aba, a rich man. He had been financially wiped out, but he said he could not complain, many others had lost all their property, and many, many others had lost their families and their lives.

A clerk finally handed him a long strip of gummed brown paper and a wet sponge in a glass dish. Tiger took it to a writing desk and began to tear the brown paper into small strips, his thick fingers careful and precise, the fingers of a man who taped his own hands.

When he finished the package he proudly held it up for me. "Now I know there is something else I can do."

We waited for the registry clerk silently. "Okay," he said, nodding at the package, then flipping it. "What's in it?"

"A medal," said Tiger softly.

"What's it worth?"

"I don't know. Fifty, hundred dollars?"

"No value," said the clerk, to himself. He weighed it, registered it, asked Tiger if he wanted it to go airmail. Tiger said, "Yes."

"One sixty."

Tiger gave him two dollar bills and counted his change. He adjusted his scarf as he walked out into the bright street, and smiled, and shook my hand gravely and could only say, "Well . . ." and shrug, and start down the steps. I never saw him again.

In the summer of 1971, after working briefly as a guard in the Metropolitan Museum of Art, Dick Tiger returned to his native land. He was penniless and brought nothing except the cancer in his liver. He died that December, in Aba, at the age of forty-two.

Lawdy, Lawdy, He's Great

Years after the events recorded here, Ali passed on this admission to Mark Kram, who covered the epic 1975 battle for *Sports Illustrated*: "We went to Manila as champions, Joe and me, and we came back as old men." Neither would be the same afterwards; each left too much of himself in that faraway place under that hot morning sun. In 2001, Kram again sparred with the fight and its legacy in his full-scale study, *Ghosts of Manila: The Fateful Blood Feud Between Muhammad Ali and Joe Frazier.*

    🥊   🥊   🥊   🥊

It was only a moment, sliding past the eyes like the sudden shifting of light and shadow, but long years from now it will remain a pure and moving glimpse of hard reality, and if Muhammad Ali could have turned his eyes upon himself, what first and final truth would he have seen? He had been led up the winding, red-carpeted staircase by Imelda Marcos, the First Lady of the Philippines, as the guest of honor at the Malacañang Palace. Soft music drifted in from the terrace as the beautiful Imelda guided the massive and still heavyweight champion of the world to the long buffet ornamented by huge candelabra. The two whispered, and then she stopped and filled his plate, and as he waited the candles threw an eerie light across the face of a man who only a few hours before had survived the ultimate inquisition of himself and his art.

The maddest of existentialists, one of the great surrealists of our time, the king of all he sees, Ali had never before appeared so vulnerable and fragile, so pitiably unmajestic, so far from the universe he claims as his alone. He

301

could barely hold his fork, and he lifted the food slowly up to his bottom lip, which had been scraped pink. The skin on his face was dull and blotched, his eyes drained of that familiar childlike wonder. His right eye was a deep purple, beginning to close, a dark blind being drawn against a harsh light. He chewed his food painfully, and then he suddenly moved away from the candles as if he had become aware of the mask he was wearing, as if an inner voice were laughing at him. He shrugged, and the moment was gone.

A couple of miles away in the bedroom of a villa, the man who has always demanded answers of Ali, has trailed the champion like a timber wolf, lay in semi-darkness. Only his heavy breathing disturbed the quiet as an old friend walked to within two feet of him. "Who is it?" asked Joe Frazier, lifting himself to look around. "Who is it? I can't see! I can't see! Turn the lights on!" Another light was turned on, but Frazier still could not see. The scene cannot be forgotten; this good and gallant man lying there, embodying the remains of a will never before seen in a ring, a will that had carried him so far—and now surely too far. His eyes were only slits, his face looked as if it had been painted by Goya. "Man, I hit him with punches that'd bring down the walls of a city," said Frazier. "Lawdy, Lawdy, he's a great champion." Then he put his head back down on the pillow, and soon there was only the heavy breathing of a deep sleep slapping like big waves against the silence.

Time may well erode that long morning of drama in Manila, but for anyone who was there those faces will return again and again to evoke what it was like when two of the greatest heavyweights of any era met for a third time, and left millions limp around the world. Muhammad Ali caught the way it was: "It was like death. Closest thing to dyin' that I know of."

Ali's version of death began about 10:45 a.m. on Oct. 1 in Manila. Up to then his attitude had been almost frivolous. He would simply not accept Joe Frazier as a man or as a fighter, despite the bitter lesson Frazier had given him in their first savage meeting. Esthetics govern all of Ali's actions and conclusions; the way a man looks, the way he moves is what interests Ali. By Ali's standards, Frazier was not pretty as a man and without semblance of style as a fighter. Frazier was an affront to beauty, to Ali's own beauty as well as to his precious concept of how a good fighter should move. Ali did not hate Frazier, but he viewed him with the contempt of a man who cannot bear anything short of physical and professional perfection.

Right up until the bell rang for Round One, Ali was dead certain that Frazier was through, was convinced that he was no more than a shell, that too many punches to the head had left Frazier only one more solid shot removed from a tin cup and some pencils. "What kind of man can take all those punches to the head?" he asked himself over and over. He could never come up with an answer. Eventually he dismissed Frazier as the embodiment of animal stupidity. Before the bell Ali was subdued in his corner, often looking down to his manager, Herbert Muhammad, and conversing aimlessly. Once, seeing a bottle of mineral water in front of Herbert, he said, "Watcha got there, Herbert? Gin! You don't need any of that. Just another day's work. I'm gonna put a whuppin' on this nigger's head."

Across the ring Joe Frazier was wearing trunks that seemed to have been cut from a farmer's overalls. He was darkly tense, bobbing up and down as if trying to start a cold motor inside himself. Hatred had never been a part of him, but words like "gorilla," "ugly," "ignorant"—all the cruelty of Ali's endless vilifications—had finally bitten deeply into his soul. He was there not seeking victory alone; he wanted to take Ali's heart out and then crush it slowly in his hands. One thought of the moment days before, when Ali and Frazier with their handlers between them were walking out of the Malacañang Palace, and Frazier said to Ali, leaning over and measuring each word, "I'm gonna whup your half-breed ass."

By packed and malodorous Jeepneys, by small and tinny taxis, by limousine and by worn-out bikes, 28,000 had made their way into the Philippine Coliseum. The morning sun beat down, and the South China Sea brought not a whisper of wind. The streets of the city emptied as the bout came on a public television. At ringside, even though the arena was air-conditioned, the heat wrapped around the body like a heavy wet rope. By now, President Ferdinand Marcos, a small brown derringer of a man, and Imelda, beautiful and cool as if she were relaxed on a palace balcony taking tea, had been seated.

True to his plan, arrogant and contemptuous of an opponent's worth as never before, Ali opened the fight flat-footed in the center of the ring, his hands whipping out and back like the pistons of an enormous and magnificent engine. Much broader than he has ever been, the look of swift destruction defined by his every move, Ali seemed indestructible. Once, so long ago, he had been a splendidly plumed bird who wrote on the wind a singular kind of poetry of the body, but now he was down to earth, brought down by the changing shape of his body, by a sense of his own vulnerability, and by the years of excess. Dancing was for a ballroom; the ugly hunt was on. Head up and unprotected, Frazier stayed in the mouth of the cannon, and the big gun roared again and again.

Frazier's legs buckled two or three times in that first round, and in the second he took more lashing as Ali loaded on him all the meanness that he could find in himself. "He won't call you Clay no more," Bundini Brown, the spirit man, cried hoarsely from the corner. To Bundini, the fight would be a question of where fear first registered, but there was no fear in Frazier. In the third round Frazier was shaken twice, and looked as if he might go at any second as his head jerked up toward the hot lights and the sweat flew off his face. Ali hit Frazier at will, and when he chose to do otherwise he stuck his long left arm in Frazier's face. Ali would not be holding in this bout as he had in the second. The referee, a brisk workman, was not going to tolerate clinching. If he needed to buy time, Ali would have to use his long lift to disturb Frazier's balance.

A hint of shift came in the fourth. Frazier seemed to be picking up the beat, his threshing-blade punches started to come into range as he snorted and rolled closer. "Stay mean with him, champ!" Ali's corner screamed. Ali still had his man in his sights, and whipped at his head furiously. But at the end of the round, sensing a change and annoyed, he glared at Frazier and said, "You dumb chump, you!" Ali fought the whole fifth round in his own corner. Frazier worked his body, the whack of his gloves on Ali's kidneys sounding like heavy thunder. "Get out of the goddamn corner," shouted Angelo Dundee, Ali's trainer. "Stop playin'," squawked Herbert Muhammad, wringing his hands and wiping the mineral water nervously from his mouth. Did they know what was ahead?

Came the sixth, and here it was, that one special moment that you always look for when Joe Frazier is in a fight. Most of his fights have shown this: you can go so far into that desolate and dark place where the heart of Frazier pounds, you can waste his perimeters, you can see his head hanging in the public square, may even believe that you have him, but then suddenly you learn that you have not. Once more the pattern emerged as Frazier loosed all of the fury, all that has made him a brilliant heavyweight. He was in close now, fighting off Ali's chest, the place where he was to be. His old calling card—that sudden evil, his left hook—was working the head of Ali. Two hooks ripped with slaughterhouse finality at Ali's jaw, causing Imelda Marcos to look down at her feet, and the President to wince as if a knife had been stuck in his back. Ali's legs seemed to search for the floor. He was in serious trouble, and he knew that he was in no-man's-land.

Whatever else might one day be said about Muhammad Ali, it should never be said that he is without courage, that he cannot take a punch. He took those shots by Frazier, and then came out for the seventh, saying to him, "Old Joe Frazier, why I thought you were washed up." Joe replied, "Somebody told you all wrong, pretty boy."

Frazier's assault continued. By the end of the 10th round it was an even fight. Ali sat on his stool like a man ready to be staked out in the sun. His head was bowed, and when he raised it his eyes rolled from the agony of exhaustion. "Force yourself, champ!" his corner cried. "Go down to the well once more!" begged Bundini, tears streaming down his face. "The world needs ya, champ!" In the 11th, Ali got trapped in Frazier's corner, and blow after blow bit at his melting face, and flecks of spittle flew from his mouth. "Lawd have mercy!" Bundini shrieked.

The world held its breath. But then Ali dug deep down into whatever it is that he is about, and even his severest critics would have to admit that the man-boy had become finally a man. He began to catch Frazier with long right hands, and blood trickled from Frazier's mouth. Now, Frazier's face began to lose definition; like lost islands reemerging from the sea, massive bumps rose suddenly around each eye, especially the left. His punches seemed to be losing their strength. "My God," wailed Angelo Dundee. "Look at 'im. He ain't got no power, champ!" Ali threw the last ounces of resolve left in his body in the 13th and 14th. He sent Frazier's bloody mouthpiece flying into the press row in the 13th, and nearly floored him with a right in the center of the ring. Frazier was now no longer coiled. He was up high, his hands down, and as the bell for the 14th round sounded, Dundee pushed Ali out saying, "He's all yours!" And he was, as Ali raked him with nine straight right hands. Frazier was not picking up the punches, and as he returned to his corner at the round's end the Filipino referee guided his great hulk part of the way.

"Joe," said his manager, Eddie Futch, "I'm going to stop it."

"No, no, Eddie, ya can't do that to me," Frazier pleaded, his thick tongue barely getting the words out. He started to rise.

"You couldn't see in the last two rounds," said Futch. "What makes ya think ya gonna see in the 15th?"

"I want him, boss," said Frazier.

"Sit down, son," said Futch, pressing his hand on Frazier's shoulder. "It's all over. No one will ever forget what you did here today."

And so it will be, for once more had Frazier taken the child of the gods to hell and back. After the fight Futch said: "Ali fought a smart fight. He conserved his energy, turning it off when he had to. He can afford to do it because of his style. It was mainly a question of anatomy, that is all that separates these two men. Ali is now too big, and when you add those long arms, well . . . Joe has to use constant pressure, and that takes its toll on a man's body and soul." Dundee said: "My guy sucked it up and called on everything he had. We'll never see another one like him." Ali took a long time before coming down to be interviewed by the press, and then he could only say, "I'm tired of bein' the whole game. Let other guys do the fightin'. You might never see Ali in the ring again."

In his suite the next morning he talked quietly. "I heard somethin' once," he said. "When somebody asked a marathon runner what goes through his mind in the last mile or two, he said that you ask yourself why am I doin' this. You get so tired. It takes so much out of you mentally. It changes you. It makes you go a little insane. I was thinkin' that at the end. Why am I doin' this? What am I doin' here in against this beast of a man? It's so painful. I must be crazy. I always bring out the best in the men I fight, but Joe Frazier, I'll tell the world right now, brings out the best in me. I'm gonna tell ya, that's one helluva man, and God bless him."

Donnybrook Farr

A . J . L I E B L I N G

Through four decades at *The New Yorker,* A. J. Liebling (1904–1963) was never at a loss for opinions. Considered one of the godfathers of New Journalism, his World War II dispatches from Europe were legendary; so were his critiques of the press, his zest for Paris, his appetite for food, and his passion for *The Sweet Science,* the apt title of his 1956 collection of essays on the sport and the milieu that surrounds it. He filled his work with jabs of cheerfulness, and followed with combinations of elation and elan. He never sniffed a gym he didn't like.

"Nobody," assured Red Smith, "wrote about boxing with more grace and enthusiasm than Joe Liebling." Add to that perspective, erudition, wit, and a fabulous nose for details. High standards? Sure. But the beauty of Liebling— evident throughout this excursion into what in other hands might have been a forgettable night of Irish boxing—is that while he takes the standards quite seriously, he doesn't follow suit with himself.

🥊   🥊   🥊   🥊

The Sweet Science, like an old rap or the memory of love, follows its victim everywhere. When Phil Drake, a horse, not a prize-fighter, won the Epsom Derby of 1955 at odds of 12 to 1, I had five nickers (Mayfair for pounds) on his nose. After deducting another five I had bet on one of the losers I had a net profit of fifty-five quid, better than one hundred and fifty dollars, which I took with me to the Champagne Bar under the grandstand. After a race won by a 12–1 shot, it is the most accessible section of the buffet. While there, I caught sight of some

English boxing writers I know and wanted to see; they were struggling to reach a more animated and less expensive sector of the bar. It was a shame I had to down my champagne so quickly, but there wasn't enough to go around, so I finished it off and then sneaked up behind them, saying something about the smallness of the world.

It was at the bar, with my profits in my pocket and my champagne in me, that I learned there was soon to be a fifteen-round fight in Dublin for the featherweight championship of Europe. The defending champion, a Frenchman named Ray Famechon, had been induced to go there to fight the challenger, a boy from the North of Ireland, but not a Protestant, known as Billy Spider II Kelly. This Kelly, my friends said, was the British and British Empire champion, and a man of promise. One could fly to Dublin in a little more than an hour, and return just as expeditiously the morning after the battle. But what decided me to go was the news that the fight was going to be held in Donnybrook, an outlying part of Dublin that is universally synonymous with an unofficial, free-for-all fight. Professional fights have been less numerous in Dublin, but some of them have been illustrious. Pierce Egan, the Blind Raftery of the London prize ring, was a part-time Dublin man himself, and has recounted the triumphs of Dan Donnelly, the first great Irish heavyweight, against two Englishmen, whose names escape my memory. They fought on the turf of the Curragh, a racecourse where, I am reliably informed by Tim Costello, a restaurateur of my acquaintance, small boys are still led out to view Donnelly's heelprints. Dan was no tippytoes fighter, and although he fought the Englishmen separately, he could have beaten them both together, make no doubt of it. Within my own lifetime, Battling Siki, the ingenuous Senegalese known to legend as the Ignoble Savage, was lured to Dublin to defend the world's light-heavyweight title, which he had acquired from Georges Carpentier, against Mike McTigue, an Irishman polished by travel. The bout was on March 17, 1923, and McTigue got the decision. McTigue's home-grounds success appeared to be the precedent most plausibly applicable to the proposed match at Donnybrook, for I knew that Famechon, who has boxed in the United States, was hardly likely to fell Kelly like an ox; the biggest piece of an ox Famechon has ever felled, I imagine, is a *tournedos*. The boxing writers told me that the referee was to be a neutral, appointed by the European Boxing Union, but even a neutral might prove suggestible at Donnybrook.

When I got my Aer Lingus ticket and reservation (Aer Lingus is the Irish airline), I found that the line had put on extra flights, rolling out old DC-3s, which take two and a half hours for the trip, to supplement their new

English-built Viscounts, which take only an hour and twenty-five minutes. Because I applied late, I was put on a DC-3. When I came aboard, the only vacant seat was next to a large, fair-haired man of resolute and familiar appearance. The seats were narrow, the leg room was limited, and it was easy to see why the place next to the big fellow had been left to the last. To establish relations, I asked him how much he weighed, and he said, as if used to being asked the question, "Fourteen stone eleven and a half," which works out to two hundred and seven and a half pounds. I said, "I weigh sixteen stone, very nearly"—very nearly seventeen, I meant. We scrunched together like bulls in a horse trailer, and he grunted, "I'm only three pound more than when I fought Joe Louey."

"*Did* you?" I asked politely.

"If I didn't, I don't know 'oo put the rooddy loomps on my 'ead," he said pleasantly, and the hand-stitched face, with the high cheekbones, narrow eyes, and Rock of Gibraltar chin, came back to me out of the late thirties. He was Tommy Farr, the old Welsh heavyweight who went fifteen rounds with Joe Louis in 1937. There is a half-established legend in Britain that he was twisted out of the decision, which he wasn't. Farr does nothing actively to favor the myth, but he doesn't discourage it, either. He also fought a series of savage bouts, with varied fortunes, against fellows like Max Baer, and against them, he thinks, he got all the worst of it when he lost. "But I love the States," he said. "I made a lot of money there. That's what I fought for, eh? Money." He rubbed a thumb like a hammer against a rectangular index finger. "Two hundred and ninety-six fights I had. Do you think it was for a rooddy lark?"

I said no, and he said, "It was my profession. I well and truly served my apprenticeship, and then I wanted money. That's why they didn't like me over there at first—the press didn't like me. Because I didn't let them mess me about, that's why. I wanted my rest. Didn't want them banging about downstairs after eleven. My manager had a fridgeful of liquor for them, and 'e'd bring them in all hours. All right for 'im wasn't it? 'E didn't 'ave to fight. They liked 'im fine. Robbed me of fifty or sixty thousand quid, they did."

I asked him how the American press had robbed him of fifty or sixty thousand pounds, and he explained that it was by saying he would have no chance against Louis. "Spoiled the gate, they did," he said.

I tried to console him by recalling how extravagantly they had praised him after the fight, but he grumbled, "That didn't 'elp the gate."

Somehow the money had slipped between the hard knuckles. So now, he said, he was launched on a second career. I asked him what it was. He was looking fit and prosperous, in a smashing dark-gray pin-striped suit, and wearing a good thin watch. In the light of this exterior, I was scarcely prepared for his answer.

"I'm a write-ter," he said. "I love write-ting. I give it to them straight. No split affinitives, you know, or other Oxfer stooff. Oh, of coorse I split an affinitive now and then, to show I know how, but I don't believe in it." He was writing boxing, he told me, for the *Sunday Pictorial,* a once-a-week tabloid, with a circulation of five and a half million, that was creeping up on the eight million circulation of that older-established phenomenon, the *News of the World.* "I thank God I 'ave found a way to make a living for my dear wife and kids," Farr said. "It seems I'm a natural-born write-ter. I've hod five revisions of contract since I came with the *Pictorial.*"

He was going to report the fight, and I asked him for a bit of professional inside on Kelly. "He's a very good methodical boxer," he said, "with a fine sense of anticipation." It was to prove a practically perfect synopsis of Kelly; he might have added only that Kelly too often anticipates the worst. Farr's experience in the United States was much in his mind. "I couldn't be a good-time Charlie," he said. "When I was a kid, I was taught not to talk or joke or laugh at the table. 'You come 'ere to eat,' my old man used to say to me. 'When you eat, go.' A man can't change from what 'e's brought up to be, can he? He wasn't a bad old man. He taught me the importance of a good left. He was very aggressive. When he was fighting, they used to say 'e was a throwback to the caveman. 'When you go into the ring, you're a hoonter,' he'd say. 'Don't hop about like you were fighting in a rooddy balloon on the end of a stick.'"

Farr told me he had written in the *Pictorial* that Don Cockell, the Englishman who recently tried to take Marciano's heavyweight crown in San Francisco, had no sympathy coming. "He had sixteen pound on Marciano," Farr said. "'E should of set about 'im. I got 'oondred and eight letters, all approving. My boss got nineteen letters, all disapproving. He phoned me up. 'That's grand,' he said. 'Keep up the good work. They'll be something extra in the post for you tomorrow.'"

Farr said he was going to spend the night at the Royal Hibernian Hotel, where his paper had reserved a room for him, and it was there that I, too, eventually found a room. I met him again at dinner; he was eating with three businessmen from Derry, young Kelly's hometown, whom he had taken into the aura of his greatness. Between courses he autographed cards for the young busboys and the waiters. "Is it true that you fought Joe Louey, Mr. Farr?" they would ask him, and he would reply, with a rugged laugh, "If I didn't, I don't know 'oo put the rooddy loomps on my 'ead." It had happened before the little busboys were born, and they thought of it as something historic.

After dinner—a modest collation of honeydew melon and *darne de saumon au Chablis,* the Irish salmon being exceptional—the five of us drove to Donnybrook in the Derrymen's car. The streets were full of automobiles from the North of Ireland and the three free counties of Ulster; my associates could pick them out by the license plates. One car we came up behind had a hand-lettered sign on its rear window reading "Won't you come into my parlor? said the Spider to the Ray." Farr, who, like most Welshmen, can sing, paid his passage with "The Londonderry Air." "It used to be my speciality," he said, and broke forth:

> "Oh, Danny Boy—ta loora loo loo loora loo,
> Oh, Danny Boy—ta loora loora loo!
> Oh, come ye BACK—"

We were the success of the cavalcade.

The fight, as I knew by that time, having had a chance to read an evening newspaper, was to be held in a monster garage, just built by the municipality to house all the omnibuses of Dublin. Six thousand seven hundred and fifty chairs had been borrowed from caterers and undertakers; the one I got was tagged "O'Connell's," but I don't know which line of work O'Connell is in. The bout was being staged by Jack Solomons, the London promoter, with the cooperation of the officials in charge of An Tóstal, a kind of Gaelic old home week, which included an ecclesiological exhibition at Maynooth, a children's art competition, and an event listed in the papers as "Dun Laoghaire— Blackrock Ceili—an Tóstal, Aras an Baile (8 P.M.)," and evidently reserved for Gaelic speakers. Famechon was to get three thousand pounds, which makes a tidy sum in francs (three million), or even in dollars (eight thousand four hundred). Kelly was to get two thousand pounds and, in the unanimous opinion of the Derrymen, the European featherweight championship as well, after which Solomons had promised him a match with Sandy Saddler for the world's title. Saddler fought Famechon in Paris last year, and knocked him out in six rounds. Now Famechon was thirty years old and Kelly twenty-three, and both had made the featherweight limit of a hundred and twenty-six pounds at two o'clock that afternoon. Famechon had been around a long time—a very good fighter by European standards but not top-class by ours. I had heard at the

Neutral Corner Restaurant, in New York, which is an international exchange for trade information, that he was definitely on the downgrade.

I had expected a delay at the gate, but Mr. Farr swept me in with him—in the double capacity of journalist and celebrity, he had the run of the house—and an usher conducted me to the O'Connell chair, in the second row ringside, where my neighbors regarded me with the respect due my illustrious sponsorship. The low ceiling of the bus garage kept the cigarette smoke down, and, although the soirée had not progressed past the first preliminary, the ring was envcloped in a blue haze, giving the scene the look of a painting of a club fight by Bellows. The strained, awkward boxers in the ring carried out the motif; the salient feature of "Stag at Sharkey's," I have always thought, is that both the central figures are simply ushers. The principals in this bout were a Dublin man and a Belfast man, of whom the former was the more inept. After the fifth round the master of ceremonies announced that the Dublin man had "retired," and a buzz of sympathy ran through the hall. The restraint was studious, as if each member of the audience had come to the hall determined to keep his temper.

The ushers, who wore badges denominating them "stewards," were fanatical about making customers crouch in the aisles while any boxing was going on, and conducted them to their chairs only during the one-minute intervals between rounds. It was like Town Hall during a séance of the New Friends of Music. Since horizontal distances were great in the garage, it took some arrivals from two to four rounds to reach their seats. The round before the Dublin man retired, a small, merry-looking man with a pointy nose and an even more finely pointed waxed mustache passed along the aisle in front of the first ringside row, bent over like a crab. The man next to me pulled my arm. "It's Alfie Byrne, the Lord Mayor," he said. His Lordship was taking no chances of alienating a voter. There was a large Irish harp in electric bulbs on one wall and another, in green paint, on the wall opposite. I saw no tricolors.

The *ambiance* warmed a bit with the next bout—a lightweight match between a heavy-muscled, pyknic Galwayman, not much more than five feet tall, named McCoy, and a more conventionally constructed fellow from Belfast, named Sharpe. (Belfast, like most industrial cities, produces a large crop of boxers.) Galwaymen, in popular myth, are hot-tempered and unpredictable, and transplanted Galwaymen, of whom there were many in the audience, are vociferously loyal. The little fellow started out at a terrific pace, moving his arms as if in a pillow fight. A cry of "Up, Galway! Come on, McEye!" spontaneously dispelled the decorum of the evening. It seemed impossible that McEye could keep on moving his arms at that rate for more than a minute, but he did, and the astonished Belfast man, after waiting for him to run down, joined in the fun. But each time Sharpe administered to the animated half keg a conventional uppercut to the chin—he knew the antidotes academically prescribed for a violent attack by a short opponent— McEye would loose a flurry of blows that reminded me of a passage in "The Song of Roland": "I will strike seven hundred or a thousand good blows." Six hundred and ninety-nine or nine hundred and ninety-eight would miss, but for the Belfast man it was like trying to hit through an electric fan. The fellow sitting next to me jiggled with the effort of maintaining his composure; he seemed to be in the grip of an electric vibrator. After every round, he would grab me and ask, "Would you say the little fellow is ahead now?" I would nod, and he would turn and grab the fellow on the other side, a sporty type who was escorting a platinum blonde. This Blazes Boylan—it is impossible to be in Dublin without Joyce—was a purist. "Sharpe is landing the cleaner punches," he would say. The man between us would wait until Blazes turned back to the blonde, and then pluck my arm again. "Do you know," he would say in a conspiratorial way, "I don't agree with that man at all." Neither did the referee, who gave the decision to McEye and perpetual motion. There are no judges at European professional bouts, and the referee decides. My neighbor and I exchanged friendly glances, secure in our connoisseurship.

The announcer now had his great moment. "My Lord Mayor, ladies and gentlemen!" he called, and began introducing visiting celebrities—Freddie Mills, the Englishman who briefly held the light-heavyweight championship of the world before Joey Maxim won it; my sponsor Farr, who got a great hand; and, climactically, "the original" Spider Kelly, the father of the hero of the evening. (I had heard of at least one earlier Spider Kelly, the man who said to his seconds, "What I need ain't advice—it's strength." But that had been in California, and it would have been a quibble to bring it up at Donnybrook.) The original Irish Spider Kelly was a puckish little man with a red face and heavy black eyebrows. He had held the British and British Empire featherweight championships himself twenty years before, I knew from my newspaper fill-in, and had guided Spider II's instruction from his first tottering essays at footwork. The audience included many fathers, more sons, and quite a number of mothers and sisters. (There was also a good speckling of Roman collars.) A cheer for old Spider was an endorsement of the principle of the family, and he got it.

A fanfare of hunting horns was sounded at the remote end of the garage, and another cheer began, distant at first, louder as its object approached the ring. It was Spider II, surrounded by his faction. He was a baby-faced boy with a crew cut, who looked more like eighteen than twenty-three. The calves of his legs resembled those of a school quarter-miler—large and rounded— but his torso and arms, white and boyish, were less impressively developed. The Frenchman, whose entry was heralded by another but less enthusiastic fanfare, was sleek, wide-shouldered, long-armed, and spindle-shanked. He looked not much younger than Spider I, but his antiquity inspired no comparable demonstration of respectful affection by the crowd. The master of ceremonies implored the audience to stop smoking during the coming contest, and all the men within my sight extinguished their cigarettes. He next introduced the boxers, giving their weights to the ounce—Kelly had a ten-ounce weight advantage—and, finally, the referee, who received a polite, unsuspicious cheer. I did not hear his name, but the man next to me said, "Some kind of a Dutchman." It appeared likely, for the referee had the buttery tint so common among Hollanders, and walked about the ring with the exaggerated spryness of a Teuton being dashing. He had a snipe nose that pointed at the ceiling, and held himself so straight that his Adam's apple created a noticeable deviation from the vertical, pushing a neat bow tie in front of it.

The gong rang, and the men came timidly from their corners amid thunderous cheers. "Don't let us pretend to be impartial," a fellow wrote in the *Irish Press* the next morning. "We all wanted the best man to win, and Billy Kelly was the best man for us." Confirming Farr's description, Kelly went to work methodically; he landed a light tap on the Frenchman's nose, parried a return with his right, and then tapped twice more. Famechon floundered at him a bit, like a fellow reaching over a man's shoulder to shake hands with someone behind him, and the round ended with no damage to either. The man next to me turned his face from the carnage and said, "Is he doing all right?" I showed him my program, on which I had marked the round even, and he said, "That other fellow has a very dangerous look."

After the second round, Kelly settled down to work, and a very promising workman he looked, drawing leads, popping the slower Frenchman with fast, precise jabs, and once, in the fourth, even landing a really good right uppercut to the diaphragm in close. When Famechon started a punch, Kelly would be going in another direction. Usually when the Frenchman got close to him, Kelly would cease trying to do harm and concentrate on escape, as if he were fighting a middleweight instead of a gaffer his own size. He was good at ducking and slipping away, but nobody was ever hurt by being ducked away from. Still, he outboxed his man round after round—I gave him four in a row—and the bus garage swelled with the sound of shouting. The jabs had little sting, but since Kelly was younger than Famechon, it appeared reasonable that he would keep on piling up points as the fight went on, and at the end would take the decision. By the seventh, Famechon, having apparently decided that the boy couldn't hurt him at all, was rushing after him, slapping and pushing but unable to accomplish much. And so they went, round after round—Kelly almost never using his right except to block and never following an advantage beyond a second or third light pop when he had his man set up for a real one. At the beginning of every round he crossed himself, and whenever Famechon's slaps strayed low he would look appealingly at the referee. As they came up for the fifteenth, I had them all square on my card—six rounds for each and two even—but I had a feeling that Kelly's margins had been a trifle clearer. I gave him the final round, which was as tantalizingly ineffectual as all the others, and as hard to pick a winner in. Just the same, I was sure that Spider II deserved the decision—and meanly suspected that he would be sure to receive it even if he hadn't done quite so well. It was then that the Dutchman, to quote one Irish writer, "rose" Famechon's hand. I thought I could write a fair account of what followed, but when I saw the story on the first page of the *Irish Press* next morning, I realized that the writer, a Mr. John Healy, had probably had more experience in that kind of going:

> There was a long pause as a stunned audience, who had watched the young Spider swap punches at a terrific pace in the last two rounds, slowly gathered what it meant—Billy Kelly had lost the fight.
>
> And then, slowly at first, until it gathered momentum and burst like a rumbling volcano, they got to their feet and cut loose with a solid barrage of catcalls, boos, whistles and shouts. Angry spectators swarmed up to and tried clambering over the Press table. A bottle whizzed over my head into the ring. [I missed this, or at any rate it missed me.] A coat, flung in rage, flapped on the ropes. [It did.] Chairs were bumbled. A squad of Gardai and plainclothes detectives surrounded the ring. ["Gardai" is Gaelic for uniformed police, and monstrous big ones these were.]
>
> They were still booing and cheering Billy when he was escorted from the ring minutes later. All down that long

avenue of jam-packed people, they screamed their admiration. "You're the winner, Billy!" or "You're the champ!"
Grown men cried their rage in the sea of faces. . . .

That's just about the way it was. Taking a more moderate line, a Mr.
Ben Kiely, on the sports page, wrote, "There's no doubt in the world about
it—the raising of Ray Famechon's hand was one of the greatest shocks in
Franco-Irish history. Because for the crowd in the Donnybrook Garage Billy
Kelly was the man for their money."

Famechon, whose hundred-and-third professional fight it was,
looked relieved but not astonished. He probably thought he had won, as any
fighter does who has made it at all close. Kelly sat in his corner with head almost between his knees, the picture of dejection, like a bright boy who has
failed to get 100 in an arithmetic test because the teacher came up with the
wrong answer. He had played it safe for fifteen rounds and failed to obtain the
reward of thrift and diligence. The most interesting figure in the ring, for
many reasons, was the referee; the man about to get lynched is undeniably the
center of attention at a lynching. It is unlikely that it had occurred to him
when he rose Famechon's hand that he would be immoderately happy to see
the Amsterdam airport again. The Kelly rooters were standing in the aisles
and on the undertakers' chairs, which assumed a new significance. Devil an
usher could make devil a customer sit down. The referee, encouraged by a
number of big men in mufti, probably detectives, who had entered the ring,
got as far as the ropes, climbed through them to the ring apron, and stood
there like a fellow who has never gone off a diving board and wishes he
hadn't walked out to the end. He was as pale as the inside of a Gouda cheese.
The Gardai marched to the edge of the ring below him and formed a pha-
lanx, into which they lowered him down. They then marched forward, with
the Dutchman in the center. A small man in a raincoat tried to cut in from
the rear, swinging a punch under a cop's armpit. The Gardai turned around,
laughing, and slung him about twenty feet, using the man's raincoat as a hammer thrower uses the wire on the hammer. The Lord Mayor slunk out as self-
effacingly as he had entered. The wild shouting continued, the ushers were
ignored for another five minutes, and then everybody began to laugh and
chat and light up cigarettes again, in preparation for the bouts that would
wind up the program. (It was apparently permissible to suffocate all boxers
except those in the main event.) Since the tag end of the program was of
small interest, I soon made my way out into the night and a pouring rain.

By the time I got back to the Royal Hibernian, Mr. Farr was established before a late snack of cold chicken and cold ham, with a few bottles of Guinness. He said he had already filed his story for the *Sunday Pictorial,* and readily recited what he thought the best bits of it for me. Like me, he thought Kelly had deserved to win. "Kelly hos nothing for the seeker of blood and thunder, but those who enjoy the grace of movement and textbook poonching will be fully satisfied by the Derry craftsman," he said, which is the way it appeared in the *Pictorial,* except for the Welsh stresses. He writes a very pretty style. He thought, though, that Kelly had been overcautious—that he had had little to beat. We adjourned to the lounge, in which bona-fide residents are allowed to drink as late as the night porter, a crabbed old humorist, will serve them, and there were joined by a number of gentlemen from Northern Ireland, including the trio who had transported us to the fight. Before bringing us a new round of drinks, the porter would make each of us give his room number, and we would count off, beginning with a Mr. Cassidy from Derry—I think he had No. 58—and going all the way round to a man from Donegal whose name I forget but who weighed eighteen stone seven and collected first editions. It was not so much that the porter expected our bona-fide status to change between rounds, I think, as that he wished to determine our degree of responsibility. A fellow who forgot the number of his room might have been refused the next drink. But nobody did forget.

Mr. Farr, who had switched from Guinness to Cointreau, was naturally the oracle of the occasion, and won the golden opinion of all until he burst out ingenuously, "The truth is that the lod fights like he was in a rooddy balloon at the end of a rooddy stick. Every time t'other lod 'it 'im in the goot, 'e looked of the referee. Is the referee 'is rooddy grondmother? Was he too prruud to reciprrocate?" He rose, granitic and dignified. "I must take an early plane in the morning," he said. "Bock to my sweet wife and wonderful children. Each Saturday ofternoon I take the kids to the cinema and tea. High tea." He made his way to the lift, the pattern of a literary man who leads a sane family life.

I stayed on until the porter himself decided to go to bed, at dawn. He has insomnia in the dark, he said.

Onward Virgin Soldier: Johnny Owen's Last Fight

author HUGH MCILVANNEY

In the hyperbolic playpen of 21st-century sports journalism the phrase "Living Legend" is a one-two combination so overused it's lost its sock. Still, there's no way around this: Hugh McIlvanney is a living legend. Just look at the stats. Seven times he's been voted the UK's Sports Writer of the Year, and he's the only member of the sporting press ever to be named Britain's Journalist of the Year. A three-decade veteran of *The Observer,* he rose to become that paper's chief sportswriter before taking on the same title, in 1993, for *The Times.*

In September of 1980, McIlvanney was ringside at the Olympic Auditorium in Los Angeles when banatamweight champ Lupe Pintor knocked out Johnny Owen. The challenger, who never regained consciousness, died six weeks later.

McIlvanney's account of the fight and the fighter is utterly moving, often poetic, beautifully reported, and always in clear focus. It's final line may carry the most heartbreaking observation ever penned on the sport.

🥊 🥊 🥊 🥊

Johnny Owen's mother worries when he fights, and so does every other mother who has ever seen him stripped. The British and Commonwealth bantamweight champion has the kind of physique that makes him elusive when he is standing still. His 118 pounds are elongated over 5 feet 8 inches, so that his biceps are scarcely more prominent than his Adam's apple or the veins on his forearm. Indeed, most of Owen's muscles come disguised as skin and bone. His ears protrude endearingly from a face that is small, shy, and much younger than could be expected of a twenty-three-year-old who has been boxing competitively since he was ten. When that appearance is juxtaposed with the thought of what he is asked to do in the ring, hearts that are not at all maternal find themselves melting.

On a recent night in Bedlinog, a South Wales village a couple of valleys away from his hometown of Merthyr Tydfil, a friendly man in the crowd turned to the boxer's father. "Dick, you have a lovely son," he said. "And I hope you won't be insulted if I tell you how he makes me feel. When I look at him I want to pick him up, put him in a shawl, carry him home, and give him a good basin of broth."

Dick Owen wasn't insulted. He and his wife were accustomed to far more indignant misconceptions about a boy so obsessively dedicated to a fighting career that he has never once allowed himself to be distracted by a girl, has never as much as kissed one in earnest. When her virgin soldier goes off to war, Johnny's mother, stubbornly refusing to watch him take punches, sits at home until she can bear the waiting no longer and then goes to pace around a telephone box higher up the hilly council estate of Gelli-deg in Merthyr, painfully delaying her call until she knows the *Western Mail* sports desk in Cardiff will be able to tell her the result. "The main reason we've never had the phone put in," says Dick, "is that we know we'd be pestered to death by people telling us we should be locked up for letting Johnny fight. Dai Gardiner, his manager, has had to take some terrible stick over that, especially from women. They've called Dai something rotten. He's more like one of the family than a manager, but these characters seem to think he is starving Johnny, then sending him out to get knocked about by sturdier lads. They don't bother to notice that Johnny won more than a hundred amateur fights and lost only eighteen, or that he's unbeaten after seventeen as a professional and has stopped eight of those professional opponents inside the distance."

Around midnight next Saturday, in Almeria, southern Spain, Owen will attempt to effect a dramatic improvement in that already exceptional record by taking the European bantamweight title away from Juan Francisco Rodriguez. A glance might suggest that Rodriguez, with only thirteen paid fights, is even less experienced than the Welshman, but that statistic is deceptive, because the Spanish authorities were so proud of their man's achievements at the amateur level—where he held a European championship and earned an Olympic bronze medal—that for a long time they severely discouraged ambitions of defecting to professionalism. Since joining the harder school, he has kept respectable company, not only making himself head boy on the Continent but putting himself in the way of the world champion, the intimidating Mexican Carlos Zarate. Admittedly, that argument was comprehensively lost after five rounds, but the defeat may be considered less than disgraceful when set against Zarate's record of having stopped fifty-two out of fifty-three opponents and having been beaten only once—and that just recently at the so-called super-bantamweight mark of 122 pounds by Wilfredo Gomez. Yet, if the form book invites caution in the approach to Rodriguez, it does nothing to make Owen pessimistic. If there is a line of comparison, perhaps it emerges from Owen's latest success, the points victory last November over the seasoned and impressively capable Sicilian Australian Paul Ferreri, who had previously given Zarate plenty of aggravation over twelve rounds before succumbing to cuts. The Welshman's apparent fragility has never looked more like Nature's con trick than it was at Ebbw Vale as he came from behind to subdue Ferreri in the last third of the fifteen-round match.

Rodriguez is known as a boxer of skill and style but one who is inclined to seek rests during rounds and continues to exhibit too many of his amateur habits. He is unlikely to be more slippery than Ferreri and he can forget about taking breathers against Owen, who seems to harbor a deep resentment of the rule that gives him a minute's break between rounds. So the biggest threat to the British champion's challenge may be the eccentricities of scoring in Spain: "We accept that we'll have to stop the fella to get the title and I expect Johnny to do that, maybe after about twelve rounds," says Dai Gardiner. After watching Owen in training last week, it was easy to accept that forecast as merely realistic.

Whether running on the scarred hills around Merthyr or working at the gym above the local Labour Club, where the harsh poverty of the facilities makes the fight emporia of New York or Philadelphia look like suites at the Savoy, his application to work is frightening. When the recent snow and ice made the sheep-paths of his roadwork hazardous, he wrapped rags and old socks around his heavy running boots and did his best to maintain his daily schedule of nine-mile slogs. On the one day a week when he is excused gym sessions, he likes to extend the run to twelve miles. His sparring has the intensity of warfare and a night's business can include as many as fifteen rounds of it. He has used a handful of experienced and active pros in this his second full preparation for a championship match that has been postponed three times. None has been less than nine pounds heavier than he is but all have had trouble coping with his pressure. On Thursday evening it was the turn of Les Pickett, the local featherweight who is due to fight an eliminator for the British championship in the midweek following the Almeria date. Pickett is not naturally accommodating but he was forced rather than forcing through the eight hard rounds and at the end of each he was gulping down extra air while Owen wandered his corner impatiently with hardly a hint of rise and fall about his narrow chest.

His floor exercises gave further evidence of freakish stamina and, through it all, from the moment he began slowly to accouter himself for work with the ritualized care of a bullfighter dressing for the ring, there was something even more remarkable: the sense of a man being stimulated and enlarged by submergence in his true métier. Earlier, in the council-house living room bright with a spreading clutter of trophies and decorated on one wall with a lurid green painting of a skeleton presented by a fan, his personality had come across as diffident almost to the point of being fugitive. But in that incomparably shabby gym, with its makeshift ring, patched punch-bag and medicine ball, wrinkling fight posters and an old bath puddled with spit and littered with dog-ends, he grew and brightened visibly with the knowledge that he was a hero at the game in hand, the certainty that he would go out from there to cause a stir in the world. Win or lose in Almeria, he will be doing what he is happiest doing. "I don't expect to lose," he says, both the accent and the quietness of voice demanding a straining alertness from the listener. "I know they say Spain is a hard place to win but it's just him and me at the finish. I really love boxing and I really love training, too, for itself as well as for the confidence it gives me. I've got a job as a machine setter in a components factory but I'm happy when I take a fortnight off for a big fight. After all the running and the other stuff in the gym, I know I'm not going to fade. I can go all out from the first bell. It's a great feeling."

It's not usually so good for the opponent, who finds Owen coming at him with an incessant variety of sharp, hurtful punches, crowding and hustling, undeterred by any but the most forceful counters. Owen's nose has been thickened and polished by all the years of aggressive attention but he has never been stopped and as a pro he has only once been briefly bemused, by George Sutton, who was eventually beaten out of sight. "The only mark I can remember him getting since turning professional was a tiny one under the left eye in his thirteenth fight," says his father. "His mother played hell when he came home. That was to be the end of it, no more boxing. He wouldn't even let me put something on the bruise. He was so proud about the thought of having a black eye to show."

Dick Owen did some amateur boxing (the family connection goes back at least as far as Dick's own grandfather, who inflicted a bit of damage in the booths) and all five of his sons were so keen that he had to set up an al-fresco gym on the drying green of 22 Heol Bryn Padell, Gelli-deg. "The boy older than Johnny was really good but gave it up too early and the one im-mediately beneath him, Kevin, was a Welsh international until he took to the courting lark and packed in the boxing," he says. "Johnny's different. He lives for the game and has never looked at a girl. There are enough of them com-ing for him now but there's plenty of time for that." John agrees. "I'd like to be still unbeaten this time next year and we could think about going for the world title. Ferreri's manager said he thought I was near the top class now but we're not rushing. Whatever happens, I think I want to be out of the game by the time I'm around twenty-seven. It seems young but, do you see, I'd have been boxing nearly twenty years by then."

Dai Gardiner, the manager, bearded and still, at thirty-eight, carrying the briskness that took him through thirteen professional fights with only one loss before a detached retina ended his career, acknowledges that the punching strength of someone like Zarate will represent the decisive ques-tion for Owen. "Can he take one on the chin from a man like that and keep going? That's the only question he's got to answer for me, and we'll just have to find out about that when it comes along. What is sure is that he won't fail because of lack of fitness or temperament, lack of skill or heart."

In short, Johnny Owen is a legitimate heir to the fighting traditions of South Wales and Merthyr Tydfil in particular. "This was a hard town in the days when the pits and the ironworks were booming," says Dick, himself a former miner. "It had 100,000 people, with Irish, Geordies, Spanish, Italians, and all sorts mixed in. Even the women were hard. They had to be. My grandmother had a job underground in the pit and my own mother handled a wheelbarrow in the Dowlais Ironworks."

The charm of Johnny is that he has inherited that toughness and kept his gentle side. His father again: "He's mine and maybe I shouldn't say this, but he *is* a lovely boy. He still washes the dishes and clears out the ashes to light the fire in the morning. Nothing changes with Johnny." Even the Spaniards may find it difficult to complain if he changes things just a little by taking that title next Saturday.

Johnny Owen's Last Fight

It can be no consolation to those in South Wales and in Los Angeles who are red-eyed with anxiety about Johnny Owen to know that the extreme depth of his own courage did as much as anything else to take him to the edge of death. This calamitous experience could only have happened to an exceptionally brave fighter because Lupe Pintor, the powerful Mexican who was defending his World Boxing Council bantamweight championship against Owen, had landed enough brutal punches before the twelfth and devastatingly conclusive round to break the nerve and resistance of an ordinary challenger. The young Welshman was, sadly, too extraordinary for his own good in the Olympic Auditorium.

Given the basic harshness of boxing as a way of earning a living, no one could blame Owen or his father or his manager, Dai Gardiner, for going after the biggest prize available to them, but some of us always felt that the right to challenge Pintor in Los Angeles was a questionable privilege. Making some notes about the background to the fight on Friday morning, I found myself writing: "Feel physical sickness at the thought of what might happen, the fear that this story might take us to a hospital room." This scribble was not meant to imply any severe criticism of a match which, on the basis of the relevant statistics, could not be condemned as outrageous. Indeed, the apprehension might have been illogically excessive to anyone who set Pintor's career figures of forty-one wins, seven losses, and a draw against the fact that Owen's one defeat had been a blatant case of larceny in Spain and the further, impressive fact that he had never been knocked off his feet as a professional boxer.

Yet it is the simple truth that for weeks a quiet terror had been gathering in me about this fight. Perhaps its principal basis was no more than a dread that the frailty that the boy's performances had hitherto dismissed as illusory would, some bad time in some bad place, prove to be terribly real. There is something about his pale face, with its large nose, jutting ears, and uneven teeth, all set above that long, skeletal frame, that takes hold of the heart and makes unbearable the thought of him being badly hurt. And, to my mind, there was an ominous possibility that he would be badly hurt against Pintor, a Mexican who had already stopped thirty-three opponents and would be going to work in front of a screaming mob of his countrymen, whose lust for blood gives the grubby Olympic Auditorium the atmosphere of a Guadalajara cockfight, multiplied a hundred times.

No fighters in the world are more dedicated to the raw violence of the business than Mexicans. Pintor comes out of a gym in Mexico City where more than a hundred boxers work out regularly and others queue for a chance to show that what they can do in the alleys they can do in the ring. A man who rises to the top of such a seething concentration of hostility is likely to have little interest in points-scoring as a means of winning verdicts. So it was hard to share the noisy optimism of the hundred-odd Welsh supporters who made themselves conspicuous in the sweaty clamor of the hall and brought a few beer cups filled with urine down on their heads. But they seemed to be entitled to their high spirits in the early rounds as Owen carried the fight to Pintor, boring in on the shorter, dark-skinned champion and using his spidery arms to flail home light but aggravatingly persistent flurries of punches.

The first round was probably about even. Owen might have edged the second on a British scorecard and he certainly took the third, but already Pintor's right hooks and uppercuts were making occasional dramatic interventions, sending a nervous chill through the challenger's friends around the ring.

It was in the fourth round that Pintor's right hand first struck with a hint of the force that was to be so overwhelming subsequently, but this time it was thrown overarm and long and Owen weathered it readily enough. He was seen to be bleeding from the inside of his lower lip in the fifth (the injury may have been inflicted earlier) but, since both Pintor's eyebrows were receiving attention from his seconds by then, the bloodshed seemed to be reasonably shared. In fact the laceration in the mouth was serious and soon the challenger was swallowing blood. He was being caught with more shots to the head, too, but refused to be discouraged, and an American voice behind the press seats said incredulously: "I don't believe this guy."

Pintor was heaving for breath at the end of the fifth but in the sixth he mounted a surge, punished Owen, and began to take control of the contest. The official doctor, Bernhard Schwartz, checked the lip for the second time before the start of the seventh. Pintor dominated that one but Owen revived heroically in the eighth, which made the abrupt disaster of the ninth all the more painful.

Pintor smashed in damaging hooks early in the ninth but their threat appeared to have passed as the round moved to its close. Then, without a trace of warning, Pintor dropped a shattering right hook over Owen's bony left shoulder. The blow hurled him to the floor and it was here that his courage began to be a double-edged virtue. He rose after a couple of seconds, although clearly in a bad condition. There was a mandatory eight count but even at the end of it he was hopelessly vulnerable to more hooks to the head and it took the bell to save him.

By the tenth there was unmistakable evidence that the strength had drained out of every part of Owen's body except his heart. He was too tired and weak now to stay really close to Pintor, skin against skin, denying the puncher leverage. As that weariness gradually created a space between them, Pintor filled it with cruel, stiff-armed hooks. Every time Owen was hit solidly in the eleventh the thin body shuddered. We knew the end had to be near but could not foresee how awful it would be.

There were just forty seconds of the twelfth round left when the horror story started to take shape. Owen was trying to press in on Pintor near the ropes, failed to prevent that deadly space from developing again and was dropped on his knees by a short right. After rising at three and taking another mandatory count, he was moved by the action to the other side of the ring and it was there that a ferocious right hook threw him on to his back. He was unconscious before he hit the canvas and his relaxed neck muscles allowed his head to thud against the boards. Dai Gardiner and the boxer's father were in the ring long before the count could be completed and they were quickly joined by Dr. Schwartz, who called for oxygen. Perhaps the oxygen might have come rather more swiftly than it did but only if it had been on hand at the ringside. Obviously that would be a sensible precaution, just as it might be sensible to have a stretcher immediately available. It is no easy job to bring such equipment through the jostling mass of spectators at an arena like the Auditorium, where Pintor's supporters were mainly concerned about cheering its arrival as a symbol of how comprehensive their man's victory had been. The outward journey to the dressing room, with poor Johnny Owen deep in a sinister unconsciousness, was no simpler and the indifference of many among the crowd was emphasized when one of the stretcher bearers had his pocket picked.

There have been complaints in some quarters about the delay in providing an ambulance but, in the circumstances, these may be difficult to justify. Dr. Ferdie Pacheco, who was for years Muhammad Ali's doctor and is now a boxing consultant with NBC in the United States, insists that the company lay on an ambulance wherever they cover fights, but no such arrangements exist at the Auditorium and the experienced paramedics of the Los Angeles Fire Department made good time once they received the emergency call. Certainly it was grief and not blame that was occupying the sick boy's father as he stood weeping in the corridor of the California Hospital, a mile from the scene of the knockout. A few hours before, I had sat by the swimming pool at their motel in downtown Los Angeles and listened to them joke about the calls Johnny's mother had been making from Merthyr Tydfil on the telephone they had recently installed. The call that was made to Mrs. Owen from the waiting room of the California Hospital shortly before

7 A.M. Saturday, Merthyr time (11 P.M. Friday in Los Angeles) had a painfully different tone. It was made by Byron Board, a publican and close friend of the family, and he found her already in tears because she had heard that Johnny had been knocked out. The nightmare that had been threatening her for years had become reality.

She can scarcely avoid being bitter against boxing now and many who have not suffered such personal agony because of the hardest of sports will be asking once again if the game is worth the candle. Quite a few of us who have been involved with it most of our lives share the doubts. But our reactions are bound to be complicated by the knowledge that it was boxing that gave Johnny Owen his one positive means of self-expression. Outside the ring he was an inaudible and almost invisible personality. Inside, he became astonishingly positive and self-assured. He seemed to be more at home there than anywhere else. It is his tragedy that he found himself articulate in such a dangerous language.

Duran No Quitter

RED SMITH

Red Smith (1905–1982), only the second sportswriter to win a Pulitzer Prize for commentary, did more than cover the games we play. In his long life as a columnist at the *Philadelphia Record,* the *New York Herald Tribune, Women's Wear Daily,* and *The New York Times,* he managed to blend the roles of historian, sociologist, psychologist, dramatist, and poet quite seamlessly. In this 1980 column, he uses Roberto Duran's plea for "No mas" as a launch pad to display them all with particular insight and gusto.

                        🥊   🥊   🥊   🥊

This is the first opportunity for comment on the ending of the Roberto Durán-Sugar Ray Leonard bout since Durán, then the World Boxing Council welterweight champion, told the referee: "No más, no más. No more box." It would require a deal of convincing to shake the conviction here that Durán had to be sick or injured, because Roberto Durán was not, is not, and never could be a quitter.

The Sweet Science is a harsh mistress, and under her cruel rules the deadliest sin is to give up under punishment. The most damning criticism that can be made of a fighter is to say, in the parlance of the fight mob, that he is a bit of a kiyi or that he has a touch of the geezer in him, meaning a streak of cowardice. The fact that no coward walks up the steps and into the ring isn't good enough for the fight mob. It is further required that when his number comes up, the fighter must endure pain and punishment without complaint as long as he is conscious.

"Do you want me to stop it?" Harry Kessler, the referee, asked when Archie Moore was being slugged senseless by Rocky Marciano.

"No," Archie said. "I want to be counted out." He was.

"I'm going to stop this," Joe Gould, Jim Braddock's manager, told his fighter when Joe Louis was pounding Jim loose from the heavyweight championship of the world.

"If you do I'll never speak to you again," Braddock said.

This is the code. Exceptions are made only if a fighter surrenders for dishonest reasons, as Sonny Liston almost surely did in his two engagements with Cassius Clay-Muhammad Ali. (The name changed between bouts.) In other words, quitting is a disgrace, deeply to be deplored unless it is done to discharge a business obligation.

Liston's motives have never been made public, but suspicions raised by the first match were confirmed beyond reasonable doubt by the second. Liston was heavyweight champion of the world up to and including his first six peculiar rounds with Clay in Miami Beach. The bell for the seventh found him sitting sullen on his stool while the title changed hands. He said an injury had rendered his left arm useless.

They met again in Lewiston, Maine. In the first round, which was also the last, Liston went in the water with a splash that washed away whatever doubt the first performance had left.

Memory retains only one other case of a champion surrendering his title, and that was strictly on the level. In 1949 Marcel Cerdan was defending the middleweight championship against Jake LaMotta in Detroit when the supraspinatus muscle at the back of his right shoulder came loose. Right arm hanging at his side, he fought on left-handed and LaMotta was having all he could do to beat one side of Cerdan until the tenth round, when the Frenchman's seconds persuaded him to leave the rest of his fight for a better time.

The better time never arrived. Booked for a rematch, Cerdan died in the crash when the plane bringing him back to the United States flew into a mountain in the Azores.

LaMotta, the Bronx Bull, was as tough as any man of his time, yet he quit in the ring at least twice. One was for business reasons. He had agreed to a barney to ornament the gaudy record of one Blackjack Billy Fox, but Jake had never been off his feet and was too proud to hit the deck. He floundered along the ropes impersonating a carp out of water until a faint-hearted referee stopped the performance. Even when Ray Robinson pounded him loose from the middleweight title in thirteen rounds in Chicago, LaMotta was still on his feet when the referee stepped in. But in his next match he gave up. Irish Bob Murphy, who wasn't great but could hit, punished Jake until he quit after seven rounds.

That scene was reminiscent of a night in Jersey City when Max Baer, a former champion, hurled invective and right-hand shots at Tony Galento until Tony, sick from swallowing his own blood, gave up. Baer didn't know it, but he had an accomplice. On the eve of the fight, a barfly in Galento's spa in Orange, New Jersey, had asked Tony for tickets, had received a predictable answer and had shoved a beer glass into Tony's profile. Several stitches were required to close the wounds before Baer reopened them.

Willie Pep and Sandy Saddler fought for the world featherweight championship four times. All four bouts were memorable and one can't be forgotten because Willie quit when he was winning. Saddler had knocked him out and taken the title in their first match; in a gallant performance with one brow gaping like a third eye, Willie outfought Saddler to regain the title; Pep lost it back in the third meeting when he did or did not tear a muscle; in their fourth match Willie took an early lead and was winning on all cards when the ninth round ended. "No more," Willie said.

At least one onlooker who had never before and has not since seen a boxer quit while winning was reminded of Willie's story of his beginnings in Hartford. As soon as school was out, he said, he would take off on the run. He didn't have to look back; he knew bigger kids would be chasing him. On his good days he was able to run home and slam the door before his pursuers could lay hands on him. Tiring of this one-sided game, Willie went to a gym to learn boxing. There he came under the tutelage of Bill Gore, and in Gore's hands he developed into the supreme artist of the ring.

Now in his fourth fight with Saddler, the artist blotted his sketchbook. "Again this night," an onlooker thought, "he ran home and slammed the door."

Biting Commentary

JIM MURRAY

How good was *Los Angeles Times* columnist Jim Murray (1919–1998). The National Association of Sportscasters and Sportswriters named him America's Best Sportswriter 14 times. He won two National Headliner Awards, and the 1990 Pulitzer Prize for Commentary.

Before that, he had a past.

I met Jim in the early '80s when I was the Hollywood columnist for Los Angeles' other paper, the *Herald Examiner.* It turned out that before Murray evolved into the funniest, classiest, and most astute and entertaining sports columnist of his time, he'd been bitten by the Hollwood bug. He'd covered the movies in the late '40s and early '50s for *Time,* and absolutely adored the milieu. Bogie had been a buddy. So had Marilyn Monroe. He could never get enough of the stuff. In 1988, a director friend who was working on a sports picture asked if he could set up a dinner with Jim. The evening was ripe for a Murray column: the director only wanted to talk baseball and Murray only wanted to talk about what was going on in Hollywood.

But back to boxing. Thankfully, Jim was on hand when Mike Tyson took that chunk out of Evander Holyfield's ear. The moment was so surreal that even a Jim Murray couldn't make sense of it in just one column. Hence, these two, deft balances of pathos, anger, humor, and disbelief.

🥊 🥊 🥊 🥊

LAS VEGAS—Well, Mike Tyson didn't need a new referee. He needed a rabies shot.

He has been hailed as having the fighting style of a wild animal.

He sure has. He proved it here Saturday night.

He tried to bite Evander Holyfield's ear off Saturday. Twice. Referee Mills Lane disqualified him before he tried to bite his nose off.

America's Wolfman made a mockery of the Marquess of Queensberry rules. He made a mockery of sportsmanship. He took pugilism back to the cave.

He is one disturbed young man. He should not be allowed to fight again. Unless it is against a hungry grizzly.

It had to be seen to be disbelieved. We've all heard of a "hungry" fighter. But never one who tried to eat his opponent.

The funny thing is, they might have spotted Tyson the first bite. Even though part of Holyfield's ear was missing, the ref just deducted a couple of points. But when Tyson chomped down again in the next round, they decided to get him out of there before he bit off more than he could chew.

It was such a shocking bit of cannibalism, they decided to halt the proceedings before Tyson tried to put him in a pot.

I guess people in the dawn of history settled matters that way. But today only dogs and mosquitoes get forgiven for biting. Prizefighting has rules. No kicking, choking, shooting, knifing—or biting.

Mike Tyson was unregenerate to the last. He had been butted, he insisted. "My career was on the line!" he exclaimed. He was entitled to retaliate, he felt. Removing an ear seemed to him to be a suitable reaction. For a mad dog, perhaps. But for a licensed pugilist?

Even Tyson's manager didn't seem to get the point. "A little nick on his ear don't mean nothin'," he screamed at the press. "My fighter had a three-inch cut."

Even Evander Holyfield was incredulous. You encounter a bear, a leopard, you protect yourself against a bite. But how do you stop a clinching opponent? "I thought my ear had fell off! Blood was all over!"

It was boxing's lowest moment. There are many things wrong with the manly art of self-defense, but we always thought those mouthpieces were in there to protect the teeth of the wearer, not the ear of an opponent.

"He spit the mouthpiece out when he bit me!" Holyfield revealed.

The heavyweight championship was awarded once in history on a disqualification, is our recollection. But that was when Max Schmeling lay on the floor and refused to get up after being hit low by Jack Sharkey. He was awarded the title even though the low blow was unintentional.

Tyson's foul was so intentional, he repeated it. Maybe he liked the taste of Evander's ear.

We are at a low point in our history. Our prizefighters bite each other, our ballplayers spit in your face.

Mike Tyson has been suspended "temporarily" by the Nevada State Athletic Commission. He gets a hearing as to whether his purse—a mere $30 million—should not be held up.

That may be the most expensive dining-out in history if the commission tries to make the "fine" stick.

Why did Mike Tyson do it. Well, that may be like asking a Doberman pinscher why it does it.

As this is written, newsmen are asking principals whether Holyfield will give Tyson a return match. Give Tyson a return fight?! What would Evander have to do—put ketchup on his ears?! Mustard on his nose?!

Mike Tyson should be allowed to fight only a thing that can bite back. His fighting days should be over.

Biting is a tactic of the overmatched. Mike Tyson was getting properly beaten up. Defeated partisans think up horror weapons. They bring in secret weapons. That's what Tyson did. He burst his moorings and began to assault the world in the ring.

I don't know what he could do to restore his dignity and professionalism. Become a vegetarian, for starters. But, I would think, given his history, he is the last guy in the world I would want to bite back.

It's not funny, it's a sad story. Ask Evander's plastic surgeon.

🥊　🥊　🥊　🥊

The Mike Tyson He Knew Showed Humor; Not Bite

All right, Miss B., take a letter to Mr. T. That's right, Mr. T., the quondam heavyweight champion. Boxing's Dracula. Half-pug, half-vampire. The Tooth Fairy.

> "Dear Mike,
>
> "I guess I go back with you as far as any other journalist. You remember, we rode to the Roy Firestone show in a stretch limo a few years ago. You were the up-and-coming heavyweight hope and you poked me in the ribs as we got in the car and you grinned 'You know, if I were around a limo like this five years ago, I'd be stealing the hubcaps.' You seemed to have an appealing sense of humor behind that frightening exterior and those bulging muscles.

"I don't want to say I defended you to many of my friends, but I did tell them I saw another side to the brute they perceived in mid-ring.

"I knew your co-manager Jimmy Jacobs well. He had been world handball champion and a world-class fight buff who collected boxing films all the way from the days of Thomas Edison's early kinescopes.

"I knew your other co-manager, Cus D'Amato. A man of dignity and probity, he also was the most paranoid fight manager I ever knew. I drove him and Floyd Patterson to the Olympic Auditorium one night (Floyd fought a man named Jimmy Slade) and I thought Cus was going to have a heart attack when I made a wrong turn. He suspected me of being Sammy the Bull. "Who are you?! Where are you taking us!" I have told the police to be on the lookout for our kidnapping!" he shrieked before I could calm him down.

"But, in spite of these derangements, you were in good hands, Mike. Cus kept you on a pretty tight leash. Because he knew you needed it. Jacobs inculcated a love of boxing history in you and you were the only guy I ever met who knew more boxing lore than I did. (You stumped me on Mickey Walker–Pete Latzo, remember, Mike?)

"When Jacobs and Cus died, you put your career in the hands of guys who would let you do anything you wanted. They were afraid to say no to you. They were as scared of you as Peter McNeeley was. Afraid of offending by offering even good advice you didn't want to hear. "Sure, Mike!" was their idea of guidance. You were a cash cow to them. Jimmy Jacobs never needed cash and Cus D'Amato had almost no interest in it.

"You were on top of the world, Mike. Or thought you were. Don King used to chortle you were 'the baddest man on the planet Earth' and if you weren't, you were getting there.

"The rape of Desiree Washington was the signal to the world you were out of control. You thought you were a law unto yourself. Athletes get that way. All the adulation, the publicity, the hype. You get a false sense of your own importance. It's called 'How dare you turn me down?! Don't you know who I am?!'

"Yeah. You're about 87 cents worth of zinc, iron, calcium and water like everyone else. A ranch mink is worth more than you skinned.

"Prison is supposed to be about rehabilitation. There are social scientists who think you could put a man-eating shark in prison for a year or two and, with 'help' (buzz word for therapy), he will come out a goldfish. Maybe so, but don't get in a pool with one, especially if your nose is bleeding.

"I don't know how you came out of prison mentally, Mike, but it looks as if you went right back to the same syco-phants, leeches and manipulators with which most fighters surround themselves.

"The inevitable happened. The one dignity you had left was your athletic prowess. When Evander Holyfield robbed you of that, you couldn't deal with it. You became obsessed with revenge. It would make everything all right. I mean, how dare Holyfield? Didn't he know with whom he was dealing?

"When it became obvious by the second round you weren't going to make everything all right, that it was deja vu all over again (as Yogi says), you burst your moorings. Your eye was bleeding, you couldn't hurt Holyfield, I think you would have killed him if you had a knife. You did the next worst thing, something that was the most disgusting thing I have ever seen not only in a prize ring but anywhere else. Maybe Jeffrey Dahmer did it, but they didn't sell tickets. It wasn't on pay-per-view.

"I don't know whether you couldn't handle fame or fame couldn't handle you. You want to be allowed to fight again? Why, Mike? So you can get the rest of his ear? So you can punch out more cops, spit at more customers, encourage more lobby riots?

"I don't think so, Mike. We've kind of lost the capacity for indignation in this country. Forgiveness is the 'in' thing.

"But, boxing shouldn't forgive you. You made it seem like a citadel of depravity. As a student of its history, let me ask you—do you think Joe Louis would ever behave like that? Rocky Marciano? Dempsey? Jack Johnson? Ali? Lord, even Sonny Liston? I don't think so.

"Letting you back in the ring would be like letting Hannibal Lecter in a prom. If you fight Holyfield again, what are they going to release it as—'Jaws, the Sequel'?

"If we want to see things get bitten, we'll go to a cockfight. So, wipe the blood off your teeth. I wouldn't go to see you and Evander Holyfield again even if you wore a muzzle and he wore earmuffs."

He Swung and He Missed

NELSON ALGREN

So much boxing fiction steps up to slug it out with the game's demons and humanity's darker side that this lighthearted, light-heavyweight romance by Nelson Algren (1909–1981) stands out for the nobility, fidelity, and ultimate likeability of Young Rocco, its hero—and for the snappy O. Henry-like twist at the end. Algren's most famous novel, *The Man With the Golden Arm,* won the National Book Award; the movie version supplied Frank Sinatra with one of his most memorable roles.

    🥊   🥊   🥊   🥊

It was Miss Donahue of Public School 24 who finally urged Rocco, in his fifteenth year, out of eighth grade and into the world. She had watched him fighting, at recess times, from his sixth year on. The kindergarten had had no recesses or it would have been from his fifth year. She had nurtured him personally through four trying semesters and so it was with something like enthusiasm that she wrote in his autograph book, the afternoon of graduation day, "Trusting that Rocco will make good."

Ultimately, Rocco did. In his own way. He stepped from the schoolroom into the ring back of the Happy Hour Bar in a catchweight bout with an eight-dollar purse, winner take all. Rocco took it.

Uncle Mike Adler, local promoter, called the boy Young Rocco after that one and the name stuck. He fought through the middleweights and into the light-heavies, while his purses increased to as much as sixty dollars and expenses. In his nineteenth year, he stopped growing, his purses stopped growing, and he married a girl called Lili.

He didn't win every one after that, somehow, and by the time he was twenty-two he was losing as often as he won. He fought on. It was all he could do. He never took a dive; he never had a setup or a soft touch. He stayed away from whisky; he never gambled; he went to bed early before every bout and he loved his wife. He fought in a hundred corners of the city, under a half dozen managers, and he fought every man he was asked to, at any hour. He substituted, for better men, on as little as two hours' notice. He never ran out on a fight and he was never put down for a ten-count. He took beatings from the best in the business. But he never stayed down for ten.

He fought a comer from the Coast one night and took the worst beating of his career. But he was on his feet at the end. With a jaw broken in three places.

After that one he was hospitalized for three months and Lili went to work in a factory. She wasn't a strong girl and he didn't like it that she had to work. He fought again before his jaw was ready, and lost.

Yet even when he lost, the crowds liked him. They heckled him when he was introduced as Young Rocco, because he looked like thirty-four before he was twenty-six. Most of his hair had gone during his lay-off, and scar tissue over the eyes made him look less and less like a young anything. Friends came, friends left, money came in, was lost, was saved; he got the break on an occasional decision, and was occasionally robbed of a duke he'd earned. All things changed but his weight, which was 174, and his wife, who was Lili. And his record of never having been put down for ten. That stood, like his name. Which was forever Young Rocco.

That stuck to him like nothing else in the world but Lili.

At the end, which came when he was twenty-nine, all he had left was his record and his girl. Being twenty-nine, one of that pair had to go. He went six weeks without earning a dime before he came to that realization. When he found her wearing a pair of his old tennis shoes about the house, to save the heels of her only decent pair of shoes, he made up his mind.

Maybe Young Rocco wasn't the smartest pug in town, but he wasn't the punchiest either. Just because there was a dent in his face and a bigger one in his wallet, it didn't follow that his brain was dented. It wasn't. He knew what his score was. And he loved his girl.

He came into Uncle Mike's office looking for a fight and Mike was good enough not to ask what kind he wanted. He had a twenty-year-old named Solly Classki that he was bringing along under the billing of Kid Class. There was money back of the boy, no chances were to be taken. If

Rocco was ready to dive, he had the fight. Uncle Mike put no pressure on Rocco. There were two light-heavies out in the gym ready to jump at the chance to dive for Solly Classki. All Rocco had to say was okay. His word was good enough for Uncle Mike. Rocco said it. And left the gym with the biggest purse of his career, and the first he'd gotten in advance, in his pocket: four twenties and two tens.

He gave Lili every dime of that money, and when he handed it over, he knew he was only doing the right thing for her. He had earned the right to sell out and he had sold. The ring owed him more than a C-note, he reflected soundly and added loudly, for Lili's benefit, "I'll stop the bum dead in his tracks."

They were both happy that night. Rocco had never been happier since Graduation Day.

He had a headache all the way to the City Garden that night, but it lessened a little in the shadowed dressing room under the stands. The moment he saw the lights of the ring, as he came down the littered aisle alone, the ache sharpened once more.

Slouched unhappily in his corner for the windup, he watched the lights overhead swaying a little, and closed his eyes. When he opened them, a slow dust was rising toward the lights. He saw it sweep suddenly, swift and sidewise, high over the ropes and out across the dark and watchful rows. Below him someone pushed the warning buzzer.

He looked through Kid Class as they touched gloves, and glared sullenly over the boy's head while Ryan, the ref, hurried through the stuff about a clean break in the clinches. He felt the robe being taken from his shoulders, and suddenly, in that one brief moment before the bell, felt more tired than he ever had in a ring before. He went out in a half-crouch and someone called out, "Cut him down, Solly."

He backed to make the boy lead, and then came in long enough to flick his left twice into the teeth and skitter away. The bleachers whooped, sensing blood. He'd give them their money's worth for a couple rounds, anyhow. No use making it look too bad.

In the middle of the second round he began sensing that the boy was telegraphing his right by pulling his left shoulder, and stepped in to trap it. The boy's left came back bloody and Rocco knew he'd been hit by the way the bleachers began again. It didn't occur to him that it was time to dive; he didn't even remember. Instead, he saw the boy telegraphing the right once more and the left protecting the heart slipping loosely down toward the navel, the telltale left shoulder hunching—only it wasn't down, it wasn't a right. It wasn't to the heart. The boy's left snapped like a hurled rock between his eyes and he groped blindly for the other's arms, digging his chin sharply into the shoulder, hating the six-bit bunch out there for thinking he could be hurt so soon. He shoved the boy off, flashed his left twice into the teeth, burned him skillfully against the middle rope, and heeled him sharply as they broke. Then he skittered easily away. And the bell.

Down front, Mike Adler's eyes followed Rocco back to his corner.

Rocco came out for the third, fighting straight up, watching Solly's gloves coming languidly out of the other corner, dangling loosely a moment in the glare, and a flatiron smashed in under his heart so that he remembered, with sagging surprise, that he'd already been paid off. He caught his breath while following the indifferent gloves, thinking vaguely of Lili in oversize tennis shoes. The gloves drifted backward and dangled loosely with little to do but catch light idly four feet away. The right broke again beneath his heart and he grunted in spite of himself; the boy's close-cropped head followed in, cockily, no higher than Rocco's chin but coming neckless straight down to the shoulders. And the gloves were gone again. The boy was faster than he looked. And the pain in his head settled down to a steady beating between the eyes.

The great strength of a fighting man is his pride. That was Young Rocco's strength in the rounds that followed. The boy called Kid Class couldn't keep him down. He was down in the fourth, twice in the fifth, and again in the seventh. In that round he stood with his back against the ropes, standing the boy off with his left in the seconds before the bell. He had the trick of looking impassive when he was hurt, and his face at the bell looked as impassive as a catcher's mitt.

Between that round and the eighth Uncle Mike climbed into the ring beside Young Rocco. He said nothing. Just stood there looking down. He thought Rocco might have forgotten. He'd had four chances to stay down and he hadn't taken one. Rocco looked up. "I'm clear as a bell," he told Uncle Mike. He hadn't forgotten a thing.

Uncle Mike climbed back into his seat, resigned to anything that might happen. He understood better than Young Rocco. Rocco couldn't stay down until his knees would fail to bring him up. Uncle Mike sighed. He decided he liked Young Rocco. Somehow, he didn't feel as sorry for him as he had in the gym.

"I hope he makes it," he found himself hoping. The crowd felt differently. They had seen the lean and scarred Italian drop his man here twenty times before, the way he was trying to keep from being dropped himself now. They felt it was his turn. They were standing up in the rows to see it. The dust came briefly between. A tired moth struggled lamely upward toward the lights. And the bell.

Ryan came over between rounds, hooked Rocco's head back with a crooked forefinger on the chin, after Rocco's Negro handler had stopped the bleeding with collodion, and muttered something about the thing going too far. Rocco spat.

"Awright, Solly, drop it on him," someone called across the ropes.

It sounded, somehow, like money to Rocco. It sounded like somebody was being shortchanged out there.

But Solly stayed away, hands low, until the eighth was half gone. Then he was wide with a right, held and butted as they broke; Rocco felt the blood and got rid of some of it on the boy's left breast. He trapped the boy's left, rapping the kidneys fast before grabbing the arms again, and pressed his nose firmly into the hollow of the other's throat to arrest its bleeding. Felt the blood trickling into the hollow there as into a tiny cup. Rocco put his feet together and a glove on both of Kid Class' shoulders, to shove him sullenly away. And must have looked strong doing it, for he heard the crowd murmur a little. He was in Solly's corner at the bell and moved back to his own corner with his head held high, to control the bleeding. When his handler stopped it again, he knew, at last, that his own pride was double-crossing him. And felt glad for that much. Let them worry out there in the rows. He'd been shortchanged since Graduation Day; let them be on the short end tonight. He had the hundred—he'd get a job in a garage and forget every one of them.

It wasn't until the tenth and final round that Rocco realized he wanted to kayo the boy—because it wasn't until then that he realized he could. Why not do the thing up the right way? He felt his tiredness fall from him like an old cloak at the notion. This was his fight, his round. He'd end like he'd started, as a fighting man. And saw Solly Kid Class shuffling his shoulders forward uneasily. The boy would be a full-sized heavy in another six months. He bulled him into the ropes and felt the boy fade sidewise. Rocco caught him off balance with his left, hook-fashion, into the short ribs. The boy chopped back with his left uncertainly, as though he might have jammed the knuckles, and held. In a half-rolling clinch along the ropes, he saw Solly's mouthpiece projecting, slipping halfway in and halfway out, and then swallowed in again with a single tortured twist of the lips. He got an arm loose and banged the boy back of the ear with an overhead right that must have looked funny because the crowd laughed a little. Solly smeared his glove across his nose, came halfway in and changed his mind, left himself wide and was almost steady until Rocco feinted him into a knot and brought the right looping from the floor with even his toes behind it.

Solly stepped in to let it breeze past, and hooked his right hard to the button. Then the left. Rocco's mouthpiece went spinning in an arc into the lights. Then the right.

Rocco spun halfway around and stood looking sheepishly out at the rows. Kid Class saw only his man's back; Rocco was out on his feet. He walked slowly along the ropes, tapping them idly with his glove and smiling vacantly down at the newspapermen, who smiled back. Solly looked at Ryan. Ryan nodded toward Rocco. Kid Class came up fast behind his man and threw the left under the armpit flush onto the point of the chin. Rocco went forward on the ropes and hung there, his chin catching the second strand, and hung on and on, like a man decapitated.

He came to in the locker room under the stands, watching the steam swimming about the pipes directly overhead. Uncle Mike was somewhere near, telling him he had done fine, and then he was alone. They were all gone then, all the six-bit hecklers and the iron-throated boys in the sixty-cent seats. He rose heavily and dressed slowly, feeling a long relief that he'd come to the end. He'd done it the hard way, but he'd done it. Let them all go.

He was fixing his tie, taking more time with it than it required, when she knocked. He called to her to come in. She had never seen him fight, but he knew she must have listened on the radio or she wouldn't be down now.

She tested the adhesive over his right eye timidly, fearing to hurt him with her touch, but wanting to be sure it wasn't loose.

"I'm okay," he assured her easily. "We'll celebrate a little 'n forget the whole business." It wasn't until he kissed her that her eyes avoided him; it wasn't till then that he saw she was trying not to cry. He patted her shoulder.

"There's nothin' wrong, Lil'—a couple days' rest 'n I'll be in the pink again."

Then saw it wasn't that after all.

"You told me you'd win," the girl told him. "I got eight to one and put the whole damn bank roll on you. I wanted to surprise you, 'n now we ain't got a cryin' dime."

Rocco didn't blow up. He just felt a little sick. Sicker than he had ever felt in his life. He walked away from the girl and sat on the rubbing table, studying the floor. She had sense enough not to bother him until he'd realized what the score was. Then he looked up, studying her from foot to head. His eyes didn't rest on her face: they went back to her feet. To the scarred toes of the only decent shoes; and a shadow passed over his heart. "You got good odds, honey," he told her thoughtfully. "You done just right. We made 'em sweat all night for their money." Then he looked up and grinned. A wide, white grin.

That was all she needed to know it was okay after all. She went to him so he could tell her how okay it really was.

That was like Young Rocco, from Graduation Day. He always did it the hard way; but he did it.

Miss Donahue would have been proud.

Thicker Than Water

PAUL GALLICO

After a rocky start as a film critic, Paul Gallico (1897–1976) found his home on the sports pages of the *Daily News* in New York. An immensely popular columnist, he was an avid practitioner of participatory journalism, sparring with Dempsey, swimming with Johnny Weissmuller, catching Dizzy Dean, and teeing it up with Bobby Jones, Gene Sarazen, and Tommy Armour. In 1937, Gallico retired his notebook, published his seminal *Farewell to Sport*, and embarked on a life devoted primarily to fiction and screenwriting. His novels include *The Snow Goose, Mrs. 'Arris Goes to Paris, Coronation, Thomasina,* and *The Poseiden Adventure.* In 1942, he wrote his *Pride of the Yankees,* the classic biography of Lou Gehrig. Two years later, he published this tale about brothers encircled by the ring.

🥊 🥊 🥊 🥊

T he other day, I heard the story of how Tommy White came back from a grave in the hard, white coral of a South Pacific island where he sleeps under a wooden cross on which his helmet hangs, rusting in the tropic rains, and knocked out Tony Kid Marino in the seventh round at the American Legion Stadium in our town.

Tommy White was a champion, but his kid brother Joey was a dog. You often run across things like that. They were both welterweights, and young Joey could box rings around Tommy. He could have boxed those same circles around any welterweight living if the geezer hadn't started to come out in him after the first solid smack.

Tommy, on the other hand, had the heart of a lion. That is why he became a world's champion. That is why he enlisted the day after Pearl Harbor. That is why he walked into the machine-gun fire that was coming from a Japanese pillbox and murdering his company and dropped a grenade into the slit, quietly and without fuss like a man posting a letter, before he died from being shot to pieces.

That sort of put the burden on Joey White and it seemed to be more of a load than he could lug. Doc Auer, who had managed Tommy and been more like a father to him, helped out all he could, but Doc wasn't exactly rich. Tommy had won his championship in the days when nobody got rich any more.

There was Mom White, and Phil, the youngest, and Anna, age twelve, who had been living in a wheelchair ever since the hit-and-run driver had tossed her like a broken doll into the gutter. And, of course, there was Ellie, Tom's widow and their year-old baby.

Joey was a good kid. He couldn't help the yellow streak that came out in him in the ring. It often happens that way. Some boys don't like it. It was just that he would begin to blink and wince at the first solid smack, and then pretty soon he would be down, and you knew he wasn't bothering to get up.

Joey wasn't happy about his weakness. He tried to overcome it by going back into the ring, but each time he dogged it, it nearly drove him crazy, he felt so ashamed. There was the time he got pneumonia after he quit cold to Young Irish, and he hoped it would kill him. It nearly did, too, because he wouldn't fight the bug in him. Blood transfusion saved his life. Tommy, who was home on leave at the time, went to the hospital and acted as donor, though Joey never knew about it. In the first place, hospitals don't tell, and, in the second, Tommy wasn't the kind who would mention such a trifle.

You hear a lot about fighters being no-goods and bums, but there are plenty of good kids in the game. The Whites were decent. When the news came about what had happened to Tommy in the Pacific, Joey went back to the ring. He might have got a job in a factory, but there were all the mouths to feed and the payments on the house. It wouldn't have been enough. And the ring was good for money now that there weren't too many classy boys around, and cards were hard to find. Joey had picked up a ruptured eardrum in one of his early fights and was 4-F.

Doc managed him, which was rough on Doc because he had loved Tommy like a son. Doc was a square shooter with a hook nose and tender hands that could soothe pain when he dressed damage in the corner. But he was a rough guy who couldn't stand kiyi in his boys. What made it worse was that Doc knew Joey had it in him to be a bigger champion and a better fighter than Tommy ever was if he didn't curl up inside when the going got rough.

You would think after Tommy being killed the way he was, it would have given Joey the guts to go in there and pitch leather. The kid had loved his brother with a sort of doglike affection even though Tommy had always overshadowed him. But it didn't work out that way. In his first fight he quit to Ruby Schloss after being out in front five rounds and having Ruby on the floor. It was a good enough brawl so that Doc could get Joey another match, but when he folded to Arch Clement, who wasn't much more than 138 pounds, from a left hook to the chin that shouldn't have bothered a flyweight, it wasn't so good.

Four F, or no Four F, the fans want a fight when they pay their money, and you can't draw flies with a loser even in wartime. Besides, the ringworms were on to Joey. The promoters just said, "No, thanks," when Doc came around looking for a fight.

So the match with Tony Kid Marino was just sheer luck. "Soapy" Glassman, matchmaker for the American Legion Stadium, told Doc: "Lissen, if there was anybody around under fifty years old who could put his hands up, I wouldn't let a beagle like Joey into my club through the back door."

But there was nobody around, and Marino was a sensation. Discharged from the Army for some minor disability, he had swept through the South and the Middle West by virtue of a paralyzing left hook. He was headed for Madison Square Garden and the big dough. Glassman had to have an opponent in a hurry. Joey got the match but everybody knew he was to be the victim in it. It was also plainly labeled "last chance."

Doc said to Joey: "I seen Marino train at Flaherty's Gym. He don't know nothin'. A smart boxer could stab him all night and he wouldn't catch up. But he hits you with that left hook, and you need a room in a hospital. You got to stay away from him. And if you get hit a punch, you got to keep boxing."

Joey said, "I'll try, Doc. Honest, I will this time."

He always said that. He always meant it—until that first hard punch chunked home.

Doc said, "Yeah, I heard that before. If we could win this one, we go in the Garden instead of that bum. Ah, nuts! A guy can dream, can't he?"

Joey did try. He could box like a phantom. He was a tall, skinny boy with light hair and dark eyes and a pale, serious face. His long arms and smooth shoulders were deceptive because they packed an awful wallop any time he stayed on the ground long enough to get set. But the night he fought Marino he wasn't staying in one place long enough to throw dynamite. He was trying his level best to do what Doc told him—stay away, stab, box, and win.

There was a crowd of eight thousand packing the Legion Arena when they rang the bell for round one but, to a man, it was there to see Marino, the new kayo sensation, stiffen somebody, and the fact that Joey White was in there made it just that much more certain. Nobody was even interested when Joey gave as pretty a boxing show as you could want to see in that first round and jabbed Marino dizzy.

In fact, some wise guy started something by holding up one finger at the end of the round and shouting, "One!" That meant one round had gone by and Joey was still there. Pretty soon everybody in the arena took it up at the end of each round. It went on that way: "Two!" "Three!" "Four!"

Marino was muscled like a bulldog. He had short, black hair and dark skin, and he moved forward with a kind of dark sneer on his face as he tried to herd Joey into a corner where he could club his brains out.

Doc wasn't daring to breathe when round six came up, and Joey was still there and so far out ahead on points it wasn't even funny. He hadn't been hit yet. Four more rounds—then Madison Square Garden, the big dough, a shot at the championship, security for Tommy's family. In and out went Joey—feint and stab, jab and step away, jab and circle, pop-pop-pop, three left hands in a row.

So then it happened just before the end of the sixth. The ropes on the south side of the ring had got slack and didn't have the snap-back Joey expected when he came off them, which caused him to be sufficiently slow for Marino's hook to catch him. It hit Joey on the shoulder and knocked him halfway across the ring.

Now, nobody ever got knocked out with a punch to the arm. But it was all over. Everybody knew it. Everybody saw the look come into Joey's eyes, the curl to his mouth and the cringe to his shoulders. It was the promise of things to come conveyed by the punch, that did it. The swarthy Marino leaped after Joey to find a lethal spot, but the bell rang, ending the round.

The crowd stood up, held up six fingers and yelled, "Six!" and the wag who had started it shouted, "Seventh and last coming up!" and everybody howled with laughter.

Joey went to his corner and sat down, but Doc who was usually in the ring before the echoes of the bell had died away, cotton swabs sticking out of his mouth, sponge in hand, ready to loosen trunks and administer relief and attention, remained outside the ropes. He didn't so much as touch Joey. He just leaned down with his head through the space between the top and second strand, and talked out of the side of his mouth into Joey's ear.

He said, "Ya bum! You going to quit in the next round, ain't you?"

Joey moved on the stool and touched his shoulder. "My arm. It's numb."

Doc went right on talking quietly out of the side of his mouth as though he were giving advice: "Makin' out to quit and you ain't even been hurt yet. You got the fight won and you're gonna go out there and lay down, ain't you?"

Joey didn't say anything any more but licked his lips and shuffled his feet in the resin and tried to hide his eyes so nobody would see the fear that was in them.

Doc said, "I ought to bust the bottle over your head. You, with the blood of a champion in your veins, makin' to go out there and lay down like a dog."

Joey turned and looked at Doc, and his lips moved. Under the hub-bub he said, "What are you talking about?"

"What I said. A guy you ain't even fit to think about. You got his blood in you. He give it to you when you was sick in the hospital and had to have a blood infusion."

"I . . . I got Tommy's blood?"

The ten-second buzzer squawked.

Doc said, "Yeah. You got it, only it dried up when it come to your chicken heart. Okay, bum, go on out there and take the dive." Then he quietly climbed down the ring steps. The bell rang for the seventh round.

Everything happened then as expected. Joey came out with his hands held too low and he seemed to be trembling. Marino ran over and swept a clublike left to the side of his head, and Joey went down as everybody knew he would.

Only thereafter he did what no one expected or had ever seen him do before. He rolled over and got on one knee, shaking his head a little, and listened to the count until it got to eight. Then he got up.

His head was singing, but his heart was singing louder. Tommy's blood! His brother's blood, the blood of one of the gamest champions in the world, coursing through his veins. A part of Tommy's life was alive inside of him. . . .

The referee finished wiping the resin from his gloves and stepped aside. Marino shuffled over, his left cocked. Joey dropped his hands still lower and stuck out his chin. The stocky little Italian accepted the invitation and hit it with all his power, knocking Joey back into the ropes.

But he didn't go down. Marino followed up, pumping left and right to Joey's head, rocking him from side to side. The crowd was screaming and above the roar someone was shouting, "Cover up! Cover up, you fool!"

Cover up for what? This bum? He couldn't hit hard enough to knock out a man with a champion's blood in his veins. Joey seemed to feel his blood stream like fire all through his body. He could take it, take it, take it now, he could sop it up, punch after punch, and not go down, never again go down as long as in his heart there beat and pulsed the warm life of his brother.

Marino fell back wheezing and gasping for air and strength to carry on the assault. Joey laughed and came off the ropes. Marino had punched himself out, had he? That was how Tommy used to get them.

Joey came down off his toes. His stance changed abruptly, hands at belt level, but nearer to his body. He edged close to Marino and chugged two short blows into his middle, whipping the punches with body leverage, and the crowd roared to its feet. Men sitting in the back rows swore it was as though they were seeing Tommy White again.

Marino grunted, turned ashen and retreated. Strength coursed like hot wine through Joey's limbs. He pressed forward, anchored to the canvas floor like a sturdy tree and raised his sights. The short, sharp, murderous punches whipped to Marino's swarthy jaw. Through the smoky air the gloves flew—punch, punch, punch!

When there was nothing more in front of him to punch, Joey leaned from a neutral corner and bawled at the body on the canvas as the referee's arm rose and fell, "Get up. . . . Get up and fight! I ain't finished yet."

Then somehow he was in Doc's arms. Doc was kissing him and there were tears on Doc's face and he was crying, "Tommy . . . Tommy . . . Joey boy. . . . It was just like Tommy was alive again. Joey, baby, there ain't nothing goin' to stop you now. . . ."

ABOUT THE EDITOR

Jeff Silverman, a former columnist for *The Los Angeles Herald Examiner*, has written for *The New York Times*, *The Los Angeles Times*, and several national magazines. The editor of *The Greatest Baseball Stories Ever Told*, *The Greatest Golf Stories Ever Told*, and *The First Chapbook for Golfers*, he now lives with his family in Chadds Ford, Pennsylvania.

Permissions Acknowledgments

Nelson Algren, "He Swung and He Missed" from *The Neon Wilderness*. Copyright © 1947 by Nelson Algren. Reprinted with the permission of Doubleday, a division of Random House, Inc.

James Baldwin, "The Fight" from *Nugget* (February 1963). Later collected in *The Price of a Ticket* (New York: St. Martin's Press, 1985). Copyright © 1963 by James Baldwin. Copyright renewed. Reprinted by arrangement with the James Baldwin Estate.

Robert Benchley, "Ringside (Formal)" from *The New Yorker* (1927). Reprinted with the permission of Conde Nast Publications, Inc.

Jimmy Cannon, "You're Joe Louis" from *Nobody Asked Me But* . . . Copyright © 1978 by Jimmy Cannon. Reprinted with the permission of Henry Holt and Company, LLC.

Ralph Ellison, excerpt from *Invisible Man*. Copyright © 1952 by Ralph Ellison. Reprinted with the permission of Random House, Inc. and the William Morris Agency.

Richard Ford, "In the Face" from *The Fights* (San Francisco: Chronicle Books, 1996). Copyright © 1996 by Richard Ford. Reprinted with the permission of International Creative Management, Inc.

Paul Gallico, "Thicker Than Water" from *Collier's* (1944). Reprinted with the permission of Harold Ober Associates, Incorporated.

Dashiell Hammett, "His Brother's Keeper" from *Nightmare Town*. Reprinted with the permission of Alfred A. Knopf, a division of Random House, Inc.

W.C. Heinz, "The Greatest Pound for Pound" from *Once They Heard the Cheers* (New York: Doubleday, 1979). Copyright © 1979 by W.C. Heinz. Reprinted with the permission of the William Morris Agency.

Homer, excerpt from *The Iliad*, translated by Robert Fitzgerald. Copyright © 1975 by Robert Fitzgerald. Reprinted with the permission of Doubleday, a division of Random House, Inc.

Mark Kram, "Lawdy, Lawdy . . ." from *Sports Illustrated* (1975). Copyright © 1975 by Time, Inc. Reprinted by permission of *Sports Illustrated*.

John Lardner, "The Sack of Shelby" from *The New Yorker* (1948). Reprinted by permission.